PENGUIN

ARKANA

THE HIDDEN TRADITION IN EUROPE

Yuri Stoyanov was born in 1961 and graduated from the University of Sofia, where he obtained his BA in 1987 and his MA in 1989. He has subsequently done research at Oxford and the University of London, where he is currently a Frances A. Yates Fellow at the Warburg Institute. He has written and lectured extensively on Jewish and Christian mysticism, medieval Balkan history, and heretical and mystical movements in the Middle Ages.

YURI STOYANOV

———

THE HIDDEN TRADITION
IN EUROPE

ARKANA
PENGUIN BOOKS

ARKANA

Published by the Penguin Group
Penguin Books Ltd, 27 Wrights Lane, London W8 5TZ, England
Penguin Books USA Inc., 375 Hudson Street, New York, New York 10014, USA
Penguin Books Australia Ltd, Ringwood, Victoria, Australia
Penguin Books Canada Ltd, 10 Alcorn Avenue, Toronto, Ontario, Canada M4V 3B2
Penguin Books (NZ) Ltd, 182–190 Wairau Road, Auckland 10, New Zealand

Penguin Books Ltd, Registered Offices: Harmondsworth, Middlesex, England

First published 1994
3 5 7 9 10 8 6 4 2

Copyright © Yuri Stoyanov 1994
All rights reserved

The moral right of the author has been asserted

Filmset by Datix International Limited, Bungay, Suffolk
Printed in England by Clays Ltd, St Ives plc
Set in 10/12 pt Monophoto Garamond

Contents

CONTENTS

CONTENTS

List of Maps

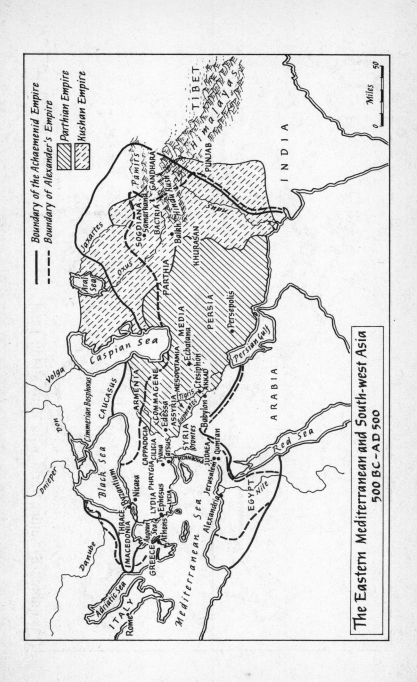

The Eastern Mediterranean and South-west Asia
500 BC–AD 500

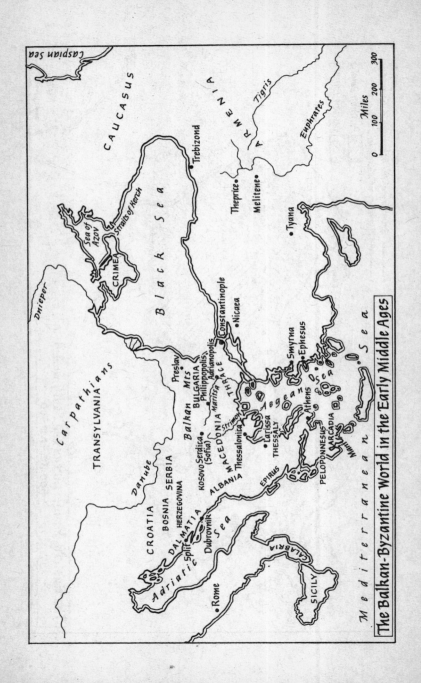

The Balkan-Byzantine World in the Early Middle Ages

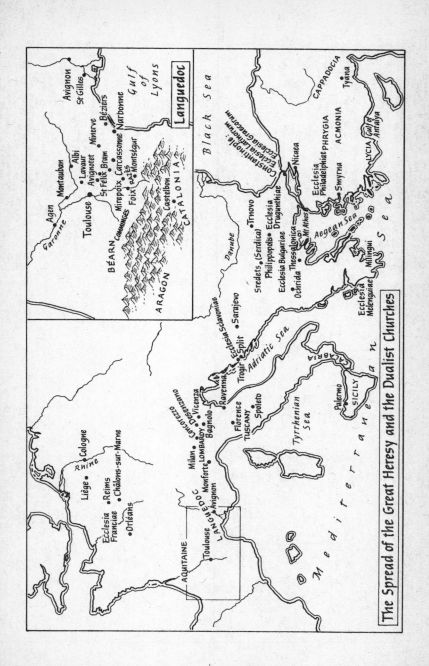

The Spread of the Great Heresy and the Dualist Churches

Preface

In the last few decades a number of ambitious publications have ventured to confront, with varying success, the historical riddles and myths traditionally associated with the Knights Templar, the Rosicrucians and the early Freemasons.[1] Cutting through seemingly inextricable tangles of fable, fact and fancy, these studies have made deep forays into the notoriously treacherous terrain which had long been an exclusive reserve of established secret-society mythology. What was unveiled were the vague outlines of an obscure but valid history which run beneath the surface of the recorded historical events and the later legendary embellishments. The partial exposure of this 'hidden history' has made it possible to investigate the ever-vexing question of the role of secret societies, Rosicrucianism and Freemasonry in the early modern era from several new angles. Fresh light was cast on some of the most shadowy and intricate developments and fluctuations in the European historical arena during the Renaissance and Reformation. Moreover, the rediscovery of the wealth and historic significance of certain trends of European esotericism (the Hermetic-Kabbalistic and Hermetic-Rosicrucian, in particular) opened new, intriguing vistas for the exploration and understanding of the great transformations in western Christendom between the fourteenth and seventeenth centuries.

However, while the religious landscape of the Renaissance has been steadily redrawn, the medieval religious history of Europe remains fraught with unsolved problems and complexities which are still being unravelled. Perhaps the most intricate and controversial of these religious problems are posed by the sudden rise and spread of medieval dualism, the 'Great Heresy' of the Bogomils and the Cathars. In the west the 'Great Heresy' emerged with claims of being a hidden tradition that had lain concealed in Greece and 'some other lands' since the era of the early Christian martyrs.[2] This 'hidden tradition', routinely defined as Christian dualism, came to be manifested in medieval Europe in two main strands. According to the first, 'monarchian' strand there was one sublime God, Father of All, but the material universe was created and ruled by His rebellious first-born, Satan or Lucifer, the Lord of the Old Testament, while His younger Son, Jesus Christ, was sent in a semblance of the human body to 'save that which was lost' during the satanic reign through his baptism in the Holy Spirit and with fire. The second, radical branch of the 'Great Heresy' taught that Satan–Lucifer was a son of the eternal Evil God whose attack on the heaven of the Good God caused the fall of the angels and the mission of the angel Christ was to redeem angelic souls from their imprisonment in human bodies. Opinions still vary widely as to whether these teachings represent merely a Christian heresy or, indeed, in the case of the radical doctrine of the eternal principle of evil, an extra-Christian religion in its own right.

The phenomenon of a highly mystical and ascetic dualist movement evolving into a powerful social and historic force and a threat to the spiritual supremacy of the Church in various parts of Europe has always been much more than a religious puzzle. Many medieval churchmen saw in the 'Great Heresy' a dangerous revival of that ancient rival to Christianity, Manichaeism; hence both the Bogomils and the Cathars came to be condemned again and again as new 'Manichaeans'. The history of European 'neo-Manichaeism' is known mainly from the acrimonious and distorted witness of its orthodox opponents and persecutors. Among the most renowned and dramatic episodes of this history are the infamous Albigensian Crusade against the Cathars in Languedoc, the siege of the Cathar citadel of Mont-ségur and the first devastating anti-heretical campaigns of the Holy Inquisition. The saga of the collision between Catharism and Catholicism has long been among the most favoured subjects for research, fascination, myth-making, romance and controversy. The fall of the Cathar citadel Montségur and the following mass burning of the Cathar *perfecti*, reputedly at the 'Field of the Cremated', is traditionally deemed to represent what Lawrence Durrell called 'the Thermopylae of the Gnostic soul', and the Cathars still retain their peculiar mystique and long-lasting hold on the European imagination.

The Cathar saga in the thirteenth century, of course, does not exhaust the complicated and elusive history of neo-Manichaeism in Europe. As attested in the extant evidence, the western and eastern wings of neo-Manichaeism were inseparably linked, both historically and doctrinally. It would be impossible to survey the rise and evolution of Catharism without charting the far-reaching missionary routes of Bogomilism following its inception in the tenth-century Bulgarian empire and diffusion throughout the Balkan–Byzantine world. With its crucial role in the revival of Gnostic–dualist traditions in medieval Europe, Bogomilism is without doubt among the most important developments in the complex and elusive religious history of the Balkans during the Dark Ages. In the Balkan–Byzantine world Bogomilism was to spread from Cappadocia in central-eastern Asia Minor to Dalmatia and Bosnia but its early history is inextricably linked to the religious ferment in the first Bulgarian empire following its turbulent Christianization in the second half of the ninth century.

Centred on the eastern Balkans, the first Bulgarian empire was one of the most powerful political formations in early medieval Europe and at various stages its boundaries stretched from Ukraine and central Europe to the Adriatic and Albania. Founded at the old Balkan crossroads of European and Asian civilizations, it marked the beginning of a new era in Balkan history when new monarchies and peoples competed for ascendancy in the medieval Balkans until the region was conquered by the Ottomans in the fourteenth–fifteenth centuries and integrated into the new, Ottoman version of the Caliphate. Since the annexation of the Balkans by the Ottoman empire, the Balkan world was largely isolated from the sweeping political and religious changes in western Europe but its European rediscovery in the nineteenth century led to the gradual untangling of its turbulent medieval history. With its strategic position at the bridge between Europe and Asia and with a history rich in invasions and protracted wars of conquest, in the Middle Ages the Balkan peninsula was subjected to still more invasions and colonizations which resulted in astonishing blends of races and cultures and the formation of the unique Balkan multi-national and multi-religious conglomerate. The increasing interest in the Balkan past in the last two centuries has shown that the Balkans, besides being the stage of contending faiths, have long served as a repository of many diverse archaic religious and cultural traditions, some of which are still being uncovered and explored.

The Balkans constituted the core of the oldest prehistoric European civilization, the so-called 'Old Europe' (7000–3500 BC), which extended from the Adriatic to western Ukraine and from the Aegean to the Middle Danube area, the eastern Balkans being the homeland of the world's oldest golden treasure (c. 4500–4000 BC).[3] At the time Greek civilization flourished in the southern Balkans, the northern and eastern Balkans were dominated by the Indo-European Thracians, who were described by Herodotus as the most numerous race after the Indians. The Thracians emerge in the *Iliad* as allies of the Trojans against the Greeks and, indeed, appear related more closely to the cultural and religious sphere of Asia Minor, Iran and the Scythian world than to Greece proper. None the less, the Thracians were increasingly exposed to Greek influences and later to Hellenization, but some of their own religious practices and concepts, with their distinct focus on the immortality of the soul and afterlife, were also to have their impact on Greece; Thrace was closely associated with the 'mysteric' trends in Greek religion. Renowned for their failure to unite, the Thracians intermittently founded their Balkan kingdoms amid periods of Persian, Macedonian and Celtic supremacy, but in the early Christian era the Balkans became an integral part of the Roman empire and were to enjoy general prosperity in the *Pax Romana*. From the fourth century AD onwards, however, Roman, and later Byzantine, rule in the area was crippled by the successive, 'barbaric' invasions of Goths, Huns and Avars and the ensuing massive Slav influx into the peninsula. In the late seventh century the Bulgars, whose origin has been much disputed but who had developed close ethnic and cultural affinities with the northern Iranians, founded in the eastern Balkans the first Bulgarian empire, which competed with Byzantium for control of the Balkan interior.

On the eve of the first Christian millennium the Bulgarian empire provided the setting for the rise of Bogomilism, which would claim to represent the true and hidden Christian church, the church of Bethlehem and Capernaum. From Bulgaria, Bogomilism soon spread in Greece, Asia Minor and the western Balkans and, in the early

thirteenth century, chronicles were already warning against the
heresy of the Bulgars. According to the chronicle of the canonist
Robert the hidden and 'calamitous' heresy of the Bulgars was
permeating many places in Europe in the early thirteenth century,
particularly southern France, while in the chronicle of the monk
Alberich the Bulgarian heresy appears as the new name of the
ancient 'Persian' Manichaean heresy.[4] There is abundant evidence
that the early missionary inroads of Bogomilism into central and
western Europe precipitated the emergence of Catharism and was
traditionally recognized by western churchmen and inquisitors as
the 'hidden tradition' behind Catharism and, as with its western
counterpart, the spread of Bogomilism was marked by persecution,
autos-da-fé and crusades. Inevitably, Bogomilism has been routinely
implicated in the time-honoured debates about the alleged heretical
guilt of the Knights Templar or the mystery of the Cathar treasure
of Montségur. Yet the role of the Bogomils in the Cathar saga and
in the spiritual history of Europe, with some notable exceptions, is
still more often acknowledged than explored. This seems somewhat
odd since the Bogomils have left their indelible imprint on the
European religious scene and the inquisitorial archives, where the
western dualist heresy is sometimes defined as *Haeresis Bulgarorum*.
The prominence of the Bulgarian Bogomils as the heretics *par
excellence* was particularly strong in France, where the Cathars were
known variously as *Bulgares*, *bogri*, *bugres* or *bougres*; *bougres* and
'heretics' were to become interchangeable terms in French. Yet
when Rabelais's sophist in Chapter 20 of *Gargantua* (1534) threatens
his adversaries that they would be burned alive 'like *bougres*', it is
used as an abusive term, apparently synonymous with 'heretics', but
it has already lost its historical association with the medieval dualist heretics. This association was more than clear for the great
preacher and defender of Catholicism, Jacques Bénigne Bossuet
(1627–1704). In his *Histoire des variations des églises protestantes*, Bossuet
avers that western 'Manichaean' heresies had their roots in Bulgaria and
alludes to the old Catholic tradition that the western and eastern
churches of medieval 'Manichaeism' had their own supreme pontiff, *le
Pape des Albigeois*, residing in Bulgaria.[5] In his *Dictionnaire philosophique*,
Voltaire also draws attention to the phenomenon of *bougres* becoming a
generic name for heretics.[6] In Protestant scholarship Bogomilism

was sometimes recognized as a revival of true, apostolic Christianity and, on account of the austere standards of their ethical and moral conduct, the Bogomils have been praised as 'the greatest puritans of the Middle Ages'.

Such long-lasting celebrity is hardly surprising, as Bogomilism was the principal force behind the spread of neo-Manichaeism in Europe and was itself one of the most elusive and tenacious heretical secret sects of the Middle Ages. The history of Bogomilism is even less documented than that of Catharism; wide gaps abound owing to the fragmented and inimical ecclesiastical records of the encounter between orthodox Christianity and neo-Manichaeism. Fitting diverse and discrepant shreds of evidence into conceivable historical patterns is often shrouded in conjecture; inevitably, reconstructions of Bogomil history and teachings have generated continuous debate.

Recent works, however, with subjects ranging from the Holy Grail cycle to the medieval transformation of Hellenistic alchemy, have opened new avenues for the study of the history and doctrine of medieval neo-Manichaeism. The importance of Bogomilism as a religious intermediary between east and west, as a depository of traditions – best described as Gnostic–dualist – which seemed to have been vanquished irretrievably by the establishment of 'normative' Christianity, is now widely accepted. To appreciate the descent, essence and continuity of these traditions it is necessary to trace their prehistory in some detail and to set European neo-Manichaeism in a wider historical and religious context. This book will chart some of the vital phases and patterns of this early history in the Near East and the Balkan–Byzantine world, which could have important bearings on the teachings and evolution of medieval dualism.

Studies of the Great Heresy have regularly been prejudiced by the theological, ideological or indeed nationalistic tenor of its investigators and often tend to advance sweeping conjecture and scenarios based on metaphysical and ideological presumptions. This book will attempt to provide a synthesis of the extant evidence and place it, where possible, in its rich historical and religious context. Recently advanced theories and recently recovered relevant data will also be included in the account, as they could lead to alternative approaches to the historical and religious problems posed by the Great Heresy. As has been mentioned already, the recoverable history of Catharism has received exhaustive treatment, if not over-elaboration, of late, varying from scrutinies of the Albigensian Crusade to a detailed and vivid reconstruction of life in the Pyrenean Cathar village of Montaillou. The present book will also try to bring into sharper focus the eastern wing of European neo-Manichaeism in the Balkan–Byzantine world, from its obscure beginnings in the tenth century to its even more obscure disappearance five centuries later.

CHAPTER ONE

The Dualist Reformation

Bogomilism and Catharism resurrected dualist religiosity in medieval Europe centuries after orthodox Christianity had formally triumphed over its main dualist adversary, Manichaeism, the only universal religion to emerge from the great spiritual turmoil in third-century Mesopotamia. In Manichaeism, the traditional dualist religious vision, which divided divine reality and the world into two wholly opposed realms of good and evil, reached its most elaborate and influential expression. What is more, Mani, the founder of Manichaeism, proclaimed that his intricate dualist system formed the core of all religions and underlay the teachings of Zoroaster, Buddha and Christ. Before it reached this universalist phase, the dualist tradition had passed through a centuries-old evolution in Iran and the eastern Mediterranean world and its Manichaean incarnation was destined to spread from Mesopotamia to north Africa and Mediterranean Europe and further to the Far East.

In the Middle Ages the diffusion and popularity of Bogomilism and Catharism marked another high point in the history of the dualist tradition after it had fallen into almost complete oblivion during the Dark Ages. The renaissance of dualism in medieval Christendom coincided with the spread of diverse reformist and anti-clerical movements amid the religious ferment in western Europe during the twelfth and thirteenth centuries. The dualists shared with reformist sectarians the pursuit of apostolic life, piety and asceticism coupled with opposition to the Church hierarchy, which was deemed to have abandoned the apostolic traditions. Although the medieval dualists claimed that they represented the true, pure Church of Christ and were successors to the apostles, their teachings differed from the fundamentals of Christian dogma in many important aspects. The Great Heresy was associated with some of the most significant and challenging religious developments in the Middle Ages but, despite its apparent parallels to the medieval reformist movements, it cannot be approached simply as a precursor of the Protestant Reformation, as is often claimed by both Catholic and Protestant writers. With its cardinal teaching of the world as a creation and battleground of two opposing principles, a good creator and an evil creator, rather than a pre-Lutheran reformation the Great Heresy appears to be an attempt at a dualist reformation. Investigation of the historical and religious milieu of Bogomilism and Catharism is, of course, of primary importance to understanding their combined role in the history of medieval Christendom. However, this role cannot be fully assessed if considered separately from the origins, transformations and convoluted stemma of the dualist tradition.

Two Principles

Within the dualist tradition itself dualism is repeatedly defined as the teaching of the two principles. According to the celebrated Cathar tract *The Book of the Two Principles*, besides the good principle, as manifested in God and Jesus Christ, there is another principle, 'one of evil, who is mighty in iniquity, from whom the power of Satan and of darkness and all other powers which are inimical to the true Lord God are exclusively and essentially derived'.[1] The tract elaborates an exhaustive theological defence of divine justice and omnipotence in the face of the presence of evil in the world. In this dualist theodicy the cosmos is viewed as the outcome and the battleground of two opposed principles, good and evil or light and darkness. Among its numerous and varied arguments for the coexistence of the principles of good and evil the tract refers to Jesus saying in Matthew (7:17–18), 'but a corrupt tree bringeth forth evil fruit. A good tree cannot bring forth evil fruit, neither can a corrupt tree bring forth good fruit' (*KJV*).

There have been many endeavours to explore dualism of the type expounded in *The Book of the Two Principles* as a religious and historical phenomenon and to classify its basic variants.[2] Some early theories – that dualism arose as a reaction against monotheism or served as a passage from polytheism to monotheism – have been largely abandoned. Dualist trends or tendencies exist in all major religions, of course, often being professed and developed by fringe or outright sectarian groups. Traditionally a sharp distinction is made between ethical dualism, where good and evil are regarded as moral opposites, and religious dualism proper, where good and evil represent two fundamental, mutually antagonistic and irreconcilable absolutes. Religious dualism is also to be distinguished from the various types of philosophical dualism like that of Plato, with his dualities between the mortal body and the immortal soul, or between the world perceived by the senses and the world of the eternal ideas comprehended by the mind. The core of religious dualism usually lies in the cosmic battle between the forces of good and evil and, while expounding the course of the all-embracing collision between the two principles, the different versions of religious dualism may furnish contrasting solutions to the principal theological riddles of divine reality, creation and the origins of evil. In so-called cosmic dualism, as exemplified by Zoroastrianism, the physical world is in essence a 'Good Creation' and, although assaulted by evil, sin and death, it is designed to bring about the ultimate destruction of the evil agency. Conversely, anti-cosmic dualism equates the physical world, the body and matter with evil, delusion and darkness, which are conceived as totally opposed to the spiritual realm, soul and light. Anti-cosmic dualism reached its most dramatic and evocative incarnation in the mythological systems of some Gnostic schools where the rejection of a Creator–God (the Demiurge) and his universe assumed extreme and occasionally drastic forms.

The Platonic type of soul–body dualism, as advanced in Plato's dialogues *Timaeus* and *Phaedo*, came to influence important Jewish and Christian traditions. A dualist spirit–matter opposition along with rigorous asceticism was cultivated in the esoteric-initiatory trends of Orphism and Pythagoreanism in antiquity. The Orphic-Pythagorean teaching of the physical body as a tomb for the divine and immortal soul is shared in the Gnostic type of religiosity with its implicit focus on the rescue of the 'divine spark' in man from the bodily prison.

Other important lines of distinction within the dualist tradition concern the source and destiny of evil. The evil principle could be considered variously as primordial and eternal, as primordial but doomed to be vanquished at the end of history or as a secondary agency stemming from one sublime prime cause. The last type is usually defined as moderate, mitigated or 'monarchian' dualism and it is exhaustively elaborated, for example, in the classical Gnostic systems. The doctrine that good and evil, light and darkness, derive from two independent coeternal principles irreducibly set against each other, is commonly described as absolute or radical dualism.

In certain religious traditions diverse types of dualism could coalesce and appear in tortuous combinations with monotheistic and polytheistic conceptions. However, the most potent and influential formulations of dualism were fostered in the Iranian religious universe when it was impregnated by the Zoroastrian dualist reformation with its dramatic revelations of the all-pervading war between the twin primordial Spirits, a war waged in 'thought, word and deed'.

Twin Spirits

The early chronology of the great Iranian religious leader and reformer Zoroaster (Zarathustra) and his revealed faith, admittedly 'the only prophetic religion ever produced by the Aryan race',[3] still remains obscure and controversial. Sharply conflicting theories continue to fix the era of his prophetic mission variously at either 1700–1400 BC, or 1400–1000 BC or 1000–600 BC. If the earliest date could be verified it would make Zoroastrianism the world's oldest revealed religion; some of the cardinal Zoroastrian teachings appear to have been accepted and elaborated, whether directly or indirectly, in Judaism, Christianity and Islam. While some classical Greek traditions place Zoroaster in prehistory, 5,000 years before the Trojan war or 6,000 years before Plato, in sacred Zoroastrian chronology, as elaborated in the Zoroastrian opus, the *Greater Bundahishn*, the advent of the priest and prophet Zoroaster opens the tenth millennium, that of Capricorn, and his traditional date is 258 years before the era of Alexander the Great (336–323 BC).[4] Recent research has dated Zoroaster's reformation around the beginning of the first millennium BC[5] and has indicated the central-eastern Iranian world as the cradle of original Zoroastrianism (also known as Mazdaism or the 'Good Religion of the Worshippers of Mazda'). A legendary tradition, reiterated by Eusebius and Augustine, located Zoroaster's homeland in the ancient region of Bactria, locked between the Oxus (Amu Darya) river and the western extension of the Himalayas, the Hindu Kush.[6] Praised later as the 'Jewel of Iran', Bactria certainly played a very important role in the expansion of nascent Zoroastrianism; indeed, in the religious history of Eurasia, its main city, Balkh, the 'mother of all towns', was destined to become successively a celebrated centre of Hellenism, Buddhism and Islam.

Both in Iran and outside the Iranian world, the life of Zoroaster came to be embroidered with vivid legends and parables. His alleged violent death at the age of seventy-seven also spawned prolific lore: according to one Persian tradition he was slain at the height of a Turanian invasion in a Balkh fire temple along with eighty priests, whose blood quenched his fire.[7] Outside Iran the figure of Zoroaster also reached astonishing prominence: in Greece the early enthusiasm of the Platonic Academy for Zoroaster has been described as amounting 'to intoxication, like the rediscovery of Indian philosophy through Schopenhauer'.[8] With the diffusion of Zoroaster lore outside Iran the prophet came to be extolled in diverse religious and cultural traditions as the archetypal philosopher, magus and master of science and astronomy. Apart from magician and prophet, Zoroaster emerged in some traditions as a Magus–King of Bactria who fought the semi-mythical Assyrian queen Semiramis (Sammuramat),[9] who shared some of the features of the Babylonian goddess of love and war, Ishtar, and passed into legend as the founder of Babylon and the temple of her tutelar deity, Bel Marduk. Jewish traditions came to identify Zoroaster with Baruch, Jeremiah's scribe, while Syriac tradition associated Zoroaster, 'the diviner of the Magians', with the biblical Balaam. In Christian lore, Zoroaster can be recognized as Nimrod or else as Noah's son, Ham, and was portrayed as an arch-sorcerer who conjured up stars to be consumed ultimately by heavenly fire.[10] The tradition of Zoroaster as the arch-magician, his name being deciphered as 'living star' or 'stream of the star', persisted into the Middle Ages. In the *Historia Scholastica* of Peter Comestor (d. 1179), which charted biblical history from the Creation to the time of the Acts of the Apostles, Zoroaster appeared as the inventor of magic who inscribed the Seven Arts on seven columns.[11] In the fifteenth century, at the height of the Renaissance, the head of the new Platonic Academy in Florence, Marsilio Ficino, argued for a pagan theological tradition, descending from Zoroaster via Hermes Trismegistus to Orpheus and Pythagoras and culminating in Plato.[12] Four centuries later Nietzsche adopted the figure of Zoroaster as the spokesman of his new gospel in his most influential work, *Thus Spoke Zarathustra*, rendering further homage to Zoroaster and what he saw as the Persian vision of history as a 'great whole', a succession of cycles of a thousand years, each presided over by a prophet.[13] In *Ecce Homo* Nietzsche attributed to the historical Zoroaster the introduction of the notion of the struggle between good and evil as the 'very fly-wheel of existence' and the creation of 'the most portentous of errors', morality. For Nietzsche the uniqueness of the Persian prophet in history was that he was exactly 'the reverse of an immoralist' and now has to be invoked in Nietzsche's new 'Zoroastrian' gospel of the 'self-surpassing of the moralist in his opposite' – in Nietzsche himself, the self-acclaimed 'first immoralist'.

The religious message of Zoroaster was indeed underpinned by the new morality and dualist vision of the universal struggle between good and evil that confronted man with the opposing ways of Truth and Untruth. As Zoroastrianism arose and spread, initially in the eastern Iranian region, it inevitably took over and transformed the traditional beliefs and deities of the archaic religions of the Indo-Iranian branch of the Indo-European peoples. What sharply distinguishes original Zoroastrianism from the polytheism of Vedic India with its multitude of gods and semi-gods is the elevation of one supreme deity, Ahura Mazda (Wise Lord), as 'the first and the ultimate', the sole creator and upholder of the spiritual and material world, who is alone worthy of worship. Ahura Mazda was probably one of the 'lords' or *ahuras* (the Hindu *asuras*) of the Aryan pantheon but with Zoroastrian reform he overshadowed the other *ahuras* and transcended ancient Aryan deities like Mithra, the god of light and covenant. An uncreated and perfectly good God, Ahura Mazda is the Creator of everything (*Yasna* 44:7) and source of the lesser beneficent divinities.

The traditional view of early Zoroastrianism as 'dualist monothe-ism' has been continuously challenged and redefined against the background of the monotheistic worlds of Judaism, Christianity and Islam. What remains undisputed is that dualism and the struggle of good and evil lie at the heart of the Zoroastrian vision of divine reality: its classical formulation is found in the hymnic *Gathas* that form the oldest 'psalmic' part of the Zoroastrian scriptures, the *Avesta*,[14] and are attributed to Zoroaster himself. The *Gathas* of Zoroaster are contained in the Avestan section of *Yasna* (Acts of Worship) (28–53), and with their visionary, allusive and often abstruse verses they still appear a 'book bound with seven seals'.[15] The ambiguities and the intricacies that recur in the *Gathas* also distinguish *Yasna* 30, where Zoroaster declares the teaching of the opposing ways of the twin, primordial Spirits who are 'renowned to be in conflict'. These two Spirits are Spenta Mainyu ('Beneficent' or 'Holy Spirit') and Angra Mainyu ('Hostile' or 'Destructive' Spirit) and while they are alluded to as twins, Ahura Mazda is styled the father of the 'Holy Spirit' (*Yasna* 47:3). Both Spirits seem to proceed from Ahura Mazda but Zoroaster's utterances are difficult to interpret and laconic, forging a theological riddle that has contin-ued to provoke arguments and differing solutions both in Zoroas-trian theology and modern scholarship.[16] When the twin Spirits met in the beginning, they established life and not-life (death) and evolved into antithetical spirits of good and evil by making conflict-ing moral choices between *asha* (Truth) and *druj* (Untruth), the two primal principles that underlie Zoroastrian ethical dualism. Yet the position of the twin Spirits, particularly that of Angra Mainyu, prior to this split remains somewhat enigmatic. The traditional debate concerning the status of Angra Mainyu in early Zoroastrian-ism is whether he was regarded as evil by nature or by choice, i.e. whether his selection of 'Untruth' was predetermined by his nature or whether it was the result of his free choice.[17] The idea of free choice is fundamental to Zoroastrianism and it seems more probable that the origin of evil lies not in the innate nature of Angra Mainyu, supposedly activated by choice, but in his selection of untruth and doing the 'worst things'. What is certain is that Angra Mainyu, the evil Spirit, chose in the beginning to incarnate and to inaugurate the way of evil thoughts, words and deeds and become the great adversary of Ahura Mazda and his Good Creation. The antagonism between Ahura Mazda and the Destructive Spirit is irreconcilable and the Holy Spirit approaches his evil twin Spirit with this uncompromising formulation of the opposition: 'Neither our thoughts nor teachings nor intentions, neither our preferences nor words, neither our actions nor conceptions nor our souls are in accord' (*Yasna* 45:2).

In Zoroastrianism, Angra Mainyu's 'wrong choice' – to do the 'worst things' – was adopted by the class of the *daevas* (gods) like Indra from the traditional Indo-Iranian (Aryan) pantheon. While in India the *daevas* ultimately ousted the *asuras*, in Iranian Zoroastrianism they were forcibly relegated to demonic 'offspring stemming from evil thinking, deceit and disrespect' (*Yasna* 32:3). At the time of the primal choice the *daevas* were approached by the 'Deceiver' and accordingly chose the 'worst thought' and 'rushed into fury, with which they have afflicted the world and mankind' (*Yasna* 30:6). While the demonic *daevas* were condemned as the evil progeny of Angra Mainyu, he himself was styled *Daevanam Daeva*, the Demon of Demons.[18]

The choice of Angra Mainyu and the *daevas* and their onslaught on the world remained fundamental to the religious vision of Zoroastrianism, and a separate section of the *Avesta*, the *Vendidad* (Law against the Daevas), comprises prescriptions for ritual purification and exorcism of the *daevas*. The spiritual beings that should be entreated are the Amesha Spentas, the six 'Beneficent' or 'Holy' Immortals, who were evoked by Ahura Mazda and, together with Spenta Mainyu, became the divine 'bounteous' septet of Zoroastrianism that is mirrored in the class of the seven archangels in the later Jewish and Christian traditions. The Amesha Spentas embodied the virtues of Ahura Mazda, like Good Thought, Best Truth, Desirable Dominion, etcetera, and along with the Wise Lord proceeded to evoke more beneficent divinities, a process which was to recover more ancient divinities among the Zoroastrian *yazatas* ('the worshipful ones').[19]

The new system of spiritual and moral values introduced by

Zoroaster provoked an epoch-making reformation of the archaic
Indo-Iranian religion and cast aside some of its initiatory and
sacrificial practices, like the blood sacrifice. What was strenuously
rejected were the orgiastic and frantic rites which were associated
with the worship of some of the demoted, warlike *daevas*, while its
priests were condemned as 'whisperers and sacrificers' who evoked
the violent forces of evil and deceit, the way of Angra Mainyu.
Despite the break with some of the formalistic ritualism of the
Indo-Iranian priestly tradition, early Zoroastrianism developed some
of the concepts of Indo-Iranian or Aryan mysticism, with its focus
on supernatural vision and mystical light, and preserved certain
cultic traditions which could be spiritualized and reconciled with
Zoroastrian ethics.[20] The cult of fire was also retained and became
fundamental to Zoroastrianism, where it was seen as possessing the
'power of Truth' (*Yasna* 43:4) and was associated with the Holy
Spirit of Ahura Mazda (*Yasna* 36:3).

In the Zoroastrian solution to the perennial enigma of the origin
of evil, as an absolutely good and just Creator of the spiritual and
material world, Ahura Mazda (later contracted to Ohrmazd) was
stripped of all culpability for the presence of evil and suffering in
his Creation. According to some Parsis, the modern Zoroastrians,
the twin Spirits emerged as the opposing but complementary forces
of maintenance and destruction, the two poles of Ahura Mazda's
power,[21] but whether this view could be projected backwards on to
early Zoroastrianism remains an open question. In traditional Zoroastrianism evil seems to be revealed as stemming from the free choice
of Untruth by Angra Mainyu (later called Ahriman) who is, however, destined to be defeated and paralysed by Ahura Mazda at the
end of historical time. The Zoroastrian sacred history came to be
divided into 'Three Times': the First Time of the original perfection
of Ahura Mazda's 'Good Creation' in its ideal and material side; the
middle Time of Mixture, of good and evil caused by the incursion
of the Destructive Spirit in the material universe; and finally the
eschatological Time of Separation of the two hostile Spirits, of
good and evil, and the ultimate purification of the world.[22] In the
First Time, Ahura Mazda's Creation exists in two states, spiritual or
ideal, *menog*, and material, *getig*, while Angra Mainyu is unable to
corrupt its ideal side, being incapable of transferring his own

creations from the spiritual to the material state. The physical aspect of Ahura Mazda's creation is vulnerable to the encroachment of Angra Mainyu and, following the formation of the material world, it is subjected to the onslaught of the Destructive Spirit which marks the beginning of the second Time of Mixture of the opposing principles of good and evil.

The Zoroastrian view of world history received considerable elaboration in later stages and, in one scheme of the cosmic process, it was held to last 12,000 years, of which the first 3,000 are the period of 'ideal creation'. The remaining 9,000 years are an era of cosmic strife when, according to the scheme in the *Greater Bundahishn* (1:28), three millennia would be dominated entirely by Ohrmazd (Ahura Mazda), three millennia would pass in a mixture of and struggle between the will of both Ohrmazd and Ahriman (Angra Mainyu) and finally, in the last three millennia, Ahriman would be defeated and rendered powerless. In Zoroastrian eschatology the last era will culminate in the advent of a virgin-born World Saviour, Saoshyant, conceived from Zoroaster's seed, miraculously preserved in a lake, while some traditions refer to three posthumous sons of Zoroaster who appear as Saoshyants (saviours) at the end of each of the last three millennia. Saoshyant, the messianic leader of the Pure Ones, wages the last holy wars against the forces of evil and resurrects the bodies of the dead which are reunited with their souls. Their resurrection sets the stage for the Last Judgement and the separation of the saved from the damned, who must face a terminal ordeal by fire and pass through rivers of molten metal, the 'pure fire' and the 'molten iron', the sign of Ahura Mazda's retribution (*Yasna* 51:9). While mankind is being purified from evil and corruption, the molten metal would burn the last vestiges of 'Untruth' and would flow even into Hell to cleanse its putrescence. In the redeemed world material creation becomes immortal.

Man is confronted with the moral task of choosing freely between the two ways of good or evil in the vast cosmic drama of the unfolding warfare between the Holy and the Destructive Spirits. His use of his free will is to be judged at the immediate individual judgement of the soul at death on the so-called 'Bridge of the Separator' and at the universal judgement during the final renovation of Ahura Mazda's Good Creation. The first judgement elevates the righteous souls to the Zoroastrian Heaven, the 'House of Song', and consigns the wicked ones and the 'destroyers of this world' to the Zoroastrian Hell, the 'House of Worst Thinking' or 'House of Untruth', where they are condemned to 'a long age of misery, of darkness, ill food and the crying of woe' (*Yasna* 31:20). Those whose good and evil deeds appear in exact balance (*Yasna* 33:1) are sent to the intermediary sphere of Hamistagan (the region of the mixed). Following the resurrection of the bodies during the Last Judgement, the saved will be sent for three days in Paradise, while the damned will face another three days of punishment in Hell. In the ensuing trial by fire, as depicted vividly in the *Greater Bundahishn* (34:18–19), the saved will pass through the rivers of molten metal as if walking through warm milk, while for the damned the ordeal would be exactly like walking through 'pure fire' and 'molten iron', which would destroy the deceitful and save the truthful (*Yasna* 31:19; 51:9). In the *Gathas* the damned appear to be condemned to eternal perdition,[23] but in later Zoroastrian eschatology after this final crucible all human beings will be purged of sin to become one voice praising Ahura Mazda, immortalized in his renewed Good Creation (*Greater Bundahishn* 34:20–21). At the resurrection, Saoshyant would perform 'the sacrifice of the raising of the dead', in which the bull Hadhayans is slain and from its fat the drink of immortality is prepared, which is to be given to all men who now become immortal. The eschatological renewal of the macrocosmos epitomizes the preordained victory of Ahura Mazda over the principle of evil and destruction and the ensuing universal salvation. The Good Creation is restored to perfection and bliss prior to the assault of evil and henceforth remains incorruptible under the eternal reign of the Wise Lord. Angra Mainyu is thrown out of the sky and rendered powerless, cast into 'the darkness and gloom', where his destructive potency and weapons will be sealed up forever (*Greater Bundahishn* 34:30).

The Zoroastrian reformation gave apparent priority to the doctrine of the predestined final transfiguration of the world, as opposed to the archaic religious scenario of the cyclic regeneration of the cosmos. The fervent expectation of the Last Judgement and the ultimate glorification of existence is one of the dominant themes of the *Gathas*. The other texts of the *Avesta*, the greater part of which seems to have been lost, reflect later periods of the growth and expansion of the Good Religion of Ahura Mazda. Throughout its history Zoroastrianism was to undergo vicissitudes and permutations but it retained Zoroaster's dualist vision of two spiritual principles warring from the beginning of the world and the inevitable triumph of Ahura Mazda, the creator and the judge, in the last days. Zoroastrianism retained also its praise for the Good Creation of Ahura Mazda where the spiritual and material world are connected inextricably, man himself being the image of the macrocosmos and his body being the garment and the weapon of his soul.

Spirit and Flesh

Zoroastrianism remained essentially a life-affirming and active religion. The dualism of the two spirits of good and evil did not comprise an opposition between the soul and the body. The body was regarded as an essential and indispensable part of the Good Creation, an instrument of the soul, and accordingly celibacy and asceticism were renounced consistently throughout the history of Zoroastrianism. A distinct dualism between the soul and the body was to become the core of the religiosity of Orphism, an important trend in the Greek mysteries which seems to have emerged in the sixth century and, apart from the Balkans, came to exert influence in Crete, Cyprus and southern Italy.

Traditionally described as a 'drop of alien blood in the veins of the Greeks', Orphism owed its name to the pre-Homeric fabled Thracian poet and musician Orpheus to whom were ascribed many Orphic works.[24] In antiquity the mythical genealogy of Orpheus varied and he was depicted as a son of Apollo or the Thracian king Oeagres of the dynasty reputedly established by Dionysus (Bacchus) when the god invaded Europe from Asia by the Hellespont and deposed the hostile Thracian king Lycurgus (Diodorus Siculus 3:65.4–7). According to Diodorus the new Dionysian dynasty in Thrace was initiated into the secret rites of the Dionysian (Bacchic) mysteries and although seemingly of Anatolian descent, Dionysus himself was seen by ancient authors as a Thracian god.[25] Various mythological stories recount the conquests of Dionysus and his cult in Thrace, Greece and even in India, which the god was said to have traversed with a great army, the 'soldiers of Dionysus', bringing to the Indians civilization and the discovery of wine (Diodorus Siculus 2:38.3–39). Ancient Orphism had strong links with the Dionysian (Bacchic) mysteries and Diodorus assigns the origins of Orphic rites to Orpheus' changes in the inherited Dionysian initiatory rites (Diodorus Siculus 3:65.6). As in Greece, the Dionysian mysteries in Thrace were intended to lead the Dionysian initiate, the *bacchus*, into 'the empire of the god', into a transformative ecstatic experience of his divinity, but were also associated with prophecy. The legendary figure of Orpheus appears closely linked with the Thracian religious sphere, with its intense spiritualist currents and renowned Thracian preoccupation with the afterlife, which was to impel some Thracians to weep at the birth of children and to rejoice at the burial of the dead (Pomponius Mela 2:2.18, Herodotus 5:4). The belief in the immortality of the soul was thought to be behind the brave Thracian conduct on the battlefield and the celebrated *appetitus mortis* (appetite for death) of the Thracians, their belief in the 'beauty' of death (Martianus Capella 6:656). The northern Thracian tribes of the Getae were known as 'the immortalizing ones' or 'those who make themselves immortal', while some Thracians were renowned for their ascetic practices and abstinence (Strabo 7:3.3–6, 11).[26] The old thesis of Erwin Rohde and W. Guthrie that the belief in the immortality and divinity of the human soul arose and entered Greece through Thracian worship of Dionysus has been consistently challenged, but ultimately Thracian religiosity is viewed as having enriched the classical world with 'a more total vision of humanity and of its destiny'[27] and seems to have left its impact on the crystallization of some concepts in Orphism.

Apart from their obvious associations with Thrace, the myths of Dionysus and Orpheus often alluded to the interaction between the rival cults of Apollo, the god of order and reason, and Dionysus, the god of wine and ecstasy. A notoriously dual deity, who was believed to drive men to a frenzy (Herodotus 4:79), the divine 'madness' (*mania*), Dionysus could be praised as a redeemer, healer and benefactor; he could appear as a lion or a leopard, but most famously in the form of a bull, and could be revealed as the 'render

of men' and the one 'who delights in the sword and bloodshed'.
When Dionysus led his force from Asia into Europe he fought the
Thracian king Lycurgus (Diodorus Siculus 3:65.5), who was apparently associated with the worship of Apollo and is recognized as a
great adversary of the crazed Dionysus in the *Iliad* (7:130–34). In
the *Iliad*, Lycurgus is blinded, in Diodorus' account he is defeated,
mutilated and crucified by the invading Dionysus. In another mythical account, while hastening through Thrace, Dionysus was insulted
and expelled by Lycurgus but the god drove the king mad and he
slashed down his own son, whom he saw as a vine shoot (Apollo-
dorus 3:5.1). In the wake of the murder, Thrace endured a great
drought and, as was revealed by the oracle, was to be relieved only
through the death of the god-fighting king. Lycurgus was accordingly tied to horses and rent apart at Mount Pangaeus, the traditional
site of a famous Dionysian oracle, while Dionysus reached India
and set up pillars in the land. Whereas these myths seem to allude to
the antagonism of the principles of Dionysus and Apollo, the figure
of Orpheus, his genealogy likewise, could appear ambiguous – he
could be described as 'sent by Apollo' (Pindar, Pythian Ode, 4:176)
or raised to prominence by Dionysus. What remains certain is that
Orpheus was or became closely associated with worship of Apollo
and, according to Aeschylus, he came to praise the sun-god, Helios,
whom he recognized as Apollo, as 'the greatest of the gods',
provoking the wrath and revenge of Dionysus, who sent against
him his frenzied female devotees, the Bassarides (the Maenads).[28]
Traditionally, Orpheus was envisioned to have been rent to pieces
by the Maenads and in one mythical account of his death his
severed head was buried in Lesbos, where a temple of Dionysus was
erected on the site of the head's burial. Orpheus' lyre was reputedly
installed in the temple of Apollo and Orpheus has been seen as
epitomizing the 'purely masculine', the *catharos*, as embodied in
Apollo.[29] In accordance with Diodorus' testimony of Orpheus'
changes in Dionysian rites and Olympiodorus' comment that, according to Orpheus, Helios has much in common with Dionysus
through Apollo's medium,[30] Orpheus' mythical feats are often seen
as a reformation of the Dionysian mysteries, a reconciliation and
synthesis of Apollonian or solar and Dionysian cultic traditions
which were attested in both Greece and Thrace.

In Orphism, Apollo and Dionysus appear reconciled, but the supposed link between Orpheus' reputed reforms of the Dionysian cult and Orphic teachings remains controversial and bitterly debated. Concern for the hereafter certainly was or came to be one of the prominent features of the Dionysian mysteries,[31] which comprised ecstatic and orgiastic rites, including the *omophagia* (eating raw flesh), which were vividly realized in Euripides' masterpiece, *The Bacchae*. In *The Bacchae*, Dionysus comes from Asia's land, from the mountains of Phrygia and Lydia, to the 'broad highways of Hellas', along with his Maenads to establish his cult on Greek soil but it is suppressed by the king of Thebes, Pentheus, who is destined, however, to be torn asunder by the Maenads. Agave, his own mother, smitten by Dionysian madness, wrenches off and raises his head as prey, which she sees as a lion's head. The ecstatic Bacchic rites could reach extreme forms and the Bacchanalia were eventually proscribed by the Roman senate in 186 BC. Orphism, which was associated with the Dionysian and Eleusinian mysteries and the Pythagorean movement, fostered ascetic and cathartic practices focused essentially on the afterlife and the fate and salvation of the soul. What appears to be a cardinal and originally secret myth of Orphism recounts the fate of Dionysus–Zagreus, Zeus's child from his incestuous intercourse with his daughter, Persephone, herself scion of Zeus's union with his mother, Rhea–Demeter. In Orphic cosmogony, after the first divine generation, Zeus emerged eventually as both creator and sovereign of the world, he was exalted as the beginning, the middle and the end, and upon the birth of Dionysus the divine child was enthroned as a ruler of the world and of the gods. The old race of gods, Zeus' enemies, the Titans, enticed the child Dionysus with toys and, while looking into a mirror, he was slain, dismembered and devoured by the Titans.[32] The Orphic myth of the dismemberment of Dionysus, which was represented in the rites initiated by Orpheus (Diodorus 5:75.4), recalls the myth of Osiris' dismemberment in Egypt and, indeed, Diodorus refers to the Greek translation of Osiris as Dionysus (1:11.3). Zeus avenged the horrible death of Dionysus by destroying the Titans with lightning and while Dionysus was later revived, it was out of the ashes of the Titans that man was created. According to a widespread reading of the myth, man inherited both the Dionysian and Titanic elements and has a dual nature, his soul being of divine Dionysian descent and his body of evil Titanic material.[33] An alternative reading of Orphic soul–body dualism argues that, rather than being associated with man's bodily and mortal nature, the Titans – with their rebellious, destructive and disorderly conduct – had established models to be followed by humans and limited the human soul to within their boundaries.[34] What is certain is that, in Orphism, the soul was viewed as pre-existing and separate from the body and was held to be undergoing punishment in the 'enclosure' and the 'prison' of the body until it had paid the due penalty (Plato, *Cratylus* 400c). The equation of the human body (*soma*) with the *sema* (tomb) of the soul is traditionally associated with the Orphic–Pythagorean current in Greek religious thought; the purification of the soul was to be achieved through an ascetic life, purifications (*katharmoi*) and initiations (*teletai*). Observation of the Orphic way of life, with its initiatory, ethical and ascetic rules, was supposed to grant salvation of the soul from the Titanic nature and primordial guilt and punishment.[35] The Orphic cultivation of the divine element in man was aimed at delivering the soul from punishment in the afterlife and from the chain of transmigration of the soul through various bodies, the sorrowful wheel of rebirth. It is widely assumed that Orphic–Pythagorean concepts of the soul and its destiny influenced Plato, while Orpheus was hailed not only as the archetypal poet–enchanter who led all things by the charm of his voice (Aeschylus, *Agamemnon* 1630) but also as a founder of the Mysteries, the first to introduce initiatory rites in Greece. Evolving ultimately into 'the greatest emblematic character of the Greek mystical consciousness',[36] the figure of Orpheus was also to be subjected to numerous cultural transformations, from Virgil's *Georgics* to Cocteau's *Orphée*.

In Orphism the body and the soul were brought together as a result of the primordial crime of the Titans – the dismembering and the devouring of Dionysus. The revived Dionysus appears to have been perceived as a saviour–god, releasing entrapped souls from a 'Titanic' prison, and Orphism is credited with introducing into European religiosity the pattern of soul–body dualism, whether in terms of distinct antithesis or mere separation.[37] In Zoroastrianism, although created after the soul, the body was regarded as being of like substance and man was described as formed of five parts – body, vital spirit, soul, form (image) and pre-existent soul (*Greater Bundahishn* 3:13). In alternative Zoroastrian systems man could be described as possessing four spiritual constituents – soul, vital spirit, pre-existent soul and consciousness – or being composed of three constituent powers, associated respectively with the body, the vital spirit and the soul, each of which is divided further into three parts.[38] Far from undergoing punishment in the body, in the Good Religion, the soul puts on its bodily garment of its free will as part of Ohrmazd's initial design to conquer Ahriman, his spiritual adversary in the material world. The visible world, *getig*, is the battleground of the forces of good and evil, and as the 'lord of the creation' man is at the forefront of the contest between the powers of Truth and Untruth. The cosmological dualism of the spiritual and material planes of existence does not imply opposition between the soul and the body. Rather they could be likened to a horse and horseman: the mission of the soul is to fight and vanquish the forces of Untruth as a knight mounted on his horse smites his enemies (*Denkart* 3:218). At death – itself introduced by Ahriman – the soul separates from the body to face its individual judgement; the 'form' of man remains with Ohrmazd and is reunited with the soul at the resurrection to face trial at the Last Judgement.

The united soul and body lead the battle against the powers of evil and accordingly Ahriman struggles to rend their union, to drive a wedge between man's essence, the soul, and its weapon and garment, the body.[39] Moreover, while Ohrmazd turned his spiritual creations into materiality, Ahriman's dark and evil spiritual essence, which has the 'substance' of death, cannot be transmuted into materiality. The spiritual evil of Ahriman does not have actual material being and can only invade the already created physical world of Ohrmazd, where it can achieve 'only a secondary kind of existence, the evil substance being clothed inside a material being, and taking on an alien shape'.[40] Ahriman's indwelling in the visible world remains in the bodies of humans, whom he tries to corrupt and to make his own; accordingly the divine and demonic coexist and fight for supremacy in man. Through adherence to the Good Religion, through good deeds, piety and righteousness man cultivates the divine element in himself and becomes a 'Good Man', a 'friend' and 'helper' of the gods. Conversely, the wicked and sinful are possessed by the *daevas* and incarnate the spiritual evil and will of Ahriman. The division between the righteous and the wicked is emblematic of the Time of Mixture of good and evil upon Ahriman's aggression: Ohrmazd has to appoint a fixed period of contest against him to prevent that mixture in his creation becoming eternal. The material world itself is to serve as a prison-house for the Destructive Spirit and eventually he will be banished from human beings at the Last Judgement, after which spirit and flesh will finally be wed together.

Although Zoroastrian dualism and its vision of the soul's destiny differ significantly from the soul–body dualism in Orphism and Platonism, traditions emerged in Greece that tried to associate the origins of the two forms of dualism. Some late classical authors asserted that Plato, who stated in the *Republic* (379c) that the cause of evil lay outside God, was himself introduced to the Zoroastrian dualist doctrine in Phoenicia. Within Platonism itself there emerged tendencies that sought to associate Zoroastrian and Platonic dualism and tried to make 'Zoroaster a precursor of Plato or Plato a reincarnation of Zoroaster'.[41] The placing of Zoroaster six millennia or two cycles of 3,000 years before Plato, served to link the figures as two seminal stages in the transmission of knowledge and implied 'the return of dualism'[42] with the advent of Plato. One legendary tradition, reiterated by the first antipope, Hippolytus, relates that Pythagoras went to Babylon to receive the teachings of 'Zaratas (Zoroaster) the Chaldean'.[43] Some scholars have argued for possible Iranian influences on the Pythagorean and Orphic movements but their suggestions have been consistently opposed. Affinities have also been suggested between Zoroastrianism and the specific teachings of Empedocles (c. 490–430 BC) of the dual and alternating action of the two forces of love and strife on the four eternal roots or elements – earth, fire, air and water.[44]

While Zoroaster's renown persisted in the pagan Greek world from the time of Plato to late antiquity, in Iran itself the original rigour of his teachings was to undergo gradual mitigation. As Zoroastrianism spread and matured it reintegrated some of the ignored deities and cultic traditions of the Aryan past, and Zoroaster's own utterances in the *Gathas* about the opposition between the twin Spirits were to receive new theological translations. With the rise of the Iranian empire of the Achaemenids as a world power in the sixth century BC and the ensuing Zoroastrian progress in its dominions, the Good Religion of Ahura Mazda was bound to encounter the rich religious world of Mesopotamia.

Creator and Destroyer

In the sixth century BC, which saw the rise of Confucianism in China, Buddhism in India and Orphism in Greece, Zoroastrianism rose to religious prominence in the first world empire, the Persian empire under the Achaemenid dynasty (550–330 BC),[45] and entered an era of expansion and transformation.

The spectacular growth of Achaemenid Persia as the new ascendant power in the Middle East was secured by the conquests of its founder, Cyrus the Great, who succeeded in uniting much of the Iranian world in what was to become the first Iranian *imperium*. The beginning of his meteoric ascent to imperial prominence can be traced to 550 BC, when he united the Medes and the Persians by taking over the Median kingdom, which had already established its control over northern Mesopotamia. In 612 BC the Median kingdom had entered into a crucial alliance with the renascent Babylon to deliver the mortal blow to the Assyrian empire, the reputed 'rod' of Yahweh's anger (Isaiah 10:5), which for centuries had dominated most of western Asia. Now it was Babylon's turn to fall to Cyrus, whose birth was reputedly foreshadowed by a dream of a vine growing from his mother's womb to cover the whole of Asia (Herodotus 1.108), while in Isaiah 45 he was recognized as the 'anointed' of Yahweh, destined to destroy Babylonian power and save Israel. Following Cyrus' conquests in Anatolia (Asia Minor) and Mesopotamia, the Persian empire began to expand to both the east and the west. Under Cyrus' successors, Achaemenid Persia consolidated its dominion over western Asia, conquered Egypt and encroached upon the Balkans, where it extended its control to the Danube delta and annexed most of Thrace and Macedonia. Around 500 BC, the boundaries of the Persian empire were already stretching from the Danube to the Indus river and from Nubian

Sudan and the Nile to the Caucasus and the Caspian Sea. For the Achaemenid monarchs, Thrace apparently seemed a vital gateway for further advance into Europe and the Persian armies repeatedly burst into the southern Balkans, threatening to overrun Greece. In 481 BC Xerxes the Great (485–465 BC) ventured to bridge the Hellespont from Asia to Europe and cursed its waters when his first bridges were destroyed in a storm. Before crossing ceremonially into the Balkans, Xerxes invoked the gods of Persia to let nothing hinder his conquest of all Europe, to annex and unite her according to the will and under the 'shadow' of Ahura Mazda. The collision between Persia and Greece has been traditionally seen as the first and archetypal clash of the 'monarchical, hierarchic and priestly' east and the 'republican, egalitarian and secular' west.[46] Despite Xerxes' occupation of Athens in 480 and the Persian burning of the Acropolis, his invasion was repelled and the Achaemenids failed to conquer peninsular Greece and advance further into the Balkans. Though the Achaemenid empire was to lose its hold of its European possessions, it continued to play an important role in the Greek world and to interfere in Greece's affairs until, under Alexander the Great, Macedonian troops finally led the triumphant pan-Hellenic crusade against Persia.

The Achaemenids divided their empire into twenty satrapies and presided over numerous satraps and vassal dynasts as sacrosanct 'Kings of the World'. The Achaemenid royal ideology synthesized both Aryan and Near Eastern monarchic traditions; it was the Achaemenid monarch, Darius the Great (521–486 BC), who was the first to proclaim that he was king by the will of Ahura Mazda, 'the greatest of the gods'. Achaemenid Persia succeeded to the rich and varied Babylonian civilizations but, unlike the Assyrians and Babylonians, the Achaemenid rulers recognized and largely tolerated the native religions, customs and loyalties in their dominions. Under their aegis the many disparate cultures and faiths of the Persian empire were integrated and reconciled, sparking off a rich and vibrant civilization. The Achaemenid 'Kings of the World' honoured and even patronized the old cults of Mesopotamia. To legitimize his succession to Babylonian kingship the founder of the empire, Cyrus the Great, assumed the role of a benefactor and protector of Marduk's famous temple complex, Esagila, and other main Babylonian shrines like Ezida, the temple of the Babylonian god of wisdom, Nabu. His successors largely continued this policy and the alleged anti-Babylonian excesses of Xerxes, the demolition of Esagila and the melting down of Marduk's statue – acts deemed sometimes to have virtually destroyed the 'soul' of Babylon[47] – are in all probability entirely fictitious.

Whether the first two Achaemenid rulers, Cyrus and Cambyses, were Zoroastrian adherents remains an open question, but Darius, who founded the spectacular ceremonial capital of the empire at Persepolis as a sacred centre of Achaemenid kingship, was a Mazda-worshipper and proclaimed that all his deeds were in accordance with the will of Ahura Mazda.[48] Herodotus tells (1:209) how, in a dream, Cyrus had seen Darius with two wings on his shoulders, overshadowing Asia with one wing and Europe with the other. During his reign Darius campaigned far and wide, from the Punjab in Asia to the Balkans in Europe, where his offensive against the Scythians carried the Persian advance further to the north-east, into Ukraine. In one of his inscriptions, Darius solemnly declared: 'Ahura Mazda, when he saw this earth in commotion thereafter bestowed it upon me, made me king. By the will of Ahura Mazda I put it down in its place', and proclaimed that no one should rebel against the command of Ahura Mazda who had created earth, sky, and man and had made Darius king, 'one king of many, one lord of many'.[49] The elevation of Zoroastrianism in the Achaemenid empire led to considerable growth of the Zoroastrian priesthood and changes in Zoroastrian worship, including the inauguration of temple cults and the establishment of the temple worship of fire in the so-called 'houses of fire' during the later Achaemenid era. While the Good Religion flourished and expanded under the Achaemenids, the fortunes of *daeva*-worship, castigated and proscribed earlier by Zoroaster, are extremely obscure and largely untraceable. Xerxes had apparently banned *daeva*-worship in the Achaemenid empire and proclaimed that he had destroyed a sanctuary of the *daevas* and uprooted their cult in a land where it was prevalent in order to establish the worship of Ahura Mazda 'with due order and rites'.[50] At the same time, his queen, Amestris, was reputed to have buried alive fourteen young Persians, sons of Persian notables, to propitiate the god of the underworld (Herodotus 7:114), a sacrifice which clearly did not follow the 'due order and rites' of Mazda-worship.

The consolidation and elevation of Zoroastrianism in the Achaemenid empire is commonly attributed to the Magi, the Median
sacerdotal tribe or caste, which appears analogous to the Indian
Brahmins or the Levites of ancient Israel and had formed the
hereditary priestly class of the Median kingdom.[51] Apart from
Media, the Magi were the acknowledged priesthood entrusted with
the conduct of religious ceremonies in western Iran. Herodotus
recounted that the Persians could not offer a sacrifice without a
Magus (1:132). In antiquity the Magi were renowned for their
expertise in divination by dreams, for fostering incestuous marriages
and for leaving the dead to be picked clean by vultures and wild
animals. Whether the Magi joined the eastern Zoroastrian priests in
a single ecclesiastical body under the Achaemenids remains unknown; their earliest contacts with the Zoroastrianism of eastern
Iran are enveloped in obscurity. While not all of the Magi associated
themselves with Zoroastrianism, those who adopted its beliefs and
practices clearly served as a vehicle for the spread of Zoroastrianism
in the western Achaemenid dominions, including Asia Minor. For
the Greeks, the teachings of the Magi were indeed the teachings of
Zoroaster and the prophet of Ahura Mazda came to be styled
'Magus'. The Magi had certainly been exposed to Mesopotamian
religious influences but since the Achaemenid era their fortunes
were inextricably linked to Zoroastrianism, although at least some
of them continued to participate in non-Zoroastrian rites. The
religious eclecticism of the Magi was to make possible the assimilation of Near Eastern traditions within Zoroastrianism in an era
when the religious policy of the Achaemenids allowed coexistence
and prolonged interchange between varying religions and cults.
Among the important religious developments of the Achaemenid
era was the Zoroastrian rehabilitation of the Lord Covenant, Mithra
'of the broad pastures', as the supreme of the divine *yazatas* (the
worshipful ones), who came to be revered as the omniscient master
of the world and its wakeful guardian against the powers of evil and
darkness. Another significant religious phenomenon of the period
was the spread of the cult of the Iranian Great Goddess Anahita,
the Immaculate Lady of the 'strong undefiled waters', which arose
under strong Assyrio-Babylonian influence. The Achaemenid King
of Kings Artaxerxes II (404–359 BC) is credited with erecting many

statues of Anahita throughout the empire and since his reign Mithra and Anahita came to be invoked along with the supreme god Ahura Mazda as the divine protectors of the Iranian monarchy.[52]

The religious transformations of the Achaemenid era also affected the original Zoroastrian dualist scheme, which had set in absolute opposition the principles of Truth and Untruth and the related opposing modes of being of the two twin Spirits beneath Ahura Mazda, the Holy and the Destructive Spirits. While in the *Gathas* of Zoroaster Ahura Mazda is clearly above the twin Spirits, in Achaemenid Zoroastrianism the process began of the coalescence of Ahura Mazda (Ohrmazd) with Spenta Mainyu, the Holy Spirit. From 'the first and the ultimate' supreme God, Ahura Mazda was gradually equated with the holy one of the twin Spirits and came to confront what was now his symmetrical opposite, the virtual anti-God, Angra Mainyu (Ahriman). The new, Zoroastrian dualist formula, in which Ohrmazd and Ahriman were positioned as two primordial and independent principles, swiftly gained currency, even outside the Iranian world. Aristotle reported in his work *On Philosophy* (fourth century BC) that the Magi believed in the existence of two principles, the good spirit, Zeus or 'Oromasdes', and the evil spirit, Hades or 'Arimanius'. Aristotle's statement on Magian dualism is recorded in Diogenes Laertius' *Lives of Eminent Philosophers* (1:8), where Diogenes also attributes to Aristotle the belief that the Magi were more ancient than the Egyptians. In modern research, the Magi have indeed been credited with the hardening of early Zoroastrian dualism in the doctrine of Ohrmazd versus Ahriman and Babylonian influences are also thought to have played a role in this Magian revision of the teaching of the twin Spirits.[53] How much this fully-fledged dualism affected Achaemenid Zoroastrianism may only be conjectured but it received theological elaboration and eventually emerged as the orthodoxy of the Zoroastrian state–church of the Sassanid empire in Iran (*c.* AD 224–640).

In classical Zoroastrian accounts of the new strict dualist system, Ohrmazd and Ahriman appeared as two separate prime causes existing from the beginning – two absolutely independent and diametrically opposed spirits. Ohrmazd is the Creator who is 'all goodness and all light' and dwells in the Endless Light above, while Ahriman is the Destroyer who is 'all wickedness and full of death' and dwells in the abyss of Endless Darkness below. Another dualist polarity contrasts the hot, moist, bright and light substance of Ohrmazd to the cold, dry, heavy and dark essence of Ahriman, whose abode is traditionally located in the northern realms (*Vendidad* 19:1). In the beginning Ohrmazd and Ahriman, Light and Darkness, are separated by the Void; Ohrmazd, who is ever in the light, is infinite in time but limited in space by Ahriman, who is slow in knowledge, possessed by the will to smite and limited in time, as he is to be vanquished in the last days (*Greater Bundahishn* 1:1–12). While originally Ahriman was unaware of the existence of Light, the omniscient Ohrmazd knew of the existence of the Destructive Spirit, with his constant desire for aggression and destruction. The unfolding conflict between the Creator and the Destroyer is recounted in the dramatic opening section of the *Greater Bundahishn*. Ohrmazd was aware that Ahriman would attack and try to merge with him. As a defence he fashioned in the Void an ideal creation which remained motionless, without thought and intangible for three thousand years. At the same time, Ahriman perceived the light of Ohrmazd and, obsessed with envy and desire for destruction, fashioned from his own darkness his destructive 'black and ashen' creation and the essence of the demons, an 'evil (disorderly) movement', designed to bring destruction to Ohrmazd's creatures. Ohrmazd offered peace to Ahriman, promising him immortality if he would abstain from battle to praise and aid Ohrmazd's creation. Ahriman forcefully rejected the offer and threatened not only to destroy Ohrmazd and his creation, but also to bring Ohrmazd's creatures to hate their Creator and to love him, the Destructive Spirit (*Greater Bundahishn* 1:22).

To counter the threat of Ahriman's aggression and everlasting struggle and mixture in his creation, Ohrmazd succeeded in securing from him a pact that the conflict was to last for the finite period of nine thousand years. Mithra was seen as watching over the pact. Ahriman was then expelled from Ohrmazd's ideal creation and cast down in his abyss of darkness, where he remained powerless for three thousand years. Ohrmazd proceeded with fashioning his material creation to repulse the future attack of the Destructive Spirit, the source of the 'disorderly movement'. Following the creation of the sky, water, earth and plants, Ohrmazd fashioned the primal 'Lone-created Bull' and the radiant Gayomart, the primal 'Righteous Man'. Ohrmazd presented the pre-existent souls of men, the *fravashis*, with the free choice: either to incarnate in material form, fight the Untruth and ultimately be immortalized with their bodies, or to be sheltered in the ideal world from the onslaught and enmity of the Destroyer, Ahriman. Confronted with the menacing prospect of Ahriman's inevitable aggression and corruption of the world, but also with the vision of the final rehabilitation of the Good Creation and immortalization of man, the souls chose to descend and carry out Ohrmazd's struggle against Ahriman.

After being ejected from Ohrmazd's spiritual world, Ahriman lay in his realm of Darkness in lethargy, his fear of Righteous Man prolonging his passivity. After three millennia, however, Ahriman was finally restored to action by the 'Accursed Whore'. Seen sometimes as the first woman, she was created by Ohrmazd but defected to the Destructive Spirit, by whom she was defiled and elevated as 'the demon Whore queen of her brood'.[54] Roused by her frenzy to demolish the dignity of the 'Righteous Man' and the Bull, Ahriman rallied his demons and weapons and, rising up in the form of a serpent, burst into the visible world at the time of the vernal equinox. The beginning of Ahriman's assault seemed to justify his sinister appellation as a 'destroyer of the world' – the whole of creation was assailed, ravaged and made powerless and at noon it was invaded by darkness.

In his triumphant oration in the *Selections of Zadspram* (4:3), Ahriman claimed 'perfect victory' and recounted his feats of destruction which had despoiled the sky, waters and earth. Besides withering the plants and blending fire with darkness and smoke, Ahriman assailed the primal Bull, which died, soothed by a narcotic mercifully provided by Ohrmazd. Ahriman, moreover, let loose the 'Demon of Death', Atvihad, along with a thousand minions, upon the Righteous Man, who, though severely weakened, survived the assault of the Destroyer and lived for another thirty years.

Ahriman's offensive also set the planets against the constellations in a heavenly war in which the planets, described as 'pregnant with darkness', fought on Ahriman's side. The so-called 'dark Sun and Moon', seen as responsible for the eclipses, were bound to the 'chariot' of the true Sun and Moon and hence were incapable of harm. In the unfolding war, the leader of the constellations, the Pole Star, confronted the planets' commander, Saturn, as the Great Bear, Vega, Scorpio and Sirius fought respectively Jupiter, Mars, Venus and Mercury. The Great Bear and Scorpio defeated their adversaries, but the planets also had their victories: Mars and Saturn prevailed in their contests, while Mercury and Sirius proved equally balanced. Feared thereafter as the planet of death, in Zoroastrian lore Saturn gained the title of 'he whose aggression reaches far', whereas Jupiter, having succumbed to the Great Bear, became the planet of life. In the Zoroastrian astrological scheme the death of the Righteous Man was caused by the predominance of Saturn, the death-bringer, placed in Libra, and 'victorious' over the life-bringer, Jupiter, weakly positioned in Capricorn.

Ahriman might have despoiled the Good Creation but his strong-hold in the material world proved to be his perennial prison, as the sky was made a fortress which he could not overcome to return to his realm of darkness. After battles with Ohrmazd's spiritual forces, Ahriman was cast into the middle of the earth and firmly ensnared in the world, which itself now had to go through transformation to 'duality, opposition, combat and mingling of high and low' (*Greater Bundahishn* 4:28). On the death of the primal Bull his limbs gave rise to plant life, his seed to animal life and his blood to the fruit of the vine, while the seed of the dying Righteous Man generated the first human couple, Mashye and Mashyane, the Zoroastrian counterparts of Adam and Eve. The 'father and mother of the world' were inducted into Ohrmazd's 'righteous order', but none the less were led astray by Ahriman to proclaim him the creator of water, earth and the plants, and thus committed 'the root sin against dualism',[55] mistaking the Destroyer for the Creator. After indulging in more crimes, Mashye and Mashyane were consigned to Hell until the time of the final transfiguration and salvation.

Despite the transgressions of the first human couple, the human race, endowed as it is with free will, remained in the forefront of Ohrmazd's battle against Ahriman throughout the remaining millennia of the original pact. The demonic hosts of Ahriman are not only compelled to fight a losing battle against Ohrmazd's forces, but also the genius of 'disorderly motion' is bound to finally provoke their self-ruin. While Ahriman's infernal world was doomed to be exterminated at the hands of Ohrmazd's commanders amid demonic orgies of self-destruction, Ahriman himself was to be hurled out of the sky through the very hole he had pierced into the Good Creation. With the decimation of the calamitous potency of the Destroyer Ahriman, described sometimes as the cutting off of his head, the Creator Ohrmazd finally becomes infinite not only in time, but also in space, to reign over the transfigured world for all eternity.

Although prevalent during long phases in the history of Zoroastrianism, the strict dualism of Ohrmazd and Ahriman, the two first principles, was not the only theological solution to Zoroaster's riddle of the twin Spirits, 'renowned to be in conflict' (*Yasna* 30:3). While Aristotle alluded to the two primordial principles of the Magi 'Oromasdes' and 'Arimanius', Eudemus of Rhodes recorded another form of Magian dualism. According to Eudemus the Magi and the 'whole Aryan race' called the 'whole intelligible and unitary universe' Space or Time, from which were extracted a good god and an evil demon, light and darkness, the first ruled by Ohrmazd, the latter by Ahriman.

The Father of Light and Darkness

Besides their contribution to the transformation of the original Zoroastrian dualism in the Achaemenid era the Magi encouraged religious syncretism which prepared the ground for the assimilation of new religious concepts in Zoroastrianism. The cults of ancient Mesopotamian deities persisted in what were now the Near Eastern domains of the Achaemenid empire in the fertile climate of the encounter between the Iranian and Mesopotamian civilizations. In parallel with Iranian dualism, neo-Babylonian thought seems to have already begun to develop a dualist antagonism between the patron god of Babylon, Bel Marduk, and the Mesopotamian archetypal deity of war, death and the underworld, Nergal, the consort of the queen of underworld and darkness, Ereshkigal.[56] As a personification of the destructive power of the sun and fire and with solar attributes, like the gryphon and the lion, Nergal is sometimes associated with the Mesopotamian sun-god Shamash. With his underworld association, Nergal was sometimes equated with the Phoenician netherworld deity Moloch (Molech), who, besides having close connections with the cult of the dead and necromancy, was said to be worshipped with human sacrifice, the victims being 'passed through fire'. Extolled as 'Lord of the Gods' and bringer of light, Bel Marduk came to be conceived of as a deity of good, while the formidable death-god Nergal, the dreaded bringer of fever and pestilence, predictably emerged as his antipode. The rival cults of the two deities persisted into the Achaemenid era and there are indications that the worship of Nergal merged with vestiges of archaic Iranian pre-Zoroastrian traditions.[57]

In the Achaemenid period Zoroaster's Good Religion not only increased its influence and authority but also felt the impact of new religious developments in the Near East: under Babylonian influence, certain novel religious and astrological notions concerning the nature and functions of time brought about a new transmutation of the Iranian dualist scheme with the emergence of a new trend in Zoroastrianism, Zurvanism.

In Zurvanism, Ohrmazd and Ahriman were regarded as twin offspring of the higher and supreme being Zurvan, the god of Time, later identified also with Destiny. While Zurvanism has sometimes been considered an independent pre-Zoroastrian Iranian religion of a time-god, with its own teachings and ritual, the prevailing view is that Zurvanism arose as a new form of modified Zoroastrian dualism which sought the common origin of Ohrmazd and Ahriman in a deified Time–Destiny.[58] The origin and early fortunes of Zurvanism, as well as its potential links with other religious trends, such as Orphism and early Buddhism and Greek philosophical traditions, are still in dispute. What seems certain is that the Zurvanite trend in Zoroastrianism developed during the middle or late Achaemenid era in western Iran and was particularly influential throughout the Persian domains in Asia Minor.

Zurvan, as the deity of Infinite Space–Time and Destiny, was raised to the supreme status of the first principle, the boundless 'Great and Just God', who is without origin and is the source of all things. Extolled as the Lord of the Zoroastrian 'Three Times', Zurvan came to be worshipped as a quaternity, a four-fold god, associated with Light, Power and Wisdom in addition to Time. He is the primal, intelligible unitary All that has begotten both Ohrmazd and Ahriman and the related antitheses of good and evil, light and darkness, et cetera. As the sole ultimate *fons et origo* of all cosmic dualities, Zurvan seems essentially a coincidence of opposites, a pre-existing and eternal Being that transcends good and evil. Zurvanism came to develop its own elaborate mythology, which is preserved in fragmentary and sometimes slightly discrepant versions, expounding its central concepts of the pre-eminence of Zurvan, the primeval birth of Ohrmazd and Ahriman and their alternating rule of the world.

In Zurvanite mythology,[59] before anything existed, there was the boundless and eternal Zurvan who yearned to father a son who would create and preside over heaven and earth as a Creator and Cosmocrator. To provoke the birth of a creator-god, Zurvan was set to offer sacrifices for a whole millennium but eventually came to doubt their efficacy and conceived twin sons – Ohrmazd, the embodiment of his wisdom, and Ahriman, the incarnation of his doubt. In some versions of the myth, Zurvan originally appears androgynous, while other variants introduce a mother goddess figure who was brought into existence early in cosmic history and conceived Ohrmazd and Ahriman after Zurvan's plea. As Zurvan had pledged that the first-born should be consecrated king, Ahriman, the would-be Lord of darkness and evil, ventured to 'tear the womb open', and came forth to claim his right to kingship. In other versions Ahriman inaugurated Untruth and proclaimed that he was Ohrmazd, but was betrayed by his 'dark and stinking' nature. The luminous and fragrant Ohrmazd was born immediately after him but although Zurvan aspired to bestow the kingship on the younger twin son, the Lord of goodness and light, he had to cede to the first-born the kingdom of the world for the finite period of 9,000 years. While unwillingly granting the kingship to Ahriman, Zurvan conferred on Ohrmazd the priesthood with its emblem, the barsom twigs. After Zurvan offered sacrifices for his son, Ohrmazd had to offer sacrifices for his father. Bestowed with divine priest-hood, Ohrmazd was made king over Ahriman, apparently in the heavenly realm, and after the fixed nine millennia of Ahrimanic dominion in the world, he was to reign and order everything according to his will.

Zurvan endows his two sons with their respective weapons or 'garments', which they choose freely according to their will and which invest them with their contrasting essences. The substance of light, Ohrmazd's essence, that 'form of fire – bright, white, round and manifest afar' (*Greater Bundahishn* 1:44), was regarded in Zurvanism as an implement granted by his father. The weapon chosen by Ohrmazd was also associated with the robes of priesthood, the 'shining white garment' that furthered good and destroyed evil. In contrast, the ashen-coloured garment chosen by Ahriman as his essence was associated with heretical priesthood, 'evil knowledge' and the Ahrimanic planets, mostly with Saturn, the bringer of death. In *The Selections of Zadspram*, the 'black and ashen garment' that Zurvan conferred on Ahriman incorporated an implement that was like blazing fire, containing the substance of *Az*, greed or lust; the garment was also described as fashioned from the substance of darkness, 'mingled with the power of Zurvan'.[60] The investiture of Ahriman with the 'black and ashen garment' was part of a treaty centred on Ahriman's archetypal threat to bring the material creation to love him and to hate Ohrmazd, a threat defined as the belief in one principle, that 'the Increaser and the Destroyer are the same'. If at the end of his nine-millennia reign Ahriman had not fulfilled this threat, his creations would be devoured by his very own weapon of greed and lust. Unlike that of Ohrmazd, Ahriman's investiture contained the seed of self-destruction and was bound to bring about the ultimate extinguishing of the dark personification of Zurvan's doubt.

In Zurvanism both Ohrmazd and Ahriman exercised their creative potential, Ohrmazd mastering heaven, earth and all that was good and right, whereas Ahriman's counter-creations were confined to the demons and all that was evil and twisted. Yet the cosmogonic role of Ahriman appears ambiguous in some Zurvanite myths. One fable recounts that despite his beautiful creations, Ohrmazd did not know how to create light; it was Ahriman who imparted to him through the demon Mahmi the formula for the creation of the luminaries: through incest. Ohrmazd's intercourse with his mother generated the Sun, while his union with his sister gave birth to the Moon: these luminaries finally illuminated his creation.[61] Otherwise, in later Zurvanism the fortunes of man and the world were seen as being determined in the cosmic conflict between the twelve zodiacal signs, the commanders on Ohrmazd's side, and the seven planets, Ahriman's commanders, which oppress creation and inflict death and evil on it. These tendencies in Zurvanism gave rise to extreme, fatalist Zurvanite circles, whose focus on the all-pervading dominance of Time–Destiny was clearly in sharp contrast to the ethos of Zoroastrianism as a religion of free will. Apart from this fatalism, materialist trends also emerged in Zurvanism which rejected the cardinal Zoroastrian beliefs in reward and punishment, heaven and hell, and proclaimed all things material and that they stemmed from Infinite Time, the first principle of the world. According to another form of Zurvanism, prior to the birth of Ohrmazd and Ahriman Zurvan created fire and water, considered in Zoroastrian lore as brother and sister, the male and female principles. In this Zurvanite system both Ohrmazd and Ahriman derived from the combination of the first two principles of fire and water and it is plausible that Ohrmazd owed his essence to the heat of the fire and the moisture of water, while Ahriman inherited the coldness of water and the dryness of fire.[62]

In Zoroastrian literature Zurvanism is described as the teachings of Ohrmazd and Ahriman, as 'two brothers of one womb'. In modern scholarship Zurvanism has been evaluated variously as an intellectual–philosophical current within Zoroastrianism, as a dangerous heresy verging on materialism and fatalism, but also as the 'supreme effort of Iranian theology to transcend dualism and to postulate a single principle that will explain the world'.[63] In its search for a single unitary principle Zurvanism modified the original dualist message of Zoroaster, which had condemned evil as a force entirely separate from and alien to the supreme Wise Lord. Far from being an eternal and independent principle, evil in Zurvanism emanates from a 'doubt', a kind of divine fall or imperfection within the First Cause, the Great and Just God Zurvan. The ensuing cosmic struggle between Ohrmazd and Ahriman is virtually designed to restore the unity and integrity of the absolute Godhead. Moreover, the fixed nine millennia of strife and mixture between Ohrmazd and Ahriman in orthodox Zoroastrianism was transformed in Zurvanism into a time of Ahriman's rule in the world, fixed in a treaty with Zurvan. By enthroning Ahriman as Prince of the World for 9,000 years Zurvanism radically reshaped the traditional Zoroastrian sacred history, which had always rejected the idea of an era of

Ahrimanic supremacy over the Good Creation and an Ahrimanic worldly *imperium*. None the less, in the first century AD, in his *De Iside et Osiride*, Plutarch described the notion of an aeon ruled by Ahriman as one of the tenets of the original teachings of the 'Magus Zoroaster'. In his account of Zoroastrian doctrine both 'Horomazes' (Ohrmazd) and 'Areimanius' (Ahriman) enjoy 3,000 years of supremacy and wage war for another 3,000 years. The belief that the evil principle came to preside over creation for a limited period became the crux of later religious and esoteric traditions. One of the cosmogonic systems of Bon, the pre-Buddhist religion of Tibet, which was said to have been introduced from Tazig (Iran), closely parallels Zurvanite concepts, possibly reflecting either earlier Iranian influences or the later impact of Manichaean missions in central Asia and China. In this Bon cosmogony, from the one and self-created 'Master of Being' two lights emanated, white and black, which respectively begat a white man, the radiant god of Being (The Master who loves Existence), associated with the principle of good and order, and a black man who embodied Non-Being (Black Hell), the source of the constellations, demonic forces, evil, pestilence and tribulations.[64]

Besides this Bon cosmogonic trinity, direct or indirect Zurvanite influences are often held to have underlain the New Testament allusion to the Devil as the 'Prince of this world' (John 16:11) and the 'god of this passing age' (2 Corinthians 4:4). While, however, the Iranian influences in the New Testament are still keenly debated, it is beyond doubt that the Christian concept of the Devil as the head of the realm of evil and originator of sin and death was determined by the radical transformations in Jewish notions of evil and Satan in the centuries that followed the dramatic vicissitudes that transformed and left their lasting imprint on the Jewish world in the sixth century BC – the Babylonian Captivity and the return to Zion. Apart from annexing the Judaean kingdom and deporting a great part of its population to Babylonia in 586 BC, the Babylonian king Nebuchadnezzar had destroyed Jerusalem and burned Solomon's Temple, but forty-seven years later Babylon herself was to fall to Cyrus the Great and the Persian conquest set the stage for the 'second Jewish Exodus', the restoration of Jerusalem, the rebuilding and consecration of the new Temple and the advent of the Second Temple era.

The 'Anointed' and the 'King of Babylon'

In 539 BC the short but historic war between the nascent Achaemenid and the neo-Babylonian (Chaldean) empires ended with Cyrus' bloodless capture of Babylon. Amid what the Persian imperial propaganda described as jubilant scenes of celebration he established himself in the Babylonian palace of the kings. Cyrus' manifesto, the so-called *Cyrus Cylinder*, and the *Verse Account of Nabonidus*, which was apparently composed in Babylonian priestly circles, praised Cyrus' capture of Babylon as an act of salvation for the city of Bel Marduk, which was lamented for having suffered desecration during the reign of the last king of the neo-Babylonian empire, Nabonidus. Both versions of Cyrus' collision with Nabonidus contrast the image of Cyrus as a saviour-king, chosen by Marduk to bring peace to Babylon, to that of Nabonidus as a heretical king, a royal adversary of Marduk, opposed to his priesthood and his worship in Esagila, 'the temple of heaven and the underworld'.[65]

Nabonidus may have been a son of the high priestess of the moon-god Sin at Harran and a zealous patron of his cult extolled him in his inscriptions as the 'Divine Crescent, the king of all gods' and even 'god of gods'. Towards the end of his reign Nabonidus sought to elevate Sin to the head of the Babylonian pantheon and declared that Esagila, Ezida and other major Babylonian sanctuaries belonged to Sin and were his indwellings.[66] While the extent of the priestly and general opposition to Nabonidus' reforms has to be conjectured, the hostile testimony to his proclivities portrayed the last Chaldean king of Babylon as a self-styled visionary, guided by revelations, dreams and miracles, who had irrevocably offended the Babylonian priesthood with his eccentric endeavours to introduce the cultic image of the moon in eclipse. Portrayed as a self-deluded and heretical ruler, Nabonidus was also accused of erecting a replica of Esagila, a type of counter-Esagila, near Marduk's old temple, interrupting the regular temple offerings, mixing up rites, uttering blasphemies at temple images and finally omitting the crucial Babylonian New Year feast. Nabonidus, who had proclaimed that all his military operations executed the will of the Divine Crescent, campaigned for ten years in northern Arabia; during his absence the

New Year festival was not celebrated, while his son, the crown-prince Belshazzar, remained as co-regent in Babylon. In the dramatic scriptural version of Babylon's fall (Daniel 5) Belshazzar emerged as the last king of Babylon; warned of the imminent fall of his 'numbered' and 'divided' kingdom by the mysterious writings on the wall, he was 'weighed in the balance' and 'found wanting', doomed to be killed the very night Babylon passed to the Medes and the Persians.

Nabonidus' return to Babylon was marked by another controversial and enigmatic act: on the eve of the Persian invasion he collected in Babylon images from the traditional Mesopotamian shrines of the 'gods of the Sumer and Akkad'. During the latter part of Nabonidus' rule Babylonia was beset by plague and famine, and Cyrus' propaganda proclaimed that, with their sanctuaries in ruins, the inhabitants of Sumer and Akkad had become like the 'living dead'. The propaganda extolled Cyrus as a vehicle of Marduk's grace upon the Mesopotamian 'living dead', returning them to life, and an instrument of Marduk's judgement on the 'mad king' Nabonidus who had plunged the worship of the Babylonian tutelar god into abomination.

The account of Cyrus' ceremonial entry into Babylon eulogized him as a messianic saviour-king, chosen by Marduk, the 'king of the gods', as the 'king of the world' to re-establish Marduk's divine supremacy in god's own 'golden city', to assume the Babylonian kingship and to return the 'images of Babylonia', removed from their 'thrones' by Nabonidus, to their ancient sacred sites. Following the pattern of Babylonian kingship, Cyrus apparently ordered the immediate restoration and beautification of temple sites throughout Babylonia and as the new 'beloved' of Marduk he is heralded in the *Cyrus Cylinder* as 'King of the World, Great King, King of Babylon, King of Sumer and Akkad and of the four rims of the earth'. After the defeat of the last Chaldean king, Babylon was to pass under Achaemenid suzerainty for more than two centuries and according to the propaganda of the new rulers, despite Nabonidus' claims to hidden wisdom and revelations, his arcane exploits and creations were finally effaced and consigned to the flames in the first religious campaigns of the righteous Cyrus.

The divine judgement on Babylon and her king is among the

dominant themes of Jewish prophetic literature and one of its most dramatic embroideries is the parable in Isaiah 14 where the king of Babylon is metaphorically associated with *Helel ben Shahar* (the Shining One, Son of Dawn, or, as translated in the Vulgate, Lucifer). As the 'son of the morning' the king of Babylon had boastfully wished to ascend into heaven, to exalt his throne 'above the stars of God' and to make himself equal to the Most High (Isaiah 14:12–19) but is doomed to be brought down to Sheol where he is greeted by the shades of the dead kings. Having desolated his land and slain his people, the king of Babylon, the former conqueror of nations, is destined to fall to the utmost depths of the abyss, cut out of his grave like an abominable shoot, 'a corpse trampled underfoot'.

In Isaiah 47 the unleashing of divine vengeance dethroned and cast into the shadows the 'virgin daughter of Babylon', the evil-struck 'daughter of the Chaldeans', who, with her shame finally exposed, is no longer to be called the queen of kingdoms, and who is betrayed by her own wisdom, for all her 'monstrous sorceries' and 'countless spells' (9–10). Notwithstanding the tenor of the prophetic utterances, Cyrus' treatment of defeated Babylon was famously lenient, unlike earlier conquests of the 'golden city', such as that of the Assyrian king Sennacherib, who captured and sacked rebellious Babylon in 689 BC, removed Marduk's statue to Assyria and proclaimed that he had made Babylon's destruction more complete 'than that by a flood' so that its 'temples and gods might not be remembered'. While Cyrus was to assume the Babylonian kingship and to be honoured as a builder and 'lover' of the temples of Esagila and Ezida, his triumph over Nabonidus was bound to mark the end of the 'Babylonian captivity' of the Jews that had been deported from Judaea to the 'rivers of Babylon' in several successive waves, the last of which dated from the final fall of Jerusalem to Babylon in 586 BC. Inevitably, the founder of the Achaemenid empire is extolled in the Old Testament, where it is Yahweh, the Lord God of Israel, who calls upon Cyrus, 'the ravenous bird from the east', to dethrone the 'virgin daughter of Babylon'. In the so-called Deutero-Isaiah (or Second Isaiah, composed of Chapters 40–55 of the Book of Isaiah) Yahweh unequivocally proclaims that he holds the right hand of his 'anointed', Cyrus, 'to subdue nations before him' and to 'undo the might of kings', 'before whom gates shall be opened and no doors be shut' (Isaiah 45:1). Yahweh promises Cyrus 'treasures of darkness, and hidden riches of secret places' (Isaiah 45:3, *KJV*) and raises him as his 'shepherd' who will fulfil all his purpose (Isaiah 44:28) and execute the divine judgement upon Babylon, which 'has been a golden cup in the Lord's hand to make all the earth drunk' (Jeremiah 51:7). As God's anointed, Cyrus emerges as a type of Gentile Messiah, a mediator of the divine grace to Israel, the prophesied 'shepherd of Yahweh', who would deliver the Jews from the 'Babylonian burden' and summon them to rebuild Jerusalem and Solomon's Temple destroyed by the Babylonian royal 'servant of Yahweh', King Nebuchadnezzar II in 586 BC.

Cyrus' historical edict of 538 BC, recounted in Ezra 1:1–4, decreed the restoration of Yahweh worship in Jerusalem and initiated the gradual return of many Babylonian Jewish deportees to Zion, which in the expression of Deutero-Isaiah had been left desolate like a widow bereaved of her children (Isaiah 49:21). The edict reflects the general religious policy of Cyrus, who, according to the *Cyrus Cylinder*, had returned Mesopotamian exiles to their homeland and had reinstated their gods to their original abodes. Cyrus had already legitimized his succession to the Babylonian kingdom: by authorizing the rebuilding of the Jerusalem Temple he apparently proclaimed his succession to the Davidic royal line in a restored and 'consoled' Jerusalem. Although for historical reasons the later rabbinic attitudes to Cyrus appear ambivalent, his renown as a pious ruler, who assisted the rebuilding of the Temple, endured and, according to some Jewish traditions, as a 'Cosmocrator' he was found worthy to ascend and sit on the throne of Solomon.[67]

The return of the Jewish exilic community to Zion under the aegis of Cyrus was perceived as a new Exodus guided by the God of Israel. The completion of the new Jerusalem Temple was presided over by Zerubbabel, a scion of the royal House of David. Its rebuilding, 'as commanded by the God of Israel and according to the decrees of Cyrus and Darius' (Ezra 6:14–15), was completed early in the reign of Darius and it was consecrated on 12 March 516 BC. The renewal of Yahweh temple-worship in Jerusalem was inevitably conceived as a re-establishment of the covenant between

Yahweh, 'who chooses Jerusalem', and his chosen people. The dawning of the Second Temple era (516 BC–AD 70) was marked by fervent anticipation of the return of the divine presence and favour to a restored and redeemed Israel: 'Now, says the Lord, I have come back to Zion and I will dwell in Jerusalem' (Zechariah 8:3). Besides the restoration of the temple the new era was expected to bring the coming of God's kingdom on earth, foretold in Isaiah 2:1–4, as well as justice, salvation and renewal to the world. The dramatic redemption of Israel was seen as the herald of the impending universal conversion of the nations to Israel's faith, when Yahweh's judgement and salvation would reach 'the end of the earth' and all men would turn to the 'Holy One of Israel' to be saved and to 'serve him with one consent' (Zephaniah 3:9). The writings of post-exilic prophets like Zechariah and Haggai are pervaded by intense anticipation of the coming eschatological age and the cataclysmic 'Day of Yahweh' when he would 'shake heaven and earth, sea and land' along with all nations (Haggai 2:6–7) to create the 'new heavens and a new earth' where, as foretold in Isaiah 65:17, 'former things shall no more be remembered'.

These expectations were closely intertwined with prophetic hopes for the ultimate restoration of the Davidic kingdom under the rule of a messianic king of the royal line of David, the prophesied 'shoot' from the 'stock of Jesse' (Isaiah 11:1), the 'righteous Branch from David's line, a king who shall rule wisely' (Jeremiah 23:5). Besides his role of a rightful King of Israel, the Davidic Messiah was sometimes envisioned as a superhuman saviour, as the ideal king of justice who would rule in 'the last days' and whose 'rule shall extend from sea to sea, from the River to the ends of the earth' (Zechariah 9:10). In the period of the Second Temple Jewish messianism received new vigour and generated traditions which were to have profound and lasting effects on Jewish, Christian and Islamic religious thought. The Book of Zechariah already distinguished two messianic figures, 'two anointed ones', the priestly Messiah and the royal Messiah, figures that are further elaborated in Jewish apocalyptic literature and the Dead Sea Scrolls. They were to be associated later with the star 'out of Jacob' and the comet 'from Israel' of Balaam's prophecy in Numbers 24:17, while in the Dead Sea Scrolls there appears also a third messianic figure, the prophet of the last days.

The expectations of the re-establishment of the Davidic kingdom were apparently centred initially on the Davidic princely 'shoot', Zerubbabel ('scion of Babylon'), governor of Jerusalem, who along with the high priest Joshua, conducted the rebuilding of the Second Temple, also known as the 'Zerubbabel Temple', as Zerubbabel was portrayed as laying the foundation of the Temple with his own hands, finishing it 'neither by force of arms nor by brute strength' but by the spirit of the Lord (Zechariah 4:6–10). In the Book of Haggai (2:20–23), on the very day of the foundation of the Second Temple, the Lord of Hosts was to shake heaven and earth, to overturn the heathen realms and to 'wear' Zerubbabel, the chosen one, as a 'signet-ring'. Apparently seen as the prophesied righteous 'Branch of David', he was expected to ascend the Davidic throne to rule as the royal Messiah alongside the priestly 'anointed', Joshua (Zechariah 6:12–13). However, Zerubbabel's sudden and baffling disappearance from the biblical narrative obscures his actual role in the Jewish messianic ferment during the building of the Second Temple.

Although Davidic restoration proved impossible, the ensuing two centuries of Achaemenid reign over the Jews in Palestine and Mesopotamia marked a watershed in Jewish religious and political history. Favoured by the tolerance of the Persian monarchs, the Jewish community in Judaea succeeded in establishing a theocratic state under Achaemenid authority and in completing the religious and legal reforms which had matured during the Babylonian captivity. Achaemenid monarchs like Darius I took care of the maintenance of the Jerusalem Temple (Ezra 6:1–11); later Jewish literature repeatedly acknowledges the cardinal role of the Achaemenids in the restoration of the Jewish national and religious polity. The Jewish leader Nehemiah, who rebuilt the walls of Jerusalem, was a cupbearer to the Achaemenid King of Kings Artaxerxes I, from whom he received the governorship of Judah, where he introduced wide-ranging political and religious reforms. Another celebrated Jewish reformer and religious leader, Ezra, was invested by Artaxerxes with the authority to restore and enforce the 'Law of Moses' as the imperial law in Israel. As a 'scribe versed in questions concerning the commandments and the statutes of the Lord laid upon Israel' (Ezra 7:11) Ezra brought from Babylon the 'Book of the Law of Moses' which was proclaimed 'in sight of all the people' of Jerusalem. The Achaemenid endorsement of the crucial missions of Nehemiah and Ezra highlights the extent to which the consolidation and codification of post-exilic Judaism depended on Persian religious policy, as inaugurated by Cyrus the Great and sustained with few exceptions until the very end of the Achaemenid empire.[68]

The Jews owed the rebuilding of Jerusalem, the Temple and their religious life to the Achaemenids' tolerant policies. Continuing Persian royal patronage of a restored and theocratic Israel undoubtedly made them more accessible to Iranian religious influences:[69] besides the apparent impact of Iranian law on Judaism, Jewish religious thought did not remain unstirred by the unravelling of new religious syntheses in the Achaemenid empire. During the ordeals of the Babylonian exile, Jewish religion had been exposed to new and alien systems of belief. During the Second Temple era it came into close contact with Iranian religious traditions and underwent a series of significant transformations. Some of the newly developed Jewish concepts and beliefs of the period betray strong affinities with Babylonian and Zoroastrian traditions and have repeatedly been attributed to direct Mesopotamian and Iranian influences on exilic and post-exilic Judaism.[70]

Despite the apparent differences between Zoroastrian and Judaic religious vision, they shared the unifying focus of the monotheistic rule of one supreme Creator-God who guides the historical process towards its climax in the final universal judgement and salvation. Both Zoroastrianism and Judaism vehemently rejected polytheism and idolatry and their prolonged intercourse in the wake of the Babylonian exile was conditioned by what is usually described as mutual religious sympathy. The seminal encounter between the Iranian and Jewish religious worlds certainly left its imprint on the evolution of post-exilic Jewish messianism and eschatology and on the rise of Jewish apocalypticism. Similarly, some important developments in the angelology and demonology of post-exilic Judaism, which elaborated and classified the parallel orders and functions of the warring angelic and demonic hosts, have been generally accepted as reflecting Babylonian and Zoroastrian influences. Moreover, it was in the Second Temple era that angels came to acquire names and individuality in contrast to the impersonal and anonymous angelic figures in pre-exilic Judaism. In the rabbinic tradition re-corded in the Jerusalem Talmud the names of the angels were brought by the Jews from Babylonia and the early post-exilic Book of Zechariah, with its notion of the 'seven eyes of the Lord', was the first to acknowledge and distinguish the different angelic orders. In later Jewish angelological lore the heavenly hosts came to be classified in an intricate and carefully graded hierarchy crowned by the divine septet of the seven archangels who have entry to the presence of the glory of the Lord (Tobit 12:15). Three of the seven archangels, Michael, Gabriel and Raphael, formed the group of 'the angels of the divine Presence' together with Phanuel (later Uriel, one of the septet) and came to be envisaged as situated at the four sides of God's throne. These elaborations of Jewish angelology were at least partially motivated by the new religious ethos of post-exilic Judaism that tended to view Yahweh as a more remote and transcendent God, who acts in history through the agency of his angelic mediators. The simultaneous forging of Jewish demonology, with its demonic orders and princes, was closely related to the unfolding of new Jewish approaches to the problem of the origin of evil and its enlarged role in cosmic history. Initially part of popular Jewish beliefs, the demons came to be seen increasingly as agents of a force that was emerging as the very personification of the spirit of evil – Satan.

Creator and Accuser

In pre-exilic biblical books the term 'satan' serves to denote generally an adversary or accuser, human or supernatural, and could be applied both in regard to David as 'satan' to the Philistines (1 Samuel 29:4) and to the angel of God who was sent to obstruct Balaam's way in Numbers 22:32. However, in the Book of Zechariah and the Book of Job there already appears a distinct accusing angel, called Satan, who emerges as a type of celestial prosecutor of Yahweh's heavenly court charged with overseeing, provoking and reporting the sins of humanity. In Zechariah 3:1, while the high priest Joshua, the priestly 'anointed', represents Israel at the divine court, Satan stands at his right hand to accuse and resist him, being opposed by the benevolent 'angel of the Lord'. In the prologue of the Book of Job 'Satan' appears among the *bnai ha-elohim*, the 'sons of God', who are admitted into God's presence and were traditionally considered to form the divine council. In the Book of Job, Satan emerges more clearly as the allurer and accuser of the righteous, whom he subjects to ordeals, temptations and punishment. In his incessant pursuit of human wickedness and sins Satan descends to earth to test man and then ascends to the divine court to raise accusations against humanity. When asked by God whence he had come, Satan suggestively replied: 'Ranging over the earth . . . from end to end' or according to the King James Version, 'from going to and fro in the earth and walking up and down in it' (Job 1:7). Yet, however hostile to man, the Satan of Job and Zechariah still serves as an accusing and punishing angel under the supreme authority of Yahweh. In later Jewish thought, however, besides his ambivalent role of tester and tempter Satan came to be charged with some of the abstruse or destructive biblical exploits of the Lord of Israel.

In the so-called 'Call to Cyrus' in Deutero-Isaiah, Yahweh reveals himself to the Achaemenid monarch as the one who creates good and evil (Isaiah 45:7), a probable reaction to the Zoroastrian type of ethical dualism of good and evil. In earlier Jewish writings Yahweh could be portrayed variously as seeking the murder of Moses (Exodus 4:24–6), promising vengeance on his enemies in which his 'sword shall devour flesh, blood of slain and captives, the heads of the enemy princes' (Deuteronomy 32:42), sending an evil spirit to plague Saul (1 Samuel 16:14), or putting a lying spirit in the mouth of Ahab's prophets to lure the apostate king to his death (1 Kings 22:23). In the prophetic literature Yahweh could be envisaged as teaching Isaiah his strategy of bringing desolation to Israel (Isaiah 6:8–12) or sending Jeremiah to the nations with a 'cup of fiery wine' to make them drink it 'and go mad; such is the sword which I am sending among them' (Jeremiah 25:16). The books of the prophets reinforced the image of Yahweh as an omnipotent and omniscient Creator, sovereign of the universe and inscrutable Lord of history, whose exalted judgement is responsible for both beneficial and calamitous events in Israel's history. As told in the Book of Job (36:23) the ways of Yahweh are bound to remain inimitable, unaccountable and impenetrable or in the famous words of the earliest of the Latter Prophets, Amos: 'Shall there be evil in a city, and the Lord hath not done it?' (Amos 3:5 *KJV*).

Among the biblical episodes when Yahweh's anger falls upon his 'chosen people', particularly enigmatic is the one chronicled in Chapter 24 of the Second Book of Samuel. There Yahweh, whose wrath has been kindled again by Israel, chooses to move David against Israel and prevails upon him to number her tribes, the census itself being a sin against the divine will (2 Samuel 24:1–2). David is lured into the census sin and has to choose one of the three proposed punishments: seven years of famine in the land, three months of flight before the enemy or three days' pestilence (12–14). David chooses to fall 'in the hands of the Lord, for his mercy is great', rather than into the hands of man, and Yahweh sends upon Israel three days' plague that smites 70,000 people. In the graphic scene of 2 Samuel 24:16, the avenging angel of pestilence stretches his hand even upon Jerusalem to destroy the Holy City before Yahweh 'repented of the evil'. When this 'census and punishment' story was recounted in Chapter 21 of the First Book of Chronicles, composed in the late Achaemenid era, it was Satan who set himself against Israel and incited David to number his people. Entrusted with one of the 'inimitable' deeds of Yahweh, Satan emerged as an individual and independent force and his name was no longer a mere title but was the proper name of the spirit of evil who was now opposed to the Lord of Israel and provoked man to sin against his laws. This new, magnified role of Satan heralded and paved the way for momentous transmutations in Jewish satanology – while in Job and Zechariah, Satan sought to incite Yahweh against man, in the First Book of Chronicles he had already moved man against Yahweh.

The story of David's census in the First Book of Chronicles marks the beginning of the striking transformation of the 'celestial prosecutor', who was originally subordinate to Yahweh, into the spirit of personified evil, the arch-enemy of good and righteousness, the source of all death, sin and destruction. The course of this transformation has long been a highly complicated and controversial problem and its current reading tends to seek its origins in the intensive search for new theodicies in post-exilic Judaism. With the newly developed distinctions between ethical good and evil, between the creative and destructive features of Yahweh, Satan eventually came to personify Yahweh's destructive powers, becoming an incarnation of 'the dark side of the God, that element within Yahweh which obstructs the good'.[71] Various stages and nuances of the evolution of Jewish satanology can be discerned in Jewish literature of the period that separates the last texts of the Old Testament and the earliest writings of the New Testament, the so-called intertestamental period. The crystallization of the concept of Satan as the embodiment of cosmic evil is often attributed to Iranian dualist influence on post-exilic Judaism; but still the process of personification of evil was to follow differing courses in Judaism and Zoroastrianism. Apart from the compensating monistic tendencies in Zurvanism, Zoroastrianism, on the whole, moved gradually towards radical dualism in which the King of Darkness, Ahriman, was to evolve into an anti-god, coeval if not coeternal with Ohrmazd. Although exposed to Persian religious insights, Jewish satanology resisted the lures of such dualism and the power of the Jewish Satan remained ever-restrained by the omnipotence and omniscience of Yahweh. None the less, some of the novel developments in post-exilic Jewish thought approximated dualism as Satan came to be seen as progressively independent and hostile to Yahweh and his creation. With the increasing focus on ethical religiosity and the struggle between the forces of good and evil in the cosmos and in the soul of man, which was particularly pronounced in apocalyptic literature, trends emerged that sought and approached dualist solutions to the riddle of the origin of evil. In the apocryphal book the Wisdom of Solomon (2:24), likewise with Zoroastrian Ahriman, Satan was revealed as the superhuman agency that was opposed to God and man and had brought sin and death into the world to thwart divine purposes. Moreover, in the Wisdom of Solomon, Satan was associated with the serpent from the story of the fall in Genesis 3 and for the first time mankind appears divided into two opposing classes: the adherents of God and of Satan. The implicit association of Satan with the serpent and the bisection of humanity into men of God's and men of Satan's lot anticipated far-reaching developments of Jewish satanology which eventually set the stage for the Christian concept of the Devil. Yet, however transformed in intertestamental literature, the figure of Satan in Judaism was to retain its initial functions of a tester and accuser and in the Talmudic era one of his common appellations was still *Satan mekatreg* (Satan the Accuser).

The Prince of Light and the Angel of Darkness

The notion of a supernatural agency epitomizing the forces of evil, sin and disorder, which was introduced in the intertestamental era, came to be associated with the ambiguous biblical narrative of the union between the 'the sons of the gods', the *bnai ha-elohim*, and the 'daughters of men' (Genesis 6:2–4). In the biblical text the *bnai ha-elohim* had descended on the 'daughters of men' and their progeny was a race of giants, the 'heroes of old, men of renown'. In the intertestamental period the coming of the *bnai ha-elohim* to earth was seen increasingly as a fall from heaven and they became rebellious fallen angels who corrupted themselves with 'the daughters of men' and introduced evil and sin into the world. In Jewish apocryphal literature, and particularly in Jewish apocalyptic thought, the rebellion and fall of the angels were repeatedly assigned to the Prince of Evil, variously named Satan, Belial or Mastema. In the apocalyptic account of the downfall of the 'sons of God' or the Watchers in the early section of the Ethiopic Book of Enoch (1 Enoch),[72] the Book of the Watchers, the rebel angels were identified with fallen stars and were led by two archangels, Semyaza and Azazel, the latter being condemned as the first star to fall from heaven. Whereas Semyaza was presented as the king of the Watchers, Azazel emerged as a heavenly sage, who on his descent revealed to mankind 'the secrets of heaven' and initiated men in 'all the iniquities on earth'. However, in the later section of 1 Enoch, the Book of Parables, the Watchers were already subjects of Satan (1 Enoch 54:6), and his host of accusing 'angels of punishment' – the 'satans' – assumed a dominant position in the hierarchy of evil powers. Apart from revealing to men the 'weapons of death', one of the Watchers in the Book of Parables was already charged with leading Eve astray and the theme of the angelic–satanic seduction of Eve in some later

Jewish, Christian and Gnostic readings of the biblical story of the Fall from Paradise was luridly elaborated.

In the apocryphal Book of the Jubilees the leader of the fallen angels was Prince Mastema who, in the wake of the flood, was allowed by Yahweh to retain a tenth part of his spirits to continue exercising his will among the 'children of men'. Identified with Satan (10–11), Prince Mastema was credited with some of Yahweh's biblical exploits like the inducement of Abraham to sacrifice Isaac, the attempt to murder Moses on his way to Egypt and the hardening of the Pharaoh's heart to pursue the 'children of Israel'. Mastema–Satan was also revealed as the power that aided the Egyptian magicians against Moses and was also unleashed to smite all of the Egyptian first-born during the original Passover, the first night of the Jewish Exodus from Egypt.

In addition to such disclosures of 'satanic' intrusions in Genesis and Exodus, the apocryphal literature of the Second Temple era elaborated in greater detail the story of the sin of the Watchers – the downfall of the evil angels and their prince, a downfall variously ascribed to lust, pride or envy of Adam. In later apocryphal traditions Satan came to be identified as the main malignant agent of the fall of Adam and Eve, either by deceiving or corrupting Eve in the flesh, or through the medium of the serpent. Before tempting Eve to eat of the fruit of the tree of knowledge, Satan could be envisaged as pouring his evil venom upon the tree, which itself might be recognized as a satanic tool from the beginning, planted by Satan to lead Adam and Eve astray.[73]

Besides the title 'Satan', the leader of the fallen angels was often styled Belial ('worthlessness' or 'destruction'), who as the arch-enemy of God presided over a counter-hierarchy and counter-realm of evil and darkness. In the apocryphal Testaments of the Twelve Patriarchs man has to choose between the Spirit of Truth and the Spirit of Untruth, the law of the Lord and the law of Belial, as God has granted man two ways, good and evil, whereas Belial offered his adherents the sword, the 'mother of the seven evils'. The spirit of Truth and the spirit of Untruth waited upon man and in between was the 'spirit of understanding of the mind'. Belial was clearly associated with Satan, with the spirit of wrath being positioned at Satan's right hand and the spirit of hatred seen to work for the death of mankind, turning light into darkness. At the end of time a great many men would ally with Belial's 'kingdom of the enemy', which, however, would be terminated in a final war when the messianic agents of God's salvation would wrest the souls of men from Belial's captivity and with the 'judgment of truth' he would be cast into the eternal fire.

The increasing preoccupation with the riddle of the origins and power of evil in God's creation also led to the emergence of traditions that Satan–Belial was the cosmic force temporarily prevailing in the world. In the apocryphal Martyrdom and Ascension of Isaiah he was revealed as the 'angel of iniquity' who had ruled 'this world' from the beginning and in the last days would descend from his firmament as the 'king of this world', as an anti-Messiah, a type of Antichrist, seeking to enslave men with his signs and wonders.[74] The advent of Belial as the anti-Messiah and his miracles, which included the raising of the dead, was envisaged in some of the books of the Sibylline Oracles which also prophesied his destruction by divine fire.[75]

The belief that the passing age of 'tribulation and strife' was the dominion of Belial, destined to be annihilated for ever in an impending final war between the forces of good and evil, lay at the heart of the eschatology of the Dead Sea Scrolls, the writings of the Qumran sect.[76] In the Dead Sea Scrolls the teachings of the 'Two Ways' and the 'Two Spirits' were carried to the dualist limits that Judaism could tolerate. The Qumran Community Rule explicitly stated that, following his 'glorious design', God appointed for man two spirits in which to walk 'until the time of the final inquisition', the spirit of truth and the spirit of falsehood. Whereas the origin of truth was in the 'Fountain of Light', the source of deceit lay in the 'Wellspring of Darkness'. Accordingly the Prince of Light ruled over the 'sons of righteousness', who walked in the 'ways of light', while the Angel of Darkness presided over the 'sons of deceit' who walked in the 'ways of darkness'. Despite God's everlasting love for the spirit of light and his hatred of the spirit and ways of darkness, He designed 'according to his mysteries' the two spirits to stand 'in equal measure until the final age' (Community Rule 4). He also set them in eternal opposition and rivalry which foreordained the fierce perpetual struggle between their divisions. By his 'inscrutable design' (or 'mysteries') God appointed a time of dominion for the Angel of Darkness when he would lead the righteous astray and subject the people of Israel to ordeals and terror. The sins of humanity, which was split into the opposing leagues of the 'sons of light' and the 'sons of darkness', were provoked by Belial's hegemony. The Community Rule darkly alluded to accounts of the iniquities and the sins of the children of Israel during Belial's domination, which were recited during the induction of neophytes into the sect, who themselves had to confess their sins and resist thereafter Belial's trials. The supremacy of Belial and the existence of falsehood would finally be terminated at the time of the final inquisition when every human being would be judged in accordance with his choice of the opposing ways of the two spirits. The 'sons of darkness' would suffer torment at the hands of the angels of destruction and annihilation by fire, whereas the 'sons of light' would be immortalized in eternal light.

Yet with all their apparent parallels to Zoroastrian sacred history, the dramatic accounts of the cosmic strife and war between the forces of light and darkness in the Dead Sea Scrolls do not develop religious dualism proper. The dualism between the 'Prince of Light' and the 'Angel of Darkness' remains dualism under the one God and it is God's inscrutable will that ordains a fixed era of Belial's dominion in the world. God created Belial, the angel of hostility, 'to corrupt' and with his dominion being in the darkness, Belial's purpose was to bring about 'wickedness and guilt', while the spirits associated with him were 'angels of destruction' who 'follow only the laws of darkness' (War Rule 13). Conversely, the Angel or Prince of Light had under his dominion the spirits of truth and was charged to help the people who cast their lot 'in the portion of light'. As in the Zoroastrian paradigm, the Qumran Prince of Light and Angel of Darkness were perceived as two opposite and coexistent metaphysical entities vying in the world and in the human soul, leading respectively the warring hosts of light and darkness that were marshalled in elaborate parallel lists of spirits. Other Qumran themes betray striking affinities with traditional Zoroastrian teachings but it has been shown that they were developed in a 'scrappy and incomplete fashion' and, being without apparent Jewish antecedents, suggest indebtedness to the more complete and consistent system in

Zoroastrianism, indicating that the 'direction of influence was from Iran to Judaism'.[77]

While the Qumran scheme of cosmic opposition and conflict was almost certainly affected by the Zoroastrian dualist model, the doctrine of the 'dominion of Belial' – the notion that Belial presides over the current age and 'this world' – is reminiscent of the basic Zurvanite myth of Ahriman's finite reign over the world. Inevitably there have been attempts to associate Belial of Qumran with Ahriman of Zurvanism but again, apart from the obvious parallels, the myths of the Qumranite and Zurvanite 'Lords of Darkness' were formulated along differing lines.[78] Zurvanite Ahriman attained the right of kingship and finite rule over the world by violating the will and the sacrificial purpose of his primeval Father and was endowed with the 'black, ashen garment' of greed and self-destruction as part of a 'treaty' with Zurvan, whereas the Qumranite Belial held sway in the world according to God's inscrutable design and through his inborn power for corruption until the time of the final Inquisition. The Qumranite Prince of Light, who was envisaged as the main defender of the 'sons of righteousness' against the reign of Belial (War Rule 13:10), is often identified with the archangel Michael who came to be elevated in the post-exilic era as an *archistrategos* (commander) of the hosts, punisher of the fallen angels and heavenly protector of Israel. Following the old notion that the wars of the nations correlated to the wars of the 'host of heaven in heaven' (Isaiah 24:21–2), the Book of Daniel revealed Michael as Israel's angelic patron who vied with the prince–angels of Persia and Greece and was expected to arise and deliver Israel in the turmoil of the final 'time of trouble' (12:1). According to the Qumran War Rule (17:7), with the advent of the final age and the 'eternal light', Michael's dominion will be raised among the angels and Israel will be exalted 'among all flesh'.

As the guardian angel of Israel, Michael inevitably came to be extolled as the principal enemy of Israel's main accuser and opponent, Satan, and their 'war in heaven' was to assume cosmic and eschatological dimensions both in Judaism and Christianity. The Jewish opposition between the Prince of Light and the Angel of Darkness, between Michael and Satan, which emerged in the apocalyptic strands of post-exilic Judaism, has sometimes been seen either as a reflection or a modified and tamed version of the Iranian dualism of Ohrmazd and Ahriman, whether in its traditional Zoroastrian or Zurvanite versions. The discovery and publication of the Dead Sea Scrolls has certainly deepened the problem of Irano-Jewish religious intercourse both in the Achaemenid era and in the post-Achaemenid, Hellenistic period in the Near East. Most of the already charted developments of Jewish intertestamental thought are recorded in the Hellenistic era, inaugurated by the conquests of Alexander the Great in Asia, when the meeting of east and west gave rise to novel and lasting religious currents, when religious dualism reached striking new forms and new spheres of influence in the unfolding age of syncretism.

CHAPTER TWO

Syncretism and Orthodoxy

In 331 BC Alexander the Great defeated the armies of the last
Achaemenid King of Kings, Darius III, for the third time in what
the Macedonian king saw as a 'legitimate war for the sovereignty of
Asia' (Arrian 2:12.5). The following year Alexander sacked and
burned the ceremonial imperial capital of Persepolis, seen by the
Macedonian conqueror as the most hateful of all cities of Asia
(Diodorus 17:70.1); its devastation was to be proclaimed as retribution for Xerxes' destruction of the Athenian Acropolis. The burning
of Persepolis 'violated and ended the long cycle of sacred Achaemenid kingship'[1] and despite fierce Iranian resistance in Sogdiana and
Bactria, the great Persian empire fell to the Macedonian pupil of
Aristotle, who proclaimed himself the new 'King of Asia', guided
and protected by Zeus and Ammon. While the Achaemenids had
failed to advance deeper into Europe and were eventually repelled
from the Balkans, Alexander, who came to be seen as inspired by
the myths of Dionysus' conquest of India, advanced through western
Asia as far as the north-west extremes of the Indian subcontinent.
The conquests of Alexander, reputedly crowned in Athens as the
second Dionysus, signalled the end of the classical epoch in Greece
and the advent of the cosmopolitan Hellenistic era (323–30 BC).
Within the short space of twelve years, Alexander succeeded in
unifying most of the ancient historical world into a vast empire.

For the defeated Persians the Macedonian 'son of Zeus-Ammon'
was to become the 'accursed Iskander', the 'evil-destined' avatar of
Ahriman, a murderer of Magi, who quenched sacred fires and
brought war and devastation to Iran but was finally forced to flee
from the world.[2] In the Sibylline Oracles (3:381–5) Alexander's
conquests were portrayed as bringing suffering to Asia and Europe,
while Macedonia, having captured 'fortified' Babylon and become

'mistress of every land' under the sun, was prophesied an evil fate, leaving only a name for posterity. Notwithstanding the Persian charge that Alexander had despoiled Iran with Ahrimanic hatred and strife, his newly founded empire inherited and sought to preserve the imperial traditions of the Achaemenid *ancien régime*, encouraging further designs for Helleno-Iranian union. Alexander's empire passed its prime with his mysterious death in Babylon in 323 BC, to be split among the successor dynasties of the Antigonids, who acceded initially to its European domains, the Ptolemies, who fell heir to Egypt, and the Seleucids, whose kingdom absorbed most of the former Achaemenid domains in Asia.

With the demise of the Persian empire, Zoroastrianism inevitably seemed set to lose much of its authority and prestige secured under the Achaemenids. Following traditional Babylonian patterns, Alexander inaugurated temple-building and renovation work at Babylonian cultic sites like the old temple complex of Marduk and, according to Plutarch, it was at Babylon that Alexander was proclaimed King of Asia. Babylon may have been designed to be the eastern capital of his empire, but in Persia Alexander's reputed restoration of the tomb of Cyrus the Great failed to win renown in the Iranian world, where he was credited with burning the Zoroastrian sacred scriptures, the *Avesta*, and it is hardly surprising that in Zoroastrian eschatological traditions the unfolding era of alien rule came to be associated with the age of 'the evil sovereignty of the wicked demons' preceding the advent of the Saviour, the Saoshyant.[3] The advent of the Hellenistic era marked the beginning of the spread of Graeco-Macedonian culture in the Middle East, a far-reaching diffusion which was accelerated by the consolidation, growing influence and religious policies of the kingdoms of the Ptolemies and the Seleucids. With the advance of Hellenism in Egypt, Mesopotamia, Palestine and Iran a new syncretism developed, which blended Greek and Oriental motifs in art, architecture and literature. In the field of religion the syncretism and remarkable tolerance of the Hellenistic era were even more apparent, as the search for new religious syntheses led to the creation of composite and often exotic forms of worship. Besides the Eleusinian, Samothracian, Dionysian and Orphic mysteries, which were traditional for the classical Greek world, the late Hellenistic period saw the spread of mystery cults centred on Oriental deities like Cybele, Attis, Isis, Osiris, Sabazius and Mithra.[4] With their recondite rites of initiation and promises of secret knowledge, regeneration and salvation, the Graeco-Oriental mystery cults proved exceptionally enduring and flourished even more widely in the Roman imperial age. With the Greek political advance in the Orient, Hellenism penetrated deep into the eastern Iranian world and reached northern India, where it stimulated the rise of novel, startling forms of cultural and religious syncretism. Simultaneously, with the establishment of the Mauryan Indian empire under Chandragupta, who in 305 BC won back Punjab from the Seleucids, Indian religious influences radiated back into western Asia. When Chandragupta's grandson, the Buddhist emperor Ashoka (c. 273–c. 232 BC), inaugurated the expansion of Buddhism into a world faith, his Buddhist missions, 'the envoys of the Beloved of God', were sent to preach the Dharma not only to the Greeks in his realm but also in the Seleucid and Ptolemaic dominions and in the heartlands of the Hellenistic world – Greece and Macedonia.[5]

Three Empires

Among the Hellenistic monarchs, the Ptolemaic rulers of Egypt – who claimed descent from Heracles and Dionysus – promoted a religious policy that was perhaps the most symptomatic manifestation of the new Hellenistic *Zeitgeist* of syncretism. While Ptolemaic policy was aimed at Graeco-Egyptian religious synthesis, the convergence of Greek and Iranian traditions in the former Achaemenid domains in Asia was to breed its own cast of syncretism, particularly influential and long-lasting in Bactria, which became the easternmost outpost of Hellenism in Asia and continued to spread Hellenistic influence in India and central Asia.

The Graeco-Iranian syntheses were not confined to Anatolia and western Asia but emerged also in the large Greek diaspora in the northern Pontic–Azov (Black Sea) region, which had long been dominated by the Scythians but in the last two pre-Christian centuries had fallen under the sway of other northern Iranian tribes, the

Sarmatians and the Alans. The religious climate of the region, largely determined by the strong Greek presence, was profoundly affected by the advent of the Sarmatians with their specific Iranian religious lore, which was probably influenced by Zoroastrian traditions possibly comprising a pantheon of seven gods including fire-worship. The new cosmopolitan spirit of the Hellenistic era spawned the flourishing of a rich syncretistic culture in the area of the Cimmerian Bosphorus (the Straits of Kerch connecting the Black and Azov Seas), which was densely settled by Greek colonists in the seventh and sixth centuries. The Graeco-Iranian contacts and interplay in the Cimmerian Bosphorus, which in classical geography was regarded as the meeting point between Europe and Asia, have often been compared to those in Bactria. Under the vigorous Thracian dynasty of the Spartocids (438–110 BC) the Cimmerian Bosphorus evolved into a strong Hellenistic kingdom and later acknowledged nominal Roman sovereignty. The Bosphorus kingdom flourished in the Pontic *Pax Romana* until the fourth century AD; its culture and religion, where Greek, Sarmato-Scythian, Iranian and later Jewish elements intermingled, retained its distinct Hellenistic character into the Christian era.[6]

With its Babylonian capital and its boundaries extending initially from Asia Minor to India, the Hellenistic kingdom of the Seleucids seemed particularly suited to fostering cultural and religious fusion between expanding Hellenism and Oriental traditions. Besides their Hellenizing policies the Seleucids, who claimed descent from Apollo, tolerated the varied religions in their kingdom and encouraged a revival of Babylonian learning and cults. In 199 BC the Seleucids finally won Palestine from the Ptolemies, where the growing influence of Hellenism was to bring about deep divisions within Judaism. The conflict between the Jewish Hellenizers and the Jewish traditionalists, the Hasidim, reached its climax in 167 BC when, during the infamous crusade of the Seleucid ruler Antiochus IV Epiphanes against Judaism, the Jerusalem Temple suffered the installation of alien worship, perhaps the cult of the Canaanite god Baal Shamin, sacrifices of pigs and the 'abomination of desolation' (1 Maccabees 1:54) on the altar. In the violent Jewish backlash the militant Maccabean family restored Judaea's independence, which lasted until 64 BC when it was Rome's turn to conquer the Promised Land

and eventually to destroy Jerusalem and the Temple under Titus in
AD 70. Apart from its historic collisions with Judaism in Palestine
the Hellenistic invasion of the Seleucid age profoundly transformed
the cultural and religious make-up of Syria and Mesopotamia and
made deep inroads into the Iranian world.[7]

From the mid third century BC onwards, however, the Seleucids
began to lose hold of their eastern dominions. The first challenge to
Seleucid authority in the east was the foundation of an independent
Graeco-Bactrian kingdom, centred on Bactria and Sogdiana. In its
eclectic religious climate Hellenistic and Zoroastrian traditions co-
existed with a variety of cults, including what appear to have been
'daevic' forms of worship. While Hellenism continued to thrive in
the Graeco-Bactrian kingdom and also spread into the adjacent
Asian region, Greek expansion in Iran itself was challenged by
vigorous Iranian reaction. At the same time as the emergence of the
Graeco-Bactrian kingdom the Seleucids were faced with the rise of
a rival Iranian monarchy in the old Achaemenid satrapy of Parthia
in north-east Iran. The driving force was Iranian semi-nomads from
central Asia, the Parni, who had apparently adopted Zoroastrianism
upon their invasion of Parthia. Under the rule of the aggressive
Arsacid dynasty (c. 250 BC–AD 226), Parthia gradually extended its
sway further in Iran and Mesopotamia, establishing its authority
over an array of vassal kingdoms and principalities. The Seleucids
were driven to the west of the Euphrates and following the Parthian
conquest of Babylonia the Arsacids adopted the old Achaemenid
title *Shah-an-Shah* (King of Kings) and claimed Achaemenid descent.
As the Seleucid kingdom declined and contracted, the new Iranian
empire expanded into a world power which came to control the
crucial trade routes between Asia and the Mediterranean.

The restoration of Iranian authority over large areas of the
former Achaemenid empire breathed new vitality into the Good
Religion: in Zoroastrian lore the first collection and edition of the
texts of the *Avesta* has been attributed to an Arsacid king. In the
Arsacid era Zoroastrian worship was upheld in image sanctuaries
and fire temples, while the Arsacids themselves maintained their
ever-burning, dynastic fire. The Magi also continued to consolidate
their spiritual hegemony in the Parthian empire. While sustaining
Zoroastrian traditions, most of the Arsacid monarchs also favoured

Hellenism, while in Commagene, eastern Anatolia, Graeco-Iranian syncretistic formations emerged in which Ohrmazd was identified with Zeus, Mithra with Apollo, the war-god Artagnes with Ares or Heracles, while Anahita was often associated with Artemis. These religious formulas appeared to gain some currency in Arsacid Iran, and along with other identifications, in which Heracles was also linked with Nergal, epitomized the syncretistic tenor of most religious developments in the Near East during the Hellenistic age.[8]

Parallel Graeco-Iranian patterns of symbiosis began to emerge also in the Graeco-Bactrian kingdom. In the mid second century BC it was plunged into the turmoil of a fresh and overpowering nomadic influx from China and central Asia where the rise of the aggressive Hsiung-nu, seen sometimes as ancestors of the Huns, forced massive Iranian migration to the west. While some of the Iranian migratory waves reached the Pontic steppes to fortify the Sarmatian power in the area, particularly important were the migratory route and campaigns of Iranian nomads called by the Chinese Yueh-Chih (which probably meant the Moon race or clan).[9] Around the time when the Maccabean family was establishing its rule in Judaea, these nomads overran Sogdiana and Bactria, and the eastern Iranian world was set to become the scene of another series of convoluted political and religious transformations. The 'Moon' nomads enriched the Graeco-Iranian-Indian civilization of Bactria with new religious imports from central Asia and China and frustrated the Parthian attempts to gain firm control of the region. The Moon clan was finally unified under the Kushan dynasty, whose kings adopted the title *devaputra* (son of god), and eventually sought to 'proclaim a new imperial age in the east'[10] after the model of the Achaemenids, while their empire grew to extend its sway from northern India to Sogdiana.

The rise of the Kushan empire as a great Asian power on a par with imperial China coincided with the consolidation of the Iranian Sarmatian supremacy over large areas in eastern Europe. In the Mediterranean the Roman conquest of Greece and the Hellenistic kingdoms had already opened the way for Roman expansion in the Middle East, where it confronted the Parthian empire. However, in the first violent confrontations between Parthia and Rome in Syria and Mesopotamia the Roman forces suffered a humiliating series of setbacks and defeats, among which the most famous was at Carrhae in 53 BC, when the forty-thousand-strong legions of Marcus Crassus, who had already plundered the treasury of the Jerusalem Temple, were destroyed by a much smaller Parthian army. Crassus' severed head was triumphantly delivered to the Parthian king amid a performance of Euripides' *The Bacchae*, where it was raised in the Dionysian climax of the play to illuminate Agave's verse: 'I am bringing home from the mountains/A vine-branch freshly cut,/For the gods have blessed our hunting'. Later, with the consolidation of Roman mastery of the Mediterranean world under the first Roman emperor Octavian Augustus (27 BC–AD 16), Parthia came to confront the aggressive *Imperium Romanum* in the west and the expanding Kushan empire in the east. Sporadically faced with war on two fronts, the Parthian military machine, with its renowned heavy cavalry, succeeded in halting the advance of the Roman legions towards Iran and Armenia at the Euphrates and for a time even threatened to recover Asia Minor for the new Iranian empire. For many authors of antiquity the historical world appeared virtually divided between Parthia and Rome with the Euphrates marking the new political and spiritual frontier between the Iranian and Graeco-Roman realms.

Although separated by Parthian Iran, the Kushan and Roman empires maintained close political, cultural and trading contacts. Affected to varying degrees by Hellenistic syncretism, the three great empires brought highly diverse races, religions and cultures into intimate contact and coexistence. In a cosmopolitan age when new spiritual currents and ideas were freely traversing the religious and political frontiers, the three polyglot empires served, each in its unique manner, as vehicles for new religious syntheses and creations which determined some of the most significant and far-reaching developments in the religious history of Eurasia.

Syncretism in the East

With their abundance of cults and their capacity to assimilate and transmute alien influences the Kushan and Roman religious worlds seem tantalizingly similar. Although little is known about the religious landscape of Iran under the Arsacids, the Parthian empire was also the meeting place of diverse religious traditions. In its western dominions the old Mesopotamian cultic traditions were still active; the Jewish communities, particularly influential in Babylonia, were loyal and supportive of Parthian authority, while the eastern part of the realm was exposed to Hindu and Buddhist influences. Christianity also penetrated and spread early in the Parthian realms, as the tolerant and syncretistic religious policy of the Arsacids was to continue until the very end of their rule in AD 226.

To the east of Parthia, the Kushan empire was to develop one of the most original Asian cultures, renowned for its elaborate and ingenious synthesis of Iranian, Indian and Graeco-Roman cultural and religious elements. The extended Kushan pantheon comprised Ahura Mazda, Buddha and Heracles, while Mithra, who was increasingly assuming solar features, was identified with Apollo and Helios.[11] Some traditional Hindu forms of worship, notably the cult of Shiva, which was prevalent in north-west India, also lived on to flourish in the Kushan realm, although now Shiva was associated variously with the hero-god Heracles or Dionysus. The foundation of the Kushan empire exposed northern India to Iranian influences but eventually Indian religiosity began to gain prominence in the empire, a process that was accelerated by a radical reformation of northern Buddhism – the rise of Mahayana Buddhism.

Simultaneously with the rise of Christianity in the Roman empire the Kushan domain witnessed the crystallization of the Mahayana (Greater Vehicle) school of Buddhism with its novel gospel of 'greater', universal salvation through faith and worship. In Mahayana Buddhism the work of salvation is inaugurated through the 'Three Bodies' of the Universal Buddha: the Body of Suchness (described also as the Body of Law, pure being and absolute source of all phenomena), the Body of Bliss or Glory and finally the Body of Transformation or 'Magical Creation' as manifested by a historical line of successive Buddhas, Sakyamuni being the historical Buddha of the present world-age. Mahayana Buddhism professed the way of the high 'Beings of Enlightenment', the Bodhisattvas, devoted to bringing full enlightenment and salvation to all living beings and praised as 'the final relief of the world' and 'the guides of the world's means of salvation'. The doctrine of the threefold nature of the supreme Buddhahood and the tenfold ladder of the Bodhisattva-ship engendered many diverse Buddha and Bodhisattva figures who were elaborated in Mahayana scriptures and iconography. In the Bodhisattva pantheon particularly honoured was the figure of Avalo-kiteshvara, Lord of Compassion, whose embodiment in Tibetan Buddhism is deemed to be its spiritual head, the Dalai Lama, with his lineage of Avalokiteshvara reincarnations. Another celebrated Bodh-isattva was Maitreya (The Kind or Loving One), who was exalted as the future Buddha and with Buddhist diffusion in Asia his cult came to acquire increasingly messianic and millenarian dimensions.

In the first Christian millennium Mahayana Buddhism, with its vigorous missionary ethos, spread far and wide in Asia and became the prevalent form of Buddhism in China, Tibet, Korea and Japan, where it gave rise to new and influential Buddhist schools of thought. The great Asian expansion of Mahayana Buddhism started from the Kushan empire, which became its stronghold during the enlightened reign of the great patron and propagator of Buddhism, Kanishka I (c. 110 AD), who emerged in Buddhist tradition as a type of second Ashoka. Under the aegis of successive Kushan rulers the empire served as a vital stepping stone for the introduction of Buddhism in central Asia and China. Yet the Mahayana reformation of Buddhism did not remain unaffected by the syncretistic climate and currents bred in the Kushan empire and the Indo-Iranian borderlands. Under Kushan rule the celebrated Buddhist art school in Gandhara, to the south of the Hindu Kush, reached its zenith. The Gandhara school developed a distinctive hybrid Graeco-Buddhist art style with curious parallels to early Christian art and elaborated for the first time the images of Buddha who had never been depicted in human form in pre-Mahayana Buddhism. Moreover, it is commonly assumed that some of the early Mahayana religious themes of light and salvation may well betray Iranian influences and the very concept of the would-be-Buddha, Maitreya, is often derived from the Zoroas-trian tradition of the saviour Saoshyant. It has also been indicated that the messianic tenor of the Maitreya cult might have been kindled by assimilation of Mithra traditions in northern Buddhism during its formative period in northern India and in the Kushan empire.[12]

While Mahayana Buddhism was beginning its expansion in Greater Asia the Graeco-Oriental Mystery religions were spreading throughout the whole Mediterranean world and reaching the acme of their popularity and influence. Christianity was also gaining increasing prominence in the Roman empire and was beginning to spread in the east into Persia and Bactria. It is worth noting that certain intriguing parallels between Mahayana Buddhism and early Christianity, including its Gnostic ramifications, have long been acknowledged but never satisfactorily discussed and explained.

During the late Hellenistic period the age-old religious and cultic traditions of Mesopotamia underwent a gradual decline and the Hellenized Orient entered an age of increasing religious ferment and new syncretistic creations. Despite the political and military opposition between the Iranian and Graeco-Roman worlds, the process of religious interchange and fusion continued unabated, as cults of saviour-gods and Gnostic syncretistic faiths spread beside Zoroastrianism, Judaism and Christianity. When in the words of Juvenal, the waters of the Syrian Orontes emptied themselves into the River Tiber; the Roman empire seemed increasingly exposed to religious invasion from the east, which ultimately weakened the hold of traditional Greek and Roman paganism, as Roman emperors chose to become initiates and even patrons of imported oriental cults.

The mystery cults, which were vying with Christianity for prestige and supremacy in the Roman world, were often devoted to 'dying and rising' deities like Attis, Adonis and Osiris. Perhaps it is significant that the cult that posed the gravest challenge to nascent Christianity focused on the unconquered and invincible god Mithras, who represented a Roman development of the Indo-Iranian Mithra. However, unlike Mithra, the Judge and Guardian of the Zoroastrian Good Creation, Mithras emerged as a saviour-god entrusted with the central divine act in the mythology of Roman Mithraism – the bull-sacrifice, the shedding of the 'eternal blood'.

Mithras the Mediator

In the 'Zoroastrian' Chapter 46 of his *De Iside et Osiride* (c. AD 70), Plutarch declared that 'Zoroaster the Magian' taught that 'votive- and thanks-offerings' should be sacrificed to the god-creator of good Horomazes, (Ohrmazd), while his rival demon-creator of evil, Areimanius (Ahriman), must be offered sinister offerings to avert evil. Plutarch even provided a vivid description of the grim offerings to Areimanius in which a herb called *omomi* had to be pounded in a mortar and, after an invocation of Hades and darkness, had to be mixed with the blood of a slain wolf and finally thrown into a sunless place. Besides dwelling on the contrasting modes of sacrifice to Horomazes and Areimanius, Plutarch recounted that, according to the Persians, between these two rival powers stood an intermediary, 'Mithras the Mediator'.

In Zoroastrian texts the Iranian Mithra could also be granted the title Mediator, but in a very different context; Plutarch's version of Zoroastrian dualism, with its prescribed parallel sacrifices to Ohrmazd and Ahriman, has understandably provoked heated controversy, as it is evidently at variance with traditional Zoroastrian values and ethics. The offerings to Ahriman have been seen as a 'conscious inversion' of Zoroastrian sacred rituals but Plutarch's account has been interpreted as representing a developed form of Zurvanism, or a mid-point between 'catholic Zoroastrianism' and the Roman Mysteries of Mithras.[13] Yet it is precisely this elusive continuity between Zoroastrianism and Roman Mithraism – between the oriental Mithra 'of the wide pastures' and the occidental Mithras the Bull-Slayer – that has proved to be one of the most notorious unsolved conundrums of the religious history of antiquity.

Roman Mithraism emerged as one of the most striking religious syntheses of antiquity: in the first four centuries of the Christian era it swept across the Roman world, becoming the favoured religion of the Roman legions and several Roman emperors. As an all-male and esoteric cult, which was diffused mainly by legionnaires, imperial officials and traders, Mithraism has often been described as a type of Roman Freemasonry. In its phenomenal spread from Syria to Britain, the cult of Mithras gained a particularly strong foothold in Italy and the Roman provinces in central and eastern Europe, while Mithras was extolled to the status of *Sol Invictus* (Invincible Sun). In his crusade to revitalize the *Imperium Romanum,* in 307, four years after launching the persecution of the Christians, Diocletian dedicated a great altar to Mithras as the protector of the empire. The elevation of Mithras in the Roman empire has been seen as a potential turning point, when Europe was confronted with the real danger of becoming Asiatic, a danger that was not matched even during the later era of sweeping Islamic expansion.[14] With all his endeavours to restore the vitality and prestige of paganism, the last pagan Roman emperor, Julian the Apostate (AD 361–3), was initiated early in the Mithraic mysteries and had a Mithraic sanctuary (*mithraeum*) erected in his palace in Constantinople. Apart from adopting Mithras as his guide and guardian god Julian also came to recognize himself as a 'human replica' of Mithras in what he saw as his redeeming religious and political mission in the Roman world. In the oft-quoted, if hyperbolic, words of Renan: 'If Christianity had been halted in its growth by some mortal illness, the world would have gone Mithraic'.[15]

However exaggerated the supposed prospects for Mithraic supremacy in Europe, the transfiguration of the ancient Iranian deity of light and war, the divine 'Judge of Iran', into a patron god of Persia's sworn enemy, the Roman empire, remains abstruse and striking. Widely differing theories have endeavoured to locate the beginnings of the Mithraic mysteries in some of the border regions between the Graeco-Roman and Iranian worlds, from Syria to the Bosphorus kingdom or the Balkans, or to associate the Roman cult with the solar cult of Mithra in the Kushan empire.[16] According to the traditional and still widespread view the mystery cult of Mithras developed in the late Hellenistic period in Asia Minor, where it seems to have been affected by some Anatolian forms of worship such as the Phrygian cult of Cybele and Attis. Formerly part of the Achaemenid empire, Asia Minor had a long-established Iranian diaspora whose Zoroastrianism seems to have been predominantly of the Zurvanite type and Magian colonies in Cappadocia are attested in the early Christian era. In the wake of Alexander's conquests Asia Minor became a fertile meeting ground of Greek, Anatolian and Persian traditions but curiously the Greek world remained particularly resistant to Mithra-worship. None the less, a questionable Latin tradition claimed that the cult of Mithra passed from the Persians to the Phrygians and from them to the Romans. In the Roman world the cult of Mithras often passed as a Phrygian cult and Mithras came to be depicted wearing a Phrygian cap and was frequently styled the 'Phrygian God' or the 'Capped One'. The role of Anatolia as the possible medium for the introduction of Mithra-worship to the Roman world is supported by Plutarch's account (Pompey 24:5) of Pompey's campaign in 67 BC against the Cilician pirates who used to perform abstruse sacrifices at the Lycian Olympus and celebrated the secret mysteries of Mithras. Despite Plutarch's evidence of transferring Cilician prisoners to Greece and Pompey's resettling of some pirates in Italy, the first steps of the Mithraic Mysteries in the Roman world still remain virtually untraceable.

What adds to the atmosphere of confusion and controversy is the obscurity surrounding the fortunes of the original Iranian cult of Mithra, which, in early Zoroastrianism at least, was largely eclipsed by the monotheistic worship of Ahura Mazda. Yet the traditional cult of Mithra did not die out and sometimes is considered to have been the prevalent form of worship among the Medes and their priesthood, the Magi, or else to have persisted in some form among the unreformed and apparently inextinguishable *daeva*-worshippers. The revived Mithra-worship of the Achaemenid era was integrated into Achaemenid Zoroastrianism but had certainly preserved some pre-Zoroastrian traditions. Some Persepolis inscriptions suggest, moreover, that in Persepolis and perhaps elsewhere in the Achaemenid empire there existed in military organizations a specific cult of Mithra comparable to the Knights of Malta or Knights Templar in medieval Christendom.[17] Besides its vital role in Achaemenid Zoroastrianism and royal ideology, the cult of Mithra arguably came into contact with Babylonian astral religion and Mithra came to be associated with the old Mesopotamian solar deity, Shamash. It is also probable, as recent research has indicated, that some forms of Mithra worship, which were preserved among the Medes and were concerned with death, the underworld and the afterlife, assimilated elements from the 'underworld' cult of Nergal.[18]

In Parthian Iran, Mithra's relation to kingship, fire- and sun-worship apparently became even more pronounced, as the cult spread in the Iranian spheres of influence in the Near East, Asia Minor and Armenia. In the syncretistic climate of the late Hellenistic era, Mithra, who as a light-god was acquiring increasingly solar attributes, was identified with solar deities like Apollo and Helios and also with Hermes as a mediator between man and the gods and as a guide of souls in the afterlife. In an era when the cult of the divinized ruler was assuming marked religious dimensions and the religions of salvation were exerting growing influence Mithra was to become the focus of new syncretistic creations. However tenuous the evidence, there are theories that while evolving as a deity of salvation, Mithra was associated also with the myths of the so-called 'great Cosmocrator–Redeemer' and the messianic king–saviour.

With its spread westwards, the cult of Mithra, already modified in the Near East, was drawn deeper into the intricate and wide-ranging processes of Graeco-Oriental syncretism and was invested with new religious values. Mithra-worship received and absorbed ideas and practices derived from Greek and Anatolian mystery traditions and was also influenced by Platonism and perhaps by Orphic thought. Ultimately, the novel and composite form of Mithra-worship that developed and became widely diffused in the Roman world was virtually a new mystery religion, in which the old Irano-Babylonian core seems to have been refashioned and recast into a Graeco-Roman mould tinged with astrological lore and Platonic speculation.

Most of the ceremones, mythology and theology of Roman Mithraism, with their marked esoteric and initiatory character, have be reconstructed from widely scattered archaeological remains, inscriptions and meagre literary evidence that have attracted differing interpretations. The secret rites of the Mithraic Mysteries were celebrated in subterranean shrines, the *mithraea*, which were supposed to mirror the cave in which Mithra Tauroctonus (the bull-sacrificer) was believed to have performed the central act of Mithraic ideology – the capture and murder of the primordial Bull of Heaven. The Mithraic temple was conceived as a 'world cave', a symbol of the cosmos, and among the cult reliefs adorning its walls the scene of the bull sacrifice, the *tauroctonia* was usually placed on the rear wall of the sanctuary and on the front of the altar. The unravelling of the symbolism of the *tauroctonia,* has provoked protracted and heated controversy, since in traditional Zoroastrianism it is Ahriman who brings death to the 'Lone-Created' bull in the violent act of the first 'creative murder' which sparked off the cycle of being and generation. Symmetrically, at the time of the final resurrection of the dead the messianic saviour Saoshyant sacrifices the mystical bull Hadhayans to obtain from his body the elixir of salvation and immortality for all men. Mithraic *tauroctonia*, inevitably, has been translated as reflecting the Iranian paradigm of the divine act of sacrifice and redemption which was, however, conveyed through the prism and style of the novel Graeco-Roman syncretism. In the Mithraic version of the divine priestly sacrifice of the bull the unleashing of the 'blood eternal' bestows life and salvation but appears linked also to the myths of the primordial cosmogonic sacrifice which brought about the creation of the world.[19] Mithras' bull sacrifice, moreover, evokes unavoidable associations with Gilgamesh's slaying of the primeval heavenly bull in Mesopotamian mythology. Alternatively, Mithraic *tauroctonia* has been viewed in the framework of Graeco-Roman astronomy as portraying the equatorial 'summer constellations', Mithras himself representing the constellation of the hero Orion.[20]

In *The Cave of the Nymphs* (24:9–11) the neo-Platonist Porphyry extols Mithras of the Mysteries as creator and master of creation, while his carrying of the bull in the cosmic cave is apparently seen as signalling the beginning of genesis. Mithras is set in the line of the equinox with north to his right and south to his left and thus he is linked with the descent of the souls into the world and their ascent to heaven through the seven planetary spheres. This seems to have been associated in the Mithraic Mysteries with the seven stages of initiation which were protected respectively by Mercury, Venus, Mars, Jupiter, the Moon, the Sun and Saturn. Beginning from the first initiatory grade of *corax* (raven), and via the following grades of the *nymphus* (bridegroom), *miles* (soldier), *leo* (lion), *Perses* (Persian), *heliodromus* (courier of the sun) to the final seventh degree of *pater* (father), the Mithraic initiates were subjected to a variety of ordeals and were invested with the insignia of each stage passed. Among the Mithraic 'fathers', who were placed under the aegis and sickle of Saturn, particularly esteemed was the so-called 'Father of the Fathers (*Pater Patrum*) amongst the ten superiors' who is envisioned in the *Catholic Encyclopedia*, perhaps too luridly, as a 'sort of pope, who always lived at Rome'.[21]

The internal hierarchy and initiation of the cult, with its successive degrees and ordeals, poses numerous unresolved problems and the underlying Mithraic teachings appear similarly abstruse and elusive.

It is still difficult to establish even the outline of the doctrines and mythology of the cult that at one stage seemed set to vie with Christianity for the soul of the Roman empire. With their focus on the labours of the invincible Mithras, from his rock-birth to the *tauroctonia*, his banquet with Sol and his final ascent, the Mithraic reliefs have generated many ingenious attempts to reconstruct the theology and central myths of Mithraism. One early and influential line of inquiry saw Mithraism largely as a Roman form of Zoroastrianism which was closely linked with the theological pursuits of Zurvanite circles in Anatolia. Accordingly, Mithraic iconography was deemed to reflect the fundamental Iranian dualism of the cosmic conflict of good and evil in which the rock-born deity of light, Mithras, led the battle against the evil Ahriman and the forces of darkness. An alternative approach to Roman Mithraism tends to assume that the mystery cult took shape under the formative influence of the Platonic tradition and reflected Platonic cosmogony and myths, the ascent of Mithras being associated with the ascent of the immortal soul in Plato's dialogue *Phaedrus*. In this line of argument Roman Mithraism is supposed to reflect not the Iranian cosmic dualism of the universal struggle between the realms of good and evil but the 'Greek polar opposition of the two realms, the cosmic and the eternal'.[22] Current Platonic decoding of the Mithraic Mysteries is sometimes taken to extremes, in which even the bull-slaying reliefs can be seen as typifying what has been described as the 'Platonic dualism of maintaining a balance between good and evil'.[23]

The dilemma whether Mithraic doctrine was underlain by Iranian or Greek forms of dualism becomes glaringly acute when one confronts the most enigmatic figure in Mithraic iconography, the winged lion-headed god. Second only to Mithras in its frequency in Mithraic iconography, it is commonly portrayed as a human figure with fearful leonine head, but it also has a human-headed counterpart who appears rather less frequently in Mithraic sanctuaries. The Mithraic lion–man was usually depicted entwined, often sevenfold, by a serpent, with the serpent's head resting on his leonine visage, which often appeared menacing if not infernal. Sometimes the zodiacal signs appeared between the coils of the serpent, and the lion–man was variously portrayed with keys, sceptres and torches or standing on the cosmic globe. It seems certain that the lion-headed god was venerated primarily in the main sites of the Mithraic Mysteries where he was revealed only to initiates of the higher grades and was honoured with offerings by the supreme Mithraic dignitaries like the *Pater Patrum* himself.[24]

Early theories concerning the nature and functions of the ambiguous snake-wrapped lion-headed god regarded him as the highest deity in the Mithraic pantheon and identified him with the time-god, Aion, and also with Kronos and the Iranian Zurvan. The apparent threatening air of the lion-headed deity was attributed to the 'menacing or devouring aspect of time'. Subsequently, it came to be recognized as the Destructive Spirit of Zoroastrianism, Ahriman himself, or as a composite figure comprising both Ahriman and Zurvan. He has also been traced to the lion-headed portrayals of the Mesopotamian underworld deity Nergal.[25] Besides Zurvan and Ahriman, the Mithraic lion–man has also been linked to Plato's Universal Soul which 'drives all things in Heaven and earth' with the dualities of heat and cold, whiteness and blackness (*Laws* 10:896–7), as well as to his symbolic picture of the soul as 'a manifold and many-headed beast' joined with the forms of lion and man (*Republic* 9:588–9). In this view the Mithraic lion-headed god represented Plato's Universal Soul, with its good and evil sides, and the Platonic dualism between the 'best kind of soul' and the 'evil kind of soul' (*Laws* 10:897), the latter, the bad world–soul, being sometimes attributed to Zoroastrian influence on Plato.[26] Accordingly, the Mithraist worshipper of the lion-headed god is seen to have been addressing both the good and evil aspects of the Universal Soul through Mithras' neutral dual mediation between the extremes of good and evil to reach the final purification.[27]

What seems to be the key to the riddle of the lion–man and his role in Mithraic worship is the several Latin Mithraic dedications to *Deus Arimanius*, including the one on the headless sculpture found at York, which apparently portrays the lion-headed deity. The Mithraic dedicatory statues of *Deus Arimanius* have been linked to Plutarch's testimony of the Areimanius cult with its grim wolf sacrifices but also to a late Zoroastrian testimony of the clandestine rite of the 'mystery of the sorcerers' centred on a secret worship of Ahriman, his rival revelation and his 'evil knowledge', which compels men to desert Ohrmazd's religion and turn to that of Ahriman.[28] The Mithraic *Deus Arimanius* is thus taken to show that Roman Mithraism derived from pre-Zoroastrian and later forbidden *daevic* forms of Mithra-worship which were associated with the dreaded 'mystery of the sorcerers' and which were sustained in Mesopotamia and Asia Minor. In this view the Roman *Deus Arimanius*, who was worshipped in the Mithraic sanctuaries, was radically different from the Zoroastrian Ahriman and was no less a deity than 'the Prince of this World of time and space', 'the source of power and riches', who sought to prevent the ascent of the soul to its heavenly abode and from whose sway the initiate aspired to escape.[29]

Alternative solutions to the problem of the Roman *Deus Arimanius* and his headless statue at York seek to untangle his role in the Mithraic Mysteries against the background of the 'mysteric' and esoteric trends in Graeco-Roman paganism. Rather than a Roman vestige of an aberrant Iranian dualism which opposes the 'word of sorcery' to the 'word of Ohrmazd' to worship the former or else to pay tribute to both, the Mithraic *Deus Arimanius* is considered an inferior but not evil cosmic power, associated with time and probably with the ascent of the initiate's soul.[30] Instead of a mediator between the opposing domains of good and evil, between Ohrmazd and Ahriman, Mithras has been viewed as an intermediary between the supernal realm and the material cosmos.[31] Moreover, with his position on the equinox, if Porphyry is to be relied on, Mithras was linked to the descent and the ascent of the souls. A recent synthesis of the evidence plausibly identifies the Mithraic lion-headed deity with the figure of the 'cosmocrator', the 'astrologically conditioned embodiment of the world-engendering and world-ruling Power generated by the endless revolution of all the wheels of the celestial dynamo';[32] far from being an oppressive force, it could not only embody souls but could also release the soul from its embodiment through initiation.

It is also becoming increasingly apparent that some Mithraic concepts, like the graduated cosmos through which the soul makes its ascent to salvation or the lion-headed 'cosmocrator' himself, were also shared in contemporary Gnostic schools, where, however, they were included in an entirely different soteriological and dualist framework.

Michael and Samael

The continuous search for the source of the Mithraic Mysteries and the conflicting arguments for their dualist character are indicative of the problems posed by the religious currents in late antiquity with the rise of new syncretistic forms of religious dualism and diverse approaches to the origins and reality of evil.

Following the destruction of the Temple in Jerusalem by the Romans in AD 70, Jewish rabbinic thought tended to counterbalance the dualist trends developed in some forms of apocalyptic Judaism. Rabbinic texts from the second century AD warn against the heresy of the 'Two Heavenly Powers' linked to speculation about the exalted status of an angel or viceregent of the Lord which might have influenced nascent Gnostic thought. In rabbinic Judaism the figure of Satan and the myth of the downfall of the angels lost much of the intensity which had marked some earlier apocalyptic traditions. Rather than an ultimate embodiment of evil and leader of the fallen angels, Satan appeared in rabbinic theory more as a symbol of the evil inclination within man (*yetser ha-ra*) which was opposed to the good inclination (*yetser ha-tov*).[33] Yet in the narrative section of the Talmud, the Haggadah, and in popular Jewish lore some of the traditions associated with Satan persisted and were elaborated in new legends. In the important apocryphal work The Ascension of Isaiah, Satan had been styled also as Samael (variously etymologized as the 'venom of God' or 'the blind god') and in the early Christian era Samael became the principal name of Satan in Juadaism. Distinguished sometimes from Satan, Samael could be identified as the guardian angel of Esau, Edom and the world empire of Rome, exalted as 'the great prince of heaven', as prince of the evil angels, 'Samael the Wicked' or else prince of all Satans (Accusers). As a prosecutor Samael could be seen as standing along with the defender Michael before the *Shekhinah* (Divine Presence) during the Jewish exodus from Egypt.

Perceived as the 'venom of God' Samael was also recognized as the much-dreaded angel of death, who was believed to smite man with a drop of poison, and in later astrological lore he was regarded as the angel of Mars. The war between Satan–Samael and the guardian angel of Israel, Michael, was perceived as continuing until the last days when Samael would be finally delivered to Israel in iron fetters. Otherwise, Michael could be charged with laying the foundations of Rome, Israel's future adversary and persecutor, itself to be patronized and guarded by Samael, while the ambiguous figure of the 'Prince of the World' could be identified with both Michael or Samael.[34]

In early Christianity itself some of the concepts of Satan and his opposition to God and man, which were developed in post-exilic and particularly apocalyptic Judaism, were accepted with all their ambiguities and potential for radical new developments. The inherited opposition between Michael and Satan was reflected in Revelation, where in the 'war in heaven' Michael led his angelic hosts against the angels of the 'great dragon', the 'old serpent', that 'led the whole world astray, whose name is Satan, or the Devil' (12:7–9). Besides being the great cosmic adversary of Michael, Satan vied with the archangel for the body of Israel's lawgiver, Moses (Epistle of Jude 9). In early Christian thought the Devil was the incarnation personified and source of evil and death, a fallen angel who led the hosts of evil against the 'Kingdom of God' and Christ. He was the 'god of this world' who has blinded the minds of the unbelievers to the message of the gospel. In Paul's dramatic light-vision on the way to Damascus the future apostle was entrusted by Jesus to go to the Gentiles and convert them from darkness to light, from the hold of Satan to God. However, Satan could also disguise himself as an angel of light and his envoys could pose as agents of good and apostles of Christ (2 Corinthians 11:13–15). Apart from being recognized as the Prince of Demons (Matthew 9:34) and 'commander of the spiritual powers of the air' (Ephesians 2:2), he was also called 'Tempter', 'Accuser' and 'Father of Lies', as he deluded and accused men and endeavoured to tempt and corrupt even the Son of God, Christ himself. Satan entered one of the twelve apostles, Judas Iscariot – according to the Fourth Gospel – during the Last Supper, to prompt the betrayal and crucifixion of the Jesus Christ. Conversely, when the apostle Peter, the Rock on which Christ's church was to be built, tried to oppose Jesus' way to Jerusalem and to his Passion and Resurrection, he was rebuked by Jesus as Satan: 'Away with you, Satan . . . you think as men think, not as God thinks' (Mark 8:33).

Satan's *imperium* embraced not only the evil spirits, but also sinful and wicked men, 'Satan's synagogue', as well as 'this age' (*aion*) and this world (*kosmos*), he was the 'Prince of this World' and 'the whole world . . . lies in the power of the evil one' (1 John 5:19). Yet Satan's prevalence in 'this world', which began with the fall of man, was broken by the advent of Christ and his Passion: 'Now is the hour of judgement for this world; now shall the Prince of this world be driven out' (John 12:31). In Revelation, following his great war in heaven against the hosts of Michael, the dragon, Satan, was doomed to be cast down to earth with his angels and to be fettered in the pit for a thousand years. After being chained for a millennium Satan would be released and would win over nations from the four corners of the world for his final, satanic crusade against the city of God's people but would be consumed by heavenly fire and flung along with his disciples into the 'lake of fire', the second death (Revelation 20:7–10; 13–15). The chronology of Satan's fortunes in Revelation appears abstruse and has invited different readings. It was generally assumed that while Satan's power was crippled by the advent of Jesus Christ, the final demise of Satan would occur at the Second Coming. Satan continued, meanwhile, his struggle against the 'Kingdom of God' and the Christian was expected to put on the whole armour of God to oppose the Devil's devices in a fight that was not 'against human foes, but against cosmic powers, against the authorities and potentates of this dark world, against the superhuman forces of evil in the heavens' (Ephesians 6:11–12). The sign of the cross was also supposed to banish evil powers; in early Christian thought the Devil was repeatedly denounced for fostering paganism, heresy and sorcery in his fight against the Kingdom of God and the divine plan of salvation. Through the water of Christian baptism not only was the soul believed to be redeemed of Original Sin, but also the Devil and his powers were renounced and repelled. For the Christian apologist Tertullian, the existence and opposing works of 'the Lord and his rival, the Creator and the Destroyer' could be experienced, learned and understood 'at one and the same time'.[35]

The early Christian notions of the Devil, his rebellion, fall, reign in 'this world' and final defeat were further elaborated and conceptualized by the Fathers of the Church. The fall of Satan and the angels could be attributed to their pride or to their envy of men. The parable against the king of Babylon in Isaiah 14:12–15 was now firmly associated with the fall of Satan and linked also to Jesus' statement in Luke 10:18: 'I watched how Satan fell, like lightning, out of the sky'. The king of Tyre in Ezekiel 28:12–19, originally all-wise and blameless, but later obsessed by lawlessness and doomed to be hurled down from the mountain of God and devoured by the fire that Yahweh had kindled within him, also came to be recognized as Satan. Michael, however, was identified as the cherub who was placed at the gates of paradise to guard 'the way to the tree of life' (Genesis 3:24), and as the angel who stood like *satan* against Balaam. Venerated among the early Christians, particularly in Phrygia, as a heavenly healer and redeemer, Michael emerged as the patron of the Church and the medieval chivalric orders. Apart from leading the war against Satan in heaven, Michael was seen as being entrusted with salvaging human souls from the power of the Devil and conducting them to the place of judgement, while later Christian elaborations envisaged Satan as ruling and punishing the sinners in Hell.

In the early stages of building the normative Christian satanology, where the Devil was generally believed to have been created by God but had fallen through his pride, envy and free will, the chronology and the outcome of his fall received varying treatment. According to Origen (*c.* 185–254) the final defeat of Satan would lead to the destruction of his sinful and ungodly nature, while his original angelic essence would be resurrected and he would be saved to return ultimately to God. At the same time, the early Church Fathers had to vigorously defend their orthodox tenets of evil as privation of good and Godness against the more radical, dualist solutions of the origin of evil which were advanced in the Gnostic schools of the second and third centuries.

Demiurge and Redeemer

Despite the evident dualism of spirit and flesh in early Christianity, which was inevitably associated with the Devil's status in the New Testament as 'the ruler of this world of matter and bodies',[36] the world was viewed as a creation of the benevolent God–Creator and was not evil by nature. Though defiled by Satan and his evil spirits, it would ultimately be redeemed and purified by the Second Coming of Christ. Conversely, the multifarious Gnostic schools did share, on the whole, an anti-cosmic dualism – the material world was negated as an imperfect and evil creation of an inferior demiurgic or clearly 'Satanic' power and was opposed to the supernal spiritual world of the true but remote and unknown God. As with Orphic-Pythagorean religiosity, in Gnosticism the soul was seen as a stranger and an exile in the body, the souls of men were 'precious pearls', divine sparks from this spiritual realm and had descended into the wicked material world of the 'howling darkness' to be imprisoned in material bodies and could be released only through the redeeming mediation of *gnosis*, a revelatory knowledge of the divine secrets.[37] The divine substance was spread unevenly among men and the Gnostic schools sometimes assumed a threefold division of mankind in which the enlightened Gnostics themselves were the spiritual aristocracy, styled the Pneumatics, the Perfect or the chosen, who would be saved, as they possessed the spirit, *pneuma*. The other class, the Psychics, had soul (*psyche*) and were deficient of spirit, yet could gain some form of salvation, while the Hylics were the earthly class, the enslaved, bound to remain entrapped in matter. These three grades of being in the universe were associated with three types of 'churches': the angelic, the psychic and the earthly.

In Christian Gnosticism Christ emerged as a heavenly spiritual redeemer sent by the unknown, supreme God to mediate the *gnosis* to men (or else only to the Pneumatics) and the Demiurge vainly endeavoured to thwart his mission. Christian Gnostic traditions elaborated different versions of Christ's mission but according to most of them Christ assumed only an appearance (*dokesis*) of humanity and accordingly his Passion and Crucifixion were also apparent. This Docetic Christology distinguished the heavenly Christ from the earthly Jesus, while sometimes substitute figures like Symon of Cyrene were introduced to replace Christ at the Crucifixion.[38]

The Gnostic schools drew widely on the syncretistic heritage of antiquity and used Iranian, Jewish, Greek, Mesopotamian, Egyptian and Christian traditions to embellish their basic myths and concepts related to the creation of the world by the Demiurge, the fall of the soul, the mission of the redeemer and revealer of the *gnosis*, and finally the release and ascent of the soul to its spiritual abode. Prior to the discovery of the Coptic corpus of secret Gnostic writings at Nag Hammadi (Chenoboskion) in Upper Egypt in 1945, the various Gnostic systems were known mainly from the hostile testimony of great Christian anti-Gnostic polemicists like Irenaeus (*c.* 130–*c.* 200), Hippolytus (*c.* 170–*c.* 236) and Epiphanius (*c.* 315–403). The Nag Hammadi texts immensely enriched the picture of the convoluted and eclectic Gnostic systems and demonstrated that Gnostic mythologies adopted and transformed some of the central themes of the Jewish apocalyptic and apocryphal corpus – like the downfall of the angels, the role of Satan in the angelic apostasy and the fall of Adam and Eve. In the Nag Hammadi tract The Apocryphon of John, presented in the form of a revelation granted by the resurrected Jesus to John, the descent of the angels to the daughters of men occurred after the flood and was a mission to raise offspring of their own (29:10–20). The angels impregnated the daughters of men with 'the spirit of darkness which they had mixed for them and with evil' (29:30) to beget children out of the darkness 'according to the likeness of their spirit' (30:9) and enslave creation. In another important Nag Hammadi text, On the Origins of the World (123:4–13), as in the classical Enochic traditions, angels (demons), created by the downcast seven rulers of darkness, were charged with imparting to men the secrets of magic, idolatry, bloodshed, temple sacrifices and libations.

The fall of Adam and Eve was also subject to diverse Gnostic interpretations, among which the tradition of Eve's seduction by the Devil or the Demiurge gained particular prominence. While Cain seems to have been routinely recognized as Eve's son by the Devil in many Gnostic traditions, Abel could be credited with satanic or Adamic descent. The heavenly but satanic extraction of Cain also became part of Jewish lore where Samael, the angel of the Lord, was envisaged coming to Eve 'riding on the serpent' and hence Cain was conceived not by Adam's seed, nor in his image and likeness, while Eve's canonical statement after Cain's birth, 'I have gotten a man from the Lord' (Genesis, 4:1 *KJV*), could be transformed into 'I have acquired a man, the angel of the Lord'.[39] While Cain could be exposed as the progenitor of 'all the generations of the wicked', Seth, with his certain and legitimate Adamic parent-age, could be extolled as the father of 'all the generations of the just' and the kingdom of the house of David could be described as 'planted' from him.[40] A preoccupation with Seth and his 'genealogy' is markedly evident in some Gnostic schools where the birth of Seth and the beginning of his line were praised as the institution of justice and a higher race. In *Panarion* (39:1–5,3) Epiphanius re-counted the system of the Sethian Gnostics where the birth of Cain and Abel was revealed as having been caused by creative angelic powers whose war over the two brothers ultimately provoked Abel's murder. The races of Cain and Abel came to be mixed together because of their malice and Seth was sent into the world with his higher seed to bring purification of the seed of men and destruction to the angelic forces that had created the world and the first two men. The birth of Seth was attributed to the intercession of the Gnostic higher 'Mother', Sophia (Wisdom), who implanted in him the seed of the divine power which was the heavenly prototype of Seth's earthly seed. The Sethian Gnostics therefore traced their descent to the elect and incorruptible line of Seth, who was identified with Christ and was conceived as bringing cyclically to the human race his higher 'seed of power and purity'. Indeed there are some indications that Melchizedek, Jesus Christ and even Zoroaster were considered in some Gnostic circles as manifestations of the saviour and revealer Seth.[41] In Epiphanius' exposé of Sethian Gnosticism the Flood itself was viewed as sent by the 'Mother on high' to extinguish the evil race of Cain, while only the just progeny of Seth was meant to be saved in Noah's ark and remain in the world. Apprehensive of the impending genocide of their 'race of wickedness', the creative angelic powers succeeded in bringing Ham into the ark; Ham preserved their race and the world was again plunged into its traditional vices and disorder. Conversely, Irenaeus in his comprehensive diatribe against Gnosticism, *Against all Heresies* (1:31.1–2), exposed certain Gnostic Cainites who extolled Cain as conceived from a superior, absolute power above. Esau, Korah and the Sodomites, who were endowed with this knowledge, were hated by the Creator but protected by Sophia and it was on behalf of his knowledge of this truth that Judas Iscariot carried through 'the mystery of betrayal'.

However divergent, the different Gnostic cosmogonies were invariably underlain by a marked anti-cosmic dualism and repeatedly identified the Gnostic Demiurge of the material universe with God the Creator of the Old Testament. In the teachings of Marcion (d. 140), who is commonly described as a heretic but not yet as a Gnostic teacher, the God of the Old Testament was the just God of the Law, whose strict judgement is antithetic to the essence of Christ's gospel of love and mercy. Jesus was sent by the higher, good and 'strange' God of love and salvation to redeem man from the tyranny of the Law of the lower Demiurge. Marcion's teachings of the 'two Gods' attracted a wide following in the Roman empire and the communities of the Marcionite church spread from Italy and Egypt to Armenia. Marcion's disciple, Apelles, transformed the Demiurge, the God of the Old Testament, into a 'fiery angel' and made him responsible for the origin of evil. In the teachings of the Gnostic Basilides (second century AD) the biblical God of Abraham, Isaac and Jacob emerged as the ruler of the inferior sphere of the planets, the Hebdomad, and as he was held to rule over 365 heavens, he was also called Abrasax, a name comprising the number 365. In the convoluted system of the Gnostic teacher Valentinus (second century AD) the Father, the First Principle and his consort, Thought, begot the spiritual world of Pleroma (plenitude or fullness) which comprised fifteen pairs of aeons. A crisis in the Pleroma, the fall or else the 'abortion' of the youngest aeon Sophia, precipitated the birth of the God of Genesis in the lower spheres who in his turn created the material cosmos blind to the higher realm of Pleroma.[42]

In the Nag Hammadi treatise On the Origin of the World (100:3–25) the lion-like Demiurge, called Yaldabaoth (probably 'Son of Chaos') and identified with the biblical God–Creator, came into being after a descending series of emanations from the spiritual world that had already caused the emergence of matter. Yaldabaoth established the heavens and their powers and proclaimed after Deuteronomy 32:39: 'I am He and there is no god beside me', but with this 'monotheistic' proclamation he sinned against the 'immortal (imperishable) ones' (103:10–15). The initiator of his creation, Pistis Sophia, called him Samael – i.e. 'the blind god' – prophesied his downfall to his 'mother, the abyss' (100:17–33) and revealed to him 'in the water the image of her greatness'. In the Apocryphon of John (9:28–35; 10:1–22) the birth of Yaldabaoth was attributed to Sophia's 'desire to bring forth a likeness out of herself without the consent of the spirit' and Yaldabaoth emerged in the form of a lion-faced serpent, imperfect, created 'in ignorance', but none the less, he was the first archon who had inherited power from his mother. Among his manifold feats in the Apocryphon of John 24, Yaldabaoth was charged with the seduction of Eve, who begot from him two sons, Elohim and Yahweh, the first set over the fire and the wind and the second over the water and the earth, named respectively by Yaldabaoth, 'with the view to deceive' (24:25), Cain and Abel.

The episode of the 'monotheistic' claim of the Demiurge, the reproach of Sophia and the revelation of the higher divine powers occurs in several important Gnostic tracts. In her various incarnations the Gnostic Sophia was perceived sometimes as the Holy Spirit, the heavenly Eve or as a dual figure, separated into a higher Mother of the heavenly Redeemer and lower Mother of the Demiurge of the material universe. Moreover, while the Gnostic Demiurge could be associated with the arrogant king of Babylon in the parable in Isaiah 14, his Mother could be seen in Gnostic mythology as Babylon or else as the heavenly Jerusalem.[43] It is also apparent that while the lion-headed Mithraic deity and the lion-shaped Gnostic Demiurge Yaldabaoth share essentially 'a similar function for symbolizing the same world-ruling, world-ensouling Power',[44] in Gnostic myths the cosmos of Yaldabaoth and his reign as a 'cosmocrator' were opposed to the supernal realm of the spirit and the liberation of the entrapped souls, whose salvation was mediated by a heavenly Redeemer breaking the bondage of the Demiurge.

Apart from the Gnostic tradition of one original principle and a fall in the divine realm, other Gnostic schools forged elaborate systems with three primary principles like that of the Gnostic sect of the Naassenes (from the Hebrew *nahash*, serpent), whose doctrines were expounded by Hippolytus in his *Refutation of all Heresies* (5:6.3–11). According to Hippolytus the Naassenes regarded the belief in one principle as the source of the world as erroneous and taught that the universe proceeded from three principles – the pre-existent, the self-originated and the outpoured chaos. All temples, rites and mysteries were viewed by the Naassenes as established for the serpent *nahash*, which was further praised as good and necessary for the existence of all things mortal and immortal. The serpent was compared with the second, self-originated principle, itself called Adamas and perceived as bisexual Man, also associated with the seed as the source of all that comes into being. In this bisexual Man was the life that was 'the light of men' (John 1:4), and the generation of perfect men, or else the drinking cup which the king 'uses for divination' when he drinks (Genesis 44:4) that was hidden and found 'in the good seed of Benjamin' (8:6). Moreover, the second, bisexual principle is compared with the 'Ocean', with its unceasing ebbs and fluctuations, the 'upward' flow being related to the origin of the gods and the 'downward' movement to the origin of humanity. At the same time, the Naassenes had to introduce a fourth evil power, the fiery god Esaldaios (El Shaddai), who was a Demiurge and artificer of 'this world', where he had imprisoned mankind against the will of Adamas.

Another Gnostic sect, the Peratae, exposed by Hippolytus in *Refutation of all Heresies* (5:12.1–17; 13), formulated similar threefold partitions in the world: three gods, three words, three minds and three types of men. In the Peratae system the first principle is the 'unoriginate' 'perfect Goodness'; the second, the 'self-originate' good multitude of powers; and the third, the 'originate' and particular being. In another version of the Peratae triad these three principles appeared as the Father, the Son and matter. Christ was also perceived as three-natured and through his descent all that had been divided into three was to be saved and all that had been brought down from the higher realms was to ascend through him. The second, 'self-originate' principle of the Peratae was envisaged as moving constantly between the Father and matter and was identified with the serpent, which was credited with bringing the 'fully formed perfect race' up from the world. The serpent was also eulogized as the 'perfect word' of Eve or the mystery of Eden and was recognized as the sign marked on Cain to protect him from murder. The position of a fourth evil principle was effectively taken by the stars, the gods of generation and destruction, whose emanations conducted the beginnings and the end of everything in the created world, but did not have power over those who were illuminated by their *gnosis* of the perfect serpent.

Another system where the serpent occupied a prominent position
was elaborated by the Gnostic Ophites (from the Greek *ophis*,
serpent), as recounted in Irenaeus' work *Against all Heresies* (1:30.1–
15). In the Ophite system the first triad was formed by the Father of
All or the First Man, the Son of Man, or the Second Man, and the
feminine Holy Spirit or the First Woman, below whom were the
elements of Water, Darkness, Abyss and Chaos. The female Holy
Spirit united with both the First and Second Man to give birth to
the Third Man, Christ, but their light overflowed on her left side.
Being on the right, Christ was raised to the higher realms, while the
power that had overflowed on the left fell downwards and was
envisaged as a female being, variously called the Left, Sophia or
Man–Woman. Sophia gave birth to Yaldabaoth who fathered his
own son and the unfolding of this generative process led to the
emergence of six sons who formed, along with Yaldabaoth, the
higher hebdomad. The serpent was envisaged as begetting six
sons in the world below to form the lower hebdomad of the seven
demons or planets of the world, who were in opposition to the
human race. According to the Ophites the serpent bore two names,
Michael and Samael, who appeared thus, 'fused into the positive and
negative aspects of a single state of existence'.[45]

As well as the Naassenes and the Peratae, Hippolytus recounted
in his *Refutation of all Heresies* (5:19.1–22) a Sethian Gnostic system,
which involved not only three sharply defined principles, of Light
above, Darkness below, and pure Spirit between them, but also the
lowest principle of darkness was already perceived as negative and
maleficent, a horrible water. The division into three powers was
further associated with biblical ternaries like Adam, Eve and the
serpent; Cain, Abel and Seth; or Abraham, Isaac and Jacob. The
multitudinous powers of the three principles were at rest when they
remained in their original state but the great impact of the three
principles, which had caused the creation of heaven and earth, led
to their mixture and conflict. With its cunning intelligence Darkness
sought to detain the elements of Light and Spirit, imprisoned in its
impure and harmful 'womb of disorder', which accepted and recognized only the forms of the 'first-born' of the waters, the wind, the
serpent and the beast (19:20). The mind of man, 'perfect god'
brought down from the sublime Light, was also entrapped in

wicked and dark bodies and strove in vain to free itself from the bodily prison. The perfect word of Light had to assume the form of a snake to enter the womb of Darkness and redeem the mind from its bondage and to accomplish the division and separation of everything that had been intermixed. Jesus' statement in Matthew 10:34, 'I have not come to bring peace, but a sword', was explained as an allusion to this mission of separation when the compounded elements were to return to their original abodes.

The same system of three primeval powers received dramatic mythological elaboration in the Nag Hammadi tract The Paraphrase of Shem, where the gentle Spirit was again envisaged positioned between the exalted and infinite Light and the Darkness, itself a 'wind in the waters', with the mind 'wrapped in a chaotic fire' (1:25–35; 2:1–5). With the agitation of Darkness and the intermixture of the three roots the universe entered an era of cosmic strife which marked the creation of heaven and earth. The Gnostic saviour Derdekeas had to descend from the realm of Light and assume the form of the beast to enter the abode of Darkness and redeem the imprisoned light of the Spirit. Derdekeas' revelation of the *gnosis* to the elect brought upon him 'the wrath of the world' when the gates of fire and smoke were opened against him and he was attacked by the winds and thunder (36:12–22). Such vivid and often striking mythic imagery was used consistently to recount the unfolding of Derdekeas' redeeming mission in the world. The very time when the light was finally about to be separated from darkness was thus marked by the act of beheading the woman who was 'the coherence of the powers of the demon who will baptize the seed of darkness in severity . . .' (40:24–30). In the last days, when the evil power of Darkness would be laid low and immobilized, those who had resisted 'the heritage of death', the oppressive water of darkness, would be finally separated from its body to enter the entirely redeemed light of the Spirit (48:10–30).

In the treatise On the Origin of the World (126–7), at the time of the final consummation the Light was prophesied to cover and wipe out the Darkness and return to its own root. Yet the essence of the opposition between the two powers of Light and Darkness could vary in the different Gnostic schools and they could be perceived as brothers deriving from one 'mystery' that retained both in itself. According to the Nag Hammadi Gospel of Philip (53:15–20): 'Light and darkness, life and death, right and left are brothers of one another. They are inseparable. Because of this neither are the good good nor the evil evil, nor is life life, nor death death'. In other Gnostic traditions the dualism of good and evil appeared radical and irretrievable and rather than being retained in one original trunk, the powers of Light and Darkness were perceived as two coeternal principles that were opposed from the very beginning. The absolute dualism of these traditions is in sharp contrast to Gnostic monarchian dualism that poses one first principle and the creation of the material world as a result of a crisis or discontinuity in the divine 'fullness'.

The radical Gnostic dualism of two primordial fundamental principles, the two realms of Light and Darkness, associated respectively with spirit and matter, has been defined sometimes as 'Iranian' Gnosticism. In traditional Iranian Zoroastrianism the material universe was created by Ohrmazd as a replica of the spiritual world and man himself was created as a microcosm of universe and Ohrmazd's 'material symbol' incarnation, a harmonious unity of body and soul. At the time of the final renewal of the world the resurrected body would be reunited with its soul in the reassembled and immortalized human being, as matter and spirit would finally coalesce in the life everlasting. While in Zoroastrianism both the spiritual and material world, both the soul and the body, were created as Ohrmazd's allies against the destroyer Ahriman, in Iranian Gnosticism the spirit and matter, Light and Darkness, appeared as two primordial and antagonistic principles whose coexistence and opposition determined three main epochs of a grandiose cosmic drama. Iranian Gnosticism received its elaborate and striking formulation in the system devised by the great Gnostic visionary, missionary and artist, Mani, the self-proclaimed herald of the third final age when the conflict between the powers of Light and Darkness would be consummated. The unfolding of the mission of Mani and the early fortunes of his religion coincided and were inextricably linked with the rise of the new Iranian empire of the Sassanid dynasty and the ensuing powerful renascence of Zoroastrianism.

The Throne and the Altar

In AD 226 Arsacid rule collapsed in Iran. Plagued by internal strife, it was overthrown by a Persian dynasty, the Sassanids, who had been hereditary guardians of a great temple of Anahita at Istakhar, near ancient Persepolis. Apart from Persia the cult of Anahita enjoyed prominence in neighbouring Armenia, which had itself long been within the Iranian and Zoroastrian sphere of influence, and where a branch of the Arsacid dynasty continued to reign for another two centuries after its fall in Iran. The Parthian feudal state in Iran was replaced by the highly centralized Sassanian empire where Zoroastrianism was upheld as a well-organized and often intolerant state religion. Sassanid art and culture clearly mark the zenith of pre-Islamic Iranian civilization, but the history of the Sassanid empire was dominated by continual collisions with its western enemy, the Roman empire. The Sassanid monarchs claimed divine descent from the 'seed of the gods': from the time of Ardashir I, the founder of the dynasty, they were seen as treading in the footsteps of their Achaemenid predecessors, claiming the 'rightful inheritance' of the Achaemenid empire to recover the imperial glory of Persia. According to Ammianus Marcellinus (17:5.5–6) in about 357 the Sassanid King of Kings, Shapur II (309–79), 'partner with the Stars, brother of the Sun and Moon', was said to have written to his 'brother', the Roman emperor Constantius II (337–61), that the dominion of his forefathers had reached in the west to the river Strymon (Struma) and the borders of Macedonia and these lands belonged to and should be restored to the Persian empire. In the face of Constantius' successor, Julian the Apostate, however, Shapur II was to confront a Roman emperor, who perceived himself as an incarnation of Alexander the Great, determined to meet and reconquer the Persians, who according to Julian had once subdued the whole of Asia and most of Europe, embracing the whole known world in their aspirations. Apart from the revival of paganism, the subjugation of Persia after the example of Alexander was to become Julian's ruling passion and in 363 he led his abortive campaign against Persia, where he finally met his death, mortally wounded during the retreat of his army. A Sassanid rock relief at Taq-i

Bostan, western Iran, commemorating Shapur's triumph over Julian, depicts the three figures of Shapur, Ahura Mazda and Mithra trampling on the Roman emperor, who had adopted Mithras as his guardian.

Julian's war and death in Sassanid Persia were among the most dramatic episodes of the four centuries of violent intermittent warfare between the Sassanid empire and the Roman, and later the East Roman, empire for supremacy in the Near East, Armenia and the Caucasus region. The exhausting internecine struggle between the two rival empires, eulogized as 'the two eyes of the world', came to a striking climax in the early seventh century, when, under the Sassanid monarch Chosroes II the Victorious, the westward Persian advance reached the heartlands of the East Roman (Byzantine) empire in western Asia Minor. In 614 the armies of Chosroes, who seems to have been disliked by the Zoroastrian clergy and was suspected of being a Christian convert, captured Jerusalem and took away the fragments of the 'True Cross', on which Jesus was supposed to have been crucified. As Persian conquests progressed into Syria, Anatolia and Egypt, Chosroes recovered most of the former western Achaemenid dominions and attempted a strike at the Byzantine capital, Constantinople. In 330 Constantine the Great had moved the imperial capital to Constantinople and now, in 626, Persian troops directly threatened the second Rome. The Byzantine emperor Heraclius, however, outmanoeuvred the Persian forces completely by shipping his army to the Caucasus via the Black Sea and in 628 was already campaigning deep into the Sassanid empire where he sacked Chosroes' palace. Heraclius' invasion provoked the assassination of Chosroes and Heraclius achieved a victorious truce with Chosroes' short-lived successor, Kavad-Shiruya, himself a suspected Christian, after which Byzantium regained its control over the newly lost provinces and the 'True Cross' was restored to Jerusalem. Plunged into political turmoil, the Sassanid empire lacked the breathing space to recover and withstand the new Arab menace from the south. Within fifteen years, despite vigorous Iranian resistance, it collapsed before the rising Arab tide. As the Arab conquest swept through Iran, the last Sassanid King of Kings and 'Brother of Sun and Moon', Yazdagird III – who was crowned at Istakhar, the site of the old Sassanid shrine of Anahita – was forced to flee and was assassinated in 652. A legend persisted that a daughter of Yazdagird, Shahrbanu (Lady of the Land, a cult name for Anahita), had married the third Imam of Shiah Islam, the martyr Husain, and begot the fourth Shiah Imam, bringing Sassanid royal blood into the lineage of subsequent Shiah Imams. With the fall of Sassanid Persia the Arab armies descended on the Byzantine empire: Egypt, Palestine and Syria, which long had been a bone of contention between the Roman and Sassanid monarchs, were now annexed to the Umayyad caliphate and the 'True Cross' had to be moved to Constantinople.

The protracted conflict between the Roman and Sassanid empires was also marked by a vigorous religious rivalry as the two empires sought to establish their own religious orthodoxies. The Christianization of the Roman world after Constantine's Edict of Milan of AD 313 was completed with the Theodosian laws in 380; the installation of Zoroastrianism as the official religion of the Sassanid empire began with its founder, Ardashir I, and was accomplished under Shapur II. Inevitably, while Christianity was on the rise in the Roman empire Shapur persecuted its adherents in Iran. Portrayed as 'bound by the rites of the Magi and practitioner of secrets' (Agathias 2:26.30), Ardashir I was credited with the saying, 'kingship and religion are twin brothers, no one of which can be maintained without the other. For religion is the foundation of kingship and kingship is the guardian of religion. Kingship cannot subsist without its foundation and religion cannot subsist without its guardian. For that which has no guardian is lost, and that which has no foundation crumbles' (*Testament of Ardashir*). The great Sassanid monarch Chosroes I, 'The Just of the Immortal Soul' (531–79), declared that the 'King of Kings', as ruler of the material world, was an intermediary between humanity on earth and Ohrmazd, Lord of the spiritual realm.[46]

During the reign of Shapur II, Armenia continued to be the focus of Roman–Iranian rivalry as it drifted away from the orbit of Zoroastrianism and became the first Christian state. Early in the fourth century the Arsacid king of Armenia, Tiridates IV, who began his reign as a zealous Zoroastrian, was converted to Christianity by St Gregory the Illuminator, himself from a branch of the old Arsacid royal house, and the old cultic centres of the Zoroastrian divinities, the *yazatas*, were turned into Christian sites.[47] Yet in subsequent centuries Zoroastrianism still found support among many Armenian nobles, who defended some of the Zoroastrian shrines by force, while the Sassanids launched three major campaigns to reconvert Armenia to Zoroastrianism. Within the Sassanid empire itself anti-Christian persecution was intermittent and its intensification in the fourth century was doubtless linked to the Christianization of its western rival, the Roman empire. At the same time, with the establishment of Christian orthodoxy in the Roman world, the Sassanid realm became a comparatively secure refuge for Christian movements that were condemned in the Byzantine empire. Following the condemnation at the Council of Ephesus in 431 of Nestorian Christianity, with its teaching of the two separate persons of Christ – the divine and the human – the Nestorian Church established its Patriarchal see in Sassanid Persia, where it was favoured by some Sassanid monarchs and from where it extended its mission into India, central Asia and China. Along with the Nestorian Christians, adherents of Monophysitism – the teaching of the single divine nature of Christ, which was embraced by the Coptic and, partially, by the Armenian church – also fled to Sassanid Persia. Apart from this Christian influx, pagan philosophers also sought refuge there following the closure of the philosophical schools in Athens by Emperor Justinian I in 529.

The establishment of Zoroastrianism as the organized state religion of the Sassanid empire occurred together with the reassembling and canonization of the Zoroastrian sacred scriptures, as well as sporadic campaigns against what was perceived as heresy, *daeva*-worship or 'Ahrimanic' sorcery. In the first century of Sassanid rule and expansion, Zoroastrian worship and fire temples were established in the newly conquered areas and regions within the Sassanid orbit of influence, such as Armenia, Georgia and Caucasian Albania. From the beginning of the Sassanid era in Iran the Zurvanite form of Zoroastrianism enjoyed intermittent prevalence, while the Zoroastrian state–church adhered to the strictly dualist form of the Good Religion. Despite the establishment of Zoroastrian orthodoxy and sporadic persecution against other faiths in the Sassanid empire, the religious climate remained diverse. Within Zoroastrianism itself a division appears to have existed between a higher, élitist and restrictive type of religion, with its esoteric and spiritualized concepts, and a common, popular type of religion, a division which was further linked with the notion of three classes of people, recognized as those who were saved, those who were not guilty and those who were guilty.[48] Although it is difficult to discern the exact targets of the constant condemnations and warnings against *yatukih* (sorcery) and *daeva*-worship during the Sassanid era, diverse magical practices undoubtedly flourished throughout the empire, remnants of *daeva*-worship being apparently still active, particularly in eastern Iranian regions like Sogdiana.

An important testimony of the religious situation in the Sassanid empire refers to three religious currents in Iran, the first of which advanced a system of three principles – the good, the just and the evil, an obvious reference to Zurvanism: the good principle being Ohrmazd; the just, Zurvan; and the evil, Ahriman. The other two currents were respectively the doctrine of the two principles – clearly dualist Zoroastrianism – and that of the seven principles, which still eludes identification.[49] Besides the strict Zoroastrian dualism, elevated to the status of orthodoxy in the Sassanid empire, there also existed a 'monotheistic' version of Zoroastrianism, according to which it was a supreme God that had created Ahriman and the world was thereafter subjected to their dual treatment, the good deriving from God and the evil from Ahriman. Another Zoroastrian trend during the Sassanid era sought the origin of Ahriman in a transformation in the good principle, an 'evil thought' that gave rise to its evil opposite.[50]

The Zoroastrian religious work *Denkart* ('Acts of the Religion') alluded to another type of threefold division among the religious trends in Iran: the first, the *yatukih*, recognized the Creator as entirely maleficent; the second, 'the religion of false dogma', approached the Creator as both maleficent and beneficent; and finally the third, 'the religion of the worshippers of Mazda or Ohrmazd', extolled the Creator as wholly beneficent.[51] The religion of the believers and worshippers of a maleficent Creator, condemned by the orthodox Zoroastrians as an 'evil knowledge', was described as a hidden heresy and in its rite of the 'mystery of the sorcerers' Ahriman, the Destroyer, was praised in 'great secrecy'. The heretical sorcerers were accused of trying to spread the religion of Ahriman in the name of Ohrmazd and thus of prompting men to abandon the worship of Ohrmazd and turn to Ahriman. Their teachings were based on a drastic reversal of Zoroastrian tenets and practices; according to Zoroastrian orthodoxy Ahriman was not conciliated by their worship but was becoming more vicious and violent. Whether the heretical 'mystery of the sorcerers' differed from, coalesced or was identical with the pre-Zoroastrian *daeva*-worship, vestiges of which survived well into the Sassanid era, can only be conjectured, but certainly both were treated as equally dangerous by Zoroastrian orthodoxy and suppressed. The zealous Zoroastrian prelate Kartir, who was particularly influential in the late third century, conducted concerted campaigns against everything he regarded as *daeva*-worship. In his inscription at Naqsh-i Rustam, Kartir proclaimed that 'great blows and torment' befell Ahriman and the *daevas*, whose heresy 'departed and was routed from the empire', while the abodes of the *daevas* were 'made into thrones and seats of gods'.[52] Kartir's crusade against *daeva*-worship was accompanied by measures against the other religions in the Sassanid empire. The Zoroastrian priesthood was reformed; Kartir's inscription recorded that Zoroastrianism and the Magians were greatly exalted in the Sassanid empire.

Yet in the climate of a revived and militant Zoroastrianism and before the Zoroastrian reaction prevailed, the second Sassanid King of Kings, Shapur I (240–72), followed a generally tolerant and indeed syncretistic religious policy. In the *Denkart* he was credited with collecting philosophical and scientific writings from Byzantium and India and adding them to the Zoroastrian canon. He forbade the Magian establishment to persecute the other faiths in the Sassanid empire and even patronized the founder of new universalist but essentially Gnostic religion, Mani. A tradition existed that he had proclaimed his religion of salvation on the day of Shapur's coronation; it was under Shapur's patronage that Manichaeism thrived and began its grand expansion in Asia and Europe.

Mani, who claimed that unlike the kings of the world he had to subdue cities and lands not with military might but with the word of God, identified himself with the Paraclete (Comforter), the Holy Spirit, promised to be sent in Christ's name to continue and 'call to mind' Christ's teachings (John 14:26). Apart from the expected

Paraclete, Mani presented himself as a successor to the prophetic missions of Buddha, Zoroaster and Christ, the ultimate seal of the Prophets and 'the envoy of the true God in the Land of Babylon'.[53]

The Prophet of Babylon

Mani was born on 14 April 216 in Babylonia, with its rich, eclectic and tolerant religious climate, one decade before the fall of the old house of the Arsacids that had ruled Iran since 250 BC. Although depicted in Christian polemical tradition as the freed slave of a widow, Mani was a scion of a noble line related to the Arsacid dynasty. His father had been converted to a sect of Babylonian baptists, who were variously called *Mughtasilah* (practitioners of ablution) or *katharioi* and who have been recently identified as a branch of the Judaeo-Christian movement of the Elchasaites, named after their mysterious founder Elchasai (Hidden Power), who was active in the early second century.[54] Elchasai was said to have been in possession of a book, later called the *Book of Elchasai*, revealed by an angel of enormous size, the Son of God, accompanied by an equally large female angel, the Holy Spirit (Hippolytus, *Refutation of All Heresies* 9:13.1–4). Elchasai was supposed to have received this book of revelations in Parthia but the content remains largely unknown since only short and scattered quotations have been preserved. Parallels have been drawn between Elchasaite teachings and the Zurvanite school that assumed that Zurvan had generated two elements, the male principle of fire and the female principle of water, associated respectively with light and darkness, but in the Elchasaite system the poles appear reversed.[55] In his rejection of the fiery sacrifices, Elchasai preached that fire was leading to error and was to be avoided as abhorrent and strange to God, while the 'sound of the water' should be followed, as water was good and acceptable to God (Epiphanius, *Panarion* 19:3.7).

What seems certain is that the Elchasaites were a Judaeo-Christian baptist sect, which might have been influenced during its development by Gnosticism, but otherwise they endeavoured to live 'according to the Law', observed the Sabbath and like most Jewish Christians denounced Paul and the 'way of the Greeks'. The teachings of the *Book of Elchasai*, with its reputed secret revelations, were undoubtedly fundamental to the Elchasaite sect which apparently possessed its own version of the Gospels. The Elchasaites were said to have invoked seven elements during their baptism: 'heaven, water, the holy spirits, the angels of prayer, oil, salt and the earth' which constituted the 'astonishing, ineffable and great mysteries' of Elchasai, revealed to the worthy Elchasaite disciples (Hippolytus, *Refutation of All Heresies* 9:15.2). Otherwise, of the 'astonishing, ineffable and great mysteries' of Elchasai, little is known, apart from the evident Elchasaite preoccupation with astrology, some sets of magical practices and the belief in the cyclic manifestation of Christ or the 'True Prophet' in many bodies throughout the ages. In some Elchasaite circles Elchasai was considered the latest incarnation in the chain and all Elchasaites were obliged to pray not towards the east but always in the direction of Jerusalem. In *Panarion* (53:1.1), Epiphanius declared that the Elchasaites were not Jews, Christians or pagans, but were somewhere between them, 'keeping to the middle way'.

Within one century of Elchasai's mission, Elchasaite groups were reported in Rome, Palestine and Syria, and were said to worship as goddesses two sisters from the 'famous seed' of Elchasai, Marthous and Marthana. The Babylonian Elchasaites, joined by Mani and his father, abstained from meat and wine and observed frequent purification of food and the body by ritual ablutions with water. Indeed Mani's conflict with the sect was provoked by his denial of the Elchasaite baptismal procedures, which he judged as preoccupied with the purification of the body, which is by its nature impure and, unlike the soul, irredeemable. Real purity, according to Mani, could be achieved only through *gnosis*, the knowledge of the separation of Light from Darkness, life from death and the living waters from the foul waters.[56]

Although Mani tried to fortify his position with parables about Elchasai, where the prophet himself was credited with supporting the reality of Mani's innovations, his attempted dualist reformation was confronted with outright hostility. At a special synod of the sect Mani's *gnosis* and his attack on Elchasaite ritual ablutions were vigorously denounced amid turbulent debates: even Mani's life was threatened. Some of the Babylonian baptists fell under the sway of Mani's orations and recognized him as a prophet and *didaskalos* (teacher), as a vehicle of the 'Living Word' and perhaps as an awaited incarnation of the 'True Prophet'. The Elchasaites, however, also had a prophecy predicting the advent of a young man, a new teacher, who would reverse the precepts of their religion and for most Elchasaites Mani seemed the incarnation of this false prophet. Mani himself was to declare that his new 'mysteries' had abolished and invalidated the traditional teachings and the mysteries of the Babylonian baptists.

Mani's mysteries were proclaimed to stem from revelations from his *Syzygus* (divine twin), deemed to come from the Father and from the 'good Right (Hand)'.[57] The mysteries revealed by the *Syzygus* to Mani were seen as secret knowledge that had been kept hidden from the world, forbidden for man to see or hear. In the Manichaean text *Kephalaia*, they appear as the mystery of 'the Deep and the High', of Light and Darkness, the mystery of the Destruction, 'the mystery of the Great War that was stirred up by Darkness',[58] the merging of Light and Darkness and the creation of the world. These 'mysteries' were to become the basis of Mani's new Gnostic system of the two contrary and coeternal principles of Light and Darkness and the Three Times of their original separation, fusion and cosmic struggle and, finally, their future ultimate separation.

One of the precepts of the *Syzygus*' revelations was that it was through Mani that the blessed Father would fight the kings and rulers of the world. Despite his apprehension that all religions and sects were adversaries of good and that he would encounter kings and religious leaders,[59] Mani perceived his mission as universalist – it had to reach all regions of the world, all people and all schools of religion. His self-proclaimed spiritualist vision provoked the isolationist Elchasaites to accuse him of 'going to the Gentiles' and, following the disputes during the Elchasaite synod, he was expelled from the Babylonian sect, which continued to live 'according to the Law'.

Mani began his mission as an 'Apostle of Light' with three former Elchasaites, including his father, and his initial missionary routes were directed into north-east Iran and remained within the Sassanid and Zoroastrian orbit. Soon, however, he embarked on a greater missionary journey which took him to the Indo-Iranian borderlands, north-west India and the Kushan realm, itself then being apparently under Sassanid suzerainty. In its mature form Mani's Gnostic synthesis included elements not only of Gnosticism, Judaeo-Christianity and Zoroastrianism, but also of Mahayana Buddhism. The Buddhist influences on Manichaeism could date to Mani's missionary venture in India where he became acquainted with Hindu and Buddhist teachings and practices. Both as a missionary and theologian Mani was influenced by Paul; he perceived his mission as a spiritual war to recover the light imprisoned in the darkness of the world. In Manichaean apocalyptic thought Mani's missionary campaigns emerged as a continuation of the wars against 'Error' which had been waged by the previous great saviours, Zoroaster and Jesus.[60] Zoroaster had once banished the Error from Babylon and when it re-emerged among the Jews it was Jesus who was sent to cast the Error out from Jewish religion and who overturned the law, destroyed the Temple and was finally crucified. Following the destruction of the Jerusalem Temple the Error retreated to Mesopotamia, where it mastered the fire of the Magi, and now Mani was entrusted to launch the new, ultimate war against its renascence and its kings and nobles, a war which was set to continue until the end of time.

During his Indian journey Mani had some missionary success with local dynasts and on his return to Iran he was soon granted audience with Shapur I. Mani was presented as a 'physician from Babylon' and his encounter with the King of Kings was to prove crucial for the early missionary expansion of Manichaeism — Mani joined Shapur's entourage and was given permission to promulgate his new religion of salvation freely in the Sassanid empire. Besides securing the favour of the *Shah-an-Shah*, Mani converted two brothers of Shapur to his 'Religion of Light' and dedicated his work *Shabuhragan*, where he expounded his teachings of the Seal of the Prophecy, the Two Principles and the Three Times, to his royal patron.

Shapur's patronage of Manichaeism has been seen as proof that at the time of his great confrontation with the Roman empire he sought the means to achieve religious cohesion in his heterogeneous realm — where Zoroastrianism co-existed with Christianity, Buddhism, Judaism and other faiths – through Mani's daring religious synthesis. Whatever the designs of Shapur, Mani certainly joined his campaigns against the Romans and in 260 might have witnessed the capture of the Roman emperor Valerian, an event commemorated on a monumental rock relief at the dynastic site of Naqsh-i Rustam near Persepolis. Valerian soon died in Persian captivity and while Zoroastrianism continued to expand its sphere of influence, Mani's 'Religion of Light' also considerably widened its missionary propaganda to 'sow the corn of life from East to West'. Apart from extending into eastern Iran, Bactria, Armenia and Georgia, the Manichaean missions also spread westwards into Egypt and Syria, penetrating the Roman empire itself, where its presence was to be lasting and feared. At the same time, the threat of Zoroastrian reaction to Mani's prominence was steadily growing but during the long rule of Shapur and the following short reign of Hormizd (Ohrmazd) I – Shapur's son from his marriage with his daughter – the 'Doctor of Babylon' and his increasing flock remained safe from persecution. The Zoroastrian reaction to Sassanid toleration of Manichaeism was imminent and the accession of Bahram I in 273 marked a drastic reversal in the fortunes of Mani and his Religion of Light, which seems to have been largely provoked by the high Zoroastrian prelate Kartir, the 'Soul-saviour of Bahram'. Apparently incited by the Zoroastrian clergy and Kartir, Bahram summoned Mani and although the Doctor of Babylon claimed that he had brought only good to the royal house by exorcizing demons and healing illness, Bahram could not be persuaded that divine revelation might be granted to Mani rather than to the King of Kings, 'The Ruler of the World'. Mani, the self-proclaimed 'Apostle of Light', was heavily fettered with seven chains and cast into prison, where he continued to instruct his disciples during his twenty-six days' Passion. On Mani's death a blazing torch was thrust through his body on Bahram's orders to ensure that the 'Seal of the Prophets' was dead and his severed head was impaled over the city gate, which came to be known as 'Mani's Gate'.

In the wake of Mani's martyrdom, with which Bahram was said to have appeased 'the Magians, the teachers of Persia, the servants of fire',[61] the Manichaeans were subjected to violent persecution and many were forced to flee eastwards to Sogdiana.[62] After ten years, amid another eruption of anti-Manichaean campaigns, apparently instigated by Kartir, Mani's successor, Sisinus, was crucified. At the height of his influence Kartir proclaimed in his inscription at Naqsh-i Rustam that throughout the whole empire the rites of Ohrmazd had become superior, while Jews, Buddhists, Hindus, Christians and Manichaeans had been smitten in the Sassanid realm.

The Father of Greatness and the Prince of Darkness

The violent reaction of official Zoroastrianism to Mani's Religion of Light was provoked partly by his use of Zoroastrian concepts in his new and essentially Gnostic religion, where Iranian, Jewish, Christian, Buddhist and Egyptian traditions were synthesized in what is usually described as the supreme syncretistic system of late antiquity. Mani was clearly indebted to Marcion's teaching of the two Gods – the good Father of Jesus Christ and the Demiurge of the visible world, but at the same time appears to have been influenced also by Marcion's theological adversary, the heretical Christian evangelist Bardaisan of Edessa (154–222).[63] In Bardaisan's system the world is composed of five primal elements – Light in the East, Wind in the West, Fire in the South, Water in the North, and their enemy Darkness in the Depths below, while their Lord is in the Heavens. Following strife among the first four elements, Darkness emerged from the abyss seeking to merge with them but the pure elements were delivered by the Most High, who sent the Messiah, Christ, to hurl Darkness down to its abode below. The elements were set up in accordance with the 'mystery of the Cross', while the World was created from the amalgam of the elements with Darkness. Mani's Religion of Light, moreover, bears traces of distinct Gnostic traditions, but it remains unclear whether they were assimilated through the medium of the Elchasaite sect or during Mani's exposure to the eclectic religious currents in Mesopotamia.

The canon of the Manichaean Church comprised seven works written by Mani himself – *The Living Gospel*, *The Treasure of Life*,

Treatise, The Book of Secrets, The Book of the Giants, The Epistles and *Psalms and Prayers*, while works like the *Shabuhragan* also enjoyed great prominence. Mani's writings were lost and until the discovery of authentic Manichaean manuscripts early in this century, Manichaean teachings were known mainly through the accounts of Church Fathers like Augustine, the Syrian Theodore bar Konai or Islamic authorities like al-Nadim and al-Biruni.[64] With the discovery of Manichaean texts first in Turfan, in Chinese Turkestan, and then in Egypt, the non-Manichaean observers of the Religion of Light could be compared with the genuine Manichaean records.

In Mani's synthesis the Gnostic anti-cosmic dualism of spirit and matter coalesces with the later Zoroastrian type of dualism of the two primordial, irreconcilable principles of good and evil and the Three Times or Epochs of the tripartite cosmic drama. In Mani's *gnosis* the imprisonment and the suffering of the soul is caused by the fusion of the two contrary principles of Light (spirit) and Darkness (matter) and the soul could be released from the 'great calamity' of the prison–body only through knowledge of their duality and the destinies of their struggle and final separation. According to Mani's *historia arcana* of the cosmos in the Former Time, the sublime Realm of Light was totally separated from the infernal Realm of Darkness and was ruled by the 'Father of Greatness'. One of the important elements of Manichaean missionary strategy was to adjust Manichaean teaching to the local religious terminology: in Iran the Father of Greatness was identified with Zurvan and his fourfold dignity comprised Divinity, Light, Power and Wisdom – hence he is also styled the Four-faced God. Like Zurvan, the Father of Greatness was regarded as androgynous and could be styled 'elder brother' or 'elder sister'. Mani's identification of the Father of Greatness with Zurvan shows clearly that he formulated his system when Zurvanism was strong in Iran, but otherwise the Manichaeans rejected the teaching that Ohrmazd and Ahriman were respectively the younger and first-born sons of one supreme deity.

In Manichaean cosmology the Realm of Light consisted of five elements – Air, Wind, Light, Water and Fire – and was also the abode of the splendid Tree of Life. In the Realm of Darkness five evil archons presided over its own five worlds – Smoke, Fire, Wind, Water and Darkness – from which arose five trees of evil that formed the Tree of Death. The whole Realm of Darkness was ruled by the Prince of Darkness (in Iranian Manichaeism usually Ahriman), who was sometimes depicted as a five-shaped being – with the head of a lion, the body of a serpent, the wings of a bird, the tail of a fish and the four feet of creeping animals.[65]

The fivefold domain of the Prince of Darkness was in a state of constant and disorderly agitation, plagued by destructive, internecine struggles between its hierarchies, during which some of the demonic powers broke out of the confines of their world and encroached upon the tranquil Realm of Light. The invasion of the forces of Darkness marked the beginning of the Present Time, the era when the two principles of Light and Darkness are intermingled and warring. To oppose the demonic onslaught the Father of Greatness evoked the Mother of Life, who herself evoked the Primal Man (Ohrmazd in Iranian Manichaeism), who was armed with the five elements of the Light Sphere, and sent against the Prince of Darkness with his infernal elements. In the ensuing battle the Prince of Darkness was victorious and his forces devoured a part of the five 'luminous elements', the panoply of the Primal Man who collapsed senseless in the bondage of Darkness.

Yet the defeat of the Primal Man was a sacrifice through which the Father of Greatness entrapped and stifled the aggression of the forces of Darkness who now seemed to be 'bitten by a snake', poisoned but addicted to the Light elements they had swallowed. In the Realm of Light a second generation of gods was evoked, the Friend of the Lights, the Great *Ban* (Architect or Builder) and the Living Spirit (Mithra in Iranian Manichaeism) to save the Primal Man, the 'bright one in darkness'. The Living Spirit (Mithra) released the Primal Man (Ohrmazd) by grasping his right hand to raise him from the dark bondage and the ritual greeting with the right hand, symbolizing the mystery of salvation from the Darkness, was to become a Manichaean custom. The Living Spirit then began the work of saving the Light elements, the so-called 'Living Soul', imprisoned in the 'burning house' of matter, and with his five sons defeated the archons of Darkness to create eight earths from their bodies and ten skies from their skins. The Living Spirit was the Demiurge of the visible world, which was created according to the design of the Great *Ban*, with its different regions representing various levels of blending Light and Darkness and mechanisms for the redemption of the Light elements that were to return to the new earth or paradise fashioned by the Great Architect.

While the Sun and Moon were created from the most pure of the recovered Light particles, the plight of the remaining entrapped Light was seen as crucifixion, the Light itself being recognized as the suffering Jesus (Jesus *patibilis*), 'hanging on every tree'. None the less, the cosmos had been designed by the Great Architect to advance the salvation of the Light elements and the Prince of Darkness had to devise new stratagems to bind them to the dark matter. In the counter-attack of the powers of Darkness the male and female archons Saclas and Namrael created Adam and Eve to fortify the imprisonment of the Light elements through the lust and reproduction of the human species. In Manichaean accounts of early human procreation, Cain was born from Eve's union with the male archon and his own incestuous intercourse with Eve generated Abel and two daughters, the 'Wise of the Ages' and the 'Daughter of Corruption'. While Abel was murdered and Cain married the 'Wise of the Ages', Adam finally begat from Eve Sethel (Seth), who was recognized as a 'stranger' to the race of the archons and was inevitably threatened with death.[66]

Prior to this entangled saga Adam had been oblivious of the Light within himself, but was awakened from his sleep by a saviour from the Realm of Light, Jesus the Splendour (sometimes identified with Ohrmazd) who released him from possession by the 'deceiving demon' and the 'great archontess'. Jesus the Splendour revealed to Adam the secret history of the cosmos, the suffering of the Light taken captive in the Darkness, and made him eat of the Tree of Life. When Adam reached full awakening he deplored the archontic creator of his body and ever after the human race remained the principal battleground between the forces of Light and Darkness. Following the mission of Jesus the Splendour a succession of redeemers, bearers of gnosis-power, were sent to humanity to further the work of salvation in a continuous revelation – Seth(el), Enoch, Noah, Abraham, Shem, Zoroaster, Buddha and the historical Jesus Christ. As in other Gnostic schools, in Manichaeism Jesus Christ remained a divine being, who did not assume a material body and whose incarnation, passion, death and resurrection were only in appearance. There existed, however, Manichaean traditions concerning the actual Jewish Messiah, but they are preserved only in scattered and obscure fragments, and Mani's lost book, *Book of the Secrets*, contained a chapter about the 'Son of the Widow', the crucified Messiah.[67] Other Manichaean texts asserted that it was the son of Mary who suffered death on the cross, not the true Son of God. At least in some Manichaean circles the son of Mary was regarded as being of the evil principle and while the Enemy or Satan had planned to crucify the Redeemer, he had actually crucified himself.

Apart from the obvious Gnostic parallels, the Manichaean teachings of Jesus' crucifixion have also been compared to the Koranic version – '"We have killed the Messiah, Jesus son of Mary, the apostle of God" – But they did not kill him, neither did they crucify him, but a similitude was made for them' (Sura 4:156–7). Certain similarities to Manichaenism have been detected also in the Koranic vision of the eschatological 'terror' (Sura 56) and the Koranic notion of the revelation being transmitted by preceding prophets until its culmination in Mohammed, 'the Apostle of God and the Seal of the Prophets' (Sura 33:40).[68] In Manichaeism, following the mission of the heavenly Jesus, it was the 'Light-bringer' Mani, the Apostle of Jesus Christ and the announced Paraclete, who was sent to proclaim the complete and final revelation in his Religion of Light. Mani was extolled as the Seal of the Prophets who revealed the future final stages of the separation of Light and Darkness, when the number of souls trapped below would 'diminish day by day' and the world of Darkness, increasingly depleted of Light, would be plunged into a Great War. The Third Time would be marked by the second coming of Jesus as the 'Great King', his 'Last Judgement' followed by the destruction of the universe in a Great Fire lasting 1,468 years. The last Light elements released would be gathered in a 'statue' to be lifted and restored to the Realm of Light, while the Prince of Darkness and his powers would be imprisoned forever in a grave prepared by the Great Architect.

The Manichaean account of the threefold cosmic drama of the strife between Light and Darkness, good and evil, matter and spirit, is illustrated by rich, expressive and occasionally disturbing mythological imagery which undoubtedly made its appeal more forceful.

At the same time, the dramatic and violent narratives provided material for their adversaries for accusations of secret, unnatural and monstrous practices. Such accusations have often been made against secretive or persecuted religious groups like the early Christians, and the Manichaeans were no exception, being charged with demon-worship, human sacrifice and the use of human skulls for divination, sexual orgies, and the like.

Mani himself was a target for anti-Manichaean polemics, and his name was often translated in derogatory terms in Syriac, Greek and Chinese, from the simple 'maniac' to 'the demonic nun'. Mani had predicted that his mission would provoke the adversity of the secular and religious powers but zealously strove to extend its sphere, as he believed that the messages of his predecessors, Buddha and Zoroaster in the east and Christ in the west, remained confined to their 'Churches' and were, moreover, distorted by their followers. As a self-proclaimed prophet from the land of Babylon, Mani clearly distinguished himself from his eastern and western apostolic predecessors and perceived himself as 'placed in the centre as uniting messenger'.[69] His highly syncretistic system was intended to reach Buddhists, Zoroastrians and Christians alike and during its spread was further enriched through its contact with other religions like Taoism in China. In his designs for a world religion Mani had hoped that his 'Church of Light' would expand both in the west and the east and would thus prove superior to all previous religions, which had remained bound either to east or west or, worse, to particular cities and countries.[70] Mani predicted that his gospel would be preached everywhere and in all languages; in the millennium that followed the Passion of the prophet of Babylon, his 'Religion of Light' was to spread from the Atlantic Ocean to the Pacific.

The Diffusion of the 'Religion of Light'

Mani's 'Church of Light' was divided into two principal and distinct classes, the elect and the listeners or auditors, and this division is variously attributed to Buddhist or Marcionite influences.

The elect, the so-called 'members of Mani', were the minority élite and were associated with Seth(el), the apostle of electship.[71] The elect were entrusted with furthering Mani's vision of redeeming the Light elements from the bondage of matter and, as the 'Saviours of God', they had to observe extreme asceticism. They were bound by the rules of the 'Three Seals', the seals of mouth, hands and breast, which imposed strict abstinence from meat, wine, blasphemy, sexual intercourse and work that could damage the Light elements. The more numerous listeners followed less rigorous standards of conduct and were allowed to marry but had to avoid 'demonic' procreation. Unlike the apostolic elect, listeners could own property and had to ensure the living of the elect, who were engaged in missionary and scribal work. Upon the death of an elect his soul was supposed to immediately reach the Realm of Light, while the soul of the listener was believed to enter a series of transmigrations until reaching the ultimate goal – an incarnation as a Manichaean elect. Mani himself was said to have preached that there were three paths which divided human souls: the way of the elect led to the Gardens of Paradise; the way of the listeners, guardians of the religion and sustainers of the elect, led to the world and its horrors; the third way of the sinners led to hell.[72] The division between the elect and the listeners would persist even during the time of the Last Judgement when the elect would be transformed into angels and the listeners would be elevated to Jesus' right side.

The elect formed the Manichaean ecclesiastical hierarchy, crowned by Mani's successor, with his seat in Babylon, who was the leader of the Church of Light or the *archegos*, a title ascribed earlier to Elchasai himself. Below the *archegos* were the twelve apostles, or teachers, and this hierarchy allowed Christian polemicists to depict Mani as a type of Antichrist accompanied by 'twelve evil disciples'. The twelve Manichaean apostles were followed by seventy-two bishops or deacons and then by 360 elders or presbyters. While women could achieve the status of an elect they could not occupy a position in the hierarchy of the Church of Light.

For the Manichaean church, and for himself, Mani was not merely the prophet who revealed the mysteries of the separation and mixture of Light and Darkness, but was seen as the Seal of Prophecy heralding the advent of the final cycle of separation and salvation. In the Manichaean eschatological chronology Mani's missionary wars against the Error and the Magi, who were recognized as reigning 'in this world', were to be followed by a vigorous revival of the Error's power, when the 'Church of Light' would be subjected to renewed suppression.[73] The renascence of the Error was expected to bring about a disastrous Great War which was, however, to be succeeded by a time of peace under the rule of the Great King, when the Manichaean Church would be fully restored and would then replace the Magi. With the liberation of Light from matter nearly accomplished, the advent of pseudo-prophets and the Antichrist would lead to the last wars against the powers of Darkness and finally the Last Judgement.

These final stages of the threefold drama of the wars between good and evil were regarded by the early Manichaeans as impending events, since they saw themselves as the last generation to have received directly the message of salvation. The great anti-Manichaean persecution launched by the Zoroastrian prelate Kartir after Mani's martyrdom was inevitably associated with the time of the renewal of Error in the Manichaean eschatological chronology. If the fourth century failed to fulfil Manichaean expectations of the restoration of the Church of Light and its triumph over the Magi, it saw the great Manichaean expansion, as Mani had predicted, into both the east and the west.

With the first serious outbreaks of persecution in the Sassanid empire many Manichaeans left Mesopotamia; none the less Babylonia remained a centre of Manichaeism and the *archegos* retained his seat there. The Religion of Light entered the Roman empire during Mani's lifetime and in the fourth century continued its advance in the Mediterranean world and particularly in North Africa. In 302, five years before hailing Mithras as the 'patron of the Empire', Diocletian issued a harsh edict against the Manichaeans in the empire, where they were accused of seeking to infect and poison like a 'malignant serpent' the Roman people with the customs and laws of the Persians. Diocletian apparently perceived Manichaeism as a Persian 'fifth column' in the empire and decreed that the sectarian leaders should be burnt with their books and their followers duly punished. The persecution of the Manichaeans, whether successful or not, was relaxed with Constantine's Edict of 312 which granted universal religious tolerance. Manichaeism then began to spread more vigorously throughout the empire and from the eastern Mediterranean provinces it entered the Balkans and Italy, spread into North Africa, and reached as far as Spain and Gaul, while the first Christian anti-Manichaean works began to appear. As witnessed by St Augustine, who for nine years (373–82) had been a Manichaean listener and had ministered to the needs of the elect, Manichaeism was well-established and well-organized in Rome and the network of Manichaean conventicles was widespread throughout the empire. With the increasing missionary work of the Manichaean envoys among the Christian populace of the empire, western Manichaeism came to accept even more Christian notions into its theological vocabulary.

After an imperial decree of 372 had forbidden Manichaean gatherings, the edicts of Theodosius the Great (379–95), which suppressed Arianism and paganism, contained anti-Manichaean legislation and marked the beginning of an era of intensifying persecution of the Manichaeans in both the West and East Roman empires. Throughout the fifth and the early sixth century the Roman papacy launched a concerted campaign against the Manichaeans in Rome and many of them were exiled and their books burnt. In the East Roman (Byzantine) empire, where becoming a 'Manichaean' was like becoming 'a citizen of a theological Persia perpetually at war with the Romans',[74] the persecution was bound to be severe and Emperor Anastasius (491–518) decreed capital punishment for the Manichaeans. The beginning of Justinian the Great's reign (527–65) saw another edict prescribing the death penalty for Manichaeans which was followed by wide-ranging searches for and execution of Manichaeans occupying imperial posts. In the *Secret History* of his contemporary, Procopius of Caesarea, Justinian was condemned as a demon-incarnate, if not the Lord of the Evil Spirits himself, whose deeds were destined to inflict great calamities upon the world. Justinian might have rebuilt the magnificent church Hagia Sophia (St Sophia), boasting that he had outdone Solomon, but Procopius' insights into his 'demonic' nature must have been shared by the Byzantine Manichaeans, as the anti-Manichaean campaigns intensified and relapsed Manichaeans were threatened with capital punishment. Under Justinian, the 'many-eyed Emperor', the Church and state joined forces more effectively than ever before; two centuries after Diocletian had launched the war against the 'malignant serpent' from Persia, the Religion of Light was extinguished in the empire and thereafter seemed to have disappeared from Europe.

While the westward course of the Manichaean mission collapsed amid the barbaric invasions and the mounting persecution in the Roman empire, it was subjected to further vicissitudes in its homeland, Babylonia. The *archegos* continued to reside in Babylonia in the Sassanid era and following the establishment of the Umayyad caliphate in 661 the Manichaeans generally received relaxed treatment and some Manichaeans returned to Mesopotamia. The succeeding Abbasids, however, took more vigorous measures against the Manichaeans and unrepentant Manichaeans were executed with their heads being left on gibbets. None the less, the Manichaean movement and its *archegos* remained active in Babylonia into the tenth century, but thereafter its fortunes in the Near East are extremely obscure. By the end of the tenth century the centre of gravity of the Religion of Light seems to have been moved finally entirely to the east, to Sogdiana and central Asia; it was this eastward course that prolonged the life of Manichaeism in Asia until the end of the Middle Ages.

Manichaeism had established an early foothold in eastern Iran and the former Kushan areas in Bactria and Sogdiana, and in central Asia Manichaeism was to compete for converts both with Buddhism and Nestorian Christianity. With the persecution following Mani's death in 274 many Manichaeans were forced to flee to the east and crossed the River Oxus (Amu Darya) into Sogdiana. Amid the strong Zoroastrian traditions of the region and the increasing Buddhist influence, Manichaeism succeeded none the less in gaining ground in Sogdiana and in the sixth century Sogdiana became a stepping stone for the introduction of the Religion of Light into China. The rising prominence of the 'eastern' Manichaeans in Sogdiana and the eastward advance of Manichaeism was, however, accompanied by a schism between the eastern wing and the old Babylonian see in the late sixth century. The schismatic 'eastern' Manichaeans began to call themselves 'The Pure Ones', established their own *archegos* in the Samarkand area and carried their missionary work further east.

In 764 Manichaean priests succeeded in converting the Khagan of the Uighur Turks and the Religion of Light became the official religion of the Uighur empire in central Asia. Now Manichaeism could use Uighur political power to expand its mission in central Asia and China and the T'ang government in China soon felt compelled to found Manichaean temples in the Yangtze basin. When the Uighur empire collapsed in 840 under the onslaught of the Kirghiz Turks, the Manichaean temples in China were closed and in 843 the Manichaeans were subjected to massive persecution.

In the second Uighur empire, founded in the Tarim Basin (modern north-west China), Manichaeism continued to enjoy the patronage of the Uighur court and along with the Manichaean temples the established Manichaean monasteries evolved into important centres of learning and missionary work. Yet Buddhism and Nestorian Christianity were to become prevalent in the Uighur realm until the Mongol conquest in the thirteenth century and the forthcoming invasion of Islam.

The great anti-Manichaean persecution launched by the T'ang authorities around 843 did not halt completely the spread of the Religion of Light in China. In its expansion into central Asia and the Far East Manichaeism inevitably not only came to use Buddhist and Taoist terminology and religious themes but was subjected to Buddhist and Taoist influences, while Manichaean influences have been detected in religions in Tibet. Mani himself came to be identified with Maitreya, the would-be Buddha, and acquired the title 'Mani the Buddha of Light', while in a Taoist setting he came to be regarded as one of the manifestations of Lao-Tzu, the founder of Taoism.[75] An eleventh-century Taoist canon included a Chinese Manichaean work, *The Sutra of the Two Principles and the Three Moments*, in all probability a version of the *Shabuhragan*, which the Apostle of Light had dedicated in the third century to his royal Sassanid patron, Shapur I.[76] Manichaeism remained active as a secret religion mostly in southern China, where its history amid the rebellions and activities of various secret societies is rather obscure as well as its association with the Buddhist White Lotus and White Cloud sects. In 1292 Marco Polo encountered a group of Manichaeans during his visit to the Fukien province in southern China but the anti-Manichaean persecution of the founder of the Ming dynasty,

Chu Yuan-Chang, in 1370 seemed to greatly diminish the Manichaean presence in southern China, although vestiges of Manichaeism were still active in Fukien in the early seventeenth century.[77] In south China the Religion of Light had reached the easternmost limit of its expansion and the extant Manichaean temple in the prefecture of Chuan, built during the period of Mongol domination in China (1280–1368), is a striking witness to the vitality of Chinese Manichaeism, which apparently outlasted by centuries the other Manichaean offshoots, including the original see in Babylonia. In medieval Europe itself heretical and dualist movements were readily recognized by the Church as Manichaean but, unlike Chinese Manichaeism, their genealogy and 'renown' as successors to Manichaeism remain uncertain and controversial.

Successors in Byzantium

Justinian's crusade against the Religion of Light might have extinguished it from Byzantium, but the term Manichaean continued to be used as an equivalent of dualist and heretic and could be used to label political and religious adversaries. The problem of its survival in Byzantium is difficult as accusations of Manichaeism appeared largely arbitrary. Yet among the array of heretical and heterodox movements in early Byzantium there were two sects which are usually thought of as the possible heirs of Manichaean Gnostic dualism and as crucial links in the chain supposedly connecting Manichaeism and medieval neo-Manichaeism – the Massalians and the Paulicians.

The Paulicians emerged in the complicated religious world of sixth-century Armenia, which in 389 had been partitioned between Byzantium and Sassanid Persia. Despite Armenia's early adoption of Christianity, Zoroastrians continued to be active and the last Sassanid campaign to reclaim the Armenian lands for the religion of Ahura Mazda in 571 to 572 was supported by Armenian feudal nobles. By the time of this attempted Zoroastrian restoration, the Armenian Christian church had already made itself autonomous and had adopted a version of Monophysite Christianity, defying the authority of Constantinople. The continuous Byzantine endeavours to assert the ecclesiastical supremacy of Constantinople in Armenia failed and in the mid seventh century, when the Arabs had conquered most of the Sassanid empire, Armenia had to acknowledge nominal Arab suzerainty.

With the foundation of the Umayyad caliphate, which engulfed the former Sassanid dominions, Zoroastrianism was disestablished in Iran and the advance of Islam in the Iranian world was accompanied by sporadic anti-Zoroastrian persecution and turning fire temples into mosques. Rather than through forceful conversions, the gradual Islamization of Iran was facilitated by the political and religious conditions in the Umayyad and later the Abbasid caliphates. The emergence of a distinct, sophisticated Persianized Islam spawned important and influential mystical and esoteric trends within Islam. None the less, in the first three centuries of the caliphate, Zoroastrianism retained its prominence in various Iranian provinces, particularly in Fars, the old Achaemenid heartland, where until the tenth century it was still stronger than Islam. After a notable religious revival in the ninth and the early tenth centuries Zoroastrianism gradually diminished to a small religious minority in Iran, while migration to India established new Zoroastrian centres in Gujarat.

Although the Good Religion of Ahura Mazda declined in Iran, Zoroastrian traditions survived in Armenia into the Middle Ages and indeed might have persisted into the modern era, even until the early twentieth century.[78] Moreover, with the establishment of Christian orthodoxy in the Roman empire, Armenia became a refuge for heretics and heterodox sectarians. Marcionite and other Gnostic groups, perhaps including Manichaeans, certainly lingered in Armenia well into the fifth century, while the Paulicians, who appeared in the following century, still present numerous problems in the study of eastern Christianity and medieval dualism. In Armenia they were accused of consorting with 'sun-worshippers' (Persians, Zoroastrians), also called Arewordik (Sons of the Sun), or observing some Zoroastrian customs like the exposure of the dead on rooftops or the veneration of the sun and, indeed, some Paulician groups might have adopted such practices.[79] Later Byzantine polemical works consistently described the Paulicians as outright Manichaeans and attributed to them the radical dualist doctrine of two gods or principles, the evil creator of the present material world and the good God of the future world. The Paulicians are also described as professing Docetic Christology – Christ's incarnation was proclaimed illusory and the Virgin Mary was praised not as the mother of Christ but as the 'heavenly Jerusalem'. According to a recent persuasive reassessment of Paulician history and teachings, however, both the dualist and Docetic doctrines represent late developments in the Paulician movement and original Paulicianism adhered to Adoptionist teachings current in early Armenian Christianity according to which Christ had been adopted as the son of God during his baptism.[80] The timing and cause of the later doctrinal reorientation of the Paulicians remains enigmatic; one of the suggested solutions dates the dualist reformation of Paulicianism to ninth-century Byzantium and attributes it to the Paulician heresiarch and missionary, Sergius.[81]

What complicates the argument for a direct Manichaean influence on Paulicianism is the apparent lack of the crucial Manichaean division between the elect and the listener among the Paulicians, although there are some indications of esoteric teachings or mysteries, preserved for the few 'perfect in impiety' Paulicians.[82] The early Paulician organization also remains obscure; they did not observe the ascetic practices of the Manichaean elect, the strict abstinence from meat, wine and marriage. Forced into conflicts with Byzantium early in their history, the Paulicians came to be renowned as aggressive and dangerous warriors who inflicted some heavy defeats on the Byzantine armies.

The Paulicians entered Byzantium around the mid seventh century and in the following three centuries posed a series of problems for the Byzantine authorities. At the height of their influence the Paulicians founded seven 'churches' in Armenia and Asia Minor, among which the church of Corinth, reputedly founded by St Paul, was regarded as their mother-church. From the eighth century the Paulicians also emerged as a factor in the Byzantine–Arab confrontation in eastern Anatolia and in 759 Paulician colonies entered the Balkans for the first time, having been resettled by the emperor Constantine v, along with other eastern heretics, to plague-stricken Thrace.

In 717 a council of the Armenian Church forcefully denounced the Paulicians as 'sons of Satan' and 'fuel for the fire eternal' but earlier, in the mid fifth century, it was still the Massalians that were perceived as the greatest heretical threat in Armenia. In 447 a special council announced sweeping measures against the Massalian heresy. The Massalians (the praying people), also called Enthusiasts, were an anti-clerical, pietist sect about whose actual teachings very little is known.[83] Their main belief was underlain by a peculiar type of anthropological dualism, according to which from birth in every man dwells a demon, who cannot be banished only by baptism, but through continuous, zealous prayer and spiritual 'baptism by fire'. After a long period of strict asceticism and unceasing prayer the Massalian mystic was supposed to reach a completely passionless state, when the demon could be expelled and he could become a receptacle for the Holy Ghost. Having achieved mystical union with the Holy Ghost, the Massalian adept was believed to be able to behold the Trinity. With the demon driven away and the Holy Ghost dwelling in his soul, the Massalian adept could sin no more and could return to life in 'this world' without ascetic restrictions. The Massalians were frequently accused by their orthodox enemies of immorality and various excesses – which did not prevent them from spreading their teachings and practices in the monasteries. Monasteries remained the favourite target of Massalian proselytism, although monasteries suspected of having been infected by Massalianism could be penalized and even burned.

The Massalians appear to have emerged in north-east Mesopotamia and by the end of the fourth century they had penetrated Syria and Asia Minor. Despite persecution at the hands of the ecclesiastical authorities, in the fifth century the Massalians spread further in Asia Minor and Armenia, and remained active in Syria until the seventh century. Although there are several Orthodox testimonies of their continuing activities, from that time their history is unknown and when their name was revived in the eleventh century, they were clearly associated with the Bogomils. Historical links between the early Massalians and the Manichaeans in Mesopotamia and Byzantium are plausible but they have not been established and it is not clear whether the repeated allusions to the Massalians after the eleventh century indicated a genuine revival of the sect or were used as a label for the new heretics, namely the Bogomils.

It is possible that some Massalians were resettled along with the Paulicians during the eighth century in the Byzantine campaigns of sending Syrian and Armenian heretics to the Balkans. The influx of heretics into the Balkans added to the eclectic religious climate of the peninsula in the Dark Ages and complicated what was already a peculiar religious situation. Although the first Christian missions to the Balkans dated from the apostolic times and Balkan Christianity produced many martyrs during Diocletian's persecution, the process of Christianization was severely disrupted by the barbaric invasions of the fourth and the fifth centuries. The Visigoths, the Huns, the Ostrogoths and the Avars traversed and plundered the peninsula and in their wake came the great Slav colonization in the sixth and seventh centuries. While Justinian the Great, the adversary of Manichaeism, was campaigning to restore the western dominions of the old Roman empire, reconquering Italy, north Africa and parts of southern Spain, the Balkans were exposed to Slav invasions from the north.

Procopius might have fancifully attributed the natural disasters that befell Byzantium during Justinian's reign to the 'demonism' of the emperor, but he also acknowledged the increasing Slav influx in the Balkans that soon brought cataclysmic changes to the peninsula. The intermittent, heavy warfare with Sassanid Persia in the east did not allow Byzantium to take efficient measures to halt the Slav invasions and eventually the pagan Slav tribes were to penetrate deep even into Greece and its southernmost region, Peloponnesus. The complete transformation of the Balkan political and ethnic make-up was furthered also by the arrival of the Serbs and Croats, tribes which were apparently of Iranian extraction, but were Slavicized by the ninth century and played a crucial role in medieval Balkan history.[84]

The Slav colonization plunged the already weakened ecclesiastical order into further disarray. The reassertion of Byzantine authority in its Balkan domains was inevitably linked to their re-evangelization and the conversion of the pagan Slav settlers to Byzantine Orthodoxy. The Balkans were open terrain in the struggle between Rome and Constantinople, as the battle for ecclesiastical jurisdiction over the province of Illyricum in the western Balkans intensified. The process of the re-Christianization of the Balkans was extremely conducive to the emergence of heterodox movements over the centuries. In the late seventh century the Byzantine plans for political and religious reconquest of the Balkans were halted by the sudden rise of the first Bulgarian empire.

In Balkan antiquity, besides Orphism, some trends in Thracian religion had cultivated a distinct religiosity, based on a dualism of soul and body, of life in this world and life after death, and had fostered ascetic practices. This spirituality 'of Balkan extraction' has been defined as 'somewhat evasive, in controversy and in opposition to the life in this world'[85] and thus was at variance with traditional biblical and Zoroastrian spirituality. It has also been noted that the Gnostic type of dualism fostered by medieval neo-Manichaeism gained prominence in those east European regions where religious dualist currents had already been influential.[86] The newly founded pagan Bulgarian state in the eastern Balkans not only allowed the continuation of non-Christian religious trends but also the spread of Christian heretical movements: indeed in the mid tenth century, within a century of the beginning of its Christianization in 864, it became the scene of a revival of dualism, the rise of the medieval Great Heresy.

CHAPTER THREE

The Rise of the Great Heresy

About the time when Rome was struck by a 'demon-caused' plague, when the Merovingian cult figure Dagobert II was martyred near Stenay and the head of the slain Shiite pretender to the caliphate, Husayn, was sent to the Umayyad caliph Yazid, the Byzantine empire had to face the sudden rise of the first rival domain in its 'God-protected' Balkan territory. In 680 the imperial fleet and armies of Constantine IV Pogonatus 'The Bearded' had advanced to the Danube delta against the forces of the Bulgar dynast Asparuch but suffered one of the most crucial and humiliating defeats in all Byzantine history. In the following year Constantine IV surrendered to Asparuch the imperial land northwards of the Balkan (Haemus) mountains, already heavily colonized by Slav tribes, and the treaty marked the foundation of one of the first states in medieval eastern Europe: the First Bulgarian Empire (681–1118).

From the Steppes to the Balkans

The foundation of the Bulgarian empire in the Balkans was one of the turning points in the religious and political history of eastern Europe in the early Middle Ages when successive migratory waves of nomadic people from the Eurasian steppes poured one after another into Europe. Stretching from the Carpathians to the Altai mountains in central Asia, the Eurasian steppes are traditionally regarded as a cradle of nations that served as the homeland of the Finno-Ugrian, Turco-Mongolian and arguably the Indo-European people. Although the ancient history of the Eurasian steppes still poses numerous unsolved problems, it is becoming increasingly apparent that this vast area had a specific cultural unity[1] in which the northern Iranians were a potent and often dominant political and cultural force until the tumultuous irruption of the Huns into Europe during the fourth century AD. In the previous century the Iranian millennial hegemony in the east European steppes had already been broken by a strong Gothic influx into the area and by the establishment of a strong Ostrogothic kingdom in modern Ukraine. The Hunnic invasion spelt the end of Iranian Sarmatian power in the steppes, pushed the Ostrogoths to the west and forced the Visigoths into the lands of the Roman empire where they defeated and murdered Emperor Valens (378), burned the sanctuary of Eleusis and, finally, in 410 sacked Rome itself.

In the following two centuries, along with new peoples from the steppes, the Bulgars expanded into eastern Europe and their incursions in the Balkans multiplied with a mounting intensity. Like other masters of the Eurasian steppes – the Sarmatians, the Alans, the Avars, the Khazars – much of the ancient history of the Bulgars remains obscure. The semi-legendary era of their early conquests and domains in inner and central Asia abounds in immense gaps and riddles and is still being reconstructed from exceedingly diverse and uneven evidence. It is widely assumed that in the early Christian era most of the Bulgars inhabited areas in southern central Asia, particularly in the Pamir region and the Sogdiana lands locked between the upper reaches of Oxus and Jaxartes, described as being between Iran and Turkestan.[2] In the political transformations of the period the former Achaemenid satrapy had retained its strong Zoroastrian traditions amid the increasing presence of Buddhism, Nestorian Christianity and Manichaeism. In the turmoil of the great migrations in the fourth and fifth centuries, when the Huns achieved complete supremacy over the nomadic world for a century, the Bulgars were pushed along the westward Hunnic expansion and drawn towards the Caucasus–Caspian region and further into Europe. During their early history the Bulgars apparently had continuous contacts with the ancient Iranian tribes in central Asia and upon their entry into Europe their culture interacted considerably with the northern Iranian Sarmato-Alan culture.

In the early seventh century most of the Bulgars were united along with some of their allies in their realm of *Magna Bulgaria*, founded on the ruins of the old Sarmato-Alan and Hellenistic civilizations in the northern Pontic–Azov area. *Magna Bulgaria* incorporated large areas of what is today Ukraine and south-eastern Russia and has been defined as a 'new edition of the Bosphorus kingdom'[3] which now extended its sway into the north Caucasus steppes. In the previous two centuries the northern Caucasus region had been an arena of intense Sassanid–Byzantine rivalry and had been subjected to the dual penetration of Byzantine Christianity and Zoroastrianism, and was marked by the appearance of Christian sites and the distinctive square-shaped fire temples of the Zoroastrian cult.[4] While the Bulgars themselves had been exposed to the strong influence of Sassanid political and cultural traditions, the ruler of *Magna Bulgaria*, Kubrat, visited Constantinople to conclude an alliance with Emperor Heraclius, was baptized and granted the noble title of 'Patrician'. On Kubrat's death (*c.* 663–8), however, *Magna Bulgaria* collapsed under the vigorous pressure of the Khazars and was incorporated in the rising Khazar khaganate, a powerful steppe empire which at its height extended its authority from the Pontic–Caspian area to the Ural mountains.

The Bulgars, who remained in the Pontic–Azov lands under Khazar suzerainty, continued to be a strong political force, associated with the Iranian Alan element in the realm and sought to seize political power in the khaganate. Despite the Arab attempts to introduce Islam in the Khazar empire in the course of the eighth century the Khazar court and nobility unexpectedly embraced Judaism but in the Khazar empire, renowned thereafter as the 'Judaic domain', the Judaized elements coexisted with pagans, Christians and Muslims.[5] With its vital strategic position, the Khazar empire served effectively as a buffer shielding eastern Europe from the progress of the Muslim Holy War and, after prolonged and violent Arab–Khazar warfare, the Arab advance was finally blocked at the Caucasus.

While the Bulgars in the Khazar empire contributed significantly to the formation of its civilization, the Bulgars who escaped from Khazar overlordship separated into several branches which began to spread over Europe, from the 'Volga to the shadows of Vesuvius'.[6] A Bulgar offshoot had already sought refuge in the Merovingian dominions of *le bon roi* Dagobert I and some Bulgars were to settle permanently in northern Italy. Besides the Bulgar realm in the Balkans, the Volga branch of the so-called 'Silver' Bulgars established a strong trading domain in the Volga–Kama region which, in contrast to the Khazar empire, and struggling against its influence, was finally won over to Islam in the tenth century. Little is known of the religious life in Volga Bulgaria before the Islamization, although in a controversial statement in *Fihristi* the Islamic encyclopedist Ibn al-Nadim asserted that the Bulgars (the Volga Bulgars) had used the 'script of the Chinese and the Manichaeans'.[7] The art of Volga Bulgaria elaborated mainly central Asian and Iranian traditions, which sometimes appear to echo Zoroastrian themes, along with an array of fantastic dragon-like and sphinx-like creatures.[8] Volga or 'Silver' Bulgaria evolved as the northernmost Muslim civilization, which flourished until it was overrun by the Mongols in the thirteenth century and its vestiges were ultimately wiped out in 1552 by Ivan the Terrible, the first Grand Duke of Moscow to assume the imperial title of Tsar.

The Balkan wing of the Bulgar diaspora took full advantage of its victory over Constantine IV to consolidate its domain in the former Roman provinces in the Balkans, traditionally seen as the most contested territory in Europe. With their well-developed and complex politico-military system, which betrayed distinct Iranian influences, the Balkan Bulgars easily secured the allegiance of the Slav tribes in their expanding realm. The state-building and centralizing role of the Bulgars in the Balkans is usually compared to that of the Normans in England after 1066 or the Salian Franks in fifth-century Gaul. The Bulgar monarchy seems to have been of the dual kingship type and the sublime ruler, who bore the title Kan, apparently was regarded as an incarnation of the divine power, and combined religious and political functions. Established in close proximity to the imperial capital of the heir apparent of the old Roman empire, the Bulgar Sublime Kans were to carve out their Balkan domain with the 'ultimate ambition to create a metropolis rivalling Constantinople itself'.[9] The monumental architecture of the pagan Bulgarian empire embodies Near Eastern architectural traditions and the royal residences of the Sublime Kans are usually associated with the Sassanid palaces in Persia or with the Umayyad citadels in Syria. The Bulgar art and architecture is diverse and eclectic, but with a predominant Sassanid influence, which largely supports the thesis that the Sublime Kans perpetuated in the Balkans ceremonial and architectural traditions akin to those of the Sassanid monarchs of Persia.[10]

The imposing temples and cult centres erected by the Bulgars point to a developed religion but strangely little is known about its exact nature and pantheon. The Bulgars brought to the Balkans a well-developed astronomo-astrological system, based on the central Asian 'animal cycle' calendar, along with an array of shamanistic beliefs and practices. The complex evidence recovered from Bulgar religious monuments is still being examined but certainly it attests to the toleration and syncretism in religion and art that prevailed in the pagan Bulgarian empire. This is hardly surprising, as the Bulgars had traversed and settled in areas which were meeting places of competing religious traditions – Zoroastrianism, Buddhism, Nestorian Christianity, Manichaeism. The evidence of some Arabic authors, who styled the Bulgars 'Magians', seems controversial, yet the closest parallel to the square-shaped Bulgar temples appeared to be the Iranian fire temples of the Parthian and Sassanid epochs which spread from central Asia and the Kushan realm to northern Mesopotamia and, under the Sassanids, also appeared in the north Caucasus area.[11] The Bulgar shrines have been also compared to a contemporary type of Buddhist temple in central Asia which was itself representative of a syncretistic form of Buddhism.[12]

The problem of the Bulgars' religion remains one of the unresolved and controversial questions related to the foundation of their Balkan empire, which emerged as one of the so-called 'successor states' of the Dark Ages, similar in some respects to Frankish Gaul under the early Merovingians, Anglo-Saxon England or the Visigothic kingdom in Spain. The notable cultural achievements of the first Bulgarian empire have been defined as 'counterpart of the Carolingian culture in Western Europe' with works 'at least of the same quality'.[13] From its foundation in 681 until the end of the first Christian millennium the growth and expansion of the Bulgarian empire affected much of the political developments in south-east Europe. In central Europe its boundaries eventually met those of the Frankish empire under Charlemagne, while in the Balkans the Bulgar war-machine recurrently moved on the offensive against the Byzantine empire to beleaguer its new Rome, the 'Holy City' of Constantinople.

Kans and Emperors

The emergence of a Bulgar power block in south-eastern Europe ended Byzantine hegemony of the Balkans for more than three centuries and marked one of the great crises which affected Byzantium in the Dark Ages. In the seventh and eighth centuries the rising tide of militant Islam engulfed the Byzantine provinces in the Near East, North Africa and south-eastern Spain, while Constantinople itself suffered two major Arab assaults. Losing Syria, Palestine and Egypt to the caliphate, Byzantium succeeded in holding on to Asia Minor but was beset by chronic political infighting and endemic palace revolutions. The religious life of the empire was strongly affected by the rise of the Iconoclastic movement in the early eighth century, which condemned the veneration of images as idolatry and won the support of many Byzantine emperors before being defeated in the council of the 'Triumph of Orthodoxy' in 843.

In the Balkans the centuries-long saga of the Bulgaro-Byzantine rivalry in the eastern part of the peninsula passed through decades of violent intermittent warfare and shaky peace, short-lived military alliances and relentless political feuding behind the scenes, Byzantine reconquests of lost Balkan provinces, sieges of Constantinople, and dynastic intermarriages. The Bulgar Kans periodically sought to exploit the volatile and convoluted internal politics in Byzantium, interfering even in the palace revolutions and in the struggles for the imperial throne. In 704 the exiled and slit-nosed ex-emperor Justinian II was restored to the throne with the crucial military support of the Bulgar Kan Tervel who was granted in return the title of Caesar, second only to the imperial title. In 717 the troops of Tervel helped beleaguered Byzantium in breaking the second great Arab siege of Constantinople, considered sometimes the most critical Arab assault on Europe, threatening her 'soft underbelly' in the south-east, fifteen years before Charles Martel halted the Saracen advance in western Europe at the battle of Tours.

In the latter part of the eighth century the great Iconoclastic emperor, Constantine v Copronymus, who was accused by his Iconophile opponents of being Paulician and Manichaean, or even Mammon himself, launched nine consecutive wars to reconquer the north-east Balkans. The recovery of the Bulgarian empire under Charlemagne's contemporary, Krum (c. 803–14), led to a series of political crises in Byzantium, as the Kan succeeded in overpowering three emperors on the battlefield, laid siege to Constantinople and even seized stocks of Byzantium's ultimate secret weapon – the 'Greek Fire'. While for the German Protestant dramatist Andreas Gryphius (1616–64) Krum was the epitome of heroic warrior, for the Byzantine chroniclers he was the 'new Sennacherib', an incarnation of the sinister Assyrian king (705–681 BC) who had destroyed Babylon and besieged Jerusalem. In 811 the Byzantine emperor Nicephorus I lost his life and army in an ill-fated campaign against Krum, in which his son and co-emperor was also wounded to die several months later: the deaths of the two emperors dispelled the mystique of the traditional Byzantine myth of the invincible emperor. For nearly half a millennium, since Valens' death in 378, no Roman emperor had ever been killed in battle and now the skull of the 'invincible' Nicephorus was fashioned into a silver goblet for the palace feasts of the 'new Sennacherib'.

Meanwhile, the sudden papal coronation of Charlemagne as *Imperator Romanorum* on Christmas Day 800, coupled with his advance into traditional Byzantine spheres of influence, had brought him into a collision course with Constantinople, which refused to recognize his imperial title. In the wake of Nicephorus' death the new Byzantine emperor Michael I Rangabe, faced with the mounting Bulgarian menace, promptly recognized Charlemagne as his 'co-emperor of the West' to seek his alliance against the resurgent Bulgarian empire. Michael I was soon defeated disastrously by Krum and dethroned in Constantinople, which itself was now besieged by the 'new Sennacherib' and agonizingly awaited for months an assault as serious as the previous two Arab sieges of Constantinople. As a true priest–king, Krum conducted ostentatious pagan ceremonies and sacrifices before the very walls of the bastion of eastern Christendom, but at the height of his preparations died amid somewhat odd circumstances, in the words of a Byzantine chronicler, 'as if slain by an invisible hand'.[14]

The pagan ceremonies of the 'new Sennacherib' before the walls of Constantinople highlight the peculiar religious dimension of the Bulgaro-Byzantine collisions throughout the Dark Ages. Following the Islamic conquests in the Mediterranean world, the influence of early and important centres of Christianity in the Near East and North Africa, including the oriental patriarchates of Antioch, Alexandria and Jerusalem, inevitably declined. While losing its eastern and African provinces to Islam, Byzantium also suffered the loss of large parts of its 'historic' Roman territory in the Balkans to the pagan domain of the Bulgar Kans, who could now directly threaten the imperial capital of Constantinople.

Having survived the collapse of its western counterpart as the only legitimate heir of the old Roman empire, Byzantium saw itself as the only eternal and indissoluble empire, established by God, to be ruled by His earthly representative, the emperor. The rise of the Bulgarian empire in such menacing proximity to the New Rome was perceived as a chastening for Byzantine sins, while imperial propaganda correlated the reconquests of the Balkans with their reconversion to Christianity as part of the providential Christianizing mission of Byzantium. From the fifth century such a sense of divine election was to be shared by the newly Christianized Merovingian kingdom,[15] but in the pagan Bulgarian domain religion and royalty were also closely intertwined and in the person and the functions of the Sublime Kan the throne was wed to the altar. From its foundation the Bulgarian empire posed a determined challenge to Byzantium's inbred sense of imperial destiny and divine election. While Byzantine imperial propaganda strove to sanctify its campaigns against Bulgaria as more or less 'holy wars' against the 'most pagan and Christ-hating domain', Bulgar royal propaganda also sought to invoke divine sanction and providence for its confrontation with the New Rome.[16] Apart from becoming the Balkan arch-rivals of the emperors in Constantinople, the Sublime Kans adopted the imperial formula, 'divine ruler chosen by God', as well as the use of the cross in their inscription and regalia. The Bulgar Kans, however, remained intensely apprehensive of the universalist evangelical pretensions of the New Rome and also ever anxious to praise the virtues of their religion and its militant superiority to Byzantine Christianity. Yet the original religious policy of the Bulgar Kans was certainly tolerant, allowing for co-existence between paganism and Christianity, whether orthodox or heretical. While in Byzantium the Iconoclastic and Iconophile movements were vying to achieve the status of orthodoxy, in the pagan Bulgarian empire the meeting and syncretism of diverse religious traditions was still alive, maintaining a religious climate of complexity and eclecticism.

Paganism, Heresy and Christianity

The foundation of the pagan Bulgarian empire marked an abrupt turn in the religious history of the Balkans and opened one of its most complex and obscure periods. Any relic of the Christian ecclesiastical order which might have survived the dawning of the Balkan Dark Ages, with its devastating series of barbaric invasions, could hardly thrive in the pagan realm of the Bulgar Kans. Conversely, the early Bulgarian empire provided perfect conditions for the revival and continuation of pagan cults and traditions which had been suppressed earlier throughout the Byzantine-controlled parts of the peninsula. The very foundation of the Bulgarian domain coincided with the convocation of the Third Ecumenical Council of Constantinople (680–81) which condemned and took measures against the remains of Dionysian and other mysteries, apparently still active in the Balkans. The Bulgars themselves introduced religious influences from central Asia and the steppes and in the following centuries the peninsula was to remain open to such influences brought by the advent of new, mainly pagan settlers and invaders from the steppes. Their mythological and magical beliefs mingled freely with various pagan survivals from antiquity to engender a rich and lasting syncretistic heritage, remnants of which can be traced even today. In the northern and eastern Balkans the Bulgars and the Slavs encountered relics of ancient Balkan paganism, like the Thracian religious cults, and perhaps vestiges of mystery religions. Various beliefs and practices associated with the old mystery cults proved unusually persistent in the Balkans, having endured through the centuries in folklore and quasi-Christian customs. Apart from the recent publicizing of folkloric relics of Orphic and Dionysian mysteries in certain regions in Thrace, a set of rituals preserved in the western Balkans has been shown to bear recognizable traces of the ancient cult of the Dioscuri and the classical mysteries of Samothrace.[17]

The expansion of the pagan Bulgarian empire in the eastern Balkans was bound to precipitate a revitalization of pagan residues in its newly conquered lands but also led to an increasing Christian presence in its sphere of control. But whatever the strength of Christianity in the eastern Balkans, without proper institutions and ecclesiastical control, it was certainly exposed to pagan and heretical influences. In Byzantium itself paganism might have been defeated but besides colouring Christian beliefs and practices pagan residues endured in certain areas of the empire and as late as the early tenth century Emperor Leo VI had to lead a crusade against the still strong paganism in the Peloponnesus region of Mani. Heterodox and heretical traditions also existed and were in force in the Byzantine world, particularly in Anatolian regions like Phrygia, where the enigmatic Judaizing sect of the Athingani synthesized the observance of the sabbath with astrological and magical beliefs and practices.[18] The pagan Bulgarian domain to the north of Byzantium provided safe refuge not only for persecuted heretics but also for Jews who were reported to have fled there during the anti-Jewish persecution of Emperor Leo III in the early eighth century. The Byzantine policy of transplanting colonists from the empire's eastern provinces to Thrace further entangled the volatile religious climate of the Balkans. These colonies of Syrian and Armenian heretics were expected to form Byzantine garrisons during the intermittent Bulgaro-Byzantine wars in the disputed Thracian borderlands; while clearly failing to oppose the Bulgarian advance, some – particularly the Paulicians – established strong and lasting hotbeds of heretical agitation.

The Paulician colony, which was transplanted to Thrace in 757 by Constantine V, was probably positioned also as a counterpoise to his Iconophile opponents. At the beginning of the century Byzantine policy had driven the Paulicians into an alliance with the Islamic powers but under Iconoclastic emperors like Constantine V, who was blamed for reintroducing them into the empire, they regained imperial favour and were able to diffuse their teachings in Byzantium. Even the Iconophile emperor Nicephorus I came to be suspected of professing Paulician beliefs, but his successor Michael I Rangabe launched severe persecution with executions of the 'Manichaeans called now Paulicians' and forced them to seek new alliances with the Islamic powers on Byzantium's eastern borders, namely the emirs of Melitene and Tarsus. The Paulician heresiarch and missionary Sergius found refuge in the lands of the emir of Melitene in eastern Cappadocia where he founded the last Paulician churches. Indeed the supposed tenth-century transformation of Paulicianism from an Iconoclastic anti-ecclesiastical sect into a militant dualist movement has been attributed to the reforms of Sergius[19] whose flight to the emir of Melitene, moreover, paved the way for the emergence of an aggressive Paulician principality on the upper Euphrates. Following the restoration of Iconophile orthodoxy in Constantinople in 843 the Paulicians suffered new violent persecution which in the chroniclers' inflated estimations claimed one hundred thousand Paulician lives. Inevitably, more Paulicians sought refuge in eastern Cappadocia and their leader, Carbeas, assumed power in a separate Arab-backed state along the upper Euphrates just to the east of the Byzantine frontier. A former imperial officer, whose Paulician father had been crucified in the persecution, Carbeas established his seat at Theprice in mountainous north-eastern Cappadocia, from where he launched a series of invasions across the eastern borders of the empire. Paradoxically the foundation of the dualist Paulician principality in eastern Cappadocia coincided with the collapse of the Uighur empire, where Manichaeism had been the official religion for nearly a century, and the ensuing massive suppression of Manichaeism in T'ang China, which culminated in a massacre of an unknown number of Manichaean priests.

The final results of the great anti-Paulician campaigns in Byzantium thus turned out rather dubious – Paulicianism may have been extinguished from Byzantine soil but now it was established in a hostile Arab-backed theocratic state that directly threatened the eastern borders of the empire. The religious conflict between Byzantine Iconophile Orthodoxy and Paulician dualism evolved into a full-scale political and military confrontation in central-eastern Anatolia where the imperial armies suffered some heavy defeats and two emperors narrowly escaped capture by the Paulician forces.

Simultaneously, in south-east Europe, Byzantium had to confront the mounting prospect of a Franco-Bulgarian alliance with all its consequences for Byzantine interests in the Balkans. In the first half of the ninth century the Bulgar Kans successfully negotiated with Charlemagne's son, Louis the Pious, and grandson, Louis the German, for the exact delineation of the Franco-Bulgarian border in central Europe. By the middle of the century the Sublime Kans already controlled much of the territory between the Carolingian dominions, which then embraced most of western Christendom, and Byzantium, the stronghold of eastern Christendom. With its strategic position between the two great rival Christian powers, the Bulgarian domain was inevitably drawn into their imperial and ecclesiastical rivalries at the time when it had already witnessed itself the first bitter pagan–Christian conflicts that marked the opening stages of a protracted and exhaustive religious struggle.

Rome, Constantinople and Theprice

In 862 the Franco-Bulgarian alliance was finally concluded and it became apparent that the Bulgar Kan Boris (852–89) planned to receive Christianity from the west and had requested missions from Louis the German. Although the threefold partitioning of the Carolingian empire in 843 had largely diminished the Frankish threat to Byzantium, Constantinople was acutely aware of the manifold dangers of allowing Carolingian and Roman influences to filter into the Balkans via Bulgaria. The Byzantine armies had just defeated the Arabs and neutralized, for a time, the Paulicians in eastern Anatolia, although in 858 the emperor Michael III had nearly been taken captive by the forces of the Paulician leader Carbeas. The Byzantine main field army was moved to the Balkans and its massive attack against Bulgaria, presaged by a locust plague and earthquakes, compelled Kan Boris to renounce his pact with the Franks and to agree to accept Christianity from Constantinople. Early in 864 Kan Boris was baptized by Byzantine prelates and was converted into Prince Michael, taking the name of his imperial godfather, Michael III.

Yet unlike the solemn baptism of the Merovingian ruler Clovis, Boris's baptism was a 'nocturnal' ceremonial, reportedly conducted 'in secret and in the dead of the night'. Boris's fears of an inevitable pagan backlash proved prophetic: he was accused of apostasy and the threat of a Byzantine religious invasion aroused an immediate and fierce reaction among the bulk of the Bulgar aristocracy. In his forceful collision with the pagan Bulgar nobles, Boris, depicted as a Christian thaumaturge, emerged victorious and fifty-two Bulgar houses faced outright annihilation. In addition to the strong pagan reaction the Christianization of the Bulgarian empire was further complicated by a long and exhausting struggle between Constantinople and Rome for ecclesiastical supremacy in the realm.

Successive and opposing missions from the Constantinople patriarchate and the Roman papacy turned the Bulgarian realm into a religious battleground between the Latin and Byzantine clergy. Apart from the dispute whether the Holy Spirit proceeds only from the Father or – as accepted by the western Church – from the Father 'and from the Son' (*filioque*), the battle for the Bulgarian church was one of the main factors for the mounting confrontation between the Constantinople patriarchs and the Roman popes. The Greek–Latin confrontation was aggravated further by Boris's intricate moves for an autonomous Church. By 881 the patriarchate had altogether outmanoeuvred the papacy in the bid for the Bulgarian church and Constantinople finally seemed to have succeeded in drawing the Bulgarian empire into the Byzantine religious and cultural orbit.

While competing for ascendancy in Bulgaria, Constantinople and Rome were challenged by other religious rivals. Besides the Islamic and Jewish missions, which don't seem to have achieved any tangible success, the Greek and Latin emissaries in Bulgaria must have vied with heretical preachers from the Thracian sectarian colonies. The newly Christianized Bulgarian empire was a suitable breeding ground for heretical agitation – apart from the heretical colonies in the annexed Thracian areas it had apparently served as a refuge for Byzantine heretics and discontents.

As late as the mid ninth century a prominent Byzantine 'Manichaean and sorcerer', Santabarenus, was offered sanctuary in then pagan Bulgaria, where he promptly denounced Christianity and freely began to promulgate his teachings. What is more, the Paulicians of the Cappadocian principality were apparently in contact with their co-sectarians in the Balkans and according to the Byzantine ambassador to Theprice, Peter of Sicily, they were organizing new missions to reinforce the Paulician colonies in Bulgaria in about 870.[20] Unlike the Roman and Constantinople missions, the course of the Theprice mission remains unknown, but late and distorted echoes of the dualist mission appear to have survived in a curious tradition about the two 'disciples of the Devil' from Cappadocia who infected Bulgaria with the Paulician heresy, Subotin (probably Child of the Sabbath) and Shutil (Jester).[21]

Yet following its heyday under Carbeas, the dualist Paulician state on the upper Euphrates soon succumbed to Byzantine military pressure. Carbeas himself was murdered in the Byzantine campaigns in eastern Anatolia in 863–4 but his nephew and successor, Chrysocheir (Golden Hand), also a former imperial officer, prolonged the war with Byzantium for another decade. In 869 Chrysocheir launched a raid across the whole of Anatolia to the Sea of Marmara and sacked Ephesus. Following his irruption into the Byzantine heartlands in western Anatolia Chrysocheir arrogantly proclaimed that the new emperor Basil I should abdicate as ruler east of the Bosphorus and retire to reign in the west. A former groom who murdered Boris's godfather, Michael, to ascend the imperial throne, Basil I immediately launched a retaliatory campaign against Theprice. Basil's offensive, however, ended in a total rout and he himself had a narrow escape from Chrysocheir's forces. Chrysocheir began a new series of devastating raids into central Anatolia but in 872 his Paulician army was annihilated in a carefully orchestrated Byzantine campaign and he himself was murdered and beheaded while attempting to flee to Theprice. Chrysocheir's head was sent to Constantinople where Basil celebrated his victory by having it pierced with three arrows while the imperial armies overran the Paulician dominions and annexed Theprice to Byzantium.

Chrysocheir's beheading and the capture of the dualist stronghold of Theprice delivered the death blow to the Paulician principality in Cappadocia and indeed to Paulicianism as a political and religious factor in the eastern provinces of Byzantium. Scattered and persecuted, many Paulicians fled back to Armenia or to the Near East, where later, during the First Crusade, Paulician forces fought under the banner of Islam. Despite the demise of Paulician power in Asia Minor there remained the Paulician colonies in the Balkans which were to play their significant role in the reassertion of the dualist tradition in the newly Christianized Balkan world.

It was also becoming increasingly apparent that the Byzantine religious sovereignty over the Bulgarian empire was far more fragile than it had seemed after the Constantinople Patriarchate had finally neutralized papal intervention in the eastern Balkans. In 889 Boris's eldest son and successor, Vladimir-Rasate (889–93), described as having chosen to tread in the footsteps of Julian the Apostate rather than St Peter, staged an emphatic pagan revival and sought to renew the old Bulgaro-Frankish alliance with the Carolingian king of the Eastern Franks, Arnulf. The new pagan renascence was terminated with the dethronement and blinding of Rasate in what was to be the last vicissitude in the long and hard-fought battle between Christianity and paganism in the ninth-century Bulgarian empire. The old Bulgar pagan temples were demolished or replaced by Christian churches and the Christian records praised the abolition of the 'pagan altars, sacrifices and idols'. Yet the bitter pagan resistance to Christianization, the religious rivalry between Rome and Constantinople and the heretical proselytism had already created the religious ferment that was to provide the matrix for the resurgence of the dualist tradition in the Balkans.

The Anniversary of Zoroaster

With the turn of the last century before the first Christian millennium there began a series of religious and political upheavals that transformed the balance of forces in both the Christian and Muslim worlds and proved decisive in the shaping of later medieval geopolitics. The triumph of Christianity in the Balkans coincided with the beginning of the Christian reconquest of Muslim Spain which had been overtaken in the sweeping westward expansion of Islam in the eighth century. To oppose the Christian *reconquista* the Spanish Umayyad emir Abd ar-Rahman III unified the Moorish possessions in the Iberian peninsula and in 929 founded the caliphate of Cordoba. Further east the rival Fatimid caliphate in North Africa, founded in 909 by a supposed descendant of Mohammed's daughter Fatima, eventually conquered Egypt in 969 and spread as far as Palestine and Syria, halting the revived Byzantine advance in the Near East. While the caliphate of Cordoba was a stronghold of Sunni Islam, the official creed of the Fatimid dynasty was Ismailism, a major Shia branch which enriched Shia traditions with Neoplatonic and Gnostic doctrines but was condemned by its Sunni opponents as a revival of Zoroastrianism, and even Manichaeism, in Islamic garb. Ismailism achieved one of the most striking medieval religious syntheses, in which the universal religious history was seen as comprising seven great prophetic cycles of revelation, six of which had already been initiated by Adam, Noah, Abraham, Moses, Jesus and Mohammed and the last one was to be inaugurated by the advent of the final Mahdi (or Qaim), the expected seventh Imam of the Ismaili movement.

For the radical and schismatic Ismaili branch in Bahrain the coming of the final religious era appeared imminent and portended by a conjunction of Saturn and Jupiter in 928. The advent of the ultimate prophetic cycle was associated with the end of the era of Islam and also with the 1,500th anniversary of the supposed death of Zoroaster (or the 1242nd year of Alexander's era), for which old Persian prophecies had predicted the religious and political restoration of Zoroastrianism. The Qarmatian commemoration of Zoroaster's anniversary precipitated one of the major crises in medieval Islam – in 930, the very year of the anniversary, the Qarmatians sacked Mecca and took away the Black Stone of the Kaaba to herald the end of the era of Islam.

Following the capture of the Black Stone, Qarmatian rule in Bahrain passed into the hands of a young Persian, who claimed descent from the Persian Shahs and was declared to be the expected Mahdi. The chosen Mahdi ordered the worship of fire and abolished Islamic laws but was killed after eighty days, which marked the end of this ephemeral but vigorous Zoroastrian revival in the Qarmatian domain. The religious turbulence around Zoroaster's anniversary inevitably also affected the Zoroastrians in Babylonia and Iran, then under the control of the Abbasid caliphate, where the Zoroastrian chief priest himself was accused of collaboration with the Qarmatians and executed.

Zoroaster's reputed anniversary did not leave unstirred the Manichaeans in Babylonia, who apparently viewed it as the onset of an era for renewed missionary expansion. The revived Manichaean activities in the turmoil of the early tenth century obviously provoked Abbasid persecution, for at the end of the caliphate of al-Muqtadir (908–32) most of the Babylonian Manichaeans had to flee to Khurasan and further to Samarkand in Sogdiana, whereas those who remained in Babylonia kept their identity secret. In the new troubled times the Manichaean community in Mesopotamia entered a period of migration and secrecy, when the Manichaean *archegos* himself disappeared from his traditional seat in Mesopotamia and the 'Religion of Light' also seemed to vanish from the tumultuous arena of the Middle East.[22]

While in the early tenth century the Islamic world had seen the emergence of rival caliphates, in Christian Europe the Carolingian imperial traditions were in decline after Arnulf, the last Carolingian emperor, was stricken with paralysis in the wake of his coronation, and died in 899. Yet at the time when England was finally unified by the grandson of Alfred the Great, Athelstan, the founder of the German Saxon dynasty, Henry the Fowler (919–63), had already enforced the monarchical authority in the East Frankish kingdom. Following the conquests of his successor, Otto the Great, the East Frankish kingdom was transformed into the Holy Roman Empire, but the German empire-building had to confront another fresh pagan influx from the steppes – the coming of the Magyars. As the pagan Magyars pressed deep into central Europe they were subjected to gradual Christianization and the turn of the millennium saw the foundation of St Stephen's Christian kingdom of Hungary.

The Magyars were driven into central Europe by the diplomacy and campaigns of the Bulgarian ruler Symeon (893–927) whose Magyar venture was followed by thirty years of intermittent Balkan wars, during which he annexed Serbia, confronted Croatia and repeatedly invaded Byzantium, seeking at one stage an alliance with the Fatimids against Constantinople. What is more, Symeon endeavoured to manoeuvre himself into a new *Basileus*, a new type of Constantinople emperor, presiding over a united Byzantine–

Bulgarian empire. While in his bid for the imperial throne Symeon was outplayed by the commander of the Byzantine fleet, Romanus Lecapenus, he finally proclaimed himself 'Emperor and Autocrat of the Romans and the Bulgars' and in 926 his imperial title was ratified by Pope John x.

The failed prospect of the unification of the Bulgarian and Byzantine empires has been seen as 'one of the great missed opportunities in history'[23] which would have allowed the Orthodox east to resist the incessant pressures from both east and west. The Bulgarian monarch was an able Greek scholar, praised as the 'new Ptolemy' and vigorously sought to promote the rich cultural heritage of Byzantine Orthodoxy in his realm. The Bulgarian empire had already adopted the legacy of St Cyril and St Methodius, the Apostles of the Slavs – the Slavonic version of the scriptures, liturgy and alphabet – and Symeon's reign is traditionally seen as the Golden Age of Slavonic letters, the flourishing of a new Slavo-Byzantine civilization, through whose medium the Byzantine cultural tradition eventually reached Serbia and Russia.[24]

However, besides the translation of Byzantine sacred and secular literature, another body of translations was also beginning to find its way into the newly Christianized Bulgarian empire – secret apocryphal texts, most of which dated from the early Christian era and have been preserved and transmitted in the Christian east. Some of these apocryphal works were to prove fundamental for the shaping and elaboration of the mythology of Bogomil and Cathar dualism. Moreover, one of the outstanding Orthodox writers of Symeon's royal school, John the Exarch, was already warning against the preachings of pagans and 'Manichaeans' (at that time a stock term for dualists) who taught that the Devil was the eldest son of God.[25] This notion of pagan–'Manichaean' affiliation has been seen as the 'earliest direct indication of the alliance between paganism and heresy'[26] in Bulgaria, significantly after a century of severe pagan–Christian collisions in the realm. What is more, this 'alliance' was a crystallization around a specific teaching of the Devil's genesis, which subsequently became the crux of Bogomil monarchian dualism, with its distinctive trinity – God the Father and his two sons, Satanael and Jesus Christ.

The Descent of the 'Manichaean Darkness'

Bogomilism made its first steps in the Balkans under the reign of Symeon's son, Peter (927–69), renowned as the 'monastic reign'. In 927 Symeon died suddenly and his death came to be ascribed to a bizarre act of magical regicide orchestrated by the emperor Romanus Lecapenus in Constantinople.[27] In the wake of Symeon's death the traditional segregation of the Byzantine imperial family was broken in a peace treaty with Peter which sanctioned a dynastic intermarriage of the Bulgarian and Byzantine royal houses and recognized Peter's title of emperor (Tsar). The treaty was soon followed by another shift in the Balkan balance of power – Serbia, long a focus of rivalry between the Bulgarian and Byzantine empires, in 931 moved out of the Bulgarian sphere of control and accepted Byzantine overlordship. Moreover, new nomads from the steppes, the Pechenegs, who are sometimes seen as recipients and bearers of Manichaean influences from central Asia,[28] soon began their incursions into the Balkans from their settlements in southern Ukraine.

With the inevitable increase of Byzantine influences in Bulgaria, as in Byzantium, it witnessed a striking rise of monasticism that was patronized by the Tsar, who was himself praised as a 'teacher of Orthodoxy' and a 'Rock of Christianity'. Peter adopted the role of a 'defender of the faith' in a religious climate apparently fraught with tensions – the Byzantinization of ecclesiastical life, the repercussions of the unusual spread of monasticism and the first signs of heretical agitation. Pagan residues were still strong and Peter's younger brother, Prince Benjamin (Boyan), who was to become one of the famous medieval 'occult' personages, was an enigmatic figure, reminiscent of the traditional 'princely magus by blood' that in the early Middle Ages was still seen as a potential menace to the Church. The sketchy evidence about Prince Benjamin centres essentially on his magical expertise and his figure has inevitably attracted much romance and speculation which links him variously with Bulgar paganism, Byzantine magic and demonology or even with the rise of Bogomilism.[29]

While the first steps of Bogomilism largely remain uncharted, it is beyond dispute that by the mid tenth century it had already assumed the shape of an organized and rapidly spreading heretical movement. In the face of the rising heresy, Peter had to write twice to the princely patriarch of Constantinople, Theophylact Lecapenus, who was, however, said to spend more time in ministering to his many horses than in the cathedral. The patriarch, none the less, was able to recognize this 'ancient and newly appeared heresy' as 'Manichaeism mixed with Paulicianism' and urged Peter to burn the 'bitter and evil roots' of their teachings in the 'holy fire of truth', arming the Tsar with a list of twelve anathemas.[30] Soon after providing spiritual guidance for the Tsar, however, Theophylact suffered a grave riding accident and in the remaining few years of his life could not conduct the battle against the new Balkan heresy, or in his own words, 'that serpent-like and many-headed hydra of impiety', which signalled the revival of dualism in eastern Christendom.

Theophylact Lecapenus was not destined to become the heresiographer of the new dualist movement, but such a heresiographer did appear in the person of a Bulgarian presbyter, Cosmas, whose vehement *Sermon Against the Heretics* (c. 967–72)[31] disclosed the identity of its founder, the priest Bogomil, invariably charged in later Orthodox traditions with the spread of the Manichaean 'darkness' or heresy in Bulgaria. The *Sermon Against the Heretics* materialized a striking picture of the religious and social tensions, which, coupled with strong pagan remnants, allowed for the quick spread of the new heresy. The heretical preachers seemed won from 'hypocritical fasting' but concealed a 'voracious wolf' within and could venture to deceive the Orthodox either by open heretical preachings or by an ingenious simulation of Orthodoxy. The heretical homilies, which seemed puzzling and ambiguous to the presbyter, apparently comprised parables, allegories and unorthodox gospel interpretations. While the meaning of the gospel events could be completely transformed in accordance with their missionary purposes, the miracles of Jesus Christ were interpreted allegorically and the Eucharistic bread and wine were taken to represent the gospels and Acts of the Apostles. Their heretical dualism, which recognized the Devil as a fallen angel and the creator of heaven, earth and man, was also expounded through allegorical interpretations of the gospel parables. The Devil could be styled as the 'unjust steward', as he was identified with the unrighteous steward from the famous parable in Luke 16:1–9, whereas in the heretical reading of the Parable of the Prodigal Son (Luke 15:11–32) Christ was taken to represent the elder and the Devil the younger brother. The concept of the Devil as a creator and master of the visible world, as 'Lord of the sky, the sun, the air and the stars', was inevitably reinforced with the allusions to the 'prince of this world' in the fourth gospel.

The heretics were also described as rejecting Mosaic Law and the Old Testament prophets, denouncing the veneration of the icons and the relics of the saints, and condemning the Church hierarchy and ceremonial. The cross itself was reviled as 'God's enemy' and for Cosmas this repudiation of the cross made the heretics worse than demons, for demons feared the cross, while the sectarians were alleged to have 'cut down the Crosses to fashion tools out of them'. Not only were the crosses allegedly mutilated, but also the heretics were accused of maligning even the Virgin Mary with 'offensive words' and treating John the Baptist not as a predecessor of Jesus Christ but as a forerunner of the Antichrist.

In the tract the heretical preachers are portrayed as extreme ascetics, abstaining from marriage, meat and wine, which were condemned as coming from the Devil (Mammon). Some heretical missionaries were also arraigned for teaching their followers to defy the authority of the Tsar and the aristocracy, but there is no tangible evidence to imply that Bogomilism ever approached any-thing like a social and peasant movement,[32] while all the available data point to a dualist sect with a strong appeal to monastic circles and the lower clergy. The tract leaves a vague and discrepant picture of Bogomil teachings and its paucity is predictably justified by falling on the authority of St Paul – 'For it is a shame even to speak of those things which are done of them in secret' (Ephesians 5:12, *KJV*). Yet, however confused and meagre, the exposé of the Bogomil doctrine yields some important clues to its underlying dualism, which is clearly of a monarchian type – the evil creator is not an eternal, independent principle, but a fallen angel, secondary and inferior to God. The monarchian character of early Bogomil dualism clearly contrasts with the late Paulician radical dualist dogma of the two principles, the evil creator of this world and the good Lord of the world to come. Confusingly, in the *Sermon*

Against the Heretics Bogomil dualism treats Christ as God's eldest son and the Devil as his younger brother, whereas in the earlier warning of pagan-'Manichaean' teachings of the Devil he was represented as God's eldest son. Later versions of Bogomil and Cathar dualism traditionally regarded the Devil as God's eldest son, who, however, came to lose his seniority upon his rebellion and fall, after which Christ was elevated to the status of God's first-born. It is thus quite probable that the Devil's position in the dualist scheme in the *Sermon Against the Heretics* reflects the status quo in the wake of his fall when his seniority was already transferred to Christ.[33]

Apart from highlighting these intricacies of the Devil's reversible seniority in medieval monarchian dualism, the *Sermon Against the Heretics* leaves a striking testimony of the early Bogomil movement in which dualist, anticlerical and iconoclastic militancy was coupled with a strong ascetic and missionary fervour. Yet the formation and early history of Bogomilism remains complicated and obscure, the very origins of Bogomilism perhaps being the most controversial problem related to the rise and spread of medieval dualism.

The Riddle of Bogomil Beginnings

The precise time and place of the origins of Bogomilism remain unknown, although Macedonia and Thrace are traditionally regarded as the cradle of the new dualist movement. The crystallization and spread of Bogomil teachings apparently owed much to the personal missionary zeal and syncretistic skills of the heresiarch of the movement, the priest Bogomil. It is widely assumed that the 'turbulent priest' had synthesized elements of earlier heretical traditions, usually identified as Paulician and Massalian, but sometimes direct Manichaean, Marcionite or separate Gnostic influences are also assumed to have their impact on the formation of Bogomil dualism. Besides the customary formula of 'Manichaean heresy', medieval Orthodox authorities on Bogomilism tended to denounce its heresy as an admixture of Manichaeism and Paulicianism, Paulicianism and Massalianism or else Manichaeism and Massalianism. Yet although the influence of antecedent anti-ecclesiastical and heretical movements on Bogomilism is undisputed, such clear-cut definitions of the Bogomil heresy are extremely misleading. There are considerable differences between Bogomil and Paulician dualism, both in the underlying dualist formula and its mythological elaborations. As regards the alleged Massalian influence on Bogomilism, the very existence of authentic Massalians in the medieval Balkan–Byzantine world is disputed and the epithet 'Massalian' seems to have been applied loosely to heretics, heterodox theologians and dissenters. For all its complexities and controversies, the evidence of early Bogomilism indicates that rather than being a natural evolution from Paulicianism or from the elusive Massalianism, Bogomilism emerged in the tenth century as a distinct and indigenous dualist movement, with its independent teachings and purposes.

There have been attempts to link the rise of Bogomilism in the Balkans with the commencement of a new Manichaean diaspora from Babylonia in the wake of the religious and political agitation surrounding Zoroaster's anniversary in the early tenth century.[34] The old connections between the Bulgars and the peoples of central Asia and the steppes have also been invoked to link early Bogomilism to the presumed Manichaean missions from the Manichaean Uighur empire following its collapse in 843.[35] The Bulgars themselves might well have encountered Manichaean missions during their period in central Asia and Sogdiana, which then served as a stepping stone for the introduction of Manichaeism in China. There is, however, no existing evidence for direct Manichaean influences on the Bulgars in the Balkans, although the Volga Bulgars were recorded as having used the Manichaean script prior to their acceptance of Islam. The subsequent new nomadic waves from central Asia and the steppes could also have brought Manichaean influences to the Balkans, but at present such links between central Asian Manichaeism and medieval Balkan dualism remain conjectural.

The Bogomil trinity of God the Father and his elder and younger son, Satanael and Jesus Christ, closely approaches the analogous Zurvanite trinity of Zurvan, Ahriman and Ohrmazd to the extent that, despite the lack of strong historical evidence, no less authorities on religious history than R. Zaehner and M. Eliade have argued that it was derived from Iranian traditions.[36] More controversially, it has been suggested that early Bogomilism might have been affected by Balkan residues of Mithraism,[37] although late references to 'Mithraism' seem to allude generally to paganism; as late as the eleventh century the philosopher Michael Psellus accused monks of Chios of initiating rituals and mysteries akin to those of Mithras.

What compounds the ambiguity surrounding the origins of Bogomilism is the paucity of evidence about its founder, the priest Bogomil. He may be regarded as the 'greatest heresiarch of the Middle Ages' but it is not even certain that his name is, as has been commonly assumed, a Slavonic translation of the Greek 'Theophilus' (Beloved of God), while most Slavonic words containing the root *bog* (God) had largely been formed under Iranian influences.[38] Moreover, besides 'Beloved of God' the name Bogomil has also been translated as 'worthy of God's Mercy', 'one who entreats God' or 'one who implores God's Grace'. Apart from being recognized as the heresiarch of Balkan dualism, in later Orthodox testimonies the priest Bogomil was anathematized for preaching the Docetic teaching that Christ's passion and resurrection were illusory and for rejecting the veneration of the cross. Orthodox traditions may have depicted the priest Bogomil and his disciples as incarnations of Jannes and Jambres, the legendary Egyptian sorcerers who opposed Moses during the Exodus, but otherwise they did not shed any light on the mundane life of the heresiarch. Vague legends recount that on Bogomil's death his followers erected a chapel at the site of his grave where they gathered for prayers. Ultimately, unlike his great spiritual ancestor, Mani Bogomil's background and rise as a heresiarch remain shrouded in opaque darkness.

The priest Bogomil has sometimes been identified with another notorious and elusive priest, who lived and wrote heterodox apocryphal works in tenth-century Bulgaria. The priest Jeremiah was to become the most popular and denounced apocryphal writer in the Slavonic Orthodox world and his famous apocryphal compilation, *The Legend of the Cross*, had been widely circulated and read from Bosnia to Russia. The possibility of Jeremiah being Bogomil's *alter ego* has been long and bitterly debated, as in Orthodox traditions Jeremiah was also denounced as a 'son' and disciple of Bogomil, who himself was condemned as an author of apocryphal works. What remains undisputed is the link between the crystallization of Bogomil doctrine and the influx of a rich and diverse apocryphal literature in tenth-century Bulgaria, some of which came to be adopted for the purposes of Bogomil propaganda.[39]

Apart from the priests Bogomil and Jeremiah, Orthodox records allude to two even more elusive figures accused of having introduced heretical books into Bulgaria – Sydor Fryazin (Sydor the Frank) and Jacob Tsentsal, who is also described as 'fryazin' (Frank).[40] The names of these two heretics suggest that they came from the west but the time of their supposed activity and the character of their heretical books remain unknown. There remains, however, the intriguing possibility of an early intercourse between eastern and western heretics prior to the first serious outbreaks of heresy in western Christendom.

Another significant problem concerning early Bogomilism is the organization and hierarchy of the Bogomil movement. In their mature form both Bogomilism and Catharism were divided into two main classes, the élite grade of the *perfecti* and the lesser grade of the believers, beneath which there apparently existed another introductory and looser class – the listeners. It has often been argued that these grades developed within later Bogomilism, but it seems more likely that they were an original feature of the Bogomil movement. The presence of an élite of Bogomil *perfecti* is implied in the *Sermon Against the Heretics* and soon there appeared a clear Orthodox testimony of distinct divisions and initiations within the Bogomil sect along with a distorted account of the rite that converted the dualist believer into a *perfectus* – the spiritual baptism, known in the west as the *consolamentum*. A recent synthesis of the evidence of Bogomil hierarchy suggests that from its beginnings the movement had a religious leader assisted by an inner circle of Bogomil apostles.[41] Such reconstruction matches the later data about the twelfth-century Bogomil heresiarch Basil and his twelve apostles, which itself, apart from the obvious Christian parallel, bears a close resemblance to the upper Manichaean hierarchy – the leader (*archegos*) and the following rank of twelve apostles.

The puzzles surrounding the organization of the early Bogomil movement also extend to the dates of the formation of the first Bogomil communities or 'churches' that were later regarded by the inquisitorial authorities as the source of all dualist churches in Europe. What remains certain is that only several decades after

Patriarch Theophylact Lecapenus had sent his panoply of anti-heretical anathemas to Tsar Peter, Bogomilism had radiated into Byzantium and its spread in the empire was to be accelerated with the Byzantine reconquest of the Balkans.

The Time of Troubles

In 969 the 'monastic' reign of Tsar Peter collapsed in the chaos and devastation of a sudden Russian invasion and the Tsar finally assumed 'monastic' garb. In one of the unexpected twists of the Byzantine *realpolitik*, the heathen Duke of Kiev, Svyatoslav, who had already undermined Khazar power in the steppes, was bribed to invade the Bulgarian empire and his armies burst into the Balkans. Byzantium eventually felt threatened by the magnitude of Svyatoslav's Balkan conquests and for three years the Bulgarian lands became a battleground between the troops of Svyatoslav and Emperor John Tzimisces. When finally repelled from the Balkans, Svyatoslav was to meet a gruesome death back in the Ukrainian steppes at the hands of the old enemies of Kievan Russia, the Pechenegs, who turned his skull into a cup.

John Tzimisces forced Tsar Peter's successor, Boris II, to abdicate in Constantinople and the onset of the Byzantine reconquest of the Balkans was coupled with a steady eastward advance. In northern Armenia and Syria, however, John Tzimisces encountered strong Paulician communities, apparently remnants of the former Paulician principality in Cappadocia, and was advised by Patriarch Thomas of Antioch to remove them from the eastern imperial frontiers. John Tzimisces again chose resettlement in the Balkans and in about 975 or 976 numerous Paulicians, some sources mention 200,000, were moved to Thrace, particularly the area around ancient Philippopolis. The timely dualist blood transfusion into Thrace reinforced Balkan dualism in the crucial period of the early diffusion of Bogomilism and amid the cataclysms of another war in the Balkan interior.

Despite the initial success of the Byzantine conquest of the eastern Balkans, the Byzantine advance was blocked in Macedonia by the enigmatic tetrarchy of the sons of a Bulgarian *comes* (count) known as the Cometopuli – David, Moses, Aaron and Samuel. The rise of the house of the Cometopuli, linked by the Byzantine poet John Geometrus to an appearance of a comet in 968, is surrounded by much controversy which is by no means resolved by their appearance in a later chronicle, itself betraying Bogomil influences, as the royal 'sons of a widow-prophetess'.[42]

The youngest of the sons, Samuel, eventually succeeded in spreading his conquests into Albania and Greece, where he overran the ancient region of Thessaly and captured its main stronghold Larissa. In 997 Samuel was crowned Tsar of a renascent and aggressive Bulgarian empire, now centred on Macedonia, which had to face, however, the increasing military pressure of the ruthless warrior-monk Emperor Basil II (976–1025). The two great powers of Orthodox Christendom met the second millennium locked in an exceedingly fierce conflict but in 1001 Basil concluded a ten-year peace treaty with the Fatimid caliph and protagonist of the Druze faith, al-Hakim, during which his wide-ranging Balkan campaigns gradually put Samuel on the defensive. In 1014, after achieving a decisive victory in Macedonia, Basil blinded and sent back to Samuel thousands of Bulgarian prisoners of war and at the sight of the blinded army Samuel collapsed and died within days.

Samuel's successors, Gabriel-Radomir (1014–15) and Ivan Vladislav (1015–18), resisted Basil's offensive for another four years but in 1018 the Bulgarian empire, which had long seemed 'all-powerful and invincible' to the Byzantines, was finally conquered by the Byzantine emperor. After three centuries Byzantium had recovered most of its lost Balkan provinces, while the various rulers in the Serbian, Bosnian and Croatian lands now became vassals of Basil, who in 1019 made his triumphant march through the reconquered Balkan territories and inaugurated victory celebrations in Athens and Constantinople. In a contemporary Arab chronicle Basil is credited with seeking to destroy the old Bulgaro-Byzantine enmity through intermarriage and the surviving descendants of the Cometopuli, like other Bulgarian noble families, intermarried with the Byzantine aristocracy to give rise to the noble line of the Aaronids, who were to play an important role in Byzantine history.[43]

Less than a century after Basil sanctioned these Bulgaro-Byzantine marriages Bogomilism was said to have affected the 'great houses' in Constantinople and it is possible that the Bulgarian influx in the Byzantine aristocracy might have facilitated the spread of the heresy in the Byzantine social élite.[44] Various scholars have assumed, moreover, that the Cometopuli and Samuel himself were of Bogomil inclination, although Samuel had re-established the Bulgarian patriarchate during his reign and was himself a vigorous church-builder. Yet Samuel seemed to be tolerant of the Bogomils and did not check the spread of the heresy in his war-torn dominions. What is more, in a later controversial Greek tradition some of the descendants of the Cometopuli, namely Samuel's daughter and Tsar Gabriel-Radomir (or else Tsar Ivan Vladislav), were themselves accused of being 'enemies of the cross' and followers of the Bogomil and Massalian heresy.[45]

Whatever the religious affinities of the Cometopuli 'sons of the widow', the last years of the reign of their dynasty marked the violent twilight of the first Bulgarian empire. The protracted and severe Bulgaro-Byzantine war of 977–1018 has been described by Arnold Toynbee as the Orthodox 'Time of Troubles', an 'internecine struggle', which marked the breakdown of the old and traditional Orthodox Christian civilization.[46] Although Orthodox Christianity had been established in Kievan Russia, which was thus drawn into the Byzantine religious and cultural orbit, the Byzantine reconquests in the Balkans were at the expense of severe social and economic setbacks in Asia Minor, most of which came to be lost to the Seljuk Turks by the end of the century. The recovery of the Balkans during the Orthodox 'Time of Troubles' was bound, moreover, to leave Byzantium open to the increasing missionary activities of the new Balkan dualist movement, Bogomilism, which in the early eleventh century had already struck roots in the western Anatolian regions and particularly in the old heretical seedbed of Phrygia.

The Heresy in Anatolia

The first testimony to the magnitude of Bogomil proselytism and expansion in western Anatolia is a long letter written in about 1050 by the monk Euthymius of the Peribleptos monastery in Constantino-ple.[47] The monastery itself had been infiltrated by four Bogomil missionaries who had led Euthymius' own disciple astray and earlier a travelling presbyter, who turned out to be a Bogomil preacher, had attempted to convert Euthymius himself. In order to expose the Bogomil proselytizers Euthymius decided to risk another attempt at conversion at the hands of their first teacher and endured an exhausting heretical sermon with quotations from the gospels, St Paul's epistles, the Psalms, St John Chrysostom and the Church Fathers – as the monk said, 'from all scriptures'. The heretics were then imprisoned in separate cells and Euthymius questioned them individually about their teachings. What Euthymius comprehended was that the heretics' thorough knowledge of the scriptures derived from a 'satanic force' that entered them on their heretical baptism, the so-called 'second baptism'. Euthymius also declared that during this baptism the gospel was placed on the novices' head and they were mesmerized with well-known gospel verses, while the initiating 'teachers of evil' recited a secret 'satanic incantation' presented as a 'revelation of St Peter'. This was alleged to banish the blessing of the Holy Ghost from the soul of the proselytes and replace it with the 'seal of the devil', transforming the initiates into devil-incarnates whose sole purpose was to lure Christ's flock into the 'repulsive and godless' heresy.

This short but expressive demonological exposé is in all probabil-ity Euthymius' own garbled and diabolized version of the rite that raised the dualist neophyte, the 'listener', to the rank of the dualist 'believer', which is referred to in other Orthodox accounts of Bogomilism as the *baptisma*. Euthymius confirmed that the first heretical baptism was only a prelude to a gradual initiation to the teachings that prepare the believer for the grade of the perfect or, in Euthymius' version, for the 'unholy service to the Devil and his mysteries'. For one or two years the neophyte was lured into a series of revelations of 'evil knowledge' until finally he was initiated into the 'whole heresy and madness'. Euthymius gave another exposé of the rite that was supposed to erase all traces of Christian baptism, probably the *consolamentum*, which admitted the dualist believer to the élite ascetic grade of the perfect. Later Orthodox versions of the *consolamentum* or *teleiosis* confirmed that the rite was preceded by a period of prolonged asceticism and instruction, and that the consecration comprised laying the gospel on the head of the proselyte followed by the hands of the perfect, amid hymns of thanksgiving. Two western versions of the Cathar *consolamentum*, which was certainly formulated under Bogomil influence, have also been preserved and they present some obvious parallels to early Christian baptism.[48]

Yet for Euthymius of Peribleptos the ultimate dualist rite transformed the erstwhile heretical disciples into apostles and teachers, 'ordained by the Devil'. While denouncing them as 'apostles of darkness', 'God's enemies' and the 'Devil's henchmen', he reaffirmed that the Bogomils renounced all Church services, the veneration of the cross, the cult of relics and the efficacy of the Eucharist and baptism. Despite his claims of direct knowledge of the secret 'writings of the heresy', his exposure of the heretical teachings is scant and confused. In Euthymius' version of Bogomil cosmology, God created the seven heavens, whereas the expelled 'prince of this world', the Devil, created the eighth, visible heaven, the earth, sea, Paradise and man. In the visible universe ruled by the fallen 'prince of the world' only the sun and the soul of man are from God but were stolen by the Devil. As God's creation, however, the soul was constantly escaping from the 'satanic' body of man; finally the Devil had to resort to an ingenious technique to entrap it. He ate of the flesh of all unclean animals and emitted this impurity on the soul in order to defile it and compel it to remain in the body of Adam. These teachings evidently reflect the old Gnostic myth of the fallen demiurge coupled with the Orphic/Gnostic concept of the incarnation as an exile in a bodily prison. The heretics, moreover, apparently did not revere the traditional Christian trinity and Euthymius suspected them of worshipping some mysterious Satanic trinity in which the Holy Ghost was the 'spirit of evil', the Son was the 'son of perdition' and the Father was Satan himself. At the same time, Euthymius alluded to the claims of the Bogomil apostles for esoteric knowledge of 'God's secrets' in the gospels, hidden for the others in parables (Mark 4:11), but confusingly stated that they called themselves true Christians after 'their father, the Antichrist'. He also maintained that during the Bogomil initiation, anything taught prior to the 'second baptism' was refuted after the rite and the newly imparted Bogomil 'mysteries' were altered further after the final heretical baptism.

Besides the heretical 'mysteries' of Bogomilism, Euthymius was alarmed that the 'many-named heresy of the Bogomils' already permeated 'every region, town and diocese' in the empire. Unlike the Paulicians, whose heresy was overt and less dangerous, the Bogomils were prepared to feign Orthodoxy, build churches, worship icons and take part in services in order to further their secretive missionary work. While preaching, the Bogomil apostles were defying torture and death; the sphere of their missionary campaigns extended beyond Byzantium to the whole of Christendom, to 'all Christians under the sun'. Euthymius' report of the Bogomil missions' reach was understandably exaggerated but within a century Bogomil missionaries had already reached and spread their teachings in central and western Europe. Bogomil preaching in Anatolia was particularly successful in the Phrygian imperial district of Thracesion where it had already won over 'whole cities' to the heresy and where the Bogomil heresiarchs John Tzurillas and Raheas were active in the region around Smyrna (Izmir), the reputed site of one of the Seven Churches of Asia (Revelation 2:8). In north-west Anatolia, in the district of Opsikion, the heretics were known by the obscure name Phundagiagites, while in Cibyrrhaeot by the gulf of Antalya, in the 'west' (i.e. the Balkans) and 'in other places' the heretics were known as Bogomils. There are also indications that around that time Bogomil missions had penetrated the mountainous province of Lycia in south-west Asia Minor.

It is significant that Euthymius affirms that the Bogomil message was gaining ground in monastic and even clerical circles in Asia Minor and was forming a dualist hidden world of 'pseudo-monks, teachers and godless priests' who used their knowledge of the scriptures to beguile more souls into their heresy. Around the time of the great schism between Rome and Constantinople in 1054, the dualist underworld in Anatolia extended, on the evidence of Euthymius, from the Bosphorus to the Gulf of Antalya.

The Three Principles of the
Thracian Euchites

In the epistle of Euthymius of Peribleptos the Bogomils were also associated with the Massalians, who were known by their Greek name Euchites, and continued to be seen as a heretical threat in early medieval Byzantium. In the mid eleventh century the politician and philosopher Michael Psellus, who at that time held the chair of *hypatos ton philosophon* (Consul of the Philosophers) in Constantinople, wrote a tract, *Dialogus de daemonum operatione*, in which he condemned certain 'accursed' and 'god-fighting' Euchites,[49] who were apparently active in southern Thrace. He revealed that they believed in a trinity of the Father and His two Sons, who ruled respectively over the heavenly and material world — which in Orthodoxy was invariably attributed to Bogomilism.

The heretical teaching of the three principles, as reported by Psellus, derived from Mani's teaching of the two principles — the two Gods opposed to each other, the creator of good, who was also the heavenly ruler and the creator of evil, who was the prince of all evil on earth. To these the Euchites added a third and the new trinity comprised the Father, associated with the supramundane realm, the younger Son, who ruled over the heavenly sphere, and the elder Son, who presided over this world. As a formula, it paralleled the Zurvanite trinity: the Zurvanites had been defined as followers of the teaching of the three principles and were distinguished from the adherents of the two principles. For Zaehner the reference to Mani's two principles and 'the most exact correspondences' between the Euchitic and Zurvanite three principles demonstrated that the doctrine of the Thracian Euchites was 'directly dependent upon Zurvanism'.[50] Yet while Psellus clearly defined the Thracian heretics as followers of the three principles he also stated that it had led to the emergence of three distinct trends among the sectarians.

The first trend admitted dual worship and revered both Sons — for although they were now disparate, they had originated from one Father and would eventually be reunited. The second worshipped the younger Son, 'as a ruler of the better and superior part', but at the same time honoured the power of the elder Son, aware of his ability to cause evil. The most extreme was the third trend who sought to separate themselves completely from the prince of the heavens and 'embrace the earthly Satanael alone'. Although Satanael, the elder Son, was a destroyer, he was invoked with many adulatory names such as 'the first-born of the Father' or 'the Creator of trees, animals and other composite beings'. The third Euchite trend did not permit worship of the younger son but accused him of being jealous of the prince of this world and his ordering of the earth. They believed that, plagued by envy, the heavenly prince 'sends down earthquakes, hailstorms and pestilence' and for this reason he should be cursed and anathematized. Finally, Michael Psellus accused Euchites of celebrating their arcane mysteries with monstrous ceremonies, including licentious and incestuous sexual orgies, and black sacrifices.

Psellus' account of the Thracian heretics' dogma of the three principles and respective threefold division has inevitably sparked controversy, since it is difficult to disentangle the reliable evidence from the demonological clichés. The threefold partitioning of the Thracian Euchites in accordance with their mode of worship is not mentioned in any account of the Massalian or Bogomil movements. Moreover, while the Massalian sectarians had been accused of orgiastic excesses, the Bogomils were always renowned, among enemies and sympathizers alike, for their austere morality and asceticism. Yet the teachings of the first two Euchite groups have been found 'quite compatible with Bogomil doctrine',[51] as some Orthodox traditions state that the Bogomils felt forced to propitiate the 'prince of this world' as a defensive tactic to avert evil and destruction.

What remains undisputed is that the Euchite doctrine of the three principles in Psellus' account is of Bogomil origin and the document confirms the growing influence of Bogomilism in Thrace. By 1062 Bogomilism had also appeared in the provincial Byzantine capital Athens, where the bishopric was driven to take measures to halt its spread. Thessaly and its capital Larissa, earlier occupied by Samuel, had also been penetrated by Bogomilism[52] and Patriarch Cosmas of Jerusalem had to admonish the Metropolitan of Larissa and the prelates of the neighbouring bishoprics with a letter warning against its spread. By the end of the twelfth century Bogomilism had gained a strong foothold in Constantinople, where its great heresiarch Basil the Physician strove to convert the pious emperor Alexius Comnenus.

The Crusades of Alexius Comnenus

The spread of Bogomilism in twelfth-century Byzantium coincided with the rise of new currents in Byzantine religious thought, a marked deepening of the interest in classical antiquity and the Hellenic past, heated theological debates and, last but not least, heresy trials. Byzantine mysticism had been revitalized by the writings of the influential mystic Symeon the Theologian, who himself was charged with Massalianism and exiled, but later rehabilitated. As a Consul of the Philosophers, Michael Psellus and his pupils revived interest in Plato and the Neoplatonists like Proclus and Plotinus, and it is commonly assumed that Psellus rediscovered and probably compiled in its present form the most important and seminal Hermetic text, *Corpus Hermeticum*.[53]

However, Psellus had to defend himself against accusations of heterodoxy and in the late eleventh century some forms of Neoplatonism were considered nearly as dangerous as Bogomil dualism itself by the conservative ecclesiastics in Constantinople. In 1082 Psellus' pupil and successor, John Italus, faced, along with his pupils, trial for their Platonic transgressions and were even threatened by a hostile mob. The trial appears largely politically motivated, but in the *Synodicon of Orthodoxy* of 1082, John Italus was anathematized for paganism and heresy together with the heresiarch Bogomil and certain contemporary Bogomil preachers who were already active in Panormus (Palermo) in Sicily.[54] One of Italus' pupils, Eustratius, who was not implicated in the trial, evolved into a leading theologian and commentator of Aristotle as well as becoming Metropolitan of Nicaea, but was none the less arraigned for unorthodoxy and deposed in 1117.

Byzantium also saw the increasing activity of heterodox preachers like Nilus the Calabrian and the priest Blachernites, who had succeeded in winning converts from even the 'great houses' in Constantinople. Both preachers were eventually condemned by the Church to a 'perpetual anathema', but while Nilus was preaching some form of Monophysitism and had a strong Armenian following, Blachernites was accused of consorting with the Enthusiasts (the Massalians) and of undermining 'great houses in the capital'.[55]

The preaching and the anathematization of Nilus and Blachernites were symptomatic of the Byzantine religious climate, with its agitation and heresy trials, during the reign of the second Comnenian emperor, Alexius I Comnenus (1081–1118). In 1095 Pope Urban II had called for the recovery of the Holy Sepulchre, and the reign of Alexius was to witness the First Crusade (1095–9), the conquest of the Holy Land, the formation of the Latin Kingdom of Jerusalem and the foundation of the Knights Templar. Besides his volatile and delicate relations with the Crusaders, Alexius Comnenus turned his attention to more spiritual concerns and took vigorous measures against the spread of heresies throughout Byzantium. Alexius' own mother was suspected of heresy and, with his marked predilection for theological debates, the emperor became a vigorous, if not obsessive, defender of Orthodoxy to be eulogized by his daughter, the historian Anna Comnena, as second only to Constantine the Great. The belligerent Paulicians in Thrace had already caused trouble for the empire in the second half of the century and Alexius' confrontation with the sectarians was, according to Anna Comnena, not only military but also apostolic, trying to win them back to Orthodoxy in protracted theological discussions. Alexius focused his efforts on the area around Philippopolis in northern Thrace, where, according to Anna Comnena, nearly all the inhabitants were heretics, Armenians or 'Manichaeans' (Paulicians), so that it had become a truly 'Manichaean' city, 'a meeting place of all evils'.[56] Consequently Alexius launched an anti-heretical crusade in Thrace, where 'whole towns and districts infected by various heresies' were 'brought back by diverse means' to the Orthodox faith.[57]

Besides the heresies prevalent in Thrace the emperor also had to deal with the rising influence of Bogomilism in his imperial capital, where the 'pernicious race' of the Bogomils had arisen like 'a very great cloud' which had gone 'deep even into the great houses' and the higher clergy of Byzantium and had assaulted many souls 'like fire'.[58] In her usual imaginative style Anna Comnena likened Alexius' crusade against the Bogomils to a conjuration of 'a snake hiding in a hole' which was lurking in secrecy until the emperor 'lured it and brought it out to the light by chanting mysterious incantations'. Early in the persecution against the Bogomils it became clear that the heresy had a teacher and 'chief representative', the monk Basil, who was assisted by twelve apostles. Basil was one of the most outstanding figures in the history of the Bogomil movement who was said to have mastered the Bogomil teachings after fifteen years' training, followed by forty years of preaching, in which he had 'disseminated his wickedness everywhere'. For Anna Comnena, Basil was the 'arch-satrap' of Satanael, but for Alexius he was an alluring promise of an erudite theological debate and he finally managed to entertain him in the palace. In an encounter reminiscent of and yet very different from that between Mani and Shapur, the emperor and his brother, Sebastocrator Isaac, tried to convince Basil of their intention of becoming Bogomil neophytes and demanded a detailed explanation of the heretical teaching. The heresiarch began to elucidate the essentials of the Bogomil doctrine, apparently as taught to listeners, and when his long oration appeared to have come to an end, Alexius drew aside the curtains, behind which a secretary had written down Basil's account. The whole senate, the military élite and the elders of the Church were convened and the heresiarch was threatened with trial, torture and death at the stake but he welcomed the threats and remained, in the words of Anna Comnena, 'the same Basil, an inflexible and very brave Bogomil' who preferred to embrace 'his' Satanael.

Oddly, or perhaps predictably, Alexius Comnenus chose to keep Basil close to the royal palace in a specially prepared house, where the emperor indulged in theological arguments with him but the house was affected by a poltergeist-like phenomenon – a hailstorm of stones accompanied by an earthquake. Anna Comnena attributed the miracle to the wrath of Satanael's devils, enraged at the revelation of their secrets to the emperor and the fierce persecution of the Bogomils. The emperor had ordered a systematic pursuit of 'Basil's disciples and fellow-mystics from all over the world', and particularly his twelve apostles, with the goal of the heresy's total extermina-

tion in Byzantium. Many Orthodox Christians were also apprehended in the campaigns and to avoid misjudgement the emperor
devised a dramatic rite of passage – two pyres were erected in the
imperial *manège* on the coast of the Bosphorus, one of which had an
enormous cross attached to it. The suspects were urged to choose on
which pyre to martyr themselves – either on the one with the cross
if they were true Christians, or on the crossless pyre if they were
heretics. When the suspects had divided into two groups and were
ready to be thrown on to the fire, the pyres were suddenly extinguished on Alexius' orders. Those who had chosen the pyre with
the cross were released, while the intransigent heretics were sent to
prison, where the emperor persisted in debating their 'hideous
religion' with them.

The emperor and the patriarchate finally decided to confront
Basil with a similar choice – death in the flames or recanting at the
cross. With intense expectation of a miracle, a crowd saw Basil the
Physician approach the pyre with the psalmic words 'But it shall not
come nigh thee; only with thy eyes shalt thou behold' and finally
'the flames, as if deeply enraged against him, ate the impious man
up, without any odour arising or even a fresh appearance of smoke,
only one thin smoky line could be seen in the middle of the
flames'.[59] For Anna Comnena the *auto-da-fé* of the Bogomil heresiarch was the culmination of Alexius' apostolic mission, 'the
crowning act of the emperor's long labours and successes' which
was an 'innovation of startling boldness'.

Alexius' crusade and Basil's execution in IIII (perhaps the only
one of its kind in Byzantine history) clearly show that at the time of
the First Crusade Bogomilism was regarded as the greatest heretical
menace in Byzantium. About half a century after Euthymius of
Acmonia warned of the dangers of Bogomil proselytism in western
Anatolia, it was, according to Anna Comnena, penetrating the
higher strata of Byzantine secular and ecclesiastical circles.

However, except for the speculation that the teachings of the
Manichaeans (i.e. Paulicians) and the Massalians coalesced in Bogomilism, and some brief cursory comments, Anna Comnena preferred
not 'to defile her tongue' with its teachings, as she was 'a woman,
the most honourable of the Porphyrogeniti and Alexius' eldest scion'
and alluded to the work of the 'best authority on ecclesiastical

dogma', Euthymius Zigabenus.[60] Euthymius Zigabenus had been commissioned by Alexius to expound and refute the ancient and new heresies and his tract *Panoplia Dogmatica*[61] inevitably contained a refutation of Bogomilism. The anti-Bogomil section is apparently based on Basil's account of the Bogomil teachings before his imperial 'listeners', and is consequently by far the most exhaustive and systematic account of Bogomil doctrine. While largely confirming previous evidence of the monarchian nature of Bogomil dualism and its initiatory and ascetic practices, Euthymius made use of his privileged information to expound in greater depth on Bogomil cosmology and the concept of the Logos and the Trinity, the allegorical system of interpreting the scriptures, the mystical practices of initiates and the distinctive demonology of the sect. Euthymius' evidence is complex and often uneven, but it gives substance to the dualist–Gnostic character of Bogomil teaching and for the first time sheds light on some of its esoteric aspects.

Trials in Constantinople

Euthymius Zigabenus praised Alexius Comnenus' anti-heretical crusades as wars against the 'apostate Dragon', the 'great Assyrian mind', and saw in Basil's execution the crushing of the head of the heretical serpent of Bogomilism. Yet, in spite of the campaigns of Alexius Comnenus, Bogomilism remained a heretical force in Byzantium and extended its influence not only into the western Balkans but also western Europe. Euthymius of Peribleptos and Anna Comnena had warned that Bogomilism was using the structures of the Orthodox Church itself in its proselytism and towards the mid twelfth century several synods were convened to expose the Bogomil presence within the Church. The series of ecclesiastical scandals culminated in 1147 when the patriarch was deposed, charged with Bogomil sympathies.

In 1140 a synod at Constantinople posthumously anathematized the monk Constantine Chrysomalus for his heretical writings, the *Golden Sermons*, which were preserved and circulated in the Constantinople monastery of St Nicholas. Some of Chrysomalus' teachings,

such as the existence of two souls – sinful and sinless – in man or
the denial of the spiritual efficacy of the Christian baptism by water,
were denounced as Massalian and Bogomil. On the whole, however,
his teachings seemed to lie mainly in the traditions of Byzantine
mysticism, as elaborated by Symeon the Theologian, but were
partially coloured by heretical influences. Whether Constantine Chrysomalus attempted a synthesis between Byzantine mysticism and
Bogomil dualism is impossible to say, but prior to his anathematization his teachings had apparently gained wide currency in Constantinople monastic circles.

Three years later another synod in Constantinople deposed and
anathematized two Orthodox bishops of Cappadocia as Bogomil
adherents. The two bishops, of the diocese of Tyana, Clement of
Sosandra and Leontius of Balbissa, preached that the miracles
attributed to the power of the cross were effected by daemons and
that the cross should not be revered unless it bore the inscription,
'Jesus Christ, Son of God'. They urged their flock towards monasticism, strongly condemned icon-worship and had even ordained
certain deaconesses and allowed them to take part in the liturgies.
Several weeks later another synod was convened to condemn another heretical preacher from Cappadocia – the monk Niphon who
was charged with propagating Bogomilism. Initially consigned to
the monastery of Peribleptos, Niphon was finally excommunicated
by another synod in 1144 and condemned to prison.

Although imprisoned, Niphon was to provoke a crisis in the
patriarchate when in 1146 the patriarchal throne passed to Cosmas
II Atticus, who himself had earlier been suspected of heresy. There
are indications that during the preceding patriarchate of Michael II
several Bogomils had been sentenced to the stake in Constantinople
but the new patriarch Cosmas decided to release Niphon. What is
more, he apparently considered the heretical monk a close companion, as Niphon was frequently entertained in the patriarchal palace
and could preach freely again. It has been argued that Niphon was
actually Basil's successor in Constantinople;[62] if this could be verified,
the year of 1146 marked a unique affiliation between the heresiarch
of Bogomilism and the patriarch of Orthodoxy. Regardless of
Niphon's position in the Bogomil movement, his presence in the
patriarchal palace could not be tolerated for long in Constantinople.

In 1147 the patriarch's adversaries succeeded in staging his dethronement and the reimprisonment of his Bogomil associate. At a synod
attended by the new emperor, Manuel 1 Comnenus, Cosmas 11
Atticus tried to counter his enemies with excommunication but was
finally deposed and disgraced as a Bogomil supporter.

Opinions vary whether the patriarch had been made the scapegoat
of a political intrigue or whether he was indeed a Bogomil sympa-
thizer. What is certain is that in the twelfth century Byzantine
Orthodoxy perceived Bogomilism as its main heretical enemy and
that Bogomilism could penetrate even the patriarchate in Constantinople or could convert and use Orthodox bishops in Cappadocia
for its own propaganda. Cappadocia seemed to mark the easternmost
reach of Bogomilism in Anatolia. The Balkan fortunes and the
western course of Bogomilism in the second half of the twelfth
century are better recorded, revealing important transformations in
the Bogomil movement as it entered its third century of underground existence with the dethronement of a Constantinople patriarch, who had been condemned as a Bogomil adherent.

Manuel Comnenus and Stefan Nemanja

Emperor Manuel 1 Comnenus (1143–80) may have witnessed and
even sanctioned the dethronement of Patriarch Cosmas Atticus but
his pro-western affinities and overtures to the papacy often brought
him into open conflict with the Orthodox Church. Despite the
problems caused by the armies during the Second Crusade (1147–
9) Manuel Comnenus remained one of the most Latinophile Byzantine emperors. With his grand design to restore the old *imperium
romanum* and with his armies engaged at various stages in places as
disparate as Cappadocia, southern Italy and Egypt, Manuel Comnenus succeeded in restoring Byzantine control over the western
Balkans against the persistent encroachment of the Hungarian kingdom. By the end of his reign most of Croatia, Dalmatia and Bosnia
were under his authority; the Serbian state, recently united under
the Grand Zhupan Stefan Nemanja, was also defeated and accepted
Byzantine suzerainty.

As well as his military campaigns, one of Manuel's ruling passions was astrology and while the poet John Camaterus dedicated a poetical tract on the twelve signs of the zodiac to him, the chronicler Michael Glykas, who criticized his astrological pursuits, was partially blinded and exiled. Later Orthodox tradition asserts that Manuel was exposed to heretical influences and it is curious that two such contemporaries – the deposed patriarch Cosmas and the reigning emperor Manuel – were to become targets of Orthodox suspicions. According to the later *Life of St Hilarion*[63] it was St Hilarion, then bishop in Macedonia, who fortified the Orthodox faith of the emperor, but the bishop also encountered numerous Manichaeans (probably Paulicians), Armenians (Monophysites) and Bogomils in his diocese. To confront the increasing influence of the heretics, who were described as 'beasts of prey' attacking and corrupting the Orthodox Church, the bishop ardently preached 'pious dogmas' to his flock and challenged the heretical preachers in heated and often violent debates. He overcame the influence of the Paulicians and the Armenian Monophysites, but he needed an imperial edict from Manuel Comnenus to purge the Bogomil heresy from his flock. Some of the Bogomils were converted (or feigned conversion) to Orthodoxy, while the unrepentant Bogomils were condemned to banishment and exile. That anti-Bogomil persecution raged during the reign of Manuel Comnenus is further confirmed by the canonist Theodore Balsamon, patriarch of Antioch (1185–90), who reported that towards the end of Manuel's reign 'whole regions and fortresses' in the Byzantine empire remained infected by the Bogomil heresy.[64] The Italian theologian Hugo Etherianus, who was Manuel's advisor on Latin theological matters, deemed it necessary to compose a polemic against the Bogomils in Byzantium and styled them 'Pathereni', which by the end of the century was the standard term for the Cathars in Italy.[65]

The spread of Bogomilism in Serbia provoked a vigorous response from Stefan Nemanja, the founder of the Serbian Nemanjid dynasty (1168–1371), who restored Serbian independence soon after the death of Manuel Comnenus in 1180. He summoned a great assembly against the 'heretics' in Serbia, who were undoubtedly Bogomils, which condemned their teachings and strictly proscribed their activities and books. Bogomilism, however, had apparently won considerable support among the Serbian nobility and Stefan Nemanja had to conduct a military campaign to eradicate the heresy. The Bogomils suffered severe persecution – some met their death by fire, others were banished and their books were burnt. While Stefan Nemanja's crusade had undoubtedly dealt a severe blow to Bogomilism in Serbia, his youngest son, St Sava, the founder of the autocephalous Serbian Church, had to continue the struggle against the Bogomils, who were still active in Serbia. The combined effort of the secular and ecclesiastical Serbian authorities seems to have been effective – the Bogomils did not regain any prominence in Serbia until the mid fourteenth century.

Persecution by Manuel Comnenus and Stefan Nemanja drove the Bogomils into the western Balkans, where Dalmatia and Bosnia emerged as centres of the heresy. The reigns of the two monarchs witnessed dramatic changes in the fortunes of medieval dualism in western Europe. At some stage during the first two centuries of their history, most probably around the beginning of the twelfth century, the Bogomils in the Balkans and Asia Minor began to establish communities or 'churches' with a developed hierarchy and ritual. Two of these churches played a decisive role in the crystallization of the Cathar movement in Italy and France and entered the inquisition archives as the source of all dualist churches in the west – *Ecclesia Drugunthiae* and *Ecclesia Sclavoniae*.

CHAPTER FOUR

The Dualist Communion

Along with Gothic art and architecture, the renewed ideals of monasticism, asceticism and apostolic life, the advent of the dualist heresy in the west was symptomatic of the religious enthusiasm and permutations of the twelfth century. The diffusion of the dualist tradition in western Europe reached its climax in the growth of an organized and widespread Cathar movement in northern Italy and southern France. Contemporary Catholic accounts often refer to the crucial impact of Balkan dualism on its formation. Modern theories may differ in their estimation of the chronology and the scale of Bogomil influence on original Catharism but invariably confirm its vital role in providing a new, dualist framework for western heretical and heterodox currents. The first signs of religious dissent in western Christendom appeared as early as the eighth century, but the earliest noticeable heretical movements arose in the eleventh century.

Heresy in the West

In 991, on his consecration as Archbishop of Rheims, Gerbert of Aurillac made a solemn profession of faith in the sanctity of both the New and Old Testaments, in the legitimacy of marriage and of eating meat and the existence of an evil spirit *per arbitrarum*, not by nature but by choice.[1] Since these 'articles of faith' are in immediate opposition to the current Bogomil and the later Cathar tenets, it has been argued that either Gerbert was declaring his opposition to some proto-Cathar movement in his province or was himself suspected of dualist transgressions and had to defend his orthodoxy.

Gerbert was said to have studied in his youth in the Moorish schools in Spain; later his reputed learning in theology, mathematics and the natural sciences was popularly believed to have been achieved through magic and he was credited with having an 'oracular head'. As the first French pope, Sylvester II (999–1003), Gerbert presided over western Christendom at the turn of the millennium, but eighty years later Cardinal Benno was to attribute Gerbert's meteoric rise to his skills in sorcery. Among the feats assigned to Sylvester II was the founding of a 'papal' school of magic in eleventh-century Rome.

In the first year of Sylvester's papacy, near Châlons-sur-Marne, north-east France, a heretic named Leutard appeared who, after a dream of a 'great swarm of bees' entering his body through his genitals, entered the church to break the cross and the image of the Saviour. Leutard declared that the cross-breaking was inspired by a revelation from God and his preachings won over adherents among the common people but, being exposed by the bishop of the diocese, he threw himself into a well.

Earlier, in the late tenth century, Vilgard, a scholar from Ravenna, indulged in pagan and classical learning to the extent that he provoked the manifestation of demons in the appearance of the poets Virgil, Horace and Juvenal, who encouraged his excessive pagan studies. Vilgard's preaching led to his condemnation as a heretic but his teachings spread in Italy and are alleged to have reached and provoked persecution in Sardinia and Spain.[2] Around 1018 'Manichaeans' appeared in Aquitaine, who rejected the baptism and the Cross and apparently observed strict asceticism.[3] Four years later ten of the canons of the Church of the Holy Cross at Orléans were accused of being 'Manichaeans' and of worshipping the devil, first as an 'Ethiopian' and also as an 'angel of light'.[4] The canons were part of a larger anti-sacramental group of heretics who comprised eminent clerics and nobles, including the confessor of Queen Constance. Besides rejecting the sacraments of the Church, the heretics of Orléans denied the human birth of Christ by the Virgin and the reality of his Passion and Resurrection. They offered their disciples deliverance from 'the Charybdis of false belief' and illumination through the rite of imposition of hands which was deemed to grant salvation and the 'gift of the Holy Spirit'. Despite their manifest loathing of matter and human body, the Orléans heretics were accused of indulging in indiscriminate nocturnal orgies, cremating the children conceived in the debauchery and collecting and preserving the ashes with great veneration. The heretics were brought to trial before the French king Robert the Pious and an assemblage of bishops, and were consigned to the flames, not before Queen Constance struck out the eye of her former confessor.

In 1022 the bishop of Arras-Cambrai in northern France sought to convert another group of heretics in his diocese who denounced the sacraments, the veneration of the Cross and practised asceticism by restraining from 'carnal longings'. The heresy taught in Arras was of an Italian extraction and around 1025 a 'strange heresy' was disclosed at a castle above Montforte in north-west Italy.[5] The heretics, including the countess of the stronghold, were mostly nobles and were considered to have come into Italy 'from some unknown part of the world'. The heretical society at Montforte believed in a Trinity in which, besides God the eternal Father, the Son was 'the soul of man beloved of God' and the Holy Ghost – 'the comprehension of divine truths by which all things are separately governed'. In their belief Jesus Christ is the soul of man 'in the flesh born of the Virgin Mary' who is identified as the Sacred Scripture, whereas the Holy Ghost is the 'devout comprehension of the Sacred Scriptures'. The Montforte heretics observed severe asceticism and while abstaining from the 'corruption' of sexual intercourse they argued that if the human race would adhere to such abstention it 'would be begotten like bees without coition'. The castle at Montforte was taken by a strong force of knights sent by the archbishop of Milan, Aribert; the heretics were brought to Milan, where they had to choose between a burning pyre and a 'Cross of the Lord' fixed close to the stake.

Towards the middle of the eleventh century Châlons-sur-Marne saw another outbreak of heresy, this time diffused by 'Manichaeans', who formed secret conventicles and used the rite of the imposition of hands to confer the Holy Spirit. Yet despite the label 'Manichaeans' and the charge of extreme asceticism, as with the previous outbreaks of western heresy in the century, there are no indications that the heretics adhered to any form of religious dualism. Most of these western heretical groups shared rejection of the sacraments and the clergy, invariably coupled with asceticism and often denunciation of worship of the Cross. They could be viewed as extreme manifestations of the evangelistic *Zeitgeist* of the eleventh century, with its monastic renascence and reformist zeal. Yet certain doctrines professed by the heretics – the rejection of Christ's Incarnation, Passion and Resurrection (Orléans), the denunciation of procreation as resulting from 'corruption' (Montforte), and the repeated hostility to the Cross – depart radically from Christian dogma and have often been attributed not to overstated and distorted apostolic impulses but to early penetration of Bogomil ideas in the west. It is the Byzantine colonies in southern Italy and Sicily, which were to be conquered in the late eleventh century by the Normans, that are usually considered as the stepping-stone for the early introduction of Bogomilism to the west and Bogomil preachers are known to have been active in Palermo in Sicily in about 1082.

Yet the early spread of Bogomilism to the west and the sudden outbreaks of western heresy in the eleventh century are surrounded by obscurity and unsolved problems. While taking shape in the western reformist climate, some of the newly appeared western heretical circles seem to have also been influenced by Bogomil traditions, but without yet adopting Bogomil dualism, and accordingly their heresy has been defined as 'proto-dualism'.[6]

It was in the twelfth century that Catharism emerged as the most developed and influential form of western dualism and from its beginnings it bore the unmistakable traces of the formative influence of Balkan dualism.

The Rise of Catharism

While recounting the transgressions of Vilgard of Ravenna, the chronicler Ralph the Bald linked the emergence and the spread of his heresy to the prophecy in Revelation 20:7 of Satan's release from his prison after a thousand years. After the repeated incidents of heretical agitation in the first fifty years of the new Christian millennium, the second half of the eleventh century failed to fulfil such expectations. In the early twelfth century the popular success of the wandering preachers, with their yearning for piety, voluntary poverty and an evangelical life, was coupled with the rise and spread of new and more vigorous reformist and heretical movements often led by charismatic figures like the notorious Tanchelm of Antwerp, who was active in the Low Countries, or Henry the Monk in France. Inspired by apostolic ideals, heretical preachers and reformists attacked the Church hierarchy, sacraments and corruption. Particularly zealous among them was the apostate monk Henry, who, having plunged in 1116 the northern French city of Le Mans into anti-clerical strife, moved to stir more anti-ecclesiastical agitation in the County of Toulouse which embraced most of Languedoc. There he encountered around 1133–4 another spirited and even more extreme preacher, Peter of Bruis, who rejected also the church buildings, the Old Testament and the cult of the Cross, which was denounced as the instrument of Christ's torture and death. Peter urged his followers to revenge the torments and death of Christ by breaking and burning crosses, but was hurled into one of his bonfires of crosses at St Gilles.

Towards the middle of the twelfth century a new heresy was taking shape, which would soon confront the spiritual authority of Rome in the Rhineland in the north and from Lombardy to the Pyrenees in the south: the movement of the Cathars or Cathari (the pure ones). The earliest certain indication of the rise of the Cathar heresy is the disclosure in 1143–4 of a heretical community at Cologne which was led by its own bishop.[7] The Cologne heretics regarded themselves as the true apostolic Church, as Christ's poor, who were 'not of this world'. They were divided into three grades – listeners, believers and the elect. Through the rite of the placing of hands, the listener could enter the ranks of the believers and after a probationary period could join the elect and be 'baptized in fire and the Spirit'. Women were also initiated into the grades of the believer and the elect, but marriage, except that between virgins, was condemned as fornication. Besides sexual intercourse, the Cologne heretics abstained from milk and any food born of coition and blessed their food and drink with the *Pater Noster*. They rejected the fire of purgatory after death but taught that upon death the soul was sent either to 'eternal rest or punishment' and fell back on Ecclesiastes 11:3 – 'And if the tree fall toward the south, or toward the north, in the place where the tree falleth, there it shall be' (*KJV*). The Cologne sectarians claimed that they had numerous adherents 'throughout the world', particularly among the clergy and the monks, and that their religion had persisted in secrecy 'from the time of the martyrs' in Greece (Byzantium) and elsewhere. The unrepentant Cologne heretics were burnt along with their bishop and his assistant but their emergence and suppression was just the beginning of a determined and prolonged challenge to the western Church.

The activities of the Cologne heretics were exposed in an appeal by the prior Eberwin of Steinfeld to the churchman and theologian St Bernard of Clairvaux. In 1145 St Bernard, who had already helped the elevation of the Knights Templar and his own Cistercian order, embarked on a preaching mission to Toulouse to redeem the region from the heretical influence of the apostate monk Henry. St Bernard did not encounter the turbulent monk but wrote to the Count of Toulouse, Alphonse Jordan, who apparently patronized Henry, about the critical religious situation in the area around Toulouse – 'The churches are without congregations, congregations are without priests, priests are without proper reverence, and, finally, Christians are without Christ'.[8] St Bernard warned the count that after being expelled from all parts of France the heretical preacher had found refuge in the lands of the County of Toulouse and there 'he revels in all his fury among the flock of Christ . . .'. St Bernard's mission encountered anticlerical attitudes among some of the Languedoc nobility and detected heretical currents in Toulouse. Around the same time, the Liège clergy wrote to the pope that a new heresy seemed 'to have overflowed various regions' of France, 'a heresy so varied and manifold that it seems impossible to characterize it under one single name'. The heretical community in Liège itself, with its militant anti-ecclesiastical character, comprised the grades of the listeners and believers and had its hierarchy of 'priests' and 'prelates'.[9]

Besides anticlerical agitation in the Low Countries and Languedoc, reformist and heretical movements also appeared in Italy amid the protracted disputes between the popes and the Holy Roman emperors. Meanwhile the Crusades had brought about cultural and commercial intercourse between east and west which, in the words of M. Lambert, 'facilitated formal and informal contacts with the underground Bogomil churches in Constantinople, Asia Minor and the Balkans'.[10] Byzantium established stronger trading contacts with Italian cities like Venice and Genoa and with southern France, while the crusading movements, the foundation of the crusader domains, with the opening of trade routes, provided the possibilities for new religious exchanges in an era when the western spiritual climate was particularly receptive to new religious ideas. The Cologne heretics had acknowledged their Byzantine pedigree in 1143; besides Bogomil missionaries the orbit of Bogomil proselytism in the west was extended through crusaders and merchants returning from the east. *Tractatus de hereticis* (*c.* 1266-7), ascribed to the inquisitor Anselm of Alessandria, revealed another route of dualist penetration of the west; the earliest Bogomil dualist bishoprics were set up in Drugunthia (in Thrace), Bulgaria and Philadelphia (in western Anatolia).[11] Anselm emphasized the vital role of the Bogomil church in Constantinople in the diffusion of dualism in the west. In Anselm's tract the dualist church in the new Rome was founded by Greeks from Constantinople, who went as merchants to Bulgaria and, being converted to Bogomilism, established a community and a 'Bishop of the Greeks' in the imperial capital. The tract also related that the Bogomil church in Constantinople converted Bosnian merchants who preached the heresy in Bosnia and, 'having increased in number', established a bishop who was called the 'Bishop of Sclavonia or Bosnia'. French crusaders, who 'went to Constantinople to conquer the land', variously read as an allusion to the First or Second Crusade, were also converted and founded a dualist community led by their own heretical bishop in Constantinople, styled the 'Bishop of the Latins'.

Particularly important is Anselm's testimony to the spread of the dualist heresy in France, which he attributed to the French dualist crusaders returning from Constantinople who preached, 'increased in numbers' and established a 'Bishop of France'. Their teachings penetrated Provence to win over numerous adherents and four new heretical bishops were established, the bishops of Carcassonne, Albi, Toulouse and Agen. The tract explicitly stated that because the French crusaders were originally 'led astray by Bulgars . . . throughout France these persons are called Bulgarian heretics'. A dualist mission from France reached the Milan area and, in Concorezzo, converted the would-be first heretical bishop in Italy, Mark the Gravedigger, along with his associates John Judeus and Joseph. The newly converted heretics embarked on preaching missions in Lombardy as well as in Treviso to the east and Tuscany to the south. Mark the Gravedigger's mission apparently won a substantial following and as attested by the treatise *De heresi catharorum in Lombardia* (*c.* 1200–1214) he was eventually elevated as bishop of all Lombard, Tuscan and Trevisan heretics.[12]

While Catharism was gaining ground in Italy, western Christendom witnessed a new series of outbreaks of heresy, some of which, besides their anticlerical tenor, also seem related to the spread of Catharism. It has been argued that German crusaders returning from the ill-fated Second Crusade, preached by St Bernard of Clairvaux in 1144, revitalized the dualist heresy in the Rhineland[13] and in 1163 another dualist group was brought to trial in Cologne and 'fiercely burned' near the Jewish cemetery outside the town. The monk Eckbert of Schönau wrote a tract against the new Cologne heretics but his thirteen sermons draw freely upon St Augustine's attacks on the fourth-century Manichaeans.[14] In his first sermon Eckbert claimed that the heretics, 'the hidden men', had increased in many countries and were called 'Piphli' in Flanders, 'Texerant' in France and Cathars in Germany. Names like 'Publicans' or 'Popelicans', deriving from the term Paulicians, were also becoming common in western Europe and around 1162, when Thomas à Becket was consecrated Archbishop of Canterbury, a group of Publicans reached England and embarked on propagating their heresy. William of Newburgh[15] asserted that the Publicans had spread their heresy in France, Spain, Italy and Germany but in England the Publicans were denounced at a synod in Oxford, publicly flogged, branded, driven out of the city and left to perish in the winter cold. This 'pious severity', said William of Newburgh, not only purged England of the heretical pestilence but prevented it from ever again reaching the island.

At about the same time the Archbishop of Rheims was prosecuting another group of Publicans in Flanders, while in 1167 Publicans were questioned about the secret tenets of their heresy in a trial at Vézelay and some of them were condemned to death. Towards the end of the twelfth century in Italy the term 'Patarene' was already interchangeable with Cathar; often the names given to the dualist communities were based on the regions or the towns associated with them. The Cathars from the area around Albi, where the earliest Cathar bishopric in southern France was founded, came to be known as Albigensians and this name acquired wide currency. However, in a number of cases dualist communities in the west adopted names like Bulgars and Sclavini to acknowledge the Balkan origin of their heresy.

Catharism in Languedoc

By the end of the twelfth century Catharism was already well established in Languedoc, where it secured the favour not only of much of the rural aristocracy but also of great Midi nobles like Roger Trencavel II, Viscount of Béziers and Carcassonne, Raymond-Roger, Count of Foix, and Raymond VI (1194–1222), the Count of Toulouse. In contrast to the prevalent climate in western Europe, Languedoc society was markedly more tolerant and cosmopolitan and had also attained a high degree of prosperity. With its distinctive and diverse culture Languedoc was a prominent centre of the twelfth century 'renaissance' and the cradle of the troubadour lyric poetry, which flourished under the patronage of the noble courts, including the affluent court of Raymond VI, himself a composer of lyrics. Apart from the flowering of its secular culture the region was plagued by political pressures in the wake of the departure of Raymond IV (1093–1105), Count of Toulouse and Marquise of Provence, for the Holy Land during the First Crusade. The rule of the Counts of Toulouse in Languedoc itself was affected by the specific feudal system in the region and threatened by the conflicting ambitions for sovereignty over Languedoc of the Capetian French kings, the kings of England and the kings of Aragon (the Counts of Barcelona).

While the Languedoc religious climate was unusually tolerant, the movement for reform within the Church had not left a strong imprint on the Languedoc clergy. The Jews enjoyed good treatment and later the Counts of Toulouse were often accused of appointing Jews to public offices. In the twelfth century the Provençal Jewry underwent a cultural and religious ferment and it was the Provençal Kabbalist school that produced in 1176 the first classic book of medieval Kabbalah, the enigmatic *Sepher Bahir*.[16] Indeed religious interchange between the Cathars and some Jewish Kabbalist circles in Languedoc has been repeatedly postulated but not yet demonstrated conclusively. The sectarian and heretical preachers were rarely apprehended in Languedoc and following the anticlerical agitation in the first half of the century, a new gospel-inspired movement was spreading in the area: the Waldensians or the Poor of Lyons. The Waldensians were excommunicated as heretics by Pope Lucius III in 1184 but the reputed apostolic life of their preachers was in marked contrast to the conduct of the Languedoc clergy, which abounded in wealthy, worldly and corrupt prelates. The Languedoc Church did not enjoy a high reputation throughout the region and the lessening of her authority was to pave the way for the missionary advance of the Waldensians and the Cathars.

The Languedoc clergy was exposed to the encroachment of the local aristocracy on Church land and tithes. The conflicts between the Church and the nobility further facilitated the spread of the anticlerical teachings of the Cathars, which won the support of many Languedoc nobles, who did not bar the Cathars from preaching in their fiefs and even allowed them access to their courts where the Cathar missionaries won over new sympathizers. Whereas Catharism permeated all social classes, it was the noble patronage of the Cathars that was crucial for the firm establishment of the heresy in Languedoc. The ascetic dualist faith of the Cathars flourished in the noble courts alongside the troubadour courtly love. While courtly love embellished the chivalric cult of the chosen Lady, Catharism won numerous adherents among the noble ladies of Languedoc who included, for example, both the wife and the sister of the nominally Catholic Count of Foix, respectively Philippa and Esclarmonda. While some noble ladies who converted to Catharism, like Esclarmonda, sought and received the rite of *consolamentum* to become important figures in the Cathar movement, the male noble patrons of the Cathars did not necessarily join the heretical ranks and when accepted as believers they usually deferred the *consolamentum* until their deathbed. Even the Count of Toulouse, Raymond VI, was later rumoured by his enemies to have maintained two Cathar *perfecti* ready to grant him the *consolamentum* when in mortal danger.

St Bernard's mission in 1145 was followed by sporadic Catholic attempts to halt the heretical agitation in Languedoc but they proved entirely unsuccessful. Raymond V of Toulouse, unlike his son Raymond VI, did not tolerate the Cathars and in 1178 appealed to Louis VII of France for forceful intervention against the growing heresy. A preaching mission was sent to Toulouse where a rich heretic was exposed and punished by flogging and three years' exile in the Holy Land. The mission, however, was openly sneered at in the streets of Toulouse and a public debate with two prominent Cathar preachers ended in their excommunication but without further punishment. Viscount Roger Trencavel, who had taken the Catholic bishop of Albi captive, and in whose fief Catharism was reported to have spread widely, was also excommunicated. In 1179, after the Third Lateran Council which condemned the teachings of the 'Cathars, Patarenes and Publicans' a new mission was dispatched to Languedoc. This time its leader, Henry, Abbot of Clairvaux, conducted a mini-crusade against Roger Trencavel who was forced to denounce the heresy and to promise persecution of the heretics in his domains.

In 1184 the Holy Roman Emperor Frederick I Barbarossa, after spending the first half of his reign in a bitter struggle with the papacy, met with Pope Lucius III in Verona to establish procedures to check the growing spread of heresy which were elaborated in a joint decree, *Ad abolendam*. The Cathars and the Patarenes were anathematized and proscribed along with other sectarian movements and legal proceedings were established against both clerical and lay heretics. Convicted heretics were to be penalized with 'appropriate punishment' and bishops were entrusted to search out and charge the heretics in their dioceses, but the death penalty was not yet prescribed. While some sporadic measures were taken against the heretics in Italy, no major prosecutions were to follow in Languedoc. Roger Trencavel's pledge to suppress the heresy in his territory proved formal, while the year of 1194 saw the death of the old Count of Toulouse, Raymond V, who, apart from his appeals for action against the heresy in Languedoc, did little himself to diminish its spread. Indeed it was during his rule that Catharism acquired its distinctive church order which was settled in a Cathar Council hosted by the Cathar congregation in the Toulouse area.

As in Bogomilism, the division between the believer and the perfect in Catharism was fundamental for the organization of the sect. Following the spiritual baptism with the placing of hands, the *consolamentum*, the new 'consoled' Cathar perfect assumed a black robe to enter a life of strict asceticism, prayer and preaching. The Catholics sometimes called the perfects 'the robed heretics', while among the Cathars they were known as 'Good Christians' or 'Good Men'. Unbound by the austere standards of the Good Men, the believers, who formed the great majority in the sect, secured the livelihood and protection of the Cathar élite. Besides attending some of the ceremonies of the *perfecti*, the believers ritually saluted the Good Men with a bow and a request for a blessing and a prayer that they become 'good Christians' and be brought to a 'good end', the *consolamentum*.

The *perfecti* responded with the blessing and prayer for a final baptism and death in the Cathar sect. The whole ritual was known as *melioramentum* (improvement), although Catholic commentators such as the Inquisitor Bernard Gui preferred to style it 'adoration'.[17] The approximate number of the Cathar *perfecti* at the beginning of the thirteenth century has been estimated at between 1,000 and 1,500; in its spread throughout Languedoc Catharism rose to virtual prevalence in the areas between Toulouse, Carcassonne and Albi.

Early Catharism in Languedoc and Lombardy inherited the monarchian dualism of the Bogomil system, where the evil creator of the material world was a power ultimately subordinate and inferior to the good Father. Following the great Cathar Council at St-Félix-de-Caraman, Catharism saw the renascence of the doctrines of absolute dualism, which posed the inexorable opposition between two coeternal and coequal powers, the good God and the evil God.

The Council at St-Félix and the Dualist Churches

As the expansion of Catharism was gaining momentum, at some point between 1166 and 1176 a crucial Cathar Council was convened at St-Félix-de-Caraman near Toulouse, which brought together a 'great multitude' of Cathar men and women. This council finally settled the administrative structure of the sect in France by instituting new heretical bishoprics, electing Cathar bishops and demarcating the boundaries between some of the Cathar dioceses. The council was presided over by the bishop of the dualist church of Constantinople, Nicetas, referred to in the *Acts* of the Council[18] as *Papa* Nicetas, who apparently had exceptional authority as he was empowered to consecrate the new bishops and even to reconsecrate the bishops of the communities which were already organized as bishoprics. *Papa* Nicetas reconsecrated the bishops of the Cathar dioceses or churches of northern France, Albi and Lombardy and consecrated the elected bishops for the new churches of Toulouse, Carcassonne and *Ecclesia Aransensis* (which is usually taken to denote not Val d'Aran but Agen).

Furthermore the Cathar *perfecti* at the council were reconsoled by receiving the *consolamentum* from Nicetas. In a separate sermon to the church of Toulouse, he elaborated on the nature, the functioning and the territorial organization of the eastern dualist 'primal churches'. Besides naming five dualist churches in the Balkan–Byzantine world, Nicetas cryptically referred to the primal 'Seven Churches of Asia' which have been viewed as an allusion to either the 'seven churches of Asia' in Revelation (1:4, 11, 20) or the seven Paulician churches in Asia Minor but they still remain a conundrum. The other five churches in his sermon – '*Ecclesiae Romanae et Dragometiae et Melenguiae et Bulgariae et Dalmatiae*' – can be traced and located with more certainty: some of them appear in inquisitorial sources with modified names.

Ecclesia Bulgariae was located in eastern Bulgaria or Macedonia, while *Ecclesia Dalmatiae* was clearly in Dalmatia in the western Balkans. *Ecclesia Dragometiae* (known also as Dugunthia or Drugunthia) is usually located in Thrace or Macedonia, and *Ecclesia Romanae* is generally believed to be the Constantinople church of *Papa* Nicetas. The Bogomil church of *Melenguiae* still eludes identification as it does not figure in the unique and elaborate list of the dualist churches in Europe presented by the Dominican friar and inquisitor Rainerius Sacchoni in 1250. Before becoming an Inquisitor, Rainerius Sacchoni had been a Cathar *perfectus* for seventeen years and in his *Summa on the Cathars and the Poor of Lyons*[19] furnished invaluable information on the beliefs, activities and locations of the dualist churches.

Rainerius listed ten western Cathar churches in France and Italy: the churches of Desenzano, Concorezzo, Bagnolo, Vicenza, the Spoletan Valley, Florence, northern France, Toulouse, Carcassonne and Albi. He also mentioned six eastern dualist churches: '*Ecclesia Sclavoniae, E. Latinorum de Constantinopoli, E. Graecorum ibidem, E. Philadelphiae in Romania, E. Burgariae* (Bulgariae), *E. Dugunthiae* (Drugunthiae)'. The church of Sclavonia is generally considered to correspond to the church of Dalmatia in Nicetas' sermon and to represent the Dalmatian and Bosnian Bogomils. Sacchoni clearly differentiated the Constantinople Greek church, whose bishop had earlier been Nicetas, from the *Ecclesia Latinorum* in Constantinople which is usually viewed as a dualist order set up to minister to the Cathars in the Latin empire of Constantinople in the wake of the Fourth Crusade (1202–04).

Ecclesia Philadelphiae in Romania was also mentioned by Anselm of Alessandria among the first three dualist churches. It is suggestive of one of the seven churches of Asia in Revelation (1:11), the Philadelphian church, which is deemed to have been taught the mystery of the 'key of David' and was located at the ancient city of Philadelphia in Lydia, western Asia Minor. As with *Papa* Nicetas, Rainerius Sacchoni registered the Bogomil churches of Bulgaria and Drugunthia at the end of his list, with the comment: 'All (Cathar churches) stem from the last-named', confirming that *Ecclesia Bulgariae* and *Ecclesia Dugunthiae* (Drugunthiae) were seen as the mother-churches of all European dualist churches.

Rainerius Sacchoni did not mention *Ecclesia Melenguiae* whose most plausible location is in Peloponnesus, probably in the Melangeia area in ancient Arcadia.[20] It has been argued that a mission from the Arcadian *Ecclesia Melenguiae* was behind the sudden emergence of *Paterini* (Cathars) in the former Byzantine province of Calabria in southern Italy, where the Greek presence was still strong in the twelfth century.[21] In the period of the general expansion of dualism the Calabrian *Paterini* gained adherents, but at the same time their links to the Cathar communities in central and northern Italy remain obscure. In the late twelfth century the Calabrian mystic Joachim of Fiore warned against their proselytism and referred to the division between the perfect and the believers among the Calabrian Patarenes. In his prophetic reading of Revelation Joachim predicted an unholy alliance between the Saracens and the Patarenes, respectively seen as the beasts from the sea and from the land, who would arise to plague the Church in the wake of the fall of the New Babylon, the Roman *imperium*.[22]

The Calabrian Cathars and the Arcadian *Ecclesia Melenguiae* remain the most enigmatic of the Bogomil and Cathar communities in southern Europe. Consequently it is impossible to determine the stance of the Calabrian and Arcadian heretics in the great schism that split the European dualist movement in the wake of *Papa* Nicetas' mission to the council of St-Félix-de-Caraman.

The Schism

With *Papa* Nicetas presiding at the council at St-Félix, there were bound to be repercussions that irreversibly transformed western dualism. Far from being the habitual heretical ceremonies, his rites of reconsecration and reconsolation were in essence rites of conversion in which the Cathar *perfecti* abandoned monarchian dualism, with its belief in the lesser status of the evil principle, to embrace the doctrine of the two coeternal principles, the doctrine of absolute dualism, whose apostle was *Papa* Nicetas.

At some time in the twelfth century the foremost Bogomil churches of Drugunthia and Constantinople had adopted the classical absolute dualism of the two coeval and opposed principles. The Bogomil church of Philadelphia apparently also came to accept the radical dualist creed and the bishop of the Constantinople church, Nicetas, consoled under the order of the Drugunthian Church, was entrusted to produce a similar renaissance of absolute dualism in Catharism. *Ecclesia Bulgariae* and *Ecclesia Sclavoniae* in the western Balkans persevered with their adherence to the original Bogomil monarchian dualism and were now faced with an imminent schism.

What increased the danger of a split was the sudden apostolic fervour of the Drugunthian and Constantinople churches, which apparently considered the consecration and consolation under the order of the moderate dualist churches invalid. Claiming that the validity of these cardinal rites could be secured only by an absolute dualist consecrator, the mission of *Papa* Nicetas sought to reconsecrate the dualist bishops and reconsole the Cathar *perfecti* under the order of the Drugunthian church. As well as the mass conversion of the French Cathars to absolute dualism at St-Félix, *Papa* Nicetas also won over the Italian Cathars. In Lombardy he succeeded in converting Mark, the bishop of the Cathars in Lombardy, Tuscany and Treviso. Mark, who had been ordained in the *Ecclesia Bulgariae*, was persuaded to abandon the Bulgarian order and was reconsecrated in the Drugunthian order,[23] which was believed to stem from the head of *Ecclesia Drugunthiae*, the enigmatic bishop, Symeon. The bishop of the Drugunthian church undoubtedly played a major role in the schism, but his activities are shrouded in obscurity, unless Runciman is right to identify him with the Bogomil associate of the disgraced patriarch, Cosmas Atticus, the monk Niphon.[24]

The large-scale missionary campaign of *Papa* Nicetas had drawn the Cathar churches into communion with a renascent absolute dualism, which retained its hold on the Cathars in Languedoc until their final extirpation. The ascendancy of radical dualism in the west, however, was soon challenged by counter-missions sent by the moderate dualist churches of Bulgaria and 'Sclavonia'. Led by Petracius, 'with companions from across the sea', the first mission reached Lombardy and caused the initial division among the Italian Cathars.[25] Earlier the Lombard bishop Mark had been plunged into doubt over his Drugunthian consecration by rumours that *Papa* Nicetas had come to an evil end. Mark set out for the Balkans to obtain ordination from the bishop of *Ecclesia Bulgariae*, but only got as far as Calabria, where a Cathar deacon told him that a voyage across the sea was impossible. Unable to embark on his journey, Mark was thrown into prison, where he fell seriously ill. His failing health forced him to appeal for the election of a new heretical bishop; soon the newly elected John Judeus reached Mark and was confirmed as bishop. Mark himself was soon released and started out for Lombardy but died before meeting his successor again, the validity of whose office was to be questioned in a new debate whether 'Lord Mark' came to a good or evil end.[26]

Petracius' moderate dualist mission intensified the growing divisions among the Italian Cathars and they split at first into two then into more groups that evolved into separate Cathar churches.[27] The churches of Bagnolo, Concorezzo, Desenzano and Mosio were active in Lombardy, the church of Vicenza in Veneto and the churches of Florence and Spoleto in Tuscany. According to their orientation, the Italian Cathar churches sought to send their bishops for the *consolamentum* and consecration at the major seats of the absolute or moderate dualist churches in the Balkans. The church of Desenzano, which was later also known as the church of the Albanenses and emerged as the stronghold of radical dualism in Italy, sent its bishop to the Drugunthian church, while Vicenza and Bagnolo sent their bishops for consecration to the church of Sclavonia. Concorezzo was led initially by John Judeus, who was persuaded to go to *Ecclesia Bulgariae* to legitimate his ordination. Another bishop of Concorezzo, Nazarius, went to Bulgaria for ordination in about 1190 and brought back with him the important Bogomil tract *Liber Secretum*,[28] which was to exercise a strong influence on the Italian moderate dualists and on some Albigensian circles in Languedoc.

Following the breach in Balkan dualism those churches that professed absolute dualism came to consider *Ecclesia Drugunthiae* as their mother-church, while the moderate communities claimed descent from the *Ecclesia Bulgariae*. The Cathars in Languedoc overall remained true to absolute dualism and in the communion of the Drugunthian church, whereas the Cathars of northern France identified with the monarchian dualist churches in Lombardy and reverted to moderate dualism. In 1208, when Pope Innocent III launched the infamous Albigensian Crusade against the Languedoc Cathars and the northern crusaders of Simon de Montfort burst into southern France, absolute dualism was the dominant creed in Languedoc.

Towards the end of the crusade, however, between 1223 and

1227, one of the foremost Cathar dioceses, that of Agen, came to be administered by an apparent advocate of monarchian dualism, Bishop Bartholomew of Carcassonne. In 1223 Cardinal Conrad of Porto, papal legate to Languedoc, alleged that Bartholomew was a vicar of a heretical antipope who had arisen 'in the regions of Bosnia, Croatia and Dalmatia, next to the nation of Hungary' to whom the Albigensians flocked 'so that he could answer their inquiries'.[29] Cardinal Conrad was referring in all probability to the bishop of the moderate dualist *Ecclesia Sclavoniae* in the western Balkans; he warned that the new Cathar bishop of Agen was consecrating bishops and organizing heretical churches. It has been shown that the activities of Bartholomew of Carcassonne were a concerted campaign to win back the Languedoc Cathars to monarchian dualism by the formation of alternative moderate dualist churches and the consecration of rival Cathar bishops.[30] The former Waldensian, Durand of Huesca, who became a vigorous anti-Cathar polemicist, wrote in about 1222–5 a tract against the Albigensians in Languedoc, where he referred to a threefold division in Catharism among the followers of the Greek, Bulgarian and Dragovitsan (Drugunthian) churches. Unlike *Papa* Nicetas, however, the prestige and influence of Bartholomew of Carcassonne did not survive his death in 1227. The old absolute dualist order in the church of Agen was restored in 1229 and in 1232 the see had to move to the Cathar stronghold of Montségur. In the following turbulent decades of mounting persecution and *autos-da-fé* the Cathar churches in Languedoc maintained their radical dualist doctrinal unity. The Catholic records of the Cathars refer regularly to the formula of two principles, or gods, or lords, one of good and the other of evil, existing from eternity and without end.

It is difficult to determine what was the catalyst for the sudden revival of radical dualism in the Bogomil Drugunthian order, especially when it is remembered that the heresiarch of absolute dualism, *Papa* Nicetas, firmly declared before the Cathar *perfecti* at St-Félix-de-Caraman that all Bogomil churches were operating in perfect concordance. The most plausible explanation is that the *Ecclesia Drugunthiae* comprised Paulicians from Thrace who precipitated a doctrinal reorientation. Whatever the origins of the schism, one of the foremost authorities on Catharism, A. Borst, has argued that the mission of *Papa* Nicetas and the ensuing supremacy of the two-gods' formula in Languedoc ultimately alienated western Christians from the magnified dualism in Catharism.[31] For inquisitors like Rainerius Sacchoni the heretical transgressions of the absolute dualists, with their two-gods' belief, were inevitably graver than the 'errors' of the moderate dualists for whom the evil demiurge of the material world was secondary to the sublime Father. Medieval monarchian dualism was undoubtedly closer to the tenets of orthodox Christianity than absolute dualism, which has often been defined as a separate dualist religion altogether.

The schism remained entirely doctrinal and did not affect the concord between the moderate and absolute dualist Churches, both of which maintained the crucial hierarchical differentiation of the two principal heretical grades, the *credentes*, believers, and the *perfecti* who had received the baptism in Spirit, the *consolamentum*. Both communities shared a common church order and the heretical dioceses were, in Languedoc for example, demarcated along the boundaries of the traditional Catholic sees. The Cathar diocese of Carcassonne thus embraced the Catholic sees of Carcassonne and Narbonne along with the Catholic dioceses in Catalonia. They were administered by heretical bishops, who were assisted by two coadjutors, called the elder son (*filius major*) and the younger son (*filius minor*) as well as a number of deacons. Upon the death of the dualist bishop the elder son succeeded to the bishopric, while the younger son was elevated to the position of the elder son and the *perfecti* elected a new younger son. The absolute churches maintained these three offices although they seem to reflect the triad of monarchian dualism – God the Father, His elder son, Satanael, and His younger son, Jesus Christ.[32]

CHAPTER FIVE

The Crusade Against Dualism

The last two decades of the twelfth century brought about a drastic reversal of fortune in the crusader domains and the Byzantine empire. In 1187 Saladin, the great adversary of the crusaders, crushed their forces near Hattin and recaptured Jerusalem, while one year earlier the militant and influential Bulgarian house of the Assenids had overthrown Byzantine rule in a campaign characterized by its religious and messianic overtones. The Assenids established the second Bulgarian empire (1186–1394) and Byzantine hegemony in the eastern Balkans was finally destroyed. The Fourth Crusade, launched in 1202 by Pope Innocent III (1198–1216), inflicted still greater disaster on Byzantium – diverted from their course, the crusaders stormed and sacked Constantinople in 1204. The leaders of the Crusade and their Venetian creditors set up the Latin Empire of Constantinople (1204–61) while the remnants of Byzantium were divided into the 'empires' of Nicaea and Trebizond and the Despotate of Epirus.

Only one year after its foundation the empire suffered a severe blow: in April 1205 the armies of the Bulgarian Tsar Kaloyan totally routed the Latin troops of the first Latin Emperor of Constantinople, Baldwin I, near Adriannopolis. In the carnage Baldwin himself was captured and died in captivity in what became known as the Baldwin Tower in Kaloyan's capital. In the same year the Latin crusaders of Constantinople sought to instigate a Crusade against the Bulgarian monarch, trying to persuade Innocent III that Kaloyan had joined forces with the Turks (the nomad Cumans) and 'other enemies of the Cross',[1] perhaps implicating heretics like the Paulicians and the Bogomils. In the previous year the Bulgarian Church had recognized the formal supremacy of the Roman See and Kaloyan himself had received his crown from Innocent III. The pope was not prepared to declare a Crusade against his recent ally and over the next two years Kaloyan inflicted new defeats on the Latin armies, killing the crusaders' leader, Boniface of Montferrat, in 1207. However, while Innocent III did not launch a Crusade against the alleged alliance of Kaloyan with the heretical 'enemies of the Cross', his papacy marked the beginning of Rome's counter-offensive against the resurgence of dualism in medieval Christendom, which culminated in the Albigensian Crusade in Languedoc.

Councils and Crusades

Besides authorizing the Fourth Crusade, which caused the dismemberment of the old Byzantine empire, Innocent vigorously enforced his vision of a universal papal theocracy and ascendancy over earthly monarchs. Innocent's theocratic aspirations led to his frequent interference in the affairs of Europe's secular rulers and with the unfolding of his long conflict with the English King John he did not hesitate to place England under an interdict and to excommunicate the king in 1208.

In the first year of his papacy Innocent proclaimed heresy *lèse-majesté* against God and received alarming reports of its spread in Bosnia, which was then nominally under the jurisdiction of Rome and the suzerainty of the Hungarian kingdom. According to the inquisitor Anselm of Alessandria, the heretical church of Bosnia or Sclavonia had been established at some stage after the Second Crusade in 1147. In 1199 Innocent III was warned that the ruler (Ban) of Bosnia, Kulin (1168–1204), who sought independence from Hungary, had succumbed along with his family and 10,000 Christians to the 'significant' heresy that was seen to 'sprout' in the land.[2] In 1200 the pope was already asking the king of Hungary to take measures against heresy in Bosnia and Ban Kulin was accused of having granted asylum to Patarenes expelled from Dalmatia. Two years later Innocent III wrote to the archbishop of Split that in Bosnia there was a multitude of people suspected of being adherents of the 'condemned Cathar heresy' but Ban Kulin insisted that he believed they were actually Catholics. Ban Kulin sent some of the suspected Cathars to Rome for a profession of faith and accepted a papal legate commissioned to inspect the religious affairs of Bosnia. Innocent entrusted this to his chaplain, Johannes de Casamaris, who in 1203 witnessed the public abjuration of errors by Ban Kulin and the priors of Bosnian monasteries. Besides renouncing the schism with Rome the Bosnian priors pledged to bring altars and crosses into the churches, to read from the Old Testament as well as the New Testament, to observe fasts and church services in accordance with the Catholic Church and not to admit Manichaeans and other heretics into their orders.[3]

Apart from his endeavours to strengthen Roman authority over Bosnia, in 1199 Innocent sent a Cistercian mission to deter the spread of Catharism in Languedoc and to reform the Languedoc Church. The mission won the support of King Pedro II of Aragon, but although Raymond VI pledged to drive the Cathars out of his domain, no firm action was taken against them. In 1204 and 1205 Innocent III repeatedly appealed to the supreme suzerain, the French King Philip Augustus, for military intervention in heresy-ridden Languedoc. Preoccupied with the conquest of the English dominions in France, Philip Augustus was openly reluctant to launch a campaign in the south. The preaching missions to Languedoc in 1206–08 were reinforced by the Spanish bishop Diego of Osma and Dominic of Guzmán, the would-be founder of the 'Order of the Preaching Friars', the Dominicans. The 'apostolic' preaching by 'example and word' of the two Spaniards brought some missionary successes but did not diminish the strength and vitality of Catharism in Languedoc. In 1207 the papal legate in Languedoc, Peter of Castelnau, finally felt compelled to excommunicate the Count of Toulouse.

One year before the excommunication of Raymond VI, Innocent III had sent a cardinal-legate[4] to Kaloyan's successor, Tsar Boril, apparently to urge him to take immediate action against the Bogomils. Innocent may have been the primary instigator of the ensuing anti-Bogomil council in 1211 but it was conducted along standard Orthodox lines and was presided over by the 'most pious' Tsar Boril. The records of the council, the *Synodicon of Tsar Boril*,[5] extol Boril as a defender of the faith who was inspired with divine zeal and gathered the heretics from the whole of his realm before the tribunal. Boril apparently shared the apostolic inclinations of Alexius Comnenus and summoned the Bogomils to present their teachings, which they did by resorting to numerous quotations from the Holy Scriptures, intending to 'entice' the Tsar and his entourage. The Tsar was said to have exposed their 'obloquy' and, after being 'entrapped' into theological disputes with the Tsar, the unrepentant Bogomils were imprisoned or 'otherwise punished'. The *Synodicon* anathematized the Bogomil doctrines and practices, most of which had already been anathematized in earlier synodicons, and cursed, along with the heresiarch Bogomil, some prominent Bogomil apostles. It explicitly condemned the 'nocturnal meetings and mysteries' of the Bogomils and their custom of 'practising sorcery' on 24 June, the birth of John the Baptist, and performing 'unholy mysteries like the hellenic pagan rites'.

While Tsar Boril was indulging in theological debates with the Bogomils, the Albigensian Crusade in Languedoc had been raging for a year and a half and the northern crusaders had already taken Béziers and Carcassonne, murdering many Catholics and Cathars at Béziers, and, as declared by Arnold Aimery, 'showing mercy neither to order nor to age nor sex'.[6] In January 1208 an attempted reconciliation between Raymond VI and Peter of Castelnau ended in acrimony and the papal legate was threatened that he would come under the surveillance of the Count of Toulouse. Peter of Castelnau was killed on 15 January 1208 and Innocent accused Raymond VI of heresy and complicity in his murder. The pope appealed for an immediate Crusade against the heresy in Languedoc and proposed the indulgences granted to earlier crusaders as well as any land they might seize from the heretics. The Albigensian Crusade was vigorously promoted in northern France and in the early summer of 1209 northern feudal lords and prelates mustered a formidable army at Lyons. Yet the military orders of the Templars and the Hospitallers did not play an active military role in the Crusade, which, in the case of the Templars, was bound to attack some of their patrons, who were renowned Cathar supporters, while Raymond VI was himself patron of the Order of the Hospitallers. Since the French king had refused to take part in the Crusade, the crusaders descended on the south led by the zealous papal legate, Arnold Aimery.

The Crusade soon turned into a war of conquest in which the

northern barons strove to seize the fiefs of the southern nobility, which remained deplorably disunited in the face of the invasion. The projected alliance between Raymond VI and Viscount Raymond-Roger Trencavel of Béziers was not achieved and Raymond renewed his overtures to Innocent III. Around the time of the inception of the Crusade Raymond VI had to make a public penance at St Gilles where he was forced to admit the various charges brought against him and was flogged by the papal legate at the altar of the cathedral.

To avert attack on his domain Raymond joined the crusaders until the fall of Carcassonne in August 1209, when Viscount Raymond-Roger was captured and died in captivity. The crusaders elected as leader a northern noble, Simon de Montfort, who also claimed the English earldom of Leicester. Simon was now proclaimed Viscount of Béziers and Carcassonne and he ruthlessly overran the Trencavel dominions, burning 140 *perfecti* at Minerve and many more heretics at Lavaur. In one of the most notorious murders of the Crusade the widow Geralda of Lavaur castle was condemned as the worst of the heretics, was thrown into a well and then Simon de Montfort had her buried under stones. Meanwhile, Raymond VI was excommunicated yet again for his failure to comply with the legates' orders for turning over suspect heretics for investigation. Repeatedly accused of neglecting his obligations to purge the heretics from his lands, Raymond VI could not clear himself of the renewed charges of heresy and in the spring of 1211, after a furious encounter with the bishop of Toulouse, he expelled the prelate from the city. A direct attack on Raymond's dominions now seemed inevitable and in the summer of 1211 Simon de Montfort, supported by German crusaders, briefly and unsuccessfully laid siege to Toulouse. Following his withdrawal, Toulouse was excommunicated and Simon's army was soon reinforced with fresh French and German crusaders. After a year of assiduous campaigning Simon subdued most of the county and Raymond VI was encircled in Toulouse, retaining only the castle of Montauban.

The conquests of Simon de Montfort now directly threatened the Languedoc vassalages of King Pedro II of Aragon and he put Toulouse under his protection. For a time he succeeded in prevailing over Innocent III that the heresy of Raymond VI and southern nobles like the Count of Foix and the Viscount of Béziers had not yet been proven. The pope then tried to halt the warfare in Languedoc and to restore the crusading ideal back to its original focus – a Holy War against the infidel. Innocent's intentions were frustrated by the stern resistance of his extremist legates and he had to retreat, endeavouring to persuade Pedro that the patrons of the heresy were more dangerous than the heretics themselves. The king of Aragon was fresh from the Christian victory over the Muslim Almohades at Las Navas de Tolosa and now chose to ally himself with Raymond VI, the Counts of Foix and Comminges and the Viscount of Béarn, all newly condemned as protectors of the Cathars. In September 1213, however, Simon de Montfort, although greatly outnumbered, routed the forces of the Aragon–Toulousian alliance near Toulouse and in the carnage King Pedro was slain on the battlefield, while Raymond VI and his son found protection in the court of King John of England.

In the ecumenical council held in Rome in November 1215, Raymond VI was again accused of having protected heretics and his title and domains were ceded to Simon de Montfort, while Raymond's son inherited the Marquisate of Provence. It seemed that Innocent's plans of purging Catharism from Languedoc were soon to be achieved under Simon de Montfort, who went to Paris to be invested by Philip Augustus with the titles and lands of the disgraced Raymond VI. Within a year, however, Languedoc was plunged into renewed hostilities – Innocent III died in the summer of 1216 and amid a resurgence of Occitanian patriotism Raymond VI and his son began the reconquest of the County with help from Aragon and his noble allies from Foix and Comminges. He returned to Toulouse in September 1217, where he was acclaimed by his citizens, and repelled the first onslaughts of Simon de Montfort. In the ensuing long siege of Toulouse, Simon de Montfort, already excommunicated by the other erstwhile leader of the Crusade, Arnold Aimery, launched a series of vigorous attacks on the city and was said to have pledged to reduce it to ashes. In one of the Toulousian counter-offensives, however, he was struck by a stone from a catapult and, in the words of *La Chanson de la Croisade Albigeoise*, he fell dead, 'bloodied and pallid'.[7] Simon's son, Amaury, continued the siege for four more weeks but finally retreated to

Carcassonne and within one decade lost all the dominions won by his father during the first stage of the Albigensian Crusade.

The new pope, Honorius III, called relentlessly for a new Albigensian Crusade and repeatedly appealed to Philip Augustus for intervention, but besides a brief siege of Toulouse by the French royal army in 1219, it was the old House of Toulouse that was now on the offensive in Languedoc. Having recovered much of his County, Raymond VI died in 1222 but he was not allowed to be buried in consecrated ground. In 1224 his son, Raymond VII, finally drove Amaury de Montfort out of Carcassonne and Languedoc. Fifteen years after Béziers and Carcassonne had fallen to the crusaders and Viscount Raymond-Roger had died in captivity, his son Raymond Trencavel was re-established as 'Viscount of Béziers, Carcassonne, Razès and Albi'. Two years later, however, Raymond Trencavel was himself forced out of his newly restored dominions by the French king Louis VIII and had to flee to Aragon, while the Trencavel lands passed to the French crown.

Raymond VII's attempts to seek reconciliation with the church at the Council of Bourges in 1225 were doomed by the Catholic preoccupation with the persistence of Catharism in Languedoc. In 1226 he was proclaimed a heretic, his lands were forfeited and he was excommunicated along with the Count of Foix and Raymond Trencavel. Amaury de Montfort had resigned his rights to the County of Toulouse and Honorius III and Louis VIII finally completed the Albigensian Crusade. In the summer of 1226 Louis VIII led a strong army into the Midi, seized Avignon and occupied much of Languedoc, but without attacking Toulouse itself, he returned to the north and died at the end of the year. Under the increasing pressure of the king's cousin, Humbert de Beaujeu, regent of the occupied lands, Raymond VII had to conclude with King Louis IX the 'Peace of Paris' in 1229 and was finally released from excommunication. The Peace of Paris marked the formal end of the Albigensian Crusade; Raymond VII retained the northern and western parts of the County of Toulouse, while ceding the larger territories either to the French king or to the Church. A marriage was arranged between Raymond's daughter and one of the king's brothers under regulations which ultimately secured the annexation of the whole of Languedoc by the French crown in 1271.

The final phase of the Albigensian Crusade was dominated by the expansionist policy of the French crown and thus, paradoxically, the rise and suppression of Catharism set the stage for the unification of the French north and the Midi under Capetian rule. In the Peace of Paris, moreover, Raymond VII was obliged to assist in the pursuit and prosecution of the heresy in his dominions. His coexistence with the French king, the Church and its new weapon against Catharism, the Holy Inquisition, continued to be erratic and uneasy.

Suppression and Resistance

The Albigensian Crusade might have broken or depleted the power of many greater and lesser southern nobles, some of whom were forced to became *faidits* (rebels), but its primary aim – the eradication of Catharism – was far from accomplished. The mass burnings engulfed many *perfecti* but the reversals of the Crusade did not allow extensive and lasting persecution of the Cathars. The Cathars were driven underground in the territories occupied by Simon de Montfort and many fled to Lombardy and Aragon. The beginning of the reconquest of the County of Toulouse by the two Raymonds after 1215 was bound to renew the vigour of Languedoc Catharism and led to the return of Cathar refugees who had escaped from the Crusade in Catalonia and Lombardy. The Cathar ecclesiastical organization had survived the first, more devastating, phase of the Crusade and in 1225, following the ephemeral restoration of Raymond Trencavel to his ancestral domains, a Cathar council established a new bishopric at Razès. The revival of Catharism prompted the papal legate Conrad of Porto to summon an ecclesiastical council at Sens and he wrote to leading French prelates about the activities of the Cathar bishop of Agen, Bartholomew, the apostle of moderate dualism in Languedoc.

Following the Peace of Paris, religious conditions in Languedoc changed radically; the Council of Toulouse in the same year prohibited the possession of the Bible in the vernacular among the laity and introduced a biannual oath of orthodoxy for the people of Languedoc. The imposition of the anti-heretical decrees of the council resulted in some prosecutions and executions but on the whole these remained irregular, if not half-hearted, and the Cathars continued to be protected by much of the rural nobility in Languedoc. In 1233, however, Pope Gregory IX (1227–41) established a more effective and rigorous tribunal intended to combat and extinguish heresy in Languedoc, the Inquisition. By that time, the last Holy Roman Emperor of the Hohenstaufen dynasty, Frederick II (1220–50), who called himself 'Lord of the World', had already passed laws prescribing the death penalty for intransigent heretics. In Brescia, central Lombardy, the hostility between the noble patrons of the Cathars and their enemies had flared up in 1224; indeed, military clashes and outbreaks of violence often arose from the persecution of the Cathars in Lombardy. Pope Honorius III appealed to the Lombard cities to enforce Frederick's anti-heretical legislation but it encountered strong opposition in cities like Florence and Verona. The initial onslaught of the Inquisition on Italian Catharism proceeded more slowly and was further enervated by the renewal of the papal–imperial disagreements over Lombardy in 1236 and the ensuing turmoil in Italy.

In 1231 Gregory IX appointed the confessor of St Elizabeth of Hungary, Conrad of Marburg, as the first papal Inquisitor in Germany, but Conrad's flagrant excesses in the prosecution of the heretics were to cost him his life in 1233. Another notorious figure among the early Inquisitors was the Dominican friar Robert, called *le bougre* (the Bulgar) because of his Cathar past, but also called 'the hammer of the heretics' because he had consigned many of his former co-religionists to the flames. Robert the Bulgar was active between 1233 and 1239 in northern France and Flanders; Matthew of Paris recorded that in 1238, he had caused many thousands to be burned in Flanders.[8] His mission reached its climax in 1239 when he sent 183 *bulgri* to the stake at Mont-Aime for 'a fiery offering and propitiation of God'. Their bishop conferred the *consolamentum* on the believers before being burned with them.

The persecution forced the northern French Cathar church into exile in Lombardy, while in Languedoc the Dominicans, entrusted by Gregory IX with the inquisition of heresy, faced sustained resistance. The Dominicans' founder, St Dominic, had already distinguished himself in the struggle against the spread of Catharism and his Order of the Preaching Friars, which received papal approval in 1217, provided the first inquisitors in the anti-Cathar campaign. In their inquests for heresy in suspect areas the Dominican inquisitors initially proclaimed a month of grace when those who confessed to heresy were absolved but had to disclose the identity of other heretics or their protectors. The period of grace was followed by the arraigning of the suspects, secret trials where those who confessed were subjected to various penances, while the seemingly insincere or unrepentant heretics could be cast in prison or delivered to the secular authorities for death by fire. Even dead heretics were not safe from the Inquisition – if their heresy was disclosed posthumously, their bodies were exhumed, dragged through the streets and burned.

Inevitably, from its inception the work of the Dominican Inquisition was frustrated by the overall hostile public reaction in Languedoc: in 1234 Raymond VII was already complaining to Gregory IX about their abuses. The beginning of inquisitorial pursuits in the towns of Languedoc led to protracted strife in Narbonne and the temporary expulsion of the Dominicans from Toulouse in late 1235, when Raymond VII was excommunicated again. Gregory soon negotiated with Raymond for the return of the Inquisition to Toulouse and the Dominicans came back to the turbulent city in 1236 to search out and convict heretics. The operation of the Inquisition, however, was affected by the escalating conflict between Frederick II and the pope, following the emperor's attempts to assert imperial authority over Lombardy in direct challenge to the papal interests in northern Italy. In 1237 Gregory IX, who excommunicated Frederick two years later, was in desperate need of allies and Raymond negotiated with him for the lifting of his own excommunication and the temporary suspension of the Inquisition in Toulouse, which was to continue for another three years. The Count of Toulouse could not negotiate, however, the elimination of the Dominican friars from the Inquisition in Languedoc, nor the burial of his father's body in consecrated ground.

The collision between the ageing pope and the emperor came to its climax in 1240–41 when Frederick, who had temporarily restored Jerusalem to Christendom in 1228, now directly threatened Rome. At the same time, Raymond Trencavel, who had been dispossessed on account of the long-standing association of his house with the heresy, attempted to recapture his dominions in the old Cathar heartlands in Razès and Carcassonne. He initially led a small force of knights from Aragon but after being acclaimed with enthusiasm in Razès he was joined by many rebellious lesser nobles and laid siege to Carcassonne, which was broken by the arrival of French royal troops. Raymond Trencavel was now himself besieged in Montréal in Razès but Raymond of Toulouse was able to act as an intermediary to secure his safe withdrawal to Aragon.

In the following year Raymond VII found himself engaged in the build-up of an anti-French league with the king of England, Henry III, and the count of La Marche, Hugh of Lusignan. Seeking to redraft the Paris treaty of 1229, Raymond VII was joined in his preparations for war by most of the southern nobles, including traditional allies like Raymond Trencavel and the counts of Comminges and Foix. As the war with the French armies unfolded early in the summer of 1242 the coalition suffered immediate setbacks: King Henry was defeated by King Louis at Taillebourg on 20 July and withdrew to English-held Aquitaine, while Count Hugo capitulated one month after the English defeat. Raymond of Toulouse, who was excommunicated during his campaign, had traversed Languedoc to Narbonne and had united the populace behind his cause, but with the collapse of the coalition and desertion in the ranks, he had to surrender in the autumn. Peace was concluded in early 1243 and yet again Raymond undertook the obligation to eradicate heresy in his domains.

Raymond of Trencavel's expedition in 1240 was followed by prosecution of his noble supporters and the unsuccessful war of Raymond VII decimated the power of the traditional patrons of the Cathars, the local southern nobles. Some of them, including Raymond Trencavel, joined King Louis in his Crusade to Egypt in 1248; Raymond was rewarded afterwards with some land in his ancestral fiefs. Raymond VII himself attempted to serve as an intermediary between Frederick II and the new pope Innocent IV, who rescinded his last excommunication. Otherwise, his mediation was doomed, as Frederick's camp was to proclaim Innocent IV a type of papal Antichrist, uncovering the numerical value of *Innocencius papa* as 666, while the pope identified his imperial adversary with the beasts from Revelation and in 1245 declared him dethroned and a suspected heretic, calling for a Crusade against Frederick in Germany.

In Languedoc, meanwhile, the Inquisition had recommenced its work in 1241 with renewed vigour in spite of the continuing antagonism between Raymond of Toulouse and the Dominican friars. Yet from the beginning of its institution in Languedoc the Inquisition was exposed to reprisals; while the Count of Toulouse was preparing for war against France, in May 1242 the *faidits* of the Cathar citadel of Montségur massacred the 'squad' of the inquisitors William Arnold and Stephen of St Thibery. Like the murder of the papal legate, Peter of Castelnau, in 1208 the reprisal against the *faidits* in 1242 was to have grave repercussions for the Cathar movement in Languedoc.

The Fall of Montségur

The impressive castle of Montségur was located in the northern Pyrenean foothills in the county of Foix and was held by Raymond of Pereille who had himself been accused of heresy in 1237. With its impregnable position it had long been a safe refuge for persecuted Cathars, particularly since the suppression of Catharism in Languedoc in the wake of the Peace of Paris in 1229. In 1232 the Cathar bishop of Toulouse, Guilhabert de Castres, and the heretical bishop of Agen, Tento I, moved their sees to Montségur, which became the centre of the Cathar movement where the *perfecti* practised Cathar ceremonies and granted the *consolamentum* to tested or dying believers. Protection from a strong garrison gathered from the *faidits* was reinforced by new rebels after the collapse of Raymond Trencavel's campaign in 1240. The commander of the castle was the son-in-law of Raymond of Pereille, the *faidit* Peter Roger of Mirapoix, who apparently maintained relations with other militant malcontents opposed to the French presence in Languedoc, like the seneschal of Raymond VII at Avignotet, Raymond of Alfaro.

Amid the flurry of expectations of Raymond VII's offensive against France, Raymond of Alfaro informed the commander of

Montségur of the arrival at his castle of a group led by the two well-known and feared inquisitors, the Dominican William Arnold and the Franciscan Stephen of St Thibery. Peter Roger sent an armed force to Avignotet that was admitted into the castle and killed the two inquisitors and their nine companions but failed to bring to Peter Roger the skull of William of Arnold, which he had intended to convert into a drinking cup.

As with the fatal murder of Peter of Castelnau in 1207, rumours implicated the count of Toulouse in the killings at Avignotet but it is hardly credible that Raymond would risk his search for allies on the eve of war with France with such a flagrant act. Otherwise, in Languedoc the death of the inquisitors was met with rejoicing coupled with intense anticipation of the impending hostilities with France, while the Dominicans requested permission from Innocent IV to leave the Midi. The subsequent defeat of the anti-French coalition sealed the fate of Montségur: several months after the peace between King Louis and Raymond of Toulouse, Montségur was besieged by the royal seneschal of Carcassonne. With its impregnable position on a high plateau the castle of Montségur defied immediate conquest and the seneschal prepared for a long and exhausting siege. The besiegers could not prevent further supplies being brought into the castle or messages from other Cathar communities. At one stage, a Cathar bishop from Cremona offered refuge in Lombardy to Guilhabert de Castres' successor to the see of Toulouse, Bertrand Marty, but Bertrand preferred to stay in Montségur.

Rumours that the count of Toulouse, then mediating between Frederick II and Innocent IV, would come to the rescue were unfounded and hopes of help from mercenaries failed to materialize. After nine months the situation of the besieged Cathars and the defending *faidits* was becoming untenable and Raymond of Pereille and Peter Roger began to sue for terms. The reputed Cathar treasure, probably along with secret Cathar writings, had already been clandestinely carried away from Montségur; according to the agreed terms of surrender the defenders from the garrison were granted amnesty and safe passage from the castle, but were to give confessions before the Inquisition. The *perfecti* were offered the choice of recanting or facing death by burning. During the negotiations about twenty people received the *consolamentum* and chose 'baptism by fire'. With the enforcement of the agreement of the surrender of Montségur three or four *perfecti* made a daring secret escape, possibly connected with the Cathar 'treasure'. More than two hundred *perfecti* remained who, besides the bishop of Toulouse, included the bishop of Razès, Raymond Aguilher. They were burned, most probably in the town of Bram, but according to tradition the mass burning took place at the foot of the mountain in the so-called 'Field of the Cremated'.

If not yet the Catholic *coup de grâce*, the fall of Montségur and the cremation of such a large section of the Cathar élite dealt a severe blow to Catharism in Languedoc. The capture of the Cathar citadel was followed by large-scale inquisitorial campaigns in Languedoc during 1245–6 which were directed from the two new centres of the Inquisition in Toulouse and Carcassonne. The officials of Raymond VII now assisted the inquisitors more readily and, after a reign which had at least delayed and obstructed the wholesale persecution of Catharism in his county, in 1249, the year of his death, he himself ordered the burning of eighty heretics at Agen. Despite his late ardour, however, Raymond VII failed to secure the Christian burial of his father and his coffin remained in the precincts of the Knights of St John outside Toulouse.

In 1237 the Inquisition had already penetrated one of the centres of refuge for the persecuted Cathars, to the south of the Pyrenees in the Catalonian dominions of Viscount Arnold of Castelbo. The viscount had been a vigorous champion of the Cathars and when his daughter Ermessinda, herself a Cathar believer, married Roger-Bernard II of Foix, the Cathars continued their activities largely unabated. However, in 1237 the Dominican friars finally initiated their inquests in the viscounty of Castelbo which led to the imprisonment of forty-five heretics and the customary exhumation and burning of their dead co-sectarians.[9]

With the Inquisition operating in Catalonia and Aragon, many Cathars were forced to flee to Lombardy, where the continuing strife between the papacy and Hohenstaufens did not permit a concerted inquisitorial campaign. In about 1250, according to the *Summa* of the inquisitor Rainerius Sacchoni, the number of Cathar *perfecti* in the old churches of Albi, Toulouse and Carcassonne – along with that of Agen, which was 'almost totally destroyed' – exceeded two hundred, matching the number burned after the fall of Montségur. In contrast, the Cathar *perfecti* in Italy, including those of the exiled church of northern France, still numbered around 2,550.

The fall of Montségur marked the beginning of the real decline of Catharism in Languedoc. Despite intermittent resistance to the inquisitorial procedures and the tension between Innocent IV and the inquisitors in Languedoc, which led to a brief suspension of the Dominican Inquisition in the area between 1249 and 1255, Catharism was soon largely driven underground. The wandering missions of the *perfecti* were becoming exceedingly dangerous, although they had already exchanged their distinctive black robes for a black girdle worn next to the body. The centre of western dualism was now in Lombardy, while the crusading projects of the papacy against Balkan dualism had proved abortive.

Rome and the Balkan Heresy

Besides the 2,550 western dualist *perfecti* Rainerius Sacchoni reckoned that there were 500 in the eastern dualist churches of the Greeks, of Sclavonia, Philadelphia, Bulgaria and Drugunthia, while the Latin Church of Constantinople comprised less than fifty. During the anti-Bogomil council of 1211 the Bogomils were accused of performing 'unholy mysteries like the hellenic pagan rites' and the continuing Bogomil activity in Anatolia and Constantinople prompted Patriarch Germanus (1220–40) to warn the citizens of Constantinople against the 'dark mysteries' of the 'satanic Bogomil heresy'. From his residence in Nicaea he sent an encyclical to Constantinople, to be read in the churches on Sundays and feast days, where he condemned the Bogomil heresy as a 'stinging snake, pestering and corroding the body of the Orthodox Church'.[10]

The measures of the Council of 1211 apparently failed to suppress *Ecclesia Bulgariae*: Pope Gregory IX eventually came to accuse the Bulgarian Tsar Ivan Asen II (1218–41) of harbouring the heretics in his realm. To the anger of Gregory, Ivan Asen had released the Bulgarian Church from its allegiance to the Roman See and in about

1235, when he was the most powerful Balkan monarch, he directly threatened the Latin Kingdom of Jerusalem. Having recently insti-gated the Inquisition in Languedoc, Gregory IX prevailed on the Hungarian King Bela IV to launch a Crusade against the Bulgarian empire where, according to the pope, the whole land was 'infected' by heretics.[11] Bela IV accepted the role of the defender of the faith and Gregory IX praised his resolve to lead a Crusade against 'the blasphemous nation, the heretics and the schismatics ruled over by Ivan Asen II'.[12] Bela IV began to muster an army in Hungary but the Crusade, conceived by Gregory IX as a new 'Holy War' against heresy, was foiled by the diplomatic moves of the Bulgarian Tsar.

The projected Crusade against the Bulgarian empire may have failed to materialize, but the papacy had already succeeded in summoning Hungarian arms in a Crusade against the heresy in Bosnia. The reconciliation of the Bosnian ruler Kulin with Rome in 1203 had prevented the projected military intervention of the Hun-garian King Henry, and in the words of F. Racki, the Catholic Church 'did not find in Kulin a Bosnian Raymond and in King Henry a Simon de Montfort'.[13] In 1211 the bishop of Bosnia was already reported to have encountered a strong presence of the Patarene heresy in the land and in about 1225 Pope Honorius III urged the Hungarian archbishop of Kalocsa, Ugrin, to take immedi-ate measures against the spread of the heresy in Bosnia. According to Conrad of Porto's letter of 1223 a dualist antipope in the western Balkans, in all probability the bishop of *Ecclesia Sclavoniae*, was involved in the affairs of Languedoc Catharism. A Crusade against Bosnia, to be led in 1227 by the Byzantine prince John Angelus, failed to be established although Archbishop Ugrin had already paid 200 marks to the prince.[14]

The Crusade against Bosnia became a reality in 1235, although two years earlier the Bosnian Ban Ninoslav had followed in the footsteps of Ban Kulin and had abjured his heretical ways, embraced Catholicism and promised to persecute the heretics in Bosnia. Apparently this act had been formal, as in 1235 Gregory IX offered indulgences to the crusaders that were to fight the heretics in 'Slavonia' and a crusading army led by the son of the Hungarian King Andrew, the Duke of Croatia, Coloman, invaded Bosnia. The Crusade promptly unified the Bosnian nobility in opposition to both Rome and Hungary, as in 1236 the pope referred to a Bosnian prince and his mother as the only good Catholics in Bosnia, who, amid the heresy-infected Bosnian nobility, were like 'lilies among thorns'. The course of the Crusade is rather obscure, but in 1238 Gregory IX claimed victory and was planning to erect a cathedral chapter in conquered central Bosnia at Vrhbosna (modern Sarajevo). Like the Albigensian Crusade, the Crusade against Bosnia quickly became a war of conquest, but while losing territories to the Hungarians, Ban Ninoslav retained his hold on parts of the banate. Towards the end of 1238 the pope proclaimed that Ninoslav had relapsed into heresy and appealed to Duke Coloman to persecute the heretics in Bosnia. A year later Dominican friars were sent to Bosnia to fight the heresy. The persecution was confined to the Hungarian-occupied area of Bosnia and did not last more than three years, since in 1241 Hungary suffered a disastrous Tartar invasion, in which both the crusading champions of Rome, Coloman and Archbishop Ugrin, were killed on the battlefield.

The Hungarian crusaders had to withdraw from the occupied Bosnian areas; the Crusade seemed to have achieved nothing but increased anti-Roman feelings in Bosnia. In 1246 Innocent IV began moves to subject the Bosnian diocese to the archbishopric of Kalocsa and appealed both to the new archbishop and King Bela IV to resume the Crusade against the heretics in Bosnia. One year later, Innocent IV praised the archbishop of Kalocsa for his endeavours at eradicating – with great bloodshed and at great expense – the heresy into which the Bosnian Church had totally lapsed. The Pope stated that large parts of Bosnia were captured and many heretics were banished but the Catholic fortifications still could not resist the attacks of the heretics. Little is known of the course of the Hungarian Crusade in Bosnia,[15] but what is clear is that while Languedoc had been finally subdued by the Inquisition, the Crusade in Bosnia failed to reach its objective and in March 1248 it was suddenly halted by Innocent, as Ninoslav had again reconfirmed his Catholicism and claimed that he had favoured the heretics only as allies against foreign invasions.

Ninoslav's manoeuvres seemed to successfully check, for a time, the Hungarian and Catholic pressure on Bosnia, where the religious conditions remained extremely complicated. Religious tolerance was an overall characteristic feature of medieval Bosnian society and pagan beliefs and customs persisted side by side and mixed with Christian and heretical traditions. When the Catholic observers referred to 'heresy' in Bosnia it is not always clear whether they were alluding to outright heretical traditions like Bogomilism, to blends of Christian and pagan beliefs or to heterodox practices of the Bosnian Christians. What is certain, however, is that the Hungarian Crusades were launched against the dualist movement in Bosnia and Dalmatia where, according to the testimony of the Dominican prior Suibert,[16] *Ecclesia Sclavoniae* was active and where many souls were destroyed by 'heretical errors'.

The Decline of Catharism

Upon the death of Raymond VII in 1249 the county was inherited by his daughter Jeanne and her Capetian husband Alphonse of Poitier; when they died childless in 1270 it became part of the French kingdom. In the latter half of the thirteenth century the Inquisition perfected its machinery of suppression and enriched its procedures with the introduction in 1252 of the authorized but regulated use of torture, to be applied first in Italy and then in France. With the relentless expansion of the inquisitorial pursuits in Languedoc more Cathar *perfecti* and believers fled from Languedoc for the more secure Italy, but soon the conditions for survival in Lombardy worsened radically.

The Italian Cathars had long profited from the strife – which raged from 1236 to 1268 – between the papacy and the House of Hohenstaufen, and which was reflected in the political division between the Guelphs and the Ghibellines. Despite his harsh heresy laws and denouncement of the heretics in their seedbed of Milan, Frederick II was far from the 'hammer of the heretics', although he did use the heretical problem in his propaganda war against the papacy. The Lombardian cities, which played a major role in the papal–imperial conflict, saw only sporadic enactment of his heresy laws, while amid the battle for allies in Lombardy the papacy did not risk demands for full-scale prosecutions of the heresy.

The Cathars often associated with the imperial Ghibelline party and, as in Languedoc, their most common protectors were to be found among the rural nobility. The fortunes of Italian Catharism were, however, to be shaken in the aftermath of the dramatic conclusion of the battle between the papacy and the Hohenstaufen dynasty. Frederick II died in 1250 and his successor as king of Germany, Conrad IV, continued the struggle against the great adversary of the 'Hohenstaufen eaglet', Innocent IV, but died after four years, although not before being excommunicated by the pope. Both his son Conradin and Frederick's illegitimate son Manfred met their deaths in their fight against the champion of the Guelph or papal faction, Charles of Anjou. With the fall of the House of Hohenstaufen the papal party inevitably gained ascendancy and by the end of the century the Inquisition was operating in most cities. Although the Italian Cathars retained some of their patrons and were occasionally able to fight the persecution, the series of anti-heretical trials, although not so sweeping as in Languedoc, steadily depleted the strength of the sect. As in Languedoc the severest blow to the Cathars was a strike at their major sectarian centre in the castle of Sirmione at the lake of Garda which was followed by a mass burning of 178 captured *perfecti*. Among those burned was the last acknowledged Cathar bishop of Toulouse.

Around the time of the successive anti-heretical trials in Bologna towards the end of the thirteenth century, a Cathar *perfectus*, Peter Autier, returned to Languedoc and instigated a brief Cathar renascence centred mainly in the county of Foix. Braving the vigilant and experienced organs of the Inquisition, which had just encountered renewed opposition in Albi and Carcassonne, Peter Autier endeavoured to revive Catharism in secret missionary journeys throughout Languedoc but his mission was mostly confined to the classes of the peasants and artisans. It took the Inquisition nearly fifteen years of relentless pursuit to capture the last major Cathar apostle and his companions. Peter Autier was burned in 1311, while Guillaume Bélibaste, usually considered as the last Cathar *perfectus*, escaped to Catalonia, but was later enticed to return to Languedoc, betrayed to the Inquisition and burned in Toulouse in 1321. One of the last great enemies of Catharism and heresy in Languedoc, the inquisitor Bernard Gui, is recorded between 1308 and 1323 as having pronounced 930 sentences against heretics, among which forty-two were death penalties. In Italy the last known western heretical bishop was captured in 1321 and thereafter heretical communities survived in remote Pyrenean and Alpine areas, although some Cathars found refuge in Sicily during the reign of Frederico III of Aragon (1296–1337).

While the assiduous work of the Inquisition could largely be blamed for extinguishing Catharism in Languedoc, the Cathar decline was conditioned also by other factors, such as the rise of new spiritual currents in Catholicism that seem to have counterbalanced the traditional dualist charms of Catharism. At the same time, ever since the heretics of Orléans had been charged with unnatural practices and Devil-worship in 1022, the tendency of associating heresy with witchcraft had been growing, to lead to an amalgamation between them in the fourteenth-century inquisitorial procedures. With the gradual demonization of the medieval dualists and the orthodox assimilation of heresy to witchcraft, Cathar dualism was to play an important role in the very shaping of the medieval concept of witchcraft, as charges brought against the heretics were to be transferred to the alleged Devil-worshipping witches. In the Catholic records descriptions appeared of 'Luciferian' sects in whose beliefs the traditional Bogomil–Cathar dualism of the evil demiurge of the material world and the transcendent good God appeared in a reversed form, and where Lucifer was revered and expected to be restored to heaven, while Michael and the archangels would duly be deposed to hell. Whether such dualism 'of the left hand' really existed as a derivation from decadent forms of Catharism or was formulated in the inquisitorial imagination is still being debated.[17] The direct or indirect impact of the Bogomil–Cathar vision of Satan as a creator and master of the material world on the formation of the witchcraft paradigms, elaborated during the ensuing great witch-craze, seems apparent, although they represent a complete reversal of the dualist tenets of the Great Heresy. Moreover, in political trials, such as the suppression of the Knights Templar in 1307–14, the accusations comprised a curious combination of allegations of witchcraft and heresy, some of which evidently reflected earlier charges against the Cathars.[18]

While in western Christendom the dualist teachings of defeated

Catharism were to be assimilated in the new demonological and witchcraft models, in the Balkan cradle of medieval dualism Bogomilism endured for at least another 150 years and persistent Catholic traditions continued to allude to a supreme dualist pontiff residing in the Balkans.

The Antipope

During the suppression of Catharism by the Holy Inquisition the activities of the Bogomil churches in the Balkan–Byzantine world understandably remained a matter of continuous inquisitorial concern. Not only did the inquisitorial authorities consider these communities as mother-churches of all dualist churches in western Europe, but they also believed, as has been attested in a number of Catholic records, that the persecuted western dualists could find the *consolamentum* and safe refuge in the eastern dualist churches. What is more, some Catholic observers believed in the existence of a secret antipope, a supreme Albigensian or Bogomil pope, whose residence was in the Balkans. While the title ascribed to the heresiarch of absolute dualism, Nicetas, 'Papa Haereticorum', is apparently a mistranslation of the Greek *papas* (priest), some scholars have maintained that the medieval dualist churches had a supreme head and it has even been argued that all southern Europe was 'parcelled out into Manichaean dioceses whose bishops paid allegiance to a Manichaean pope seated in Bulgaria'.[19]

In one of the early outbreaks of heresy in the west – the activities of the heretics from the Montfort castle in 1028 – their representative, Gerard, had proclaimed, 'There is no pontiff beside our Pontiff, though he is without tonsure of the head or any sacred mystery',[20] but it is usually assumed that he was referring to the Holy Ghost. In 1143, during the first certain discernment of Catharism in Cologne, Eberwin of Steinfeld stated in his appeal to St Bernard of Clairvaux that the heretics who were called apostles had their own pope; the Calabrian mystic Joachim of Fiore also shared the belief in one supreme heretical pontiff.

The warning of Cardinal Conrad of Porto in 1223 about the rise of an Albigensian antipope in the western Balkans most probably referred to the heretical bishop of *Ecclesia Sclavoniae*.

In 1387 the Cathar Jacob Bech, from one of the last dualist communities in northern Italy (which was in constant contact with *Ecclesia Sclavoniae*), confirmed before his *auto-da-fé* that the dualists denied the authority of the Roman pope and had their own *Papa Major*.[21] As late as 1461 three heretical Bosnian noblemen were sent to Rome and among the fifty heretical articles that they rejected before Cardinal Torquemada was the belief that the heretics were the successors to the Apostles and that their heresiarch, 'the Bishop of the Church', was the true successor of Peter.[22]

The possibility that the medieval neo-Manichaean movement had a supreme leader, similar to the *archegos* of Manichaeism, has been much debated but generally the evidence is found insufficient and illustrates the lack of data about the internal history of the Bogomil movement. Yet the image of the dualist antipope residing in the Balkans remained central to the Catholic perception of the movement and was reiterated by Bossuet even in the seventeenth century, while *Papa* Nicetas, the apostle of absolute dualism in the west, came to personify the image of the '*Antipape des Hérétiques Albigeois*'.

The association of the supposed heretical antipope with Bosnia, moreover, seems hardly surprising – following the final victory of Catholicism over Catharism in Languedoc and Lombardy in the early thirteenth century, Bosnia became for Rome the irredeemable land of heresy, or in the words of Pope Urban v (1362–70), 'the cesspool of heresy of all parts of the world'.[23]

The Bosnian Church and
Ecclesia Sclavoniae

Between 1235 and 1248 Bosnia was subjected to political and religious invasions but through force of circumstances and political moves, Ban Ninoslav succeeded in reversing the course of the two Crusades that Rome had launched against Bosnia. Following his death in about 1250, however, Bosnia fell under direct Hungarian suzerainty and was divided into separate administrative areas or banates. With the accession of the adolescent King Ladislas (1272–90) Hungary itself entered a period of insecurity and internal strife that could hardly have been conducive to supervising Bosnian religious affairs. None the less, the papacy continued to urge the Hungarian court to take measures against the heresy in Bosnia and in 1280 the king's mother, Elisabeth, assured Pope Nicholas III of her intention to persecute heretics in her dominions, which included Bosnia. King Ladislas himself ordered persecution of various religious sects in the kingdom, particularly in the diocese of Bosnia, but if any action was taken its results remain unknown.

In 1282 the Orthodox king of Serbia, Stefan Dragutin, was forced to abdicate, but the Hungarian king entrusted him with important banates in Bosnia and he was credited with converting heretics in Bosnia. He requested, moreover, aid from Rome against the heretics and their patrons and was sent a Franciscan mission charged with searching out and fighting the heresy in the western Balkans. Dragutin's son-in-law, Stjepan Kotroman, was related to the old lineage of Ninoslav and in the early fourteenth century blocked the attempts of Croatian nobles to occupy all Bosnian territory. His son, Stjepan Kotromanić, who was Orthodox by faith, was supported by the first Hungarian Anjou king, Charles I, and gradually manoeuvred himself into being Ban of Bosnia. He extended his sway into Dalmatia and, profiting from internal struggle in Serbia, in 1321 took over Serbian-ruled Hum (modern Herzegovina), then predominantly Orthodox.

By the time Bosnia had become a strong Balkan state under Kotromanić, another religious factor had entered the Bosnian scene – the Bosnian church. The origins and nature of the Bosnian church are still debated: according to an early established and still widely held view, it was a result of the evolution of the Bogomil movement in Bosnia – the *Ecclesia Sclavoniae* of the inquisitors – into a national Bosnian church which in about 1250 'displaced Catholicism as the established religion'.[24] This view has been subjected to sustained criticism which rejects the dualist nature of the Church of Bosnia but admits the presence of a dualist movement in the religious life of medieval Bosnia and its potential influences on the Bosnian church.[25] In this view it emerged as a reaction against the Hungarian

Crusades but was based on the earlier Catholic monastic movement in Bosnia and developed in isolation from east and west. Another view posits a merger between the earlier Catholic monastic organization in Bosnia and the dualist movement during the Hungarian Crusade which resulted in its formation, based on the earlier Catholic monastic order but it also had some dualist features, particularly in its theology.[26] What is certain is that the Bosnian church, established in an area where the spheres of influence of the western and eastern churches met, was schismatic from both Catholicism and Orthodoxy and had its own hierarchy, its head, *dyed*, presiding over the lesser ranks of *gost*, *starac* and *strojnik*. The members of the Bosnian church were often referred to as Patarenes, the customary name for the Italian Cathars, and were sometimes associated with heterodox and heretical beliefs and practices. As with much of the religious life of medieval Bosnia, the beliefs and the practices of the Bosnian church remain elusive but they were condemned as heretical by Rome and occasionally also by the Serbian Orthodox church. For medieval Catholic observers the Bosnian church was a dualist organization and in Pope Pius' opus *Europa* the Bosnian heretics were described as living in monasteries and as being 'Manichees', believers in two principles, 'the one good and the other evil'.[27] Indeed it later acquired a Slavonic ritual[28] that bears a close resemblance to the Cathar Ritual of Lyons and was certainly brought to Bosnia by Bogomil sectarians. Some of the practices attributed to members of the Bosnian church at various stages – rejection of the veneration of icons and the cross, proscription of swearing vows – certainly betray dualist influences, but on the whole the organization, conduct and recorded beliefs of the Bosnian church differ from those of the traditional dualist churches. Yet the dualist movement in Bosnia certainly enjoyed a high reputation among the western Cathar churches and in 1325 John XXII declared that many Cathars were flocking to Bosnia which has been seen sometimes as a dualist 'Promised Land'.[29] The last Cathar communities in Piedmont maintained contacts with Bosnia and their heresy was defined as 'the faith of the heretics of Bosnia'. The Bosnian dualist movement outlasted not only western Catharism but also the Bogomil communities to the east – but still the problem of its association with the actual Bosnian church remains a puzzle. The evidence allows different solutions and even when regarded as an independent body from the dualist sect in Bosnia, the Bosnian church could still have maintained relations with the dualists and may have acquired practices or beliefs from them,[30] an interchange that may have led to the emergence of the dualist currents within the Bosnian church itself.

The problem of the origins and the nature of the Bosnian church remains unresolved and while it is certain that it cannot be considered a typical dualist church, it is equally certain that it was not merely an offshoot of a Catholic order which had broken with Rome. The evidence indicates that members of the Bosnian church could adhere to orthodox Christian beliefs and practices, but could, at times, also follow heretical, dualist or pagan traditions, surviving pagan elements remaining particularly active in the diverse religious world of medieval Bosnia. The view that the dualist movement and the monastic order in Bosnia fused to form the Bosnian church in the turmoil of the Hungarian Crusade answers most of the puzzles associated with the Bosnian church, if it is accepted, of course, that the newly formed church gradually abandoned some of its dualist beliefs and practices on its way to becoming an established ecclesiastical body. In this case the crusading designs and ventures in Bosnia not only failed but backfired by leading to a fusion of its own former Catholic order with the dualist sect, which was to have been eradicated, to a creation of a rival church in Bosnia preventing Rome from establishing firm control. At the same time, a dualist sect, with limited influence, might have remained independent from the Bosnian church, but still capable of exerting influence on members of the church and perhaps of reviving dualist concepts in its theology.

Whatever the truth about its beginnings, the first certain signs of the existence of an organized Bosnian church appeared around 1322, while three years later Pope John XXII wrote to the Bosnian Ban and the Hungarian king that numerous heretics from many different regions were flocking to the Bosnian state.[31] This report of a heretical influx into Bosnia at the same time as the Inquisition was extinguishing the last visible traces of Catharism in Languedoc and Lombardy cannot, of course, be ascertained but it is a testimony to the papal distress with the religious situation in Bosnia which was seen as allowing refuge for persecuted heretics and becoming a centre of the heretical diaspora. Several years later the Dominicans and the Franciscans began to vie for the right of sending missions to Bosnia. Ultimately the inquisitorial contest was won by the Franciscans. Whatever the success of the Franciscan mission, in 1337 Pope Boniface XII was already appealing to several strong Croatian nobles to aid the Franciscans in Bosnia with military force, as the Ban and part of the nobility were protecting the heretics. The swift military action of the Bosnian Ban prevented any Croatian interference but the Ban soon deemed it necessary to sanction the foundation of a Franciscan vicariate in Bosnia and accepted Catholicism himself.

The Bosnian state established by Kotromanić was rather decentralized and soon after his death Bosnia and Hungary found themselves vying for the fealty of vassals in northern Bosnia, and eventually his Catholic successor, Tvrtko, had to recognize the suzerainty of the Hungarian King Louis the Great in 1357. Yet warfare between Bosnia and Hungary flared up in 1363 and upon his invasion, Louis, the most notable of the Hungarian Anjou kings, pledged to annihilate what was seen as the great number of heretics and Patarenes in Bosnia. The Hungarian onslaught was repelled and during a period of political vicissitudes Tvrtko was accused by his own brother of accepting and defending heretics who flocked to his domain. Despite the continuing papal complaints of the heresy in Bosnia and appeals for Hungarian intervention, Tvrtko began to expand his sway into Serbia, annexing more Orthodox territory. After a period of ascendancy in the Balkans, Serbian power was in decline and after the death of the great Serbian ruler Stefan IV Dushan in 1355 the end of the royal Nemanjid dynasty came in 1371. On account of his relation to the dynasty, Tvrtko, already married to a Bulgarian Orthodox princess, laid claim to the Serbian kingship and in 1377 was crowned by an Orthodox metropolitan, king of Serbia, Bosnia and the 'coastal lands'.

There are many indications that while the Franciscan mission had made some headway in central Bosnia, Catholicism remained underdeveloped in the country. In 1373 the Franciscan vicar revealed to the pope that in Bosnia Catholic converts had to profess Catholicism in secret and to publicly perform heretical rites like 'adoring heretics', an obvious allusion to the Cathar rite of the *melioramentum*, described by the inquisitors as 'adoration'. However, Tvrtko tolerated different faiths in his realm and Pope Gregory IX was notified that while attending Catholic services, the Ban was sometimes accompanied by heretics and Patarenes.

That activity of the dualist movement during Tvrtko's rule is verified by the testimony of the procedures of the Inquisition against an Italian Cathar community in Chieri, Piedmont, in 1387. The trial against the Piedmont Cathars coincided with the appearance of two Catholic polemical tracts against the Bosnian Patarenes and their dualist beliefs. One of the Piedmont Cathars, Jacob Bech, revealed before the Inquisition in Turin that he had been converted by two Italian heretics and one from 'Sclavonia' and that some of his co-sectarians had already gone to Bosnia to be initiated into the heretical teachings. Bech was sentenced for following the teachings of the Cathars and 'the heretics of Sclavonia' and later the Inquisition actually found and burned the remains of one of the Chieri Cathars who had gone to Sclavonia to accept the 'faith of the heretics of Bosnia'.[32]

Whereas the Bosnian dualists apparently maintained some contacts with the remaining Cathars in northern Italy, their relations with their Balkan co-sectarians to the east remain obscure. In a turbulent century, which was to be sealed with the momentous victories of Islam in the Balkans, the encounters between the Orthodox Church and the dualist tradition entered their final stages.

The Hesychast Mystics and the Bogomils

In 1261 the Nicaean Emperor Michael III restored the Byzantine empire under the Palaeologus dynasty (1261–1453), but increasingly weakened by internal civic and religious dissension it never reached its past imperial glory. In the second half of the thirteenth century the Bulgarian empire entered another 'Time of Trouble' but when it recovered towards the beginning of the fourteenth century it was overshadowed by the rise of Serbia as the dominant Balkan power.

In the first half of the fourteenth century the Orthodox Church was plagued by new theological controversies provoked by the emphatic revival of the Byzantine mystical tradition in the teachings of the Hesychast mystics. The Hesychasts elaborated the monastic contemplative tradition of the inner mystical prayer (*hesychia*) associated with the perpetual recitation of the Jesus Prayer, 'Lord Jesus Christ, Son of God, have mercy on me, a sinner'. While Hesychast doctrine and practice is emphatically contemplative, some Hesychast method of inner prayer prescribes bodily postures and breathing control for achieving the necessary concentration during the prayer. The ultimate aim of the Hesychast contemplation was the communion with the divine and Hesychasm found its influential theological systematization in Palamism, the mystical teachings of the theologian St Gregory Palamas (1294–1357), the spiritual descendant of Symeon the Theologian. In Palamism God's essence remains inaccessible but the inner prayer could lead the mystic to a vision of God's uncreated light, transfiguration and salvation. Hesychasm was widespread in Byzantine monastic circles but its stronghold was the great monastic centre of Mount Athos in north-east Greece, the 'Holy Mountain' of Orthodoxy.

The increasing prominence of Hesychast mysticism was bitterly confronted by the anti-Palamite faction in the Orthodox Church, headed by Barlaam of Calabria, Gregory Akyndinus and the historian Nicephorus Gregoras. Among other arguments, the anti-Palamite party tried to associate the Hesychast focus on inner prayer and the deification of the mystic with Massalianism, then routinely identified with Bogomilism. Gregory Palamas himself condemned Massalianism as teaching that man could behold the unknowable essence of God and is reported to have defeated 'Massalians' in theological debates in one of the monasteries of Thrace. Indeed the reaction to Hesychasm within the Orthodox Church also reflected the concern of some Byzantine ecclesiastical circles with the extreme monastic mysticism that was viewed as fertile ground for the emergence of heresy.

Massalian and Bogomil propaganda in the monasteries had a long history and in the first half of the fourteenth century the sectarian preachers encroached even on the spiritual bastion of Orthodox monasticism and Hesychasm, the Holy Mountain of Athos. Converted to the 'Massalian heresy' in Thessalonica, a number of Athonite monks propagated the heresy in the monasteries of Mount

Athos for three years. The spread of the heresy was eventually checked by a special council which anathematized the heretics and banished them from the Holy Mountain. Following their expulsion the disgraced Athonite monks scattered from Constantinople to Thessalonica and Bulgaria. The prominent anti-Hesychast Nicephorus Gregoras alleged that even the champion of Hesychasm, Gregory Palamas, being a covert heretic himself, had to leave Mount Athos and hide in Thessalonica.

The Hesychast controversies attained political dimensions during the civil strife in Byzantium between 1341 and 1347, when Gregory Palamas was excommunicated, cast into prison and his Hesychast teachings condemned. The Council of 1347, however, released Palamas from his excommunication and supported Hesychasm, while excommunicating the prominent anti-Hesychast Akyndinos. Yet the two parties in the Church clashed again during the Council of 1351 when under Patriarch Callistus, Palamism was sanctioned again and the 'rationalist' teachings of Barlaam of Calabria were condemned. Yet the anti-Palamite faction continued to be active and even sought to discredit Patriarch Callistus with accusations of heresy. In an episode similar to the twelfth-century deposition of Cosmas Atticus, one of Callistus' closest allies in Constantinople, the monk Niphon Scorpio, who had already been accused of Bogomilism, came to be accused of Massalianism by the Athonite monks. Niphon Scorpio had formerly spent some years at Mount Athos and the exhaustive enquiries of the Athonite monks had found evidence that he had indeed been one of the heretical monks. The Patriarch faced the allegations of the anti-Hesychast faction but unlike Cosmas Atticus three centuries earlier he secured the final condemnation of his adversaries.[33] By the time Gregory Palamas, who had been raised as the archbishop of Thessalonica, was canonized in 1368, his great adversary Nicephorus Gregoras had died, anathematized and under house arrest, and his corpse had been dragged through the streets of Constantinople.

One of the key figures of the Hesychast movement, St Theodosius of Trnovo, also led the battle against Bogomilism and heresy in the fourteenth century.[34] An old ally of Patriarch Callistus, St Theodosius endeavoured to establish Hesychasm and confronted an array of heretical preachers. A monk called Theodoret attacked Hesychasm, and his own teachings, with their pagan and magical character, gained ground in the higher classes. He was banished by St Theodosius but another monk, Theodosius, after a period of asceticism, embarked on large-scale evangelization, denounced marriage and taught his adherents to follow him naked. Inevitably, he was accused of encouraging indiscriminate promiscuity, but it seems that he was preaching return to the 'paradisal state'. Even more dangerous were the preachings of two monks, Lazarus and Cyril the Barefooted, who had been ejected earlier along with the other heretical monks from Mount Athos. The two ex-Athonite monks, who were joined by a priest called Stefan, claimed to follow the ideal of apostolic poverty and incessant prayer, teaching that dreams were divine visions. They were also charged with various excessive teachings varying from the indispensability of castration to the necessary submission to the 'natural passions'. In the Council convened in 1350 by St Theodosius, approved by the Bulgarian Tsar Ivan Alexander (1331–71), the heretical trio was accused of professing the radical dualist belief in two principles, but confusingly the recorded doctrine refers to the good God presiding over the earth and his adversary reigning in heaven. The dualism and anti-sacramentalism of the heretics were, however, drastically dissociated from the customary Bogomil asceticism and rigorous morality. Following the Council and the encounter with St Theodosius Lazarus recanted, while the priest Stefan and Cyril were branded on the face and expelled from the realm.

During the decade following the Council St Theodosius had to acknowledge the rise of a powerful Judaizing movement related to a critical dynastic collision in the royal family – Tsar Ivan Alexander had cloistered his Tsaritsa in a monastery and had married a Jewess. Having succeeded in fostering the growth of Hesychasm in Bulgaria, St Theodosius eventually prevailed on the Tsar to convoke another Council in 1360 which anathematized the anti-Hesychasts along with the Bogomils and the Judaizers. The anti-Hesychasts and the Bogomils were proclaimed banished from Bulgaria, whereas the three leaders of the Judaizing movement were originally sentenced to death but were later reprieved by the Tsar; one of them repented and was converted to Orthodoxy, another was murdered by a mob and the third suffered mutilation. Some of the charges levelled against the Judaizers – the rejection of the churches, the clergy, the sacraments, the icons – reiterated traditional accusations against Bogomilism and the Council of 1360 is accordingly seen sometimes as being summoned against an association of the Judaizing and Bogomil movements.[35]

The banishing of the Bogomils from Bulgaria doubtless resulted in persecution but their scale and course remain unknown. Anti-Bogomil measures were also taken in neighbouring Serbia – a Serbian code of law, dating from the mid fourteenth century, provided different punishments, from branding to exile, for the followers of Bogomilism, condemned in the document as the 'Babun faith'.[36] There are some indications that Bogomil refugees moved to the newly established Walachian principality to the north of the Danube and thereafter their fortunes in Bulgaria largely disappear from the records. When in 1365 the king of Hungary, Louis the Great, occupied parts of north-west Bulgaria he introduced Franciscan missions aimed at the conversion of numerous Patarenes and 'Manichaeans' to Catholicism. After his prolonged battle against the sectarian enemies of Orthodoxy St Theodosius died in 1363 but even from his deathbed he was warning against the ever-dangerous Bogomil–Massalian heresy.

During the patriarchate of one of his eminent disciples, Patriarch Euthymius (1375–93), the Bulgarian empire enjoyed a remarkably flourishing culture but heretical preachers continued to enjoy prominence. Particularly influential were the teachings of two vigorous heretical preachers, Phudul and Piropul, who shared the anti-clerical tenets of the Bogomils but were also renowned for their magic practices. Their teachings and rites of 'demonic sorcery' had won a considerable following, even among the nobility and the court, but the zealous public preachings of the patriarch were said to have extinguished 'the evil seeds of their venom'.[37]

In the last phase of the confrontation between heresy and Orthodoxy in Bulgaria the Orthodox authorities were challenged mainly by syncretistic teachings which combined the old anti-clerical and anti-sacramental attitudes of the Bogomils with pagan and magical practices. Whether this indicates a movement of fourteenth-century Bogomilism towards syncretism remains a matter of conjecture but in the following century the Balkan dominions of the nascent

Ottoman empire witnessed even more striking forms of religious syncretism. By the time of the anti-Bogomil Council of 1360 the Ottoman Turks had already begun their expansion into the Balkans, and towards the close of his patriarchate the Hesychast patron Euthymius had to shield his flock not from heretics and sorcerers but from the advance of the Ottoman holy war.

The Ottoman avalanche in the Balkans found the Christian Balkan domains disunited and weakened by the usual internecine strife and the fate of the Byzantine emperor, who after 1371 was virtually an Ottoman vassal, was shared by the other Balkan monarchs. The great battle at Kosovo Polje in 1389, where allied Balkan (mostly Bosnian and Serbian) armies encountered the Ottomans, brought the deaths of Sultan Murad and the Serbian prince Lazar and opened the way for further Ottoman advance in the Balkans. In 1393 the Bulgarian patriarch Euthymius had to organize the defence of the capital, Trnovo, which fell to the Ottomans after a three-month siege and was sacked and partly burnt. The patriarch was exiled and by the end of the century most of the fragmented Bulgarian domains were engulfed by the Ottoman empire.

The first western Crusade against the Ottomans, led by the Hungarian King Sigismund, ended in disaster in 1396 and the subsequent endeavours in 1444 and 1448 failed to check the Ottoman irruption into Europe. In 1453 Constantinople, after serving for more than 1,200 years as a capital of the successive Roman, East Roman and Byzantine empires, fell to the Ottomans and the cathedral of St Sophia was converted into a mosque. The residues of Serbia were annexed in 1459, while in 1517 Sultan Selim the Grim captured Cairo to assume the caliphate, and twelve years later the Ottomans besieged Vienna for the first time.

Balkan Orthodoxy had to adapt itself to Ottoman rule and Bogomilism gradually vanished from its records altogether. The last Orthodox polemist to denounce the Bogomil heresy was Symeon, Metropolitan of Thessalonica (1417–30), who launched a fierce attack on the Bogomils, whom he styled also as 'Kudugers', in his *Dialogus contra haereses*.[38] Symeon condemned the Bogomils as the most dangerous heretics in his metropoly and, echoing Psellus' allegations against the Thracian sectarians, accused them of worshipping, in 'secret and godless ceremonies', the Antichrist, the 'Archon

of sin and darkness'. Around 1454 to 1456 the Constantinople patriarch Gennadius Scholarius, who was the first patriarch to be
appointed by an Ottoman sultan, mentioned in one of his letters
that the Bosnian Kudugers were still active and influential among the
nobility and the court in Herzegovina.[39] At that time Bosnia and
Herzegovina had not yet been conquered by the Ottoman armies
and Rome was still continuing its struggle against what the papacy
saw as 'Manichaean' heresy and 'errors' in Bosnia.

Heresy and Politics in Bosnia

Alongside the Serbian troops, the Bosnian forces played a role in
the battle with the Ottomans at Kosovo Polje, 'the Waterloo of
Balkan freedom',[40] and upon the death of Sultan Murad on the
battlefield the Bosnian king Tvrtko proclaimed a Christian victory
and was praised in Florence as a saviour of Christendom. Following
his death in 1391, the decentralizing tendencies in the Bosnian
domains prevailed again and several strong Bosnian houses came to
dominate the political scene, while the succeeding Bosnian rulers
found it extremely difficult to assert their authority and in the
climate of political dualism were sometimes challenged by anti-
kings raised by opposing noble factions. What complicated the
political situation in the western Balkans further was the struggle
for the Hungarian throne – between Ladislas of Naples and the
would-be Holy Roman emperor, Sigismund of Luxemburg – which
evolved into a war of succession that affected and divided the
Bosnian nobility.

It seems certain that most of the Bosnian nobles were associated
initially with the Bosnian church, but with the gradual penetration
of Catholicism in Bosnia some of them accepted the Catholic faith.
In the early fourteenth century, when both Hungary and Bosnia
witnessed the struggles of rival claimants for their thrones, several
of the major Bosnian noble houses were closely linked with the
Bosnian church and used Patarenes for diplomatic services. Among
the Bosnian nobles who took active part in the Hungarian dynastic
collisions, particularly important was Duke Hrvoje Vukčić, who

was himself known as a Patarene, and is traditionally described as the Bosnian king-maker.

In 1393 Sigismund of Luxemburg had forced the Bosnian king Dabisha to recognize him as successor to the Bosnian throne, but his unsuccessful bid for the Bosnian crown in 1395 had compelled many Bosnians into alliance with his rival, Ladislas. Duke Hrvoje sided initially with Ladislas and eventually became his deputy for Croatia and Slavonia, and while the Ladislas camp acknowledged that Hrvoje was a Patarene, it was declared that he would be brought back to the true faith. Whatever Hrvoje's religious affinities and designs, in 1409, after an emphatic victory of Sigismund over the Bosnians, the Patarene duke shifted his allegiance to him and was accepted along with the Orthodox Serbian and Walachian rulers into his newly founded Dragon Order intended to fight pagans and heretics. Only three years later Sigismund suddenly charged Duke Hrvoje with plotting rebellion and stripped him of his powers in the kingdom; Hrvoje pleaded that as a member of the Dragon Order he must be judged before the Order and if found guilty would allow them to have his head. He implored to be allowed to embrace the Catholic faith, as he did not wish to end his days in a 'pagan rite',[41] a cryptic confession, made, moreover, by a member of the Dragon Order. Hrvoje's plea to be delivered from the 'pagan rite', which has not yet been decoded, was rejected and the turbulent duke now joined forces with one of the claimants to the Bosnian throne, Tvrtko II. In 1415, in a crucial battle in northern Bosnia, where Turkish mercenaries were used for the first time on Bosnian soil, he crushed Sigismund's forces and effectively terminated the sway of the future Holy Roman emperor in Bosnia.

The feats of Duke Hrvoje highlight the convoluted interrelations between 'heresy', politics and religion in Bosnia, where a Patarene noble could be an important ally of Catholic rulers like Ladislas and Sigismund, join the Dragon Order and use religion for his own ends. The early fourteenth century saw the increasing importance of the Bosnian church in the volatile political situation in Bosnia and for a time the *djed* acted as a councillor at the Bosnian court. Without evolving completely into a state religion proper, the Bosnian church enjoyed the support of powerful Bosnian noble houses and was intermittently active in the Bosnian court. In Herzegovina, where the nobility remained largely Orthodox, the Bosnian church had a strong patron in the house of Stefan Vukčić who assumed the title 'Duke (Herzog) of St Sava', from which the name of the land was ultimately derived.

In 1443 the Bosnian throne passed to Stefan Tomaš, a member of the Bosnian church, who was described by Pope Nicholas v as entrapped in the Manichaean errors before his final conversion to Catholicism. According to later Catholic tradition, upon Stefan Tomaš's accession Pope Eugene vi offered him a crown but requested persecution of the Manichaeans in Bosnia and Bosnian participation in a league against the Turks. By 1445, the year when Pope Eugene v recognized him as king, Stefan Tomaš had promised to embrace Catholicism and had been engaged in a war with Stefan Vukčić, who had firmly opposed his election as king. The conversion of Stefan Tomaš was not followed by any immediate persecution against the Bosnian church or heretics and the king maintained his relations with his former co-religionists. Some Bosnian nobles were also converted to Catholicism and the Franciscans were to increase their influence in Bosnia and at court. With the new advance of Catholicism in Bosnia references to dualists ('Manichaeans') multiplied and the Bosnian heresy was now firmly recognized as 'Manichaean'. Indeed the evidence does suggest dualist agitation in Bosnia around the mid fifteenth century and the 'Manichaeans' were clearly perceived as an obstruction to the progress of Catholicism in the realm. At that time the Bosnian church acquired the Slavonic ritual which was clearly a version of the Cathar Ritual of Lyons and the Constantinople patriarch Gennadius referred to Kudugers among the Bosnians and the nobility in Herzegovina. In 1461 three Bosnian nobles, seen as powerful ringleaders of the heresy at the royal court, were sent to Rome, renounced their 'Manichaean errors' before Cardinal Torquemada and returned to Bosnia, where one of them returned to his heresy 'like a dog to his vomit' and fled to Herzog Stefan. In contrast to the old *Ecclesia Sclavoniae*, however, the Bosnian nobles had to refute in Rome the articles of the radical dualism of the two principles, the two Gods, the supremely good one and the supremely evil one.

The apparent activation of the Bosnian dualist movement, continually mentioned in Inquisition documents during the reign of Stefan

Tomaš has been assigned to a probable split within the Bosnian church which resulted in the emergence of a dualist wing.[42] For Rome, the whole Bosnian church appeared dualist, 'Manichaean', and with the conversion of King Tomaš the Catholic demands for strong action against the Bosnian heretics were mounting. In 1459 King Tomaš finally succumbed to the pressure and reversed the policy of religious tolerance, as had been generally pursued by his predecessors. The king is recorded as having offered the 'Manichaeans' in his realm the choice of conversion or exile; 2,000 chose baptism, while the others sought refuge in the neighbouring dominions of Herzog Stefan.

Herzog Stefan had already concluded peace with the Catholic king of Bosnia and besides some overtures to Rome continued to be a follower of the Bosnian church and to use Patarene diplomats. During the Herzog's war with Dubrovnik (1451–4) he was accused by his adversaries of being a Patarene 'enemy of the Cross' and of destroying churches and crucifixes, but the peace was negotiated by Patarene diplomats. Indeed by the time of Stefan Tomaš's persecution of the Bosnian church, its hierarchy had apparently moved into Herzegovina.

The measures of Stefan Tomaš considerably weakened the hold of the Bosnian church in his realm and did not meet the resistance of the pro-Patarene nobles in a period when Catholicism was finally gaining ascendancy in Bosnia. Besides traditionally Orthodox Herzegovina, the Orthodox presence in eastern Bosnia had also increased and there appeared the first visible signs of the religious contest between eastern and western Christianity in Bosnia.

Soon after the death of Stefan Tomaš in 1461 a new powerful religious factor entered the Bosnian scene – Sunni Islam. His successor, Stefan Tomašević, promptly appealed to Rome for a crown in a request that implied that the 'Manichaeans' had already been largely expelled from Bosnia. He was crowned by a papal legate in his capital but the evolution of Bosnia into a Catholic kingdom was severely curtailed only two years later when it swiftly fell to Mohammed II the Conqueror after a surprising Ottoman attack. The emphatic Catholicism of the Bosnian king and his requests for help against the Turks had failed to secure Christian aid and in the following centuries Catholicism in Bosnia lost ground to both Islam and Orthodoxy. The king himself was caught by the Turks and beheaded. Herzegovina was also initially overrun in the Ottoman attack but Herzog Stefan soon restored its autonomy and the hierarchy of the Bosnian church retained its favoured position under his protection; he himself died in 1466, still a Patarene adherent.

The swift collapse of Bosnia and the ensuing success of Islam in the land that Rome called the 'lair of all heresies' has understandably attracted much attention and speculation. A traditional and, until recently, predominant approach to the religious history of Bosnia viewed the Bosnian church as a thoroughly Bogomil organization and attributed both the fall and Islamization in Bosnia to religious and political strife in the aftermath of the persecution against the Patarenes under Stefan Tomaš. The hostility between Catholicism and the Bosnian church, which intensified in 1459, is supposed to have provoked the collaboration of the Patarenes with the Ottoman conquerors. With their hostility to Catholicism, the forcibly converted Patarenes and their unconverted co-sectarians were suspected of a mass conversion to Islam which paved the way for the establishment of an important Islamic outpost in close vicinity to central Europe. As the Bosnian church has been treated more than frequently as a wing of the Bogomil movement, the enduring collision between Catholicism and the 'Great Heresy' has been viewed as having finally secured the progress of a new religious rival in Bosnia, Islam. The supposed mass conversion of dualists in Bosnia and Herzegovina was said to have been facilitated by the alleged 'similarities' in dualist and Islamic ethics. Seen in the light of the dualist–Catholic strife and the repeated Catholic campaigns against Bosnian heresy, Bosnia has been presented as the 'best and the saddest example'[43] of the consequences of religious persecution.

Yet the Islamization of Bosnia clearly did not follow the simplistic pattern of a dualist reaction against Roman suppression of heresy and heterodoxy, through mass conversion to an advancing Islam. While there are some controversial and legendary reports of Patarene or 'Manichaean' association with Ottoman military success in Bosnia, an actual collaboration between the Ottomans and the Bosnian church (or the dualists) cannot be substantiated. Indeed the only figure that actively and successfully resisted the Ottoman occupation of Bosnia and Herzegovina was Herzog Stefan, a notable and well-known patron and adherent of the Bosnian church. The persecution under King Tomaš had undoubtedly greatly weakened the influence of the Bosnian church, but resentment against continual Hungarian and Catholic interference in Bosnian affairs, particularly among the newly and forcibly converted Bosnians, certainly played its role in the advance of Islam. The characteristic lack of religious uniformity in medieval Bosnia – where Catholicism met with Orthodoxy, the Bosnian church and the dualist heretics – allowed for a quicker spread of Islam, which was to win Catholic, Orthodox and Patarene converts. Yet the views of the early stages of Islamization in Bosnia and the fate of the Bosnian 'Krstjani', whether dualist or schismatic, continue to differ sharply and paint extremely conflicting pictures of the religious history of early Ottoman Bosnia.[44]

What seems certain is that the religious life of Bosnia prior to the mid fifteenth century, with its general toleration of religious beliefs and practices, undoubtedly favoured the longer survival of dualist traditions. After the death of the old patron of the Bosnian church, Herzog Stefan, Herzegovina was finally annexed by the Ottomans in 1481. While Herzog Stefan's immediate successor had remained in the flock of the Patarene church, his third son, like many Bosnian nobles, came to accept Islam and rose to be a grand vizir under the Ottoman ruler, Selim 1. With the commencement of Ottoman rule in Bosnia, amid the novel religious diversity and rivalries, the traces of dualist traditions and the Bosnian church itself become extremely elusive.

The Fate of Balkan Dualism

In both Constantinople and Rome, the last testimonies to the Balkan dualist heresy refer to Bosnia, and the Bosnian lands are sometimes credited with preserving another witness to Bogomil dualism in the curious symbolism of the monolithic medieval Bosnian tombstones, the *stećci*, often referred to as the 'Bogomil gravestones'. Estimated to be more than 50,000 in number and concentrated mainly in Bosnia, Herzegovina and the adjacent regions, the majority of *stećci* were erected in the fourteenth and fifteenth centuries in the shapes of standing slabs, sarcophagi and boxes. The *stećci* bear a rich variety of carvings: solar symbols, crescents, rosettes, swastikas, pentacles and crosses, along with figurative representations of hunting, dancing and jousting scenes. While the association of the carvings with traditional funeral symbolism has been acknowledged, many of their features have tantalized archaeologists and antiquaries for more than a century. Since 1876, when Arthur Evans related the *stećci* carvings to the teachings of the Bosnian Patarene movement, a number of scholars have supplemented his theory with more material and suggestions, but it has also encountered strong opposition which has highlighted the numerous difficulties in the attempts at symbolic interpretations of the engravings, apart from the fact that *stećci* had been erected by Catholics, Orthodox and Patarenes alike.[45] The suggested links to dualist beliefs, such as the proposed parallels to central Asian Manichaean iconography or the connection between the *stećci* depictions of the sun and moon and their significance in Manichaeism, necessarily rely on a series of conjectures.[46] Yet it has been shown that some of the *stećci* carvings have retained the symbolism of ancient cults in the medieval guises of the jousting and hunting scenes or in the curious combinations of the symbols of the fleur-de-lis with crosses of the type of *crux ansata*.[47] There are indications of the survival of a medieval mystery cult in Bosnia and Herzegovina as pagan practices, which were condemned as heretical, persisted in various forms, and religious syncretism has been specified as plausibly being responsible for the continual accusations of heresy against the medieval Bosnians.[48]

In the early thirteenth century the Bogomils were accused of performing mysteries like 'hellenic rites' and the latter stages of the heresy were characterized by the emergence of teachings representing a *mélange* of dualist beliefs, magic and demonology. The patterns of symbiosis between dualist and traditional pagan beliefs in various areas of the Balkans have been indicated repeatedly by scholars.[49] Such a dualist–pagan synthesis in the *stećci* carvings cannot be excluded, particularly in the cases when the recoverable pagan symbolism allows for a dualist interpretation, as in the well-represented *stećci* motif of two horsemen opposing each other, identified as a survival of the classical theme of the Dioscuri.[50]

Following the disappearance of the Balkan Bogomils the Balkan folklore remained the repository of the old dualist beliefs and legends that had spread with the dissemination of Bogomil dualist teachings. Indeed, as late as the eighteenth century, reports occurred of schismatic Patarenes and 'Manichaeans' in Bosnia, sharing an opposition to Catholicism, the latter claiming that Jesus Christ did not die on the cross and extolling the archangel Michael.[51] Conversely, in Bulgaria itself Paulician sectarians, including those from their ancient dualist strongholds in Thrace, were converted to Catholicism in the seventeenth century, although they still practised their 'baptism by fire'. Nineteenth-century journalists' reports of the existence of Bogomil colonies in Bosnia are symptomatic of the western rediscovery of Bogomilism and the Balkans, rather than any actual survival of dualist sectarians in the Balkans.[52] It seems certain that the Islamization of Bosnia marked the closing chapter of the five-centuries-long history of Balkan and, indeed, European dualism.

The reasons for the swift disappearance of the Bogomils in the early Ottoman period in the Balkans still remain largely unexplained and sometimes the 'Bosnian' argument is projected on to the whole Balkans – the Bogomils are supposed to have chosen to accept Islam and vanished without trace among the Islamized section of the Balkan population. The remains of the 'hidden tradition', which at the rise of its influence in Europe openly claimed descent from the apostles, are supposed to have finally fled to Islam. However, evidence for such a Bogomil influx into Islam is lacking and the obscurity surrounding their disappearance seems to result from the insufficient knowledge of the early religious history of the Ottoman empire, with its array of sectarian and syncretistic movements, still a controversial and largely unexplored field.

What remained 'of the sway once held over the minds of men by the most powerful sectarian movement in the Balkans', wrote D. Obolensky, was a 'vague dualist tradition which has left its imprint on south Slavonic folklore'.[53] What remains also are the heretical book, brought from Bulgaria to Italy by the heretical bishop of Concorezzo, *Liber Secretum*, the fragments of the inner teachings of the Bogomils in Zigabenus' *Panoplia Dogmatica* and the dispersed fragments of dualist legends and myths of the Bogomils and Cathars in the sermons, annals, polemics and Inquisition records of their adversaries.

CHAPTER SIX

The Dualist Legends

Medieval and modern authorities on medieval dualism agree that initiation into Bogomil and Cathar teachings proceeded gradually and that prior to the *consolamentum* the ordinary believers were not introduced to what was considered the inner doctrines, preserved for the *perfecti*, who claimed knowledge of the 'mystery of the Kingdom of God'. On behalf of their initiation and status the *perfecti* bore the title of the Blessed Virgin Mary, *Theotokos* (God-Bearer), as they were seen as a receptacle of the Holy Spirit and as giving birth to the word. The parable in Matthew 7:6, 'Do not give dogs what is holy, do not throw your pearls to the pigs', was interpreted as alluding to the need for esotericism, the pearls being 'the mysterious and precious tenets' of Bogomilism, the preserve of the *perfecti*.

However acrimonious, the Orthodox records of the Bogomil course of initiation suggest that the believers were initially introduced to teachings and ethics close to evangelical Christianity, coupled with a gradual introduction to progressively heretical precepts, until the general nature of the dualist doctrine was outlined to the neophyte. Yet according to Euthymius Zigabenus, dualist dogmas were revealed only at the end of further initiation to those believers who chose to enter upon the probationary period required before the final elevation to the highest dualist grade of the *perfecti* and receiving the *consolamentum*. The probationary period was described variously as lasting one to two or three years and after the *consolamentum* the new *perfecti* had access, in the words of Orthodox commentators, to the 'mysteries for the more advanced in impiety' and 'to the whole heresy and madness'. The élite class of the *perfecti* was fully introduced to the dualist *historia arcana*, which the Orthodox saw as the ultimate 'satanic mysteries', and, as 'accomplished theologians',[1] mastered a system of allegorical interpretation of the scriptures which was widely used during missionary tours and the theological debates pursued by the 'teachers of the heresy'.

The Bogomil missionaries and scribes elaborated a vivid polemical dualist mythology, fragments of which have been preserved in the Orthodox accounts of the heresy and denounced as 'satanic fables', 'unholy babble', et cetera. Apart from the canonical scriptures the dualist mythology made wide use of themes and imagery from the apocryphal literature circulating in the Orthodox east, which included early Christian texts and important Jewish apocalyptic texts like the Book of the Secrets of Enoch (2 Enoch) and the Apocalypse of Abraham. Among these texts, particularly important for the Bogomils was the Vision of Isaiah, an apocalypse from the early Christian era, which subsequently was taken over by the Cathars. The only extant Bogomil tract, *Liber Secretum* or *Interrogatio Iohannes*, was brought to Italy by the bishop of the Cathar church of Concorezzo, Nazarius, and became the basic text for Cathar moderate dualism in Lombardy, exerting further influence in Languedoc. Some of its concepts were in harmony with the teachings of absolute dualism and gained currency in radical dualist Cathar circles, while others were naturally at variance and were bitterly disputed. Indeed debates over certain notions in *Liber Secretum* eventually caused a split in the church of Concorezzo. The Bogomil and Cathar preoccupation with apocryphal stories and myths provoked a reaction in the Cathar church of Desenzano, the bastion of absolute dualism in Italy, where some Cathar circles attempted to advance a more literal reading of scriptural passages and to furnish a philosophical foundation for radical dualism, the tract *The Book of the Two Principles*. Yet, along with the apostolic life and the ascetic conduct of the *perfecti*, the flexibility and the picturesqueness of dualist apocryphal mythology was one of the great strengths of Bogomil and Cathar propaganda and it is not surprising that distinct dualist traditions left a firm imprint and endured in Balkan folklore.

Besides the principal dividing line between the medieval adherents of absolute and monarchian dualism, other divergencies of doctrine and scriptural interpretations inevitably emerged among the various dualist communities. Otherwise, the pattern of Cathar initiation into the inner sanctum of the *perfecti* seems essentially parallel to the Bogomil one, although there are some indications of teachings which were not shared by all *perfecti*, which might well have been a later innovation. The orthodox adversaries of medieval dualism zealously rejected the validity of the pretensions of the *perfecti* to esoteric knowledge of the 'divine mysteries' and many heretical books, both Cathar and Bogomil, were reported to have been burned. Most of the information about the teachings of the medieval dualists is preserved in Orthodox and Catholic records, invariably hostile and vilifying. *The Book of the Two Principles* is a notable exception and so is the so-called 'Manichaean Tract'[2] preserved in the polemical *Liber contra Manichaeos*, but both expound the tenets of absolute dualism. For monarchian dualism the most important texts still remain the Bogomil *Liber Secretum* as well as the various, sometimes controversial, fragments in the Orthodox and Catholic polemical literature. While the works of inquisitors like Rainerius Sacchoni, Anselm of Alessandria or the friar Moneta of Cremona give the outlines of Cathar dualism, the anti-Bogomil exposé of the Orthodox theologian Euthymius Zigabenus sheds light on some of the inner teachings in the original Bogomil dualism. Euthymius' expertise in what could be safely called Bogomil esotericism is hardly surprising, for his refutation of Bogomil teachings was based on the sermon of the Bogomil heresiarch Basil the Physician before Alexius Comnenus, recorded by Alexius' secretary. Regrettably Euthymius Zigabenus did not make full use of the teachings divulged during the heresiarch's oration and admitted that he did not proceed to disprove all Basil's arguments, in his own words, to preserve his sanity in this 'enormous sea of godlessness'.

Euthymius' disquiet with this 'godlessness' appears understandable: his exposé of the Bogomil heresy revealed teachings focused on the problems that had once divided the Gnostic teachers from the Church Fathers: the nature of the Creation, the identity of the Demiurge of the material world, the origins of evil and the plight of the human soul.

Christ–Michael and Samael–Satan

Medieval dualist lore resurrected many Gnostic and Manichaean themes and imagery and much of it was intended to reveal the hidden 'dualist reality' behind biblical accounts, like the creation, the fall of man or the flood. Yet in some dualist legends, particularly among the absolute dualists, direct dependence on the biblical text was lacking. Apart from the borrowings from apocryphal writings, preserved in eastern Christendom and medieval elaborations of the dualist scribes, the medieval dualist lore comprised traditions whose exact pedigree or background could appear elusive and untraceable.

Similar to some older Gnostic traditions, like the Valentian school, medieval dualism claimed succession to the true Christian faith and, as with older Gnostic creation myths, the Bogomil–Cathar myths of the creation of the world revealed the mystery of the Demiurge of the visible world. The unfolding of this revelation is preserved in two main Bogomil versions – the tract *Liber Secretum* and the Bogomil section in *Panoplia Dogmatica*. The two accounts epitomize the monarchian strand in Bogomil–Cathar dualism, where the Demiurge, the Lord of the Old Testament, is exposed as evil, but subordinate to the higher one God, while the establishment and activation of the material universe is inextricably linked to the story of his fall. Traditionally, Satan or Samael was God's first-born and was originally the more powerful elder brother of Christ, the Logos. In *Liber Secretum*, at the beginning Satan presided over the virtues in heaven and was 'regulator of all things', sitting with the God–Father. Satan's power was described as descending from heaven to hell and even to the throne of the Father. Similarly, in the Bogomil satanology expounded in *Panoplia Dogmatica*, Samael was the heavenly vice-regent of the good God–Father and sat on a throne at his right side as second only to him, the creator of the angelic hosts, and possessed a similar image and 'garment'. The traditional cause of Satan's fall was his pride and inevitably the parable in Isaiah about the king of Babylon (14:13–14) – 'I will set my throne high above the stars of God . . . I will rise high above the cloud-banks and make myself like the Most High' – was thought to reveal the 'evil plots' of his real aspirations. To further his designs for exaltation and eternal rule Satan proceeded to subvert the angels of the 'Father invisible' and ascended as far as the fifth heaven. Exposed by a voice from the throne of the Father, Satan was cast out of heaven along with the ensnared angels who were stripped of their garments, thrones and crowns. According to *Liber Secretum*, with his fall Satan was deprived of the light of his glory and his face became human, albeit like 'an iron glowing from the fire', while his seven tails drew away a third of God's angels. In the alternative version of the Bogomil myth Satan still possessed his divine image and 'garment' after his downfall and having retained his creative potency he decided to 'make a second heaven like a second God'. In *Liber Secretum*, after completing the creation with the assistance of the angels of air and water, Satan ordered the earth to bring forth all living beings, while the heavenly hosts, his ministering angels, were created from fire. The Bogomil elaboration of the age-old tradition of entrapping the divine soul in the prison–body followed: Satan created man in his likeness from clay and compelled the angel of the second heaven to enter the clay. With a part from man's body, Satan fashioned the body of a woman, who was brought to life by the angel of the first heaven. Now both the angels of the first and second heavens suffered imprisonment in mortal, respectively male and female, forms. In the alternative version of the Bogomil myth Satan's task proved more onerous and his creature Adam, made out of earth and water, was far from perfect – a flow of water out of his right foot and forefinger twisted on the earth and took on the shape of a serpent. In Satan's attempt to breathe spirit into Adam, the spirit followed the same course, animating the serpent that inevitably became the most subtle creature, enlivened as it was by the spirit of Satan himself. Now Satan, the second Creator, was forced to appeal to the good Father to send His Spirit to his creature, pledging that both would become masters of man and that some of his progeny would eventually fill the heavenly abodes made void by the fall of the rebellious angels. The good God consented and breathed the 'spirit of life' into man. Eve was created and animated in the same manner. The Bogomil accounts of man's creation clearly reiterated the old Gnostic soul–body dualism, where the divine soul was seen as imprisoned in the body created by the Demiurge. Another tradition, which had been current in both Gnostic and Jewish traditions, also found its elaboration in medieval dualism: Eve's seduction and corruption by Satan.

Following the creation of the first human couple Satan proceeded to defile Eve by assuming the shape of the serpent and enticing her into intercourse. The stories of the seduction of Eve also varied. In *Liber Secretum* after planting a bed of reeds in Paradise, Satan forbade Adam and Eve to eat the fruit of good and evil but lured Eve into sin. With Eve's desire 'glowing like an oven' the devil emerged from the reeds in the serpent's shape and satisfied his lust. Adam was also tricked into debauchery with Eve, who begot together the 'children of the devil and of the serpent' and Satan's reign, dependent on procreation, would last until the end of the world. In the alternative Bogomil version of the seduction of Eve by the Demiurge she begot twins, Cain and his sister Calomena, from Samael–Satan while Abel was born after her human union with Adam. Cain, the 'seed of Samael', slew Abel, 'the seed of Adam', and brought murder and death into the world. However, after his shape-changing and intercourse with Eve, Samael–Satan lost his creative potency, even his divine form, to become dark and abhorrent.

Yet Samael–Satan continued to be master of his creation and his cruel reign allowed only a few to join the good Father and ascend into the ranks of the archangels. In *Liber Secretum* Satan was permitted by the Father to reign for seven ages, during which he sent his ministering fiery angels to men, while the sacrificial rites were initiated to hide the kingdom of heaven from men. As in the older Gnostic works Satan made the futile 'monotheistic' proclamation: 'I am He and there is no god beside me' (Deuteronomy 32:39). Satan revealed his divinity to Moses, granted him the Law and sent him to deliver the children of Israel from Egypt, leading them through the Red Sea on dry ground.

The Bogomil mythology further embellished the story of the angels' downfall and in its version, aware of Samael–Satan's promise to fill their former heavenly abode with the sons of men, the fallen angels took wives from among the daughters of men. The giants born of the union began to struggle against Samael–Satan, who, enraged by their rebellion, brought the flood over the earth to destroy every living being, sparing only the life of his minister, Noah. From Adam to Christ, only Jesus' antecedents enumerated in the genealogies in Matthew and Luke were saved, along with the sixteen prophets and the martyrs who died rather than succumb to idolatry.

In Bogomil Christology the mission of Christ was to announce the name of the Father and it is in precognition of this mission that Satan gave Moses three pieces of wood for Christ's crucifixion. In one of the strands of Bogomil Christology, after 5,500 years God the Father felt compassion for the suffering of his creation, the human soul, under the satanic reign and sent the 'Son–Logos'. He was also recognized as the archangel Michael, described as an archangel because he was the most divine of all angels, Jesus because he healed every illness or affliction and Christ because his body was 'anointed'. He descended from heaven and entered the Virgin through the right ear to assume the semblance of a human body. While his Passion, death and resurrection were unreal, he was victorious in his battle against the rebellious Samael–Satanael. In this version of Bogomil Christology it was after the victory of Christ–Michael over Satanael that the God's first-born lost his last 'divine syllable' -el (Lord) and was cast fettered into the pit, while Christ–Michael ascended to Satanael's former throne to the right of the Father. It has been assumed sometimes that with his fall Satanael's seniority had automatically passed to the Son–Logos and following his triumph and the imprisonment of the God's first-born, Christ–Michael returned to his ultimate source, the good Father.

In *Liber Secretum*, before the advent of Christ, God sent His angel, called Mary, so that Christ could be received by her through the Holy Spirit but Satan also sent his angel, the prophet Elijah, now in the incarnation of John the Baptist, who baptized with water. Upon his descent Christ entered and emerged from Mary's ear to be recognized by John the Baptist as the one who baptized with the Holy Spirit and with fire, the one able to save and destroy. As in Manichaeism, baptism by water was vigorously rejected in Bogomilism and Catharism, but according to *Liber Secretum* the world had accepted John's baptism rather than Jesus' baptism by fire and thus the actions of many people remained evil, as they avoided coming to the light.

A recurrent idea that emerged both in the Bogomil and Cathar thought held that the only Old Testament figures who were saved, recognized as the sixteen prophets and Jesus' ancestors listed in the genealogies in Matthew and Luke, rose again on the death of Christ and received the *consolamentum* from Christ himself. In their trinitarian system the Son was traditionally regarded as lesser in Godhood than the Father, and the Holy Ghost lesser than the Son. Another distinct Bogomil teaching, expounded in *Panoplia Dogmatica*, concerned the way the Son and the Holy Ghost proceeded from the Father – the Son was viewed as a light emanating from the right side of the head of the Father, while the Holy Ghost emanated from the left side. The emanation was initiated 5,500 years after the creation of the world when the Father assumed these three faces. With the return of the Son and the Holy Ghost to the Father he resumed his 'one-faced' form. The process in which the Father begot the Son and the Son begot the Holy Spirit was continued by the Holy Spirit who begot Judas and the apostles. The beginning of Jesus' genealogy in Matthew 1:2, 'Abraham begat Isaac; and Isaac begat Jacob; and Jacob begat Judas and his brethren' (*KJV*) was taken as referring to the emanatory processes within the Holy Trinity.

Bogomil monarchian dualism had an eschatological character – Satan was expected to be ultimately conquered in the last days and *Liber Secretum* furnished a vivid account of the Last Judgement, with imagery dependent on the canonical Revelation and other extra-canonical apocalypses. After a period when Satan would be 'loosed out of his prison' (Revelation 20:7, *KJV*) the Son of Man would conduct the Last Judgement and separate His just from the sinners and Satan and his hosts would be cast into a lake of fire. The Son of God would then occupy for ever the place of the first-born, on the right hand of the Father and reign with his Holy Father in all eternity.

The Cathar versions of moderate dualism generally followed the Bogomil prototypes, although understandably different interpretations appeared. Cathar monarchian dualism emphatically postulated that while the one higher Father created primordial matter, it was the Prince of this World, Satan, himself created by God, who divided it into four elements. Sometimes the higher God was regarded as the Creator of the primal elements but invariably it was the Devil who divided the elements. The creation of man could be elaborated with various new details – in one variant God the Father sent a heavenly angel to observe how Lucifer had divided the elements and it was this angel that Lucifer captured and subjected to human flesh in the body–prison.[3] As in Bogomilism, the parable of the unjust steward in Luke 16:1–9 remained one of the principal parables in Catharism of the actions and fortunes of Satan, the present Prince of the world and the former Prince of the Angels.

According to some Cathar esoteric embellishments of the myth of Lucifer's fall, in the beginning there existed a certain evil four-faced spirit, the four faces being respectively those of a man, bird, fish and beast and when he was still good Lucifer encountered this evil spirit. The evil spirit was devoid of creative power but Lucifer was struck with wonder and ventured to converse with him, was led astray and prompted to seduce the angels.[4]

While charting the feats of Satan as the Lord of the Old Testament the Cathar accounts are as explicit as those of the Bogomils, recounting that Satan sent prophets to men and through their prophecies precipitated animal sacrifices, the blood offerings through which he was honoured as god. In the Bogomil account of the flood, moreover, Noah is not a thoroughly negative figure, as he ministered to Satan and was saved by the fallen Demiurge without knowing about his apostasy, whereas in one Cathar version it was the 'Holy God' who saved Noah and 'all living creatures' from Satan's flood.[5]

Yet, despite the variances, Satan in Bogomil and Cathar monarchian dualism was created by the higher God and because of his rebellion was cast out of heaven and created the material cosmos. Conversely, in medieval radical dualism Lucifer proceeded immediately from the eternal principle of evil, from an evil God, who was coeternal and coexistent with the good God.

The Good God and the God of Evil

The western accounts of medieval absolute dualism are considerably more elaborate than the eastern records and it was in Italy that the radical dualist doctrines received their theological and sometimes novel formulation in *The Book of the Two Principles*. The traditional accounts of Cathar radical dualism postulated the belief in two principles, existing for all eternity, without beginning or end. The principle of good was recognized as the Father of Christ, the God of Light, while the principle of evil was the God of Darkness, who blinded the minds of the unbelievers.

In some Cathar accounts the God of Darkness was regarded as the Lord of Genesis, the Creator of the four elements, the visible heaven, the sun, the moon, the stars and everything on earth; He was the God of Moses. The God of Light was the Creator of everlasting, eternal things and created four alternative elements of his own and another heaven, sun, moon and stars.[6]

The God of Light also created his heavenly people, comprising the body, soul and spirit, the spirit being outside the body and serving as the custodian of the soul. Satan was believed to have been envious of the God of Light and having ascended into his sublime heavens he led astray the souls created by the good God and lured them to earth and the 'murky clime'. When Satan ascended into the heavens with his legions, war ensued in heaven and he was defeated by the archangel Michael and his hosts, as recounted in Revelation. Upon his expulsion from heaven Satan entrapped the deceived souls in the prison of the body; Jesus' mission was to deliver these souls from Satan's enslavement.

Only through the *consolamentum* could the imprisoned soul receive back its heavenly custodian spirit and when, in the last days, all the ensnared souls would achieve their penance they would ascend back to their heavenly abodes and regain their heavenly bodies. This was deemed to be the resurrection of the dead in the Scriptures, not the resurrection of physical bodies but of spiritual bodies. In one form of Italian absolute dualism the Devil imprisoned the deceived souls daily in human and animal bodies and conducted their transmigration from one body to another until they – also called 'the people of God' and the 'sheep of Israel' – were to be recovered back to heaven.[7] The Desenzano Cathars, who had their consecration in the Drugunthian order, advanced a more elaborate version of the invasion of the heavenly realm of the good Lord by the powers of darkness.[8] In their belief Lucifer, the son of the evil Lord, ascended to the heavenly abodes and transformed himself into an angel of light and gained the admiration of the angels who prevailed on the good Lord to install him as a steward over the angels. There followed Lucifer's corruption and seduction of the angels, the battle in heaven and his fall along with the third part of the angels who were believed to have body, soul and spirit. The slain bodies of the angels, recognized as Ezekiel's 'dry bones', remained in heaven, while the souls were taken captive by Lucifer and imprisoned in bodies.

A brief polemical tract against the Italian Cathars reveals another doctrine concerning the feats of Lucifer which was current among the Cathars of the church of Desenzano, the so-called Albanenses. The teaching was considered 'secret',[9] which is understandable, since it envisioned Lucifer, the son of the evil God, having intercourse with the wife of the good God. Lucifer ascended to heaven, where he found the wife of the celestial king alone and finally prevailed on her to yield to him so that she begot a son that Lucifer could make 'god in his kingdom and have him worshipped as a god'. This teaching is illuminated further by a quotation from Revelation, 'The Kingdom of this world is become our Lord's' (11:15) and according to the Albanensian teaching, 'thus Christ was born and thus He brought His flesh down from heaven'; this was regarded as the Albanensian 'great secret'. Yet in Albanensian Christology Christ remained an angel incarnate and the events in the gospel were treated as having occurred only in outward appearance and Christ did not ascend in human flesh but in the flesh he had 'brought from heaven'.

The Albigensian absolute dualist circles in Languedoc shared the belief in the transmigration of souls and apparently had teachings that were held to be esoteric. A Catholic exposé of the tenets of Albigensian absolute dualists in Languedoc written around the beginning of the Albigensian Crusade recounted one of these teachings.[10] It stated that the Albigensian 'elders' taught in 'secret meetings' that it was the evil God who made his creatures first, two male and two female, a lion, a bee-eater, an eagle and a spirit. Subsequently, the good Lord took from the evil God the spirit and eagle for his act of creation and from them he fashioned his own things. Plagued by this despoilment the evil God decided to avenge himself and sent his son, Lucifer, with a host of brilliant men and women to the court of the good God, where Lucifer beguiled him and was appointed a 'prince, priest and steward' over his people. The good God also gave Lucifer a testament for the people of Israel, but in his absence the son of the evil God led them astray and scattered them throughout his dominions, while the most noble were sent to this world, styled 'the last lake', 'the farthest earth' and 'the deepest hell'. The souls were sent to this world, the bodies, abandoned by the spirit, were left in the desert and these were 'the lost sheep of the house of Israel' (Matthew 15:24) who are the focus of Christ's saving mission. Christ himself was born in the sublime 'land of the living' of Joseph and Mary, who are identified with Adam and Eve, and it was there that his Passion, Resurrection and Ascension to the good Father took place. Christ was deemed to have passed, with His testament, disciples, father and mother, through seven realms to free His people. The good God was believed to have two wives, Collam (Oholah) and Colibam (Oholiba) – the two courtesans in Ezekiel 23:4, symbolizing respectively Samaria and Jerusalem – and to have engendered sons and daughters from them.

According to the same tract another teaching that these Albigensian circles regarded as esoteric and again was taught in their 'secret meetings' claimed that Mary Magdalene was in reality the wife of Christ and she was also recognized as the Samaritan woman to whom he said, 'Call thy husband.' She was the woman that Christ freed when the Jews were trying to stone her and she was his wife as she was alone with him in three places, the temple, at the well and in the garden. This Albigensian belief in Mary Magdalene as Christ's wife is confirmed by two additional Catholic tracts on the Cathar heresy, although in their versions the Cathar attitudes to the 'terrestrial' Christ and Mary Magdalene were modified by dualism applied to the gospel story itself.

In these two exposés the precepts of absolute dualism were transposed on the nature of Christ and there appeared two Christ figures – the celestial and the terrestrial, the latter being an evil or pseudo-Christ. In the first version[11] the terrestrial Christ, who was born in the earthly Bethlehem and was crucified in Jerusalem, was virtually an evil Christ and Mary Magdalene was his concubine. The other version[12] confirms the teaching of the two wives of the good

God, adding that it was his relationship with the wife of the evil God that prompted the latter to send his son to the court of the good God. The son of the evil Lord deceived the good God and seized human and animal souls that were dispersed among his seven realms, to which Christ was sent with his redeeming mission and suffered seven times. There was a division between the true Christ, who was born in the celestial Jerusalem and suffered there, 'betrayed by His brothers', while the Christ who appeared in 'this world' was a pseudo-Christ and had pseudo-apostles. The declared belief that Mary Magdalene was Christ's wife seems to refer to the celestial Christ, although in this dualist line of argument one might have expected two distinct figures of Mary Magdalene, celestial and terrestrial.

The origins of the teachings of the two wives of the good God and particularly of Mary Magdalene's marital status appear rather obscure, although Mary Magdalene played a prominent role in the Gnostic *Pistis Sophia*, while in the Gnostic *Gospel of Philip* she was described as the 'companion' of Christ, whom he loved more than all his disciples. The teaching of Mary Magdalene as the 'wife' or 'concubine' of Christ appears, moreover, an original Cathar tradition which does not have any counterpart in the Bogomil doctrines. Some of the theological and mythological elaborations of radical dualism in Italian Catharism were also original and sometimes reformist, as attested by the influential views of John de Lugio, who, for example, came to accept the whole Bible as 'written in another world'.[13] John de Lugio restored the attribution of some of the events in the Old Testament, like the sending of the flood, to the true God, but argued that the acts of punishment sent upon Israel in Judaea and the Promised Land were provoked by his adversary. According to John de Lugio the evil god has attacked the true God and his Son for all eternity and he falls upon Yahweh's words to Satan in the Book of Job: 'Thou movest me against him, to destroy him without cause' (2:3). *The Book of the Two Principles*, sometimes attributed to John de Lugio himself, advanced a wide-ranging polemic against both Catholicism and monarchian dualism, attacking the doctrine of free will to present the paradigm of the absolute and eternal opposition between good and evil. The doctrine of the two creators was elaborated at some length and the good Creator was defined as omnipotent over good things, while the evil Creator was charged with engendering evil and wickedness which was manifested in the Old Testament. The old argument of how a good God could permit the existence of evil in his creation was invoked against monarchian dualists, with their teaching of a one higher God who had created the inferior Demiurge. Finally, the tract elaborated on the inevitability of persecution for all who 'live godly in Christ Jesus'. The tract relied heavily on its dualist readings of the scriptures, a peculiarity which, indeed, characterized the older Bogomil system of an allegorical interpretation of the gospels and parts of the Old Testament.

Bethlehem and Capernaum

The Bogomil predilection for using parables in their sermons was attested early on, but it is Zigabenus' *Panoplia Dogmatica* that sheds light on the fuller range of Bogomil allegorical readings of the scriptures. Besides the parable of the unjust steward, all-important for Bogomil–Cathar satanology, gospel themes and images could be used to support Bogomil teachings and propaganda. The Bogomil preachers proclaimed their church to be true Bethlehem, as it was viewed as the cradle of the 'word' and the true faith, while the Orthodox Church was styled Herodes, as it tried to exterminate the true 'word'. The Pharisees and the Saducees coming for John's baptism in Matthew 3:7 were identified with the Orthodox, while the two violent men possessed by devils who 'came out of the tombs' to confront Jesus in Gadarenes (Matthew 8:28) were recognized as epitomes of the clergy and monks.

Besides the polemic against the Church allegoric readings of the gospels were used for scriptural support of the Bogomil teachings. In Matthew's description of John the Baptist (3:4), the rough coat of camel's hair and the locusts were seen as the commandments of the Law of Moses, while his leather belt and the wild honey were seen as symbolizing the gospel. 'Eye for eye, tooth for tooth' certainly invited a dualist interpretation and accordingly the two eyes were the Law of Moses and the Law of the Gospel respectively, whereas the two teeth represented the broad way of Moses' Law and the narrow way of the gospel. In Jesus' precept, 'You are not to swear at all – not by heaven, for it is God's throne, not by earth, for it is his footstool, nor by Jerusalem, for it is the city of the great King' (Matthew 5:35), the great King was inevitably recognized as the Devil, the Prince of this World; the woman who 'suffered from haemorrhages' for twelve years (Matthew 9:20) was the Jerusalem church bleeding from the blood offerings among the twelve tribes of Israel and healed by Jesus and by his destruction of Jerusalem. Jerusalem was indeed seen as the old seat of Satan but following its destruction he had to move to the cathedral of St Sophia in Constantinople, the 'Queen of Cities'.

Particularly interesting is the Bogomil translation of Rachel's 'weeping for her children' (Matthew 2:18) after Herod's killing of the innocents. Rachel, otherwise the biblical mother of Joseph and Benjamin, was seen as a widow and mother of two daughters whom she unwisely dressed in men's clothes and sent to meet their death at the hands of Herod, mistaking the purpose of his search for the male infants. The widow Rachel, who had caused the death of her children in this short Bogomil story, is identified with the heavenly Father, the daughters/sons of the widow with the souls of Adam and Christ, and Herod, naturally, with the Prince of the World.

The Cathars retained this use of parables and allegories for the illustration of their dualist teachings. The parable in Luke 10:30, 'A certain man went down from Jerusalem to Jericho', was seen as an allusion to Adam's descent from the heavenly Jerusalem to the world, while, 'And fell among thieves which stripped him of his raiment' (*KJV*), was read as Adam's fall among evil spirits who stripped him of his light.[14]

Yet the extant Bogomil and Cathar parables and allegories represent only fragments of what was certainly a more developed system of scriptural interpretation. The Bogomil preachers claimed that Christ's departure from Nazareth to Capernaum (Matthew 4:13) meant the departure from the established orthodox Church to their underground and persecuted church where he had chosen to dwell. Whatever the validity of these claims for apostolic succession, until there is some substantial discovery of genuine Bogomil texts like, for example, the momentous findings of Manichaean works in the sands of Turfan early this century, most of the history and teachings of this 'Capernaum' church will remain elusive and untraceable.

Select Bibliography

Ackroyd, P. R., *Exile and Restoration*, London, 1968.

— *Israel under Babylon and Persia*, Oxford, 1970.

Acta Bosnae potissimum ecclesiastica, ed. E. Fermendžin, in *Monumenta spectantia historiam Slavorum meridionalium*, vol. 23, Zagreb, 1892.

Acta Bulgariae ecclesiastica, ed. E. Fermendžin, in *Monumenta spectantia historiam Slavorum meridionalium*, vol. 18, Zagreb, 1887.

Adam, A., *Texte zum Manichäismus*, Berlin, 1954.

Adémar of Chabannes, *Chronique*, ed. J. Chavanon, in *Collection de textes pour servir à l'étude et à l'enseignement de l'histoire*, vol. 20, Paris, 1897.

Alberic of Trois-Fontaines, *Chronica Albrici monachi Trium Fontium a monachi novi monasterii Hoiensis interpolata*, ed. P. Scheffer-Boichorst, *MGH SS*, vol. 23, cols. 631–950.

Alberry, C. R. C. (ed.), *A Manichaean Psalm Book*, Part 2, Stuttgart, 1938.

Alderink, L. J., *Creation and Salvation in Ancient Orphism*, Chico, California, 1981.

Alexander Lycopolitanus, *Contra Manichaei opiniones disputatio*, ed. A. Brinkmann, Leipzig, 1895.

Alfaric, P., *Les écritures manichéennes*, 2 vols., Paris, 1918–19.

Altheim, F. and R. Stiehl (eds.), *Geschichte Mittelasiens in Altertum*, Berlin, 1970.

Angelov, D., *Bogomilstvoto v Bulgaria* [Bogomilism in Bulgaria], 3rd edn, Sofia, 1980.

Anklesaria, B. T. (ed. and tr.), *Zand-Akasih, Iranian or Greater Bundahishn*, Bombay, 1956.

Annales S. Medardi Suessionnenses, ed. G. Waitz, *MGH SS*, vol. 26, pp. 518–22.

Arberry, A. J., (ed.), *The Legacy of Persia*, Oxford, 1953.

Artamonov, M., *Istoriya Khazar* [History of the Khazars], Leningrad, 1962.

Asboth, J., *An Official Tour through Bosnia and Herzegovina*, London, 1890.

Asmussen, J. P., *Xuastvanift, Studies in Manichaeism*, Copenhagen, 1965.

— *Manichaean Literature*, New York, 1975.

Athanassakis, A. N. (ed. and tr.), *The Orphic Hymns: Text, Translation and Notes*, Missoula, Montana, 1977.

Attaliates, Michael, *Historia*, ed. I. Bekker, *CSHB*, 1853.

Bailey, Sir Harold, *Zoroastrian Problems in the Ninth-century Books*, Oxford, 1943.

Barber, M., *The Trial of the Templars*, Cambridge, 1978.

Beaulieu, P.-A., *The Reign of Nabonidus, King of Babylon 556–539 BC*, New Haven and London, 1989.

Beck, H.-G., *Kirche und theologische Literatur im byzantinischen Reich*, Munich, 1959.

Bengston, H. (ed.), *The Greeks and the Persians from the Sixth to the Fourth Centuries*, London, 1968.

Benoist, J., *Histoire des Albigeois et des Vaudois*, 2 vols., Paris, 1691.

Benveniste, E., *The Persian Religion According to the Chief Greek Texts*, Paris, 1929.

— *Les Mages dans l'ancien Iran*, Paris, 1938.

Bernard Gui, *Manuel de l'inquisiteur*, ed. and tr. G. Mollat, *Les Classiques de l'histoire de France au moyen âge*, 8, 9, 2 vols., Paris, 1926–7.

Beshevliev, V., *Die Protobulgarische Periode der bulgarischen Geschichte*, Amsterdam, 1981.

— *Pârvobulgarite* [The Proto-Bulgars], Sofia, 1981.

Bianchi, U., *Il dualismo religioso. Saggio storico ed etnologico*, Rome, 1958.

— 'Dualistic Aspects of Thracian Religion', *History of Religions*, 10:3 (1971), pp. 228–333.

— *Selected Essays on Gnosticism, Dualism and Mysteriosophy*, Leiden, 1978.

— (ed.), *Mysteria Mithrae*, Leiden/Rome, 1979.

Bickerman, E. J., *Studies in Jewish and Christian History*, 3 vols., Leiden, 1976–86.

Bidez, J. and F. Cumont, *Les Mages hellénisés*, 2 vols., Paris, 1938.

al-Biruni, *Chronology of the Ancient Nations*, tr. E. Sachau, London, 1879.

— *Alberuni's India*, tr. E. Sachau, 2 vols., London, 1988.

Black, M. (ed.), *The Scrolls and Christianity*, London, 1969.

Bogomilstvoto na Balkanot vo svetlinata na nai novite istrazivany [Bogomilism in the Balkans in the light of the most recent research], Skopje, 1982.

Böhme, R., *Orpheus*, Bern, 1970.

Böhlig, A., *Kephalaia*, vol. 2, Stuttgart, 1966.

Bonacursus, *Manifestatio haeresis catharorum quam fecit Bonacursus*, *PL*, vol. 204, pp. 775–92.

Borst, A., *Die Katharer*, Stuttgart, 1953.

Bossuet, J. B., *Histoire des variations des églises protestantes*, 2 vols., Paris, 1688.

Bousset, W., *Hauptprobleme der Gnosis*, Göttingen, 1907.

Bowker, J., *The Targums and Rabbinic Literature*, Cambridge, 1969.

Boyce, M., *The Manichaean Hymn-cycles in Parthian*, London, 1954.

— *Zoroastrians: Their Religious Beliefs and Practices*, London, 1979.

— *Textual Sources for the Study of Zoroastrianism*, Manchester, 1984.

— *A History of Zoroastrianism*: vol. 1, *The Early Period*, 2nd edn with corrections, Leiden, 1989; vol. 2, *Under the Achaemenians*, Leiden, 1982; (and F. Grenet), vol. 3, *Zoroastrianism under Macedonian and Roman Rule*, Leiden, 1991.

Bozoky, E., *Le Livre secret des cathares*, Paris, 1980.

Brand, C. M., *Byzantium Confronts the West, 1180–1204*, Cambridge, Massachussetts, 1968.

Van den Broek, R. and M. J. Vermaseren (eds.), *Studies in Gnosticism and Hellenistic Religions presented to G. Quispel on the Occasion of his 65th birthday*, Leiden, 1981.

Brown, P. R. L., *Religion and Society in the Age of St Augustine*, London, 1972.

Browne, E. G., *Literary History of Persia*, Cambridge, 1928.

Browning, R., *Byzantium and Bulgaria*, London, 1975.

— *The Byzantine Empire*, London, 1980.

Bryder, P., *The Chinese Transformations of Manichaeism: A Study of Chinese Manichaean Terminology*, Lund, 1985.

— (ed.), *Manichaean Studies: Proceedings of the First International Conference on Manichaeism*, Lund, 1988.

Buber, M., *Good and Evil*, New York, 1952.

Burkert, W., *Lore and Science in Ancient Pythagoreanism*, tr. E. Mihar, Jr, Cambridge, 1972.

— *Greek Religion*, tr. J. Raffan, Oxford, 1985.

— *Ancient Mystery Cults*, Harvard, 1987.

Burkitt, F. C., *The Religion of the Manichees*, Cambridge, 1925.

Burn, A. R., *Persia and the Greeks: The Defence of the West, c. 567–478*, 2nd edn, London, 1984.

Burstein, S. M. (tr.), *The Babyloniaca of Berossus*, Malibu, 1978.

Bury, J. B., *A History of the Later Roman Empire from Arcadius to Irene*, 2 vols., London, 1889.

— *A History of the Eastern Roman Empire from the Fall of Irene to the Accession of Basil I (AD 802–867)*, London, 1912.

— (ed.) *The Early History of the Slavonic Settlements in Dalmatia, Croatia and Serbia*, London, 1920.

Campbell, L. A., *Mithraic Iconography and Ideology*, Leiden, 1968.

Cedrenus, Georgius, *Historiarum Compendium*, ed. I. Bekker, 2 vols., *CSHB*, 1838–9.

Charles, R. H. (ed.), *The Apocrypha and Pseudoepigrapha of the Old Testament*, 2 vols., Oxford, 1913.

Ch'en, K., *Buddhism in China: A Historical Survey*, New Jersey, 1964.

Christensen, A., *L'Iran sous les Sassanides*, Copenhagen, 1936.

Cinnamus, Joannes, *Historiae*, ed. A. Meineke, *CSHB*, 1836.

Ćirković, S., *Istorija srednjovekovne bosanske drzave* [A History of the Medieval Bosnian State], Belgrade, 1964.

Clemen, C., *Fontes historiae religionis persicae*, Bonn, 1920.

Cohn, N., *The Pursuit of the Millennium*, London, 1957.

— *Europe's Inner Demons*, London, 1975.

Colledge, M. A. R., *The Parthians*, London, 1967.

Comnena, Anna, *Alexias*, ed. L. Schopen and L. Reifferscheid, 2 vols., *CSHB*, 1839–78; also in J. Migne, *PG*, vol. 131; *The Alexiad*, tr. E. Dawes, London, 1928.

Conybeare, F. C. (ed.), *The Key of Truth: A Manual of the Paulician Church in Armenia*, Oxford, 1898.

Corbine, H., *Spiritual Body and Celestial Earth: From Mazdean Iran to Shi'ite Iran*, tr. N. Pearson, London, 1990.

Ćorović, V., *Bosna i Hercegovina*, Belgrade, 1925.

Couliano, I. P., *Les Gnoses dualistes d'Occident: histoire et mythes*, Paris, 1990.

Cross, F. M., *The Ancient Library of Qumran*, New York, 1961.

Cumont, F., *Textes et monuments figurés relatifs aux mystères de Mithra*, 2 vols., Brussels, 1896–9.

— *The Oriental Religions in Roman Paganism*, Chicago and London, 1911.

— *Lux Perpetua*, Paris, 1947.

— *The Mysteries of Mithra*, tr. T. McCormack, New York, 1956.

Daniélou, J., *Theology of Jewish Christianity*, tr. and ed. J. A. Baker, London, 1964.

Darmesteter, J. (tr.), *Le Zend-Avesta*, 3 vols., Paris, 1892–3.

— (tr.), *The Zend-Avesta*: Part 1, *The Vendidad*, *SBE*, vol. 4, Oxford, 1895, repr. Delhi, 1965; Part 2, *The Sirozahs, Yashts and Nyayaesh*, *SBE*, vol. 23, Oxford, 1883, repr. Delhi, 1965.

Debevoise, N. C., *A Political History of Parthia*, Chicago, 1938.

Decret, F., *L'Afrique manichéenne*, 2 vols., Paris, 1978.

Dhalla, M. N., *Zoroastrian Theology*, New York, 1914.

— *History of Zoroastrianism*, New York, 1938.

Dobrev, P., *Prabălgarite* [The Proto-Bulgars], Sofia, 1991.

Dodds, E. R., *The Greeks and the Irrational*, Berkeley and London, 1951.

— *Pagans and Christians in an Age of Anxiety*, Cambridge, 1965.

von Döllinger, I., *Beträge zur Sektengeschichte des Mittelalters*, 2 vols., Munich, 1890, repr. 1968.

Dondaine, A., *Un traité néo-manichéen du XIIIe siècle: Le Liber de duobus principiis, suivi d'un fragment de rituel cathare*, Rome, 1939.

— 'Nouvelles sources de l'histoire doctrinale du néo-manichéisme au moyen âge', *Revue des sciences philosophiques et théologiques*, 28 (1939), pp. 465–88.

— 'Les Actes du concile albigeois de Saint-Félix-de-Caraman', in *Miscellanea Giovanni Mercati*, vol. 5, *Studi e Testi*, Vatican City, 125 (1946).

— 'Le Manuel de l'inquisiteur (1230–1330)', *Archivum Fratrum Praedicatorum* (Rome), 17 (1947), pp. 85–194.

— 'L'Hiérarchie cathare en Italie': Part 1, 'Le "De heresi catharorum in Lombardia"': Part 2, 'Le "Tractatus de hereticis" d'Anselme d'Alessandrie', *Archivum Fratrum Praedicatorum* (Rome), 19 (1949), pp. 280–312, 20 (1950), pp. 234–324.

— 'L'Origine de l'hérésie médiévale: À propos d'un livre récent', *Rivista di storia della Chiesa in Italia*, 6 (1952), pp. 47–78.

— 'Durand de Huesca et la polémique anti-cathare', *Archivum Fratrum Praedicatorum* (Rome), 29 (1959), pp. 228–76.

Doresse, J., *The Secret Books of the Egyptian Gnostics*, New York, 1960.

Dougherty, R. P., *Nabonidus and Belshazzar: A Study of the Closing Events of the Neo-Babylonian Empire*, New Haven, 1929.

Dragojlović, D., *Bogomilstvo na Balkanu i u Maloj Aziji* [Bogomilism in the Balkans and Asia Minor]: vol. 1, *Bogomilski rodonacalnici* [Bogomil Predecessors], Belgrade, 1979; vol. 2, *Bogomilstvo na pravoslavnom istoku* [Bogomilism in the Orthodox East], Belgrade, 1982.

— and V. Antić *Bogomilstvoto vo srednovekovnata izvorna graga* [Bogomilism in the Medieval Sources], Skopje, 1978.

Drijvers, H. J. W., *Bardaisan of Edessa*, Assen, 1966.

Duchesne-Guillemin, J., *Ormazd et Ahriman: L'aventure dualiste dans l'antiquité*, Paris, 1953.

— *The Western Response to Zoroaster*, Oxford, 1958.

— *La Religion de l'Iran ancien*, Paris, 1962.

— *Symbols and Values in Zoroastrianism*, New York, 1966.

Dujćev, I., 'I Bogomili nei paesi slavi e la loro storia', *L'Oriente Cristiano nella storia della civiltà*, Rome, 1963, pp. 619–41.

— *Medioevo bizantino-slavo*, 3 vols., Rome, 1965–71.

— 'Aux origines des courants dualistes à Byzance et chez les Slaves méridionaux', *Revue des Études Sud-est Européennes*, 1 (1969), pp. 51–62.

Dumézil, G., *Naissance d'archanges*, Paris, 1945.

Dunlop, D. M., *The History of the Jewish Khazars*, Princeton, 1954.

Dvornik, F., *Les Slaves, Byzance et Rome au IXe siècle*, Paris, 1926.

— *The Slavs: Their Early History and Civilization*, Boston, 1956.

Eberwin of Steinfeld, *Epistola ad S. Bernardum*, *PL*, vol. 182, pp. 676–80.

Eckbert of Schönau, *Sermones tredicim contra Catharos*, PL, vol. 195, cols. 11–102.

Eddy, S. K., *The King is Dead*, Lincoln, 1961.

Euthymius of Acmonia, 'Euthymii monachi coenobii Peribleptae epistula invectiva contra Phundagiagitus sive Bogomilos haereticos', ed. G. Ficker, in *Die Phundagiagiten*, Leipzig, 1908, pp. 3–86.

— *Euthymii monachi coenobii Peribleptae liber invectivus contra haeresim exsecrabilium et impiorum haereticorum qui Phundagiatae dicuntur*, PG, vol. 131, cols. 47–58.

Evans, A. J., *Through Bosnia and Herzegovina on Foot during the Insurrection*, London, 1877, repr. New York, 1971.

Eznik of Kolb, *Wieder die Sekten* [Against the Sects], tr. J. M. Schmidt, Vienna, 1900.

Fallon, F. T., *The Enthronement of Sabaoth: Jewish Elements in Gnostic Creation Myths*, Leiden, 1978.

Ficker, G., *Die Phundagiagiten: Ein Betrag zur Ketzergeschichte des byzantinischen Mittelalters*, Leipzig, 1908.

Filoramo, G., *A History of Gnosticism*, tr. A. Alcock, Oxford, 1990.

Fine, J. V. A., *The Bosnian Church: A New Interpretation*, New York and London, 1975.

— *The Early Medieval Balkans*, Ann Arbor, Michigan, 1983.

— *The Late Medieval Balkans*, Ann Arbor, Michigan, 1987.

Flusser, D., *Judaism and the Origins of Christianity*, Jerusalem, 1988.

Fol, A., *Trakiiskiat Dionis* [The Thracian Dionysus], 1, Sofia, 1991.

— and I. Marazov, *Thrace and the Thracians*, London, 1977.

Forsyth, N., *The Old Enemy: Satan and the Combat Myth*, Princeton, 1987.

Frye, R. N., *The Heritage of Persia*, London, 1962.

— *The History of Ancient Iran*, Munich, 1984.

von Gabain, A., *Das uigurische Königreich von Chotscho 850–1250*, Berlin, 1961.

Garsoïan, N. G., *The Paulician Heresy*, The Hague and Paris, 1967.

— 'Byzantine Heresy: A Reinterpretation', *Dumbarton Oak Papers* (Washington, D. C.), 25 (1971), pp. 85–113.

— *Armenia between Byzantium and the Sasanians*, London, 1985.

Gaster, T. H. (tr.), *The Scriptures of the Dead Sea Sect*, London, 1957.

Genning, V. F. and A. H. Halikov, *Rannie bolgari na Volge* [The Early Bulgars on the Volga], Moscow, 1964.

Germanos II, 'Germani Patriarchae Constantinopolitani epistula ad Constantinopolitanos contra Bogomilos', ed. G. Ficker, in *Die Phundagiagiten*, Leipzig, 1908, pp. 115–25.

Gershevitch, I., *The Avestan Hymn to Mithra*, Cambridge, 1959.

— 'Zoroaster's Own Contribution', *Journal of Near-Eastern Studies*, 23 (1964), pp. 12–38.

Gibbon, E., *The History of the Decline and Fall of the Roman Empire*, ed. J. B. Bury, 7 vols., 1909–14.

Gimbutas, M., *The Slavs*, London, 1971.

Glycas, Michael, *Annales*, ed. I. Bekker, *CSHB* 1836.

Gnoli, G., *Zoroaster's Time and Homeland: A Study on the Origins of Mazdaism and Related Problems*, Naples, 1980.

Gouillard, J., 'L'hérésie dans l'empire byzantin des origines au XIIe siècle', in *Travaux et mémoires*, 1 (1965), pp. 299–324.

— 'Le Synodicon de l'orthodoxie' in *Travaux et mémoires*, vol. 2 (1967), pp. 1–316.

Grayson, A. K., *Assyrian and Babylonian Chronicles*, Locust Valley, New York, 1975.

Gregoras, Nicephorus, *Byzantina Historia*, ed. L. Schopen and I. Bekker, 3 vols., *CSHB*, 1829–55.

Guthrie, W. K. C., *Orpheus and Greek Religion*, 2nd edn, London, 1952.

— *The Greeks and Their Gods*, London, 1950.

Gyuzelev, V., *Knyaz Boris Pŭrvi* [Prince Boris 1], Sofia, 1969.

Hamilton, B., *Religion in the Medieval West*, London and New York, 1986.

Hanson, P. D., *The Dawn of Apocalyptic*, Philadelphia, 1975.

Harmatta, J., *Studies in the History and Language of the Sarmatians*, Szeged, 1970.

von Harnack, A., *Marcion*, Leipzig, 1924.

Hausherr, I., *Études de spiritualité orientale*, Rome, 1969.

Haussig, H. W., *A History of Byzantine Civilization*, tr. J. Hussey, London, 1971.

Hegemonius, 'Acta Archelai', ed. C. H. Beeson, in *Die Griechischen Christlichen Schriftsteller der ersten drei Jahrhunderte*, vol. 16, Leipzig, 1906.

Hengel, M., *Judaism and Hellenism*, 2 vols., Philadelphia, 1974.

Henneke, E. and W. Schneemelcher (eds.), *New Testament Apocrypha*, 2 vols., Philadelphia, 1963–5.

Henning, W. B., *Zoroaster, Politician or Witch-Doctor?*, Oxford, 1951.

Henrichs, A., 'Mani and the Babylonian Baptists', in *Harvard Studies in Classical Philology*, 77 (1973), pp. 23–59.

Herrmann, G., *The Iranian Revival*, Oxford, 1977.

Herzfeld, E., *Zoroaster and His World*, 2 vols., Princeton, 1947.

— *The Persian Empire*, Wiesbaden, 1968.

Hinnells, J. R., *Persian Mythology*, London, 1973.

— (ed.), *Mithraic Studies*, 2 vols., Manchester, 1975.

van der Horst, P. W. and J. Mansfeld, *An Alexandrian Platonist Against Dualism*, Leiden, 1974.

Hosch, E., *The Balkans*, tr. T. Alexander, New York, 1972.

Hussey, J. M., *Church and Learning in the Byzantine Empire 867–1185*, London, 1937.

— *The Orthodox Church in Byzantium*, Oxford, 1986.

Insler, S., *The Gathas of Zarathustra*, Leiden, 1975.

Ivanov, I., *Bogomilski knigi i legendi* [Bogomil Books and Legends], Sofia, 1925 (French tr.: *Livres et légendes bogomiles*, Paris, 1976).

Jackson, A. V. W., *Researches in Manichaeism with Special Reference to the Turfan Fragments*, New York, 1932.

Jacobsen, T., *The Treasures of Darkness*, New Haven and London, 1976.

Jaeger, W., *Aristotle: Fundamentals of the History of His Development*, tr. R. Robinson, 2nd edn, Oxford, 1948.

James, M. R. (tr.), *The Apocryphal New Testament*, Oxford, 1924.

Jonas, H., *The Gnostic Religion*, Boston, 1958.

Juan de Torquemada, *Symbolum pro informatione manichaeorum* (*El Bogomilismo en Bosnia*), ed. N. L. Martines and V. Proano, Burgos, 1958.

Jung, L., *Fallen Angels in Jewish, Christian and Mohammedan Literature*, Philadelphia, 1926.

Kakouri, K. J., *Dionysiaka: Aspects of the Popular Thracian Religion of To-day*, Athens, 1965.

Kalužniacki, E., *Werke des Patriarchen von Bulgarien Euthymius*, Vienna, 1901.

Kelly, H. A., *The Devil, Demonology, and Witchcraft*, New York, 1974.

Kent, R. G., *Old Persian: Grammar, Texts, Lexicon*, 2nd edn, New Haven, 1953.

Kerenyi, C., *Dionysos: Archetypal Image of Indestructible Life*, tr. R. Mannheim, London, 1976.

Kern, O., *Orphicorum fragmenta*, Berlin, 1922.

Klijn, A. F. and G. J. Reinink, *Patristic Evidence for Jewish-Christian Sects*, Leiden, 1973.

Klimkeit, H. J., 'Vairocana und das Lichtkreuz. Manichäische Elemente in der Kunst von Alchi (West Tibet)', *Zentralasiatische Studien*, 13 (1979), pp. 357–98.

— 'Hindu deities in Manichaean art', *Zentralasiatische Studien*, 14 (1980), pp. 179–99.

— 'Christians, Buddhists and Manichaeans in Central Asia', in *Buddhist-Christian Studies*, 1 (1981), pp. 46–50.

Kluger, R. S., *Satan in the Old Testament*, tr. H. Nagel, Evanston, 1967.

Koenen, L. and C. Römer (eds.), *Der Kölner Mani-Kodex*, Opladen, 1988.

Kruglikova, I. T. (ed.), *Drevnyaya Baktria*, 2 vols., Moscow, 1976–9.

Krumbacher, K., *Geschichte der byzantinischen Literatur*, 2nd edn, Munich, 1897.

Kuhrt, A. and S. Sherwin-White (eds.), *Hellenism in the East*, Berkeley, 1987.

— H. Sancisi-Weerdenburg, *et al.* (eds.), *Achaemenid History*, 7 vols., Leiden, 1987–91.

Lang, D. M., *The Bulgarians*, London, 1976.

Laurent, J., *L'Arménie entre Byzance et l'Islam*, Paris, 1919.

Le Roy Ladurie, E., *Montaillou: village occitan de 1294 à 1324*, Paris, 1978.

Lea, H. C., *A History of the Inquisition of the Middle Ages*, 3 vols., New York and London, 1888.

Legge, F., *Forerunners and Rivals of Christianity*, 2 vols., Cambridge, 1915.

Lieu, S. N. C., *The Religion of Light: An Introduction to the History of Manichaeism in China*, Hong Kong, 1979.

— *Manichaeism in the Later Roman Empire and Medieval China*, 2nd rev. edn, Tübingen, 1992.

Lintforth, I. M., *The Arts of Orpheus*, Berkeley, 1941.

Loos, M., *Dualist Heresy in the Middle Ages*, Prague, 1974.

Lossky, V., *The Mystical Theology of the Eastern Church*, Cambridge, 1957.

Luckenbill, D. D., *Ancient Records of Assyria and Babylonia*, 2 vols., Chicago, 1926–7.

Mandić, D., *Bogomilska crkva bosanskih krstjana* [The Bogomil Church of the Bosnian 'Krstjani'], Chicago, 1962.

Mango, C., *Byzantium: The Empire of New Rome*, London, 1980.

Manselli, R., *Testi per lo studio della Eresia Catara*, Turin, 1964.

— 'Il manicheismo medievale', *Ricerche religiose*, 20 (1949), pp. 65–94.

Mansi, J. D., *Sacrorum conciliorum nova et amplissima collectio*, 54 vols., reprint of 1901–27 edn, Graz, 1960–1.

Marquart, J., *Osteuropäische und ostasiatische Streifzüge*, Leipzig, 1903.

Martene, E. and E. Durand, *Veterum scriptorum et monumentorum historicum, dogmaticarum, moralium amplissima collectio*, 9 vols., Paris, 1724–33.

Martin, E., *A History of the Iconoclastic Controversy*, London, 1930.

Matthew of Paris, *Chronica majora*, ed. H. R. Luard, Rolls Series, no. 57, 7 vols., London, 1872–83.

Messina, G., *Der Ursprung der Magier und die zarathustrische Religion*, Rome, 1930.

Meyendorff, J., *A Study of Gregory Palamas*, New York, 1964.

— *St Gregory Palamas and Orthodox Spirituality*, New York, 1974.

Miller, W., *The Balkans*, New York and London, 1896.

Mills, L. H. (tr.), *Zend Avesta*: Part 3, *The Yasna, Visparad, Afrinagan, Gahs and Miscellaneous Fragments*, *SBE*, vol. 31, Oxford, 1887, repr. Delhi, 1965.

Minns, E. H., *Scythians and Greeks*, Cambridge, 1913.

Mitchell, C. W. *et al.* (eds.), *S. Ephraim's Prose Refutations of Mani, Marcion and Bardaisan*, 2 vols., London, 1912–21.

Mole, M., *Culte, mythe et cosmologie dans l'Iran ancien*, Paris, 1963.

— *La légende de Zoroaster selon les textes pehlevis*, Paris, 1967.

Momigliano, A., *Alien Wisdom*, Cambridge, 1975.

Moneta of Cremona, *Adversus Catharos and Valdenses libri quinque*, ed. T. A. Ricchini, Rome, 1743.

Monumenta Serbica spectantia historiam Serbiae, Bosnae, Ragusii, ed. F. Miklosich, Vienna, 1858.

Moore, R. I., *The Birth of Popular Heresy*, London, 1975.

Moulton, J. H., *Early Zoroastrianism*, London, 1913.

— *The Treasure of the Magi*, Oxford, 1917.

al-Nadim, *The Fihristi of al-Nadim*, tr. B. Dodge, 2 vols., New York, 1970.

Narain, A. K., *The Indo-Greeks*, Oxford, 1957.

Nelli, R., *Le Phénomène cathare*, Paris, 1964.

— (tr.), *Écritures cathares*, Paris, 1968.

— *La Philosophie du catharisme*, Paris, 1975.

Nicetas Choniates, *De Manuele Comneno*, in *Historia*, ed. I Bekker, CSHB, 1835.

Nicholson, H., *Templars, Hospitallers and Teutonic Knights: Images of the Military Orders, 1128–1291*, Leicester, 1993.

Niel, F., *Montségur: Temple et fortresse des cathares d'Occitanie*, Grenoble, 1967.

Nilsson, M. P., 'Early Orphism and Kindred Religious Movements', *Harvard Theological Review*, 28 (1935), pp. 181–230.

— *A History of Greek Religion*, tr. F. J. Fielden, Oxford, 1925.

— *The Dionysiac Mysteries of the Hellenistic and Roman Age*, Lund, 1957.

Nock, A. D., *Essays on Religion and the Ancient World* (sel. and ed. Z. Stewart), 2 vols., Oxford, 1972.

Nyberg, H. S., *Die Religionen des alten Iran*, tr. H. Schaeder, Leipzig, 1938.

Oates, J., *Babylon*, London, rev. edn, 1986.

Obolensky, D., *The Bogomils: A Study in Balkan Neo-Manichaeism*, Cambridge, 1948.

— *The Byzantine Commonwealth: Eastern Europe 500–1453*, London, 1971.

Oeder, J. L., *Dissertatio inauguralis prodromum historiae Bogomilorum criticae exhibens*, Gottingae, 1734.

Olmstead, A. T., *History of the Persian Empire*, Chicago, 1948.

Olschki, L., 'Manichaeism, Buddhism and Christianity in Marco Polo's China', *Zeitschrift der schweizerischen Gesellschaft für Asienkunde*, 5 (1951), pp. 1–21.

Ort, L. J. R., *Mani: A Religio-historical Description of his Personality*, Leiden, 1967.

Otto, W. F., *Dionysos: Mythos und Kultus*, Frankfurt-am-Main, 1933.

Pagels, E., *The Gnostic Gospels*, London and New York, 1979.

Pavry, J. D. C. (ed.), *Oriental Studies in Honour of C. E. Pavry*, Oxford, 1933.

Pétrement, S., *Le Dualisme dans l'histoire de la philosophie et des religions*, Paris, 1946.

— *Essai sur le dualisme chez Platon, les Gnostiques et les Manichéens*, Paris, 1947.

Petrus Siculus, *Historia Manichaeorum qui et Paulicani dicuntur*, *PG*, vol. 104, cols. 1239–1305.

Pettazzoni, R., *Essays on the History of Religions*, tr. J. H. Rose, Leiden, 1954.

Photius, *Contra Manichaeos*, *PG*, vol. 102, cols. 15–265.

Piotrovskii, B. B. (ed.), *Istoriya narodov severnogo Kavkaza s drevneishikh vremen do kontsa XVIIIv.* [History of the peoples in the North Caucasus from ancient times until the end of the 18th century], Moscow, 1988.

Pletneva, S. A., *Ot Kochevi k gorodam* [From Nomadism to City], Moscow, 1967.

— *Khazary* [The Khazars], Moscow, 1976.

Polotsky, H. J. (ed. and tr.), *Manichäische Homilien*, Stuttgart, 1934.

— and A. Böhlig (trs. and eds.), *Kephalaia*, vol. 1, Stuttgart, 1940.

Pritchard, J. B., *Ancient Near Eastern Texts Relating to the Old Testament*, 3rd edn with supplement, Princeton, 1969.

Pritsak, O., 'The Origin of Rus', An inaugural lecture, Harvard Ukranian Research Institute, Occasional Papers, Cambridge, Massachusetts., 1975.

— 'The Khazars Kingdom's Conversion to Judaism', *Harvard Ukranian Studies*, 2 (1978), pp. 261–81.

— *The Origin of Rus*: vol. 1, *Old Scandinavian Sources other than the Sagas*, Cambridge, Massachusetts, 1981.

Psellus, Michael, *Dialogus de daemonum operatione*, *PG*, vol. 122, cols. 819–76.

Puech, H.-C., *Le manichéisme: son fondateur, sa doctrine*, Paris, 1949.

— and A. Vaillant (eds. and trs.), *Le Traité contre les Bogomiles de Cosmas le prêtre*, Paris, 1945.

Quandt, G., *Orphei Hymni*, Berlin, 1941.

Quispel, G., *Gnosis als Weltreligion*, Zürich, 1951.

— *Gnostic Studies*, 2 vols., Leiden, 1974–5.

Ralph the Bald, *Raoul Glaber: Les cinq livres de ses histoires* [*900–1044*], ed. M. Prou, Paris, 1886.

Reinach, S., *Antiquités du Bosphore cimmérien*, Paris, 1892.

— *Cultes, Mythes et Religions*, 2 vols, Paris, 1905–6.

Reitzenstein, R., *Hellenistic Mystery-Religions*, tr. J. Steely, Pittsburgh, 1978.

— and H. H. Schaeder, *Studien zum antiken Syncretismus aus Iran und Griechenland*, Leipzig/Berlin, 1926.

Revard, S. P., *The War in Heaven: Paradise Lost and the Tradition of Satan's Rebellion*, New York, 1980.

Ricoeur, P., *The Symbolism of Evil*, Boston, 1967.

Robert of Auxerre, *Roberti canonici S. Mariani Autissiodorensis Chronicon*, ed. O. Holder-Egger, *MGH SS*, vol. 26, pp. 219–87.

Robinson, J. T. *et al.* (eds.), *The Nag Hammadi Library*, Leiden, 1973.
— (ed.), *The Nag Hammadi Library in English*, Leiden, 1977.
Roche, D., *Études manichéennes et cathares*, Arques, 1952.
Rohde, E., *Psyche: The Cult of Souls and Belief in Immortality among the Greeks*, tr. (from the 8th edn) W. B. Hillis, London, 1925.
Romaios, C. A., *Cultes populaires de la Thrace*, Athens, 1949.
Roquebert, M., *L'Epopée cathare*, 3 vols., Toulouse, 1970–86.
Rosenfield, J. M., *The Dynastic Art of the Kushans*, Berkeley, 1967.
Rostovtzeff, M. I., *Iranians and Greeks in South Russia*, Oxford, 1922.
— *Skifia i Bospor*, Leningrad, 1925.
Rudolph, K., *Gnosis*, ed. and tr. R. McL. Wilson, Edinburgh, 1983.
Runciman, S., *A History of the First Bulgarian Empire*, London, 1930.
— *The Medieval Manichee: A Study of the Christian Dualist Heresy*, Cambridge, 1946.
— *The Eastern Schism*, London, 1955.
Russell, D. S., *The Method and Message of Jewish Apocalyptic*, Philadelphia, 1964.
Russell, J. B., *Dissent and Reform in the Early Middle Ages*, Berkeley, 1965.
— *The Devil: Perceptions of Evil from Antiquity to Primitive Christianity*, New York, 1977.
— *Satan: The Early Christian Tradition*, New York, 1981.
— *Lucifer: The Devil in the Middle Ages*, New York, 1985.
Russell, J. R., *Zoroastrianism in Armenia*, Harvard Iranian Series v, Cambridge, Massachusetts, 1987.
Ryazanovskii, T. A., *Demolonolgiya v drevnerusskoi literature* [The Demonology in Old Russian Literature], Moscow, 1915.
St Bernard of Clairvaux, *Epistolae*, 241, 242, *PL*, vol. 182, cols. 434–7.
— *Sermones super Cantica canticorum*, in J. Leclercq, C. H. Talbot and H. M. Rochais (eds.), *Sancti Bernardi Opera*, 2 vols., Rome, 1957–8.
Scharf, A., *Byzantine Jewry*, London, 1971.
Schmidt, C., *Histoire et doctrine de la secte des Cathares ou Albigeois*, 2 vols., Paris/Geneva, 1849.
Scholem, G., *Jewish Gnosticism, Merkabah Mysticism and Talmudic Tradition*, New York, 1960.
— *Major Trends in Jewish Mysticism*, 3rd edn, New York, 1961.
— *The Messianic Idea in Judaism*, London, 1971.
— *Origins of the Kabbalah*, tr. A. Arkush, Princeton, 1987.
Scylitzes, Joannes, *Synopsis historiarum*, ed. H. Thurn, Berlin/New York, 1973.
Sedlar, J. W., *India and the Greek World*, New Jersey, 1980.
Segal, A., *Two Powers in Heaven*, Leiden, 1977.

Sharenkoff, V. N., *A Study of Manichaeism in Bulgaria with Special Reference to the Bogomils*, New York, 1927.

Shaked, S., 'Esoteric Trends in Zoroastrianism', *The Israel Academy of Sciences and Humanities, Proceedings* (Jerusalem), 3:7 (1969), pp. 175–221.

— (tr.), *The Wisdom of the Sasanian Sages (Denkard VI)*, Boulder, Colorado, 1979.

— (ed.), *Irano-Judaica*, 2 vols., Jerusalem, 1982–90.

Sharpe, E. and J. Hinnells (eds.), *Man and His Salvation: Studies in Memory of S. G. F. Brandon*, Manchester, 1973.

Sinor, D., *Introduction à l'étude de l'Eurasie Centrale*, Wiesbaden, 1963.

— *Inner Asia and its Contacts with Medieval Europe*, London, 1977.

Smith, C. E., *Innocent III: Church Defender*, Baton Rouge, 1951.

Smith, S., *Babylonian Historical Texts Relating to the Capture and Downfall of Babylon*, London, 1924.

— *Isaiah Chapters XL–LV: Literary Criticism and History*, London, 1944.

Söderberg, H., *La Religion des Cathares: Étude sur le gnosticisme de la basse antiquité et du moyen âge*, Uppsala, 1949.

Spinka, M., *A History of Christianity in the Balkans*, Chicago, 1933.

Starr, J., 'An Eastern Christian Sect: The Athinganoi', *Harvard Theological Review*, 2 (1936), pp. 93–106.

Staviskii, B., *La Bactriane sous les Kushans*, tr. P. Bernard, M. Burda, F. Grenet, P. Leriche, Paris, 1986.

Stevenson, J., *A New Eusebius*, London, 1968.

Stone, M. E. (ed.), *Jewish Writing of the Second Temple Period*, Philadelphia, 1984.

Stroumsa, G. A. G., *Another Seed: Studies in Gnostic Mythology*, Leiden, 1984.

Sulimirski, T., *The Sarmatians*, London, 1970.

Symeon of Thessalonica, *Symeonis Thessalonicensis archiepiscopi. Adversus omnes haeresis*, *PG*, vol. 155, cols. 33–176.

Tacheva-Hitova, M., *The Oriental Cults in Moesia Inferior and Thracia*, Leiden, 1983.

Tarn, W. W., *Hellenistic Civilization*, 3rd edn, London, 1952.

— *The Greeks in Bactria and India*, 2nd edn, Cambridge, 1951.

Tcherikover, V., *Hellenistic Civilization and the Jews*, Philadelphia, 1959.

Ter Mkrttschian, K., *Die Paulikianer im byzantinischen Kaiserreiche und verwandte ketzerische Erscheinungen in Armenien*, Leipzig, 1893.

Texidor, J., *The Pagan God*, Princeton, 1977.

Theiner, A., *Vetera monumenta historica Hungariam sacram illustrantia*, 2 vols., Rome, 1859–60.

— *Vetera monumenta Slavorum Meridionalium historiam illustrantia*, Rome, 1863.

Theophanes, *Chronographia*, ed. C. de Boor, Leipzig, 2 vols., 1883–5.

Theophanes Continuatus, *Chronographia*, ed. I. Bekker, *CSHB*, 1838.

Thouzellier, C., *Un Traité cathare inédit du début du XIIIe siècle d'après le 'Liber contra manicheos' de Durand de Huesca*, Louvain, 1961.

— *Catharisme et valdéisme en Languedoc à la fin du XIIe et au début du XIIIe siècle, Politique pontificale-controverses*, rev. edn, Paris, 1969.

— *Hérésie et hérétiques: Vaudois, cathares, patarins, albigeois*, Rome, 1969.

Toynbee, A., *A Study of History*, 10 vols., London, 1934–54.

— *Constantine Porphyrogenitus and His World*, London, 1973.

Trachtenberg, J., *The Devil and the Jews*, New Haven, 1943.

Tritton, A., *The Caliphs and their Non-Muslim Subjects*, London, 1930.

Tucci, G., *The Religions of Tibet*, tr. G. Samuel, London/Berkeley, 1980.

Turberville, A., *Medieval Heresy and the Inquisition*, London, 1920.

Urbach, E. E., *The Sages, Their Concepts and Beliefs*, 2 vols., Jerusalem, 1975.

Vaklinov, S., *Formirane na staro-bălgarskata kultura 6–9 vek* [The Formation of the Old Bulgarian Culture in the Sixth to Ninth Centuries], Sofia, 1977.

Valeev, F. H., *Drevnee i srednevekovoe iskusstvo srednego povolzia* [Ancient and Medieval Art in the Middle Volga Region], Joshkar Ola, 1975.

Van Cleve, J. C., *The Emperor Frederick II of Hohenstaufen: Immutator Mundi*, Oxford, 1972.

Vermaseren, M. J., *Corpus inscriptionum et monumentum religionis mithraice*, 2 vols., The Hague, 1956–60.

— *Mithras the Secret God*, tr. T. and V. Megaw, London/Toronto, 1963.

Vermes, G., *The Dead Sea Scrolls in English*, 3rd edn, Harmondsworth, 1987.

Vicaire, M. H., *Saint Dominic and His Times*, tr. K. Pond, New York, 1965.

Volpe, G., *Movimenti religiosi e sette ereticali nella società medievale italiana (secoli XI–XIV)*, 2nd edn, Florence, 1926.

Wakefield, W., *Heresy, Crusade and Inquisition in Southern France*, London, 1974.

— and A. Evans (eds. and trs.), *Heresies of the High Middle Ages*, New York, 1969.

Warner, H. J., *The Albigensian Heresy*, 2 vols., London, 1922–8.

West, E. W. (tr.), *The Bundahis, Selections of Zad-sparam, Bahman Yast, and Shayast la-shayast*, in: *Pahlavi Texts*, Part 1, *SBE*, vol. 5, Oxford, 1880, repr. Delhi, 1965.

— (tr.), *The Dadistan-i Dinik and the Epistles of Manuskihar*, in: *Pahlavi Texts*, Part 2, *SBE*, vol. 18, Oxford, 1882, repr. Delhi, 1965.

— (tr.), *Dina-i Mainög-i Khirad, Sikand-Gümanik Vigar, Sar Dar*, in: *Pahlavi Texts*, Part 3, *SBE*, vol. 24, Oxford, 1885, repr. Delhi, 1965.

— (tr.), *Dinkard*, Books VIII and IX, in: *Pahlavi Texts*, Part 4, *Contents of the Nasks*, *SBE*, vol. 37, Oxford, 1892, repr. Delhi, 1965.

— (tr.), *Dinkard*, Books VII and V, *Selections of Zad-spram* in: *Pahlavi Texts*, Part 5, *Marvels of Zoroastrianism*, *SBE*, vol. 47, Oxford, 1897, repr. Delhi, 1965.

West, M. L., *Early Greek Philosophy and the Orient*, Oxford, 1971.

— *The Orphic Poems*, Oxford, 1983.

Widengren, G., *The Great Vohu Manu and the Apostle of God, Studies in Iranian and Manichaean religion*, Uppsala/Leipzig, 1945.

— *Mani and Manichaeism*, London, 1965.

— *Les Religions de l'Iran*, Paris, 1968.

— (ed.), *Der Manichäismus*, Darmstadt, 1977.

Wilson, R. McL., *The Gnostic Problem*, London, 1958.

— *Gnosis and the New Testament*, Oxford, 1968.

Winston, D., 'The Iranian Component in the Bible, Apocrypha and Qumran: A Review of the Evidence', *History of Religions* 5 (1966), pp. 183–216.

Wolf, J., *Historia Bogomilorum*, Vitembergae, 1712.

Yadin, Y., *The Scroll of the War of the Sons of Light against the Sons of Darkness*, Oxford, 1962.

Yamauchi, E., *Pre-Christian Gnosticism*, London, 1973.

Yates, F., *Giordano Bruno and the Hermetic Tradition*, London, 1978.

Zaehner, R. C., *Zurvan: A Zoroastrian Dilemma*, Oxford, 1955.

— *Teachings of the Magi*, London, 1956.

— *The Dawn and Twilight of Zoroastrianism*, London, 1961.

Zigabenus, Euthymius, *Panoplia Dogmatica*, *PG*, vol. 130; vol. 131, cols. 39–48.

— *De haeresi Bogomilorum narratio*, ed. G. Ficker, *Die Phundagiagiten*, Leipzig, 1908, pp. 89–111.

Zonaras, Ioannes, *Annales Epitome Historiarum*, ed. M. Pinder, T. Büttner-Wobst, 3 vols., *CSHB*, 1841–1897.

Notes

Quotes from the Bible are taken from the New English Bible except in some instances where the King James Version has been used. These are followed by the abbreviation *KJV*. Other abbreviations used in the notes and bibliography are:

CMC Cologne Mani Codex
CSHB Corpus Scriptorum Historiae Byzantinae
MGH SS Monumenta Germaniae Historica, Scriptores
PG Patrologia Graeca
PL Patrologia Latina
SBE Sacred Books of the East

Preface

1 Among the most important recent works on these subjects are: R. Le Forestier, *La Franc-maçonnerie templière et occultiste aux XVIIIe et XIXe siècles* (Paris, 1970); F. Yates, *The Rosicrucian Enlightenment* (London and Boston, 1972); J. W. Montgomery, *Cross and Crucible* (2 vols., The Hague, 1973); K. R. H. Frick, *Die Erleuchteten* (Graz, 1973); *Licht und Finsternis*, Part 1 (Graz, 1975); *Licht und Finsternis*, Part 2 (Graz, 1978); M. Barber, *The Trial of the Templars* (Cambridge, 1978); P. Partner, *The Murdered Magicians* (Oxford, 1982); D. Stevenson, *The Origins of Freemasonry* (Cambridge, 1988).

2 It is generally thought that the discovery and trial of the heretical group at Cologne in 1143–4 represents the first certain sign of the rise of Catharism proper. An account of the incident at Cologne is contained in the appeal of Eberwin, prior of the Premonstratensian abbey of Steinfeld, to St Bernard of Clairvaux against the Cologne heretics. The Cologne

heretics claimed that they were heirs to a hidden 'apostolic' tradition which had been kept secret since the time of the martyrs and was sustained in Greece and 'other lands'.

3 For the designation 'Civilization of Old Europe', its scope and significance see M. Gimbutas, *The Gods and Goddesses of Old Europe* (London, 1974), pp. 17–37. A discussion of the importance of the gold treasure discovered near Lake Varna in north-east Bulgaria in 1972 may be found in C. Renfrew, *Problems in European Prehistory* (Edinburgh, 1979), pp. 377–89, where this discovery is defined as demonstrably 'the earliest major assemblage of gold artefacts to be unearthed anywhere in the world, an event of some note, comparable in significance to Schliemann's find of the Great Treasure at Troy'. The Varna finds predate those of Troy by at least 1,500 years.

4 The chronicle of the canonist Robert of Auxerre (*Roberti canonici S. Mariani Autissiodorensis Chronicon*, ed. O. Holder-Egger, MGH SS, 26, pp. 219–87) alludes to the spread of the heresy in southern France (p. 271) and to the missions and measures taken against the heretics (pp. 260, 270–71). According to the chronicle of the monk Alberic of Châlons-sur-Marne (*Chronica Albrici monachi Trium Fontium a monachi novi monasterii Hoiensis interpolata*, ed. P. Scheffer-Boichorst, MGH SS, 23, pp. 631–950), many heretical Bulgars were burned and became pseudo-martyrs of the Devil. The chronicle documents the mass burning of 183 Bulgars who were tried by the infamous Dominican inquisitor Robert the Bulgar, himself a former heretic.

5 J. B. Bossuet, *Histoire des variations des églises protestantes* (2 vols., Paris, 1688), vol. 2, pp. 100–103, 154–7.

6 Voltaire, *Dictionnaire philosophique*, vol. 2, *Oeuvres complètes de Voltaire*, vol. 38, pp. 356–60.

1 The Dualist Reformation

1 The tract was discovered and published by A. Dondaine in 1939, *Un traité néo-manichéen du XIIIe siècle: Le Liber de duobus principiis, suivi d'un fragment de rituel cathare* (Rome, 1939). See A. Borst's comments in *Die Katharer* (Stuttgart, 1953), pp. 284–318. The quotations are from the translation in W. Wakefield and A. Evans, *Heresies of the High Middle Ages* (New York, 1969), pp. 511–91.

2 A seminal analysis of the types of religious dualism has been advanced in U. Bianchi, *Il dualismo religioso. Saggio storico ed etnologico* (Rome, 1958). A

more general treatment of dualism may be found in S. Pétrement, *Le Dualisme dans l'histoire de la philosophie et des religions* (Paris, 1946). The discussion of religious dualism here will be confined to those traditions of immediate relevance to the belief system of medieval dualism. A wide-ranging survey of dualism in different religious traditions may be found in M. Eliade, 'Prolegomenon to Religious Dualism' in *The Quest: History and Meaning in Religion* (Chicago, 1969).

3 R. C. Zaehner, *The Dawn and Twilight of Zoroastrianism* (London, 1961), p. 170.

4 M. Boyce has argued consistently for early dates of Zoroaster, ranging from 1700–1500 BC to 1400–1000 BC: *Zoroastrians: Their Religious Beliefs and Practices* (London, 1979), p. 18; *A History of Zoroastrianism*, vol. 1, 2nd edn (Leiden, 1985), pp. 190–91 and vol. 2 (Leiden, 1982), p. 3. An eighth-century date (784–707 BC) has been suggested by O. Klima, 'The Date of Zoroaster', *Archiv Orientalni*, 27 (1959), p. 564. The Iranian chronology of the Zoroaster's prophetship in relation to the 12,000 years' 'life of the world' remains highly controversial, and has been accepted as historical by, among others, E. Herzfeld, 'The Traditional Date of Zoroaster' in J. D. C. Pavry (ed.), *Oriental Studies in Honour of C. E. Pavry* (Oxford, 1933), pp. 132–6; Zaehner, *The Dawn and Twilight*, p. 33, but forcefully rejected by, for example, G. Gnoli, *Zoroaster's Time and Homeland: A Study on the Origins of Mazdaism* (Naples, 1980), pp. 163–75; M. Mole, *Culte, mythe et cosmologie dans l'Iran ancien* (Paris, 1963), pp. 530ff.

5 Gnoli, *Zoroaster's Time*, pp. 167–75; M. N. Dhalla, *History of Zoroastrianism* (New York, 1938), pp. 11ff. See also the counter-arguments in Boyce, *A History of Zoroastrianism*, vol. 2, pp. 1–4.

6 The classical references placing Zoroaster in Bactria or western Iran have been assembled in A. V. W. Jackson, *Zoroaster the Prophet of Ancient Iran* (New York, 1899), respectively pp. 186–8 and pp. 189–91, while he also compiled a valuable list of the classical passages alluding to Zoroaster, pp. 226–73. In modern Zoroastrian tradition Bactria may similarly be seen as Zoroaster's homeland (P. D. Mehta, *Zaratushtra* (Shaftesbury, 1985), pp. 7–8).

7 The Iranian traditions about the death of Zoroaster are listed in Jackson, *Zoroaster the Prophet*, pp. 127–32.

8 W. Jaeger, *Aristotle: Fundamentals of the History of His Development*, tr. R. Robinson, 2nd edn (Oxford, 1948), pp. 133–4.

9 The traditions of Zoroaster as king of Bactria and his mythical wars with Assyria and Semiramis have been collected in Jackson, *Zoroaster the Prophet*, pp. 154–7, 186–7, 274–8, while an elaborate version of the Ninus–Semiramis legend is recounted in Diodorus 2:4.1–20.

10 Characteristic Christian traditions concerning Zoroaster are contained, for example, in the Clementine Recognitions 4:27–9 (*PG*, vol. 1, cols. 1326ff.); the Clementine Homilies 9:4ff. (*PG*, vol. 2, cols. 244ff.), as well as in later works like Georgius Cedrenus, *Historiarum Compendium*.

11 Peter Comestor, *Historia scholastica, PL,* vol. 198, col. 1090.

12 Marsilio Ficino, *Platonica Theologia*, ed. and tr. R. Marcel (3 vols., Paris, 1964–70), vol. 3, p. 148.

13 F. Nietzsche, *Gesamtausgabe in Großoktav*, ed. C. G. Naumann, and later A. Kröner (19 vols., Leipzig, from 1894), vol. 14, p. 303.

14 The texts of the *Avesta* have been translated into English by J. Darmesteter and L. H. Mills in *Zend-Avesta*, *SBE* (Oxford 1880–87, repr. Delhi, 1965), vols. 4, 23 and 31. Apart from Mills's translation of the *Gathas* in *Zend-Avesta: Yasna*, *SBE*, vol. 31, there exist several direct and indirect English translations of the *Gathas*. The following quotations from the *Gathas* are from the recent translation by S. Insler, *The Gathas of Zarathustra* (Leiden, 1975).

15 Insler, *Gathas*, p. 1. It has been argued that certain teachings of the *Gathas* represent esoteric and initiatory traditions associated with Zoroastrian élites and differ from the 'public' or state Zoroastrian cult in successive Persian empires. See, for example, G. Gnoli, 'Politica religiosa e concezione della regalità sotto i Sassanidi' in *La Persia nel Medioevo* (Rome, 1971), pp. 225–55. Arguments for esotericism in the *Gathas* have been advanced in Mole, *Culte*, pp. 61–70 and G. Messina, *Die Ursprung der Magier und die zarathustrische Religion* (Rome 1930), pp. 8off.

16 Apart from provoking varying theological readings within Zoroastrianism, the Gathic dualism of the two primal spirits has been a subject of continuing scholarly controversy: according to Boyce, in the *Gathas* Ahura Mazda is directly opposed to Angra Mainyu and the Destructive Spirit could in no way be seen as proceeding from him: *Zoroastrians*, pp. 19–20, 213; similarly, U. Bianchi, *Selected Essays on Gnosticism, Dualism and Mysteriosophy* (Leiden, 1978), p. 410. According to an alternative position Ahura Mazda, the supreme god, appears in the *Gathas* as a 'father' of the twin Spirits: R. C. Zaehner, 'Zoroastrianism' in *The Concise Encyclopedia of the Living Faiths*, 4th edn (London, 1988), pp. 204–5; Gnoli, *Zoroaster's Time*, pp. 210–13, and a similar theological position can be found in modern Parsi theology: see Dhalla, *History of Zoroastrianism*, pp. 36–8.

17 The view that the twin Spirits had free will and became respectively Holy and Destructive by free choice is supported in Zaehner, 'Zoroastrianism', p. 204; *The Dawn and Twilight*, pp. 4–2; Gnoli, *Zoroaster's Time*, p. 213; I. Gershevitch, 'Zoroaster's Own Contribution', *Journal of Near-*

Eastern Studies, 23 (1964), p. 13. The alternative position, according to which the twin Spirits manifested in their primordial choice their innate nature and activated their inherent opposition, is advanced in Boyce, *Zoroastrians*, pp. 20–21; Bianchi, *Selected Essays*, pp. 361–89, 415–16, where the choice of the twin Spirits is seen not as the cause but as the effect of them being respectively good and evil. According to Boyce, in the 'ancient and well-defined' dualism of genuine Zoroastrianism the twin, opposed Spirits were Ahura Mazda and his great adversary, Angra Mainyu (*A History of Zoroastrianism*, vol. 2, p. 232) and their identification as Spenta Mainyu and Angra Mainyu, the Holy Spirit and Evil Spirit, emanating from Ahura Mazda, represents the attempts of modern European scholars, 'seeking to interpret Zoroastrianism according to their own ideas of desirable monism' (Boyce, *A History of Zoroastrianism*, vol. 2, p. 232).

18 The demotion of the *daevas* has been discussed in G. Widengren, *Les Religions de l'Iran* (Paris, 1968), pp. 36ff., 97ff.; E. Benveniste, *The Persian Religion According to the Chief Greek Texts* (Paris, 1929), pp. 39ff.; Boyce, *Zoroastrians*, pp. 21–2, who argues that the *daevas* were wicked both by nature and by choice.

19 In his *Naissance d'archanges* (Paris, 1945), Chaps. 2–4, G. Dumézil argues that the Amesha Spentas appear as substitutes for some of the principal gods of the archaic Indo-Iranian pantheon, a view shared by J. Duchesne-Guillemin, *The Western Response to Zoroaster* (Oxford, 1958), Chap. 3, but rejected entirely by some Iranists like Zaehner, *The Dawn and Twilight*, pp. 49–50. The *yazatas* included the *yazata* Tishtrya, who represented the star Sirius and was elevated as a 'lord and overseer over all stars' (*Yasht* 8:44). The Amesha Spentas themselves came to be seen as forming the celestial cortège of Ahura Mazda and each of them was perceived as a protector of one of the seven creations that comprise the Good Creation.

20 Gnoli, *Zoroaster's Time*, pp. 193–7; M. Eliade, 'Spirit, Light and Seed' in *Occultism, Witchcraft and Cultural Fashions* (Chicago, 1976), pp. 103–105, and *A History of Religious Ideas*, tr. W. R. Trask (Chicago, 1978), vol. 1, p. 307. Pre-Zoroastrian Iranian religion and cults have received extensive treatment in Boyce, *A History of Zoroastrianism*, vol. 1, pp. 3–181; vol. 2, pp. 14–40.

21 The summary of Parsi beliefs quoted in J. Duchesne-Guillemin, *Symbols and Values in Zoroastrianism* (New York, 1966), pp. 3–5, illuminates sufficiently this theological position. Parsi translations of the Gathic teachings of the twin Spirits in terms of (modern) theosophic and Hegelian dialectics are discussed in U. Bianchi, 'Aspects of Modern

Parsi Theology' in *Selected Essays*, pp. 410–16. Fragments from Parsi theosophical fragments have been included by Boyce in the chapter on modern Zoroastrianism in her *Textual Sources for the Study of Zoroastrianism* (Manchester, 1984), pp. 135–9. A brief account of the rise of the theosophic currents among the Parsis may be found in K. Mistree, 'The Breakdown of the Zoroastrian Tradition as Viewed from a Contemporary Perspective' in S. Shaked (ed.), *Irano-Judaica* (Jerusalem, 1990), pp. 234–40.

22 Distinguishing between Zoroaster's original teachings and what seem to be later religious developments in Zoroastrianism poses notoriously difficult problems that remain far from resolved. The following account of Zoroastrian sacred history and eschatology makes use of later Zoroastrian (Pahlavi) texts, like the *Greater Bundahishn* and the *Selections of Zadspram*, without entering into the controversial questions of the time and background of the formulation of what may appear to be novel Zoroastrian concepts or beliefs. Principal Pahlavi books have been translated by West in the *Sacred Books of the East* (vols. 5, 18, 24, 37 and 47) and new, more reliable, translations of some Pahlavi texts are also available. For the quotations of Pahlavi texts here the following translations are used: *Select Counsels of the Ancient Sages*: R. C. Zaehner, *Teachings of the Magi* (London, 1956); the *Selections of Zadspram*: R. C. Zaehner, *Zurvan: A Zoroastrian Dilemma* (Oxford, 1955); *The Testament of Ardashir* (an Arabic version of a Sassanid work): Shaked, 'Esoteric Trends in Zoroastrianism'.

23 Zaehner, *The Dawn and Twilight*, pp. 59–60; Boyce, *Zoroastrians*, pp. 27–9.

24 The principal collection of relevant Orphic fragments remains O. Kern, *Orphicorum fragmenta* (Berlin, 1922), and some important Orphic fragments have been translated in W. K. C. Guthrie, *Orpheus and Greek Religion*, 2nd edn (London, 1952), pp. 59–62, 137–42. The Orphic hymns have been edited by G. Quandt, *Orphei Hymni* (Berlin, 1941), and recently re-edited and translated by A. N. Athanassakis, *The Orphic Hymns* (Missoula, Montana, 1977).

25 The tradition of Orpheus' Dionysian dynasty and initiations and the ensuing association between the Dionysian and Orphic mysteries is illustrated by the fragment in Kern, *Orphicorum fragmenta*, pp. 8ff. E. Rohde's discussion of the 'The Thracian Worship of Dionysus' in his *Psyche: The Cult of Souls and Belief in Immortality among the Greeks*, tr. (from the 8th edn) W. B. Hillis (London, 1925), Chap. 8, still remains a classic account of the cult of Dionysus in Thrace. Thracian religion has not yet been reconstructed sufficiently but R. Pettazzoni, 'The Religion of Ancient Thrace' in *Essays on the History of Religions*

(Leiden, 1954), pp. 81–94, U. Bianchi, 'Dualistic Aspects of Thracian Religion', *History of Religions*, 10:3 (1971), pp. 228–333, and A. Fol and I. Marazov, *Thrace and the Thracians* (London, 1977), pp. 17–37, illuminate most of the recoverable characteristic features of Thracian religion. In his recent book, *Trakiiskiyat Dionis* (Sofia, 1991), Fol distinguishes sharply between the archaic Thracian Dionysus, as a focus of Palaeo-Balkan religious tradition, and the later Hellenic Dionysus, protagonist of Greek literary tradition.

26 According to Herodotus (4:94) the Getae claim to immortality was based on the belief that they did not die but only left this life to go to Zalmoxis. On 'immortalization' among the Getae and the figure and cult of Zalmoxis see M. Eliade, *Zalmoxis, the Vanishing God* (Chicago, 1972), and for a discussion of the ascetic and spiritualist trends among the Thracians and the Getae, pp. 61ff.; also Rohde, *Psyche,·*pp. 263ff., 360; D. Popov, *Zalmoxis* (Sofia, 1989), pp. 90–110. The shamanistic features of the figure of Orpheus and their connections with shamanistic beliefs and practices in the Thracian and Scythian world have been considered in E. R. Dodds, *The Greeks and the Irrational* (Berkeley and London, 1951), pp. 147ff.; W. Burkert, *Lore and Science in Ancient Pythagoreanism* tr. E. Mihar, Jr (Cambridge, 1972), pp. 163–5; M. L. West, *The Orphic Poems* (Oxford, 1983), pp. 4–6, 146–50; B. Bogdanov, *Orfei i drevnata mitologiya na balkanite* [Orpheus and Ancient Balkan Mythology] (Sofia, 1991), pp. 80–91.

27 Bianchi, 'Dualistic Aspects', p. 231. The thesis that the belief in the immortality and divinity of the soul emerged in Thracian worship of Dionysus and entered Greece from Thrace has been advanced in Rohde, *Psyche*, pp. 254ff., 263ff., and W. K. C. Guthrie, *The Greeks and Their Gods* (London, 1950), pp. 174–7, 179ff., 317ff.

28 The tradition of Orpheus' solar affiliation and Dionysus' reaction was the subject of Aeschylus' lost play, the *Bassarides*; see Kern, *Orphicorum fragmenta*, p. 33 (fragment 113). The traditions about the death of Orpheus are assembled in pp. 33–41 (testimonies 113–35). In Guthrie's reconstruction of Orpheus' association with Apollo (*Orpheus and Greek Religion*, pp. 44–9), Orpheus is seen as a Hellenic missionary in Thrace, a champion of Apollo-worship, opposed to the excesses of the Thracian cult of Dionysus; also in his *The Greeks and Their Gods*, pp. 315ff.

29 M. Detienne, 'Orpheus', in M. Eliade (ed.), *Encyclopedia of Religion*, (New York, 1987), vol. 11, p. 114.

30 Olympiodorus' comment is included in Kern, *Orphicorum fragmenta*, p. 232 (fragment 211). The view that Orpheus or the Orphics acted as reformers of Dionysian mysteries is supported, for example, in Guthrie,

Orpheus and Greek Religion, pp. 39–46; M. Nilsson, 'Early Orphism and Kindred Religious Movements', *Harvard Theological Review*, 28 (1935), pp. 203ff.

31 For Bacchic concern with the afterlife see, for example, W. Burkert, *Greek Religion*, tr. J. Raffan (Oxford, 1985), pp. 293–6.

32 The antiquity of the myth has been debated, as it is preserved by later authors like Olympiodorus and Proclus, although it seems apparent that early authors like Plato alluded to the story, as argued in Dodds, *The Greeks and the Irrational*, p. 156; Bianchi, 'Péché originel and péché antécédent', *Revue de l'histoire des religions*, 170 (1966), pp. 118ff. Moreover, according to Bianchi, the myth of Dionysus–Zagreus and the crime of the Titans as well as Plato's utterance about the rebellious and deceitful 'Titanic nature' (*Laws* 3:701c–d) allude to an antecedent sin of divine beings preceding the existence of humanity. Arguments for the antiquity of the myth of the dismemberment of Dionysus and that it was deliberately kept secret as 'a doctrine of mysteries' are presented in Burkert, *Greek Religion*, p. 298. The Orphic cosmogonies and theogonies are discussed in Guthrie, *Orpheus and Greek Religion*, Chap. 4 (with a translation of fragments pp. 137–42); L. J. Alderink, *Creation and Salvation in Ancient Orphism* (Chico, California, 1981), Chap. 2; M. L. West, *The Orphic Poems*, Chaps. 3–7, pp. 143–51, presents further suggestions for a shamanistic background of the myth of the death and rebirth of Dionysus, a pattern of ritual initiation that is thought to have been brought into the Greek world from Thrace and Scythia. Assertions that Orphism might owe its cosmogonical and salvation beliefs to Zoroastrian influences can be found, for example, in Boyce, *A History of Zoroastrianism*, vol. 2, pp. 162, 232.

33 Rohde, *Psyche*, pp. 341ff.; Guthrie, *Orpheus and Greek Religion*, pp. 156ff.; Nilsson, 'Early Orphism', pp. 207, 229ff.; A. D. Nock, *Essays on Religion and the Ancient World* (Oxford/Cambridge, Mass., 1972), vol. 1, p. 297; Bianchi, 'Psyche and Destiny', in E. Sharpe and J. Hinnells (eds.), *Man and His Salvation: Studies in Memory of S. G. F. Brandon* (Manchester, 1973), pp. 53–65.

34 Alderink, *Creation and Salvation*, pp. 65–72, 76–7, 83–5, 92–3. For reconstructions of Orphic teachings on the afterlife, judgement and fate of the soul see Guthrie, *Orpheus and Greek Religion*, pp. 156–71, and *The Greeks and Their Gods*, pp. 322–5; Rohde, *Psyche*, pp. 344ff.; Nilsson, 'Early Orphism', pp. 216ff.; but for Alderink's alternative position, see *Creation and Salvation*, pp. 74–80, 87ff.

35 In *Laws* 6:782c, Plato refers to the vegetarianism required by the 'Orphic life', while Aristophanes alludes to the Orphic ban on killing, a

prohibition introduced by the initiations of Orpheus (*Frogs* 1032). Modern views of the Orphic way of life are to be found in Guthrie, *Orpheus and Greek Religion*, pp. 196–201; Burkert, *Greek Religion*, pp. 301–304; Alderink, *Creation and Salvation*, pp. 80–85. Alderink questions the widely accepted position that Orphism comprised the doctrine of the transmigration of the soul, *Creation and Salvation*, pp. 57ff., 83ff. Another controversy surrounds the supposed existence of an Orphic 'church' or sect. While authorities like Guthrie, *Orpheus and Greek Religion*, pp. 204ff., or M. P. Nilsson, *A History of Greek Religion*, tr. F. J. Fielden, 2nd edn (London and New York, 1945), p. 218, accept that the Orphics effectively formed a sect, others strongly deny the existence of a sectarian type of organization. According to Eliade the 'secret groups' of Orphic initiates could be compared to the similarly secret associations of the Tantric adepts (*History of Religious Ideas*, tr. W. R. Trask (Chicago, 1982), vol. 2, p. 488).

36 Bianchi, 'Dualistic Aspects', p. 231.

37 On Dionysus as a saviour–god see Alderink, *Creation and Salvation*, pp. 69–70; Guthrie, *Orpheus and Greek Religion*, p. 83. The thesis that Orphism introduced the dualism of soul and body into Greek religious thought is advanced, for example, by Nilsson, *A History of Greek Religion*, p. 229, where Orphism is credited with formulating the new idea of the body as the tomb of the soul with the inevitable re-evaluation of 'this life as compared with the other life'. Similarly, Dodds, *The Greeks and the Irrational*, p. 139, assigns to Orphism the initiation of a new, fateful religious pattern which credited man with 'an occult self of divine origin' and set soul and body in opposition. While arguing that Orphic anthropological dualism did not imply opposition between soul and body, Alderink, *Creation and Salvation*, p. 88, indicates that the Orphics 'were among the first – if not the first – to make a distinction between body and soul and to speculate about their relations'.

38 The teaching of the four spiritual constituents of man is expounded in the Pahlavi work *Denkart* (Acts of the Religion) 3:218, while the doctrine of man's three parts with their three subdivisions is advanced in another important Pahlavi text, the *Selections of Zadspram*. Both teachings have been analysed in detail in Sir Harold Bailey, *Zoroastrian Problems in the Ninth-century Books* (Oxford, 1943), which presents further material on the Zoroastrian doctrine of man and his spiritual constitution, pp. 78–119. The relationship between soul and body in Zoroastrianism has been examined, with translations of relevant fragments, in Zaehner, *The Dawn and Twilight*, pp. 268–79.

39 This is illustrated by the *Denkart* fragment translated in Zaehner, *The Dawn and Twilight*, p. 274.

40 Shaked, 'Some Notes on Ahreman, the Evil Spirit, and his Creation', in *Studies in mysticism and religion presented to G. G. Scholem*, Jerusalem, 1969, p. 230. Shaked sees the essence of Ahriman's creation as a corruption of Ohrmazd's creation (p. 233), while the 'coming into being of the material world out of the conceptual, *menog*, is only made possible through the negative participation of the evil principle' (p. 234).

41 Benveniste, *The Persian Religion*, pp. 20–21. According to Pliny, *Natural History* 30:3, both Eudoxus and Aristotle held that Zoroaster lived 6,000 years before Plato; Benveniste thought this chronological relation served to link Zoroastrian and Platonic dualism in a cyclical scheme which reflected the Iranian cycle of 12,000 years and its division into two eras of six millennia – the first period is marked by the advent of Zoroaster, while the end of the second has to bring back 'a representative of the same idea', Benveniste, *The Persian Religion*, p. 20. According to Herzfeld, *Zoroaster and his World*, vol. 1, p. 3, Eudoxus' figure of 6,000 years between Zoroaster and Plato implies 'the Zoroastrian doctrine of messianic return' and combines the notions that Zoroaster would reappear after 6,000 years and that Plato is Zoroaster's incarnation.

42 Jaeger, *Aristotle*, p. 136. Jaeger wrote: the 'originality of Eudoxus lay solely in putting Zarathustra 6,000 years ago', while it was Aristotle who, 'led by his doctrine of the periodical return of all human knowledge, first specifically connected this figure with the return of dualism, and thereby put Plato in a setting that corresponded to his profound reverence for him'. The cycle of 6,000 years between Zoroaster and Plato thus served to indicate that 'Zarathustra and Plato are obviously two important stages in the world's journey towards its goal, the triumph of the good', Jaeger, *Aristotle*, pp. 134–5.

43 Hippolytus, *Refutation of all Heresies*, 6:23.2.

44 The possibility of Zoroastrian influences on Orphism and Pythagoreanism is discussed, for example, by Duchesne-Guillemin in his *Ormazd et Ahriman*, p. 87. Zoroastrian impact on Orphic cosmogony and teachings of salvation is suggested by Boyce (see above, n. 32). The parallels between Zoroastrian traditions and the concepts of Heraclitus, along with a survey of the earlier studies and approaches to the problem, have been examined at great length in M. L. West, *Early Greek Philosophy and the Orient* (Oxford, 1971), pp. 165–202. In Chap. 7, 'The Gift of the Magi', pp. 203–42, West offers a strong argument for active Iranian influence on the development of Greek thought in the period 550–480 BC. Iranian influences on early Ionian philosophical and religious movements are discussed also in Boyce, *A History of Zoroastrianism*, vol. 2, pp. 153–63. The parallels between the concepts of Empedocles and

Zoroastrian thought are examined, for example, in J. Bidez and F. Cumont, *Les Mages hellénisés*, vol. 1, pp. 238ff., with the suggestion that they reflected Empedocles' Pythagorean affinities.

45 The Achaemenid empire, the fifth 'Great Oriental Monarchy' in Rawlinson's *Seven Great Oriental Monarchies of the Ancient World* (3 vols., New York, 1885), has been given a further full-length treatment in A. T. Olmstead, *History of the Persian Empire* (Chicago, 1948), and more recently in J. Cook, *The Persian Empire* (London, 1983), while R. N. Frye, *The Heritage of Persia* (London, 1962), pp. 16–78, offers a survey of pre-Achaemenid Iranian traditions. A. Kuhrt, H. Sancisi-Weerdenburg, *et al.* (eds.), *Achaemenid History* (5 vols., Leiden, 1984–90), contains important recent contributions to the historiography of the Achaemenid empire. Somewhat differing accounts of the history of Zoroastrianism and its relationship with the Achaemenids may be found in Boyce, *A History of Zoroastrianism*, vol. 2; Zaehner, *The Dawn and Twilight*, Part 1, Chap. 7, 'Achaemenids and Magi'; Gershevitch, 'Zoroaster's Own Contribution'; Duchesne-Guillemin, *The Western Response to Zoroaster*, pp. 52ff.; Mole, *Culte*, pp. 26ff.

46 E. J. Bickerman, 'Persia' in *Encyclopaedia Judaica*, vol. 13 (Jerusalem, 1971), p. 304. Apart from the accounts in Greek historiography, the Graeco-Persian wars have received detailed treatment in works like A. R. Burn, *Persia and the Greeks: the Defence of the West, c. 567–478*, 2nd edn (London, 1984); H. Bengston (ed.), *The Greeks and Persians from the Sixth to the Fourth Centuries* (London, 1968).

47 J. Wellard, *By the Waters of Babylon* (London, 1973), p. 188. The tradition of Xerxes' destruction of Esagila and removal of Marduk's statue has been subjected to strong criticism and rejected in A. Kuhrt and S. Sherwin-White, 'Xerxes' Destruction of Babylonian Temples' in Kuhrt and Sancisi-Weerdenburg, *Achaemenid History*, vol. 2, pp. 69–78.

48 The inscriptions of Darius and other Achaemenid monarchs have been edited and translated in R. G. Kent, *Old Persian: Grammar, Texts, Lexicon*, 2nd edn (New Haven, 1953). According to Boyce, Cyrus' religion was indeed Zoroastrianism, *A History of Zoroastrianism*, vol. 2, pp. 43ff., 51–3; M. Boyce, 'The Religion of Cyrus' in Kuhrt and Sancisi-Weerdenburg, *Achaemenid History*, vol. 3, pp. 5–31. The role of the Achaemenid ceremonial capital of Persepolis is discussed in Frye, *The Heritage of Persia*, p. 100; Olmstead, *History of the Persian Empire*, pp. 172–85; A. U. Pope, 'Persepolis, a Ritual City', *Archaeology*, 10 (1957), pp. 123–30.

49 Kent, *Old Persian*, p. 138; Boyce, *Textual Sources*, p. 105. Darius'

Mazda-worship, as reflected in his inscriptions, is discussed in Zaehner, *The Dawn and Twilight*, pp. 155–8; Gershevitch, 'Zoroaster's Own Contribution', pp. 16–19; Boyce, *A History of Zoroastrianism*, vol. 2, pp. 118–24.

50 Kent, *Old Persian,* pp. 150–51; Boyce, *Textual Sources,* p. 105. The historical significance of Xerxes' inscription has provoked debate and varying interpretations in, for example, Zaehner, *The Dawn and Twilight*, pp. 159ff.; Gershevitch, 'Zoroaster's Own Contribution', p. 18; Boyce, *A History of Zoroastrianism*, vol. 2, pp. 173–7; M. Papatheophanes, 'Heraclitus of Ephesus, the Magi and the Achaemenids', *Iranica Antiqua*, 20 (1985), pp. 107–11; H. S. Nyberg, *Die Religionen des alten Iran*, tr. H. Schaeder (Leipzig, 1938), pp. 337ff.

51 There is a considerable literature and divergence of opinion on the Magi – from the surmise in G. Messina, *Die Ursprung der Magier und die zarathustrische Religion* (Rome, 1930), and Mole, *Culte*, that the Magi were Zoroaster's disciples and heirs, to the opinion of R. Pettazzoni, *La religione di Zarathustra* (Rome, 1920), p. 84, that the Magi were the priests of the *daevas*. The problem of the Magi and Zoroastrianism has been approached and illuminated from different angles in Bidez and Cumont, *Les Mages hellénisés*; E. Benveniste, *Les Mages dans l'ancien Iran* (Paris, 1938); Widengren, *Les Religions de l'Iran*, pp. 134ff., 147ff.; Zaehner, *The Dawn and Twilight*, pp. 161ff.; Papatheophanes, 'Heraclitus of Ephesus'; Boyce, *A History of Zoroastrianism*, vol. 2, pp. 19ff., 21, 43, 46–8, 154–5; Gershevitch, 'Zoroaster's Own Contribution', pp. 24ff., 29–31; Gnoli, *Zoroaster's Time and Homeland*, pp. 206ff.

52 The question of the religious eclecticism of the Magi and their role in the religious syncretism of the Achaemenid era has been examined in Gnoli, *Zoroaster's Time and Homeland*, pp. 209ff.; Papatheophanes, 'Heraclitus of Ephesus', pp. 111ff.; Gershevitch, 'Zoroaster's Own Contribution', pp. 24ff.; Frye, *The Heritage of Persia*, pp. 75–7. Zaehner, *The Dawn and Twilight*, pp. 97–144, offers a detailed, if controversial, account of the fortunes of Mithra-worship in pre-Zoroastrian and pre-Achaemenid Iran and its reintegration into the Good Religion. The promotion of the cult of Anahita under Artaxerxes is discussed in Boyce, *A History of Zoroastrianism*, vol. 2, pp. 201–204. According to Frye, Mithra and Anahita were always revered by the Achaemenid house (*The Heritage of Persia*, p. 269, n. 91).

53 The Magi have been identified as authors of the Ohrmazd-versus-Ahriman formula in Gershevitch, 'Zoroaster's Own Contribution', pp. 29ff., where it is defined as 'an original and elegant heresy'; and in Gnoli, *Zoroaster's Time and Homeland*, pp. 210ff., with arguments for Mesopotamian influences in the creation of the new dualist opposition.

54 The figure of the 'Accursed Whore', her wickedness and her 'defection' to Ahriman is discussed in Zaehner, *The Dawn and Twilight*, pp. 231–4; *Zurvan*, pp. 74–5, 183ff.

55 Zaehner, *The Dawn and Twilight*, p. 267.

56 A. D. H. Bivar, 'Religious Subjects on Achaemenid Seals' in J. R. Hinnells (ed.), *Mithraic Studies*, vol. 1 (Manchester, 1975), pp. 95ff. Bivar contends that the Zoroastrian dualist antithesis between Ahura Mazda and Ahriman could 'to some extent reflect tensions which had arisen in neo-Babylonian religion and was not merely an abstract psychological antithesis but a concrete fact of religious history' (p. 96). In Accadian sources Nergal is identified with Moloch (Molech) and two recent books have demonstrated that rather than being a technical name for human sacrifice by fire, 'Molech' was indeed the name of a Canaanite chthonic deity. See: G. Heider, *The Cult of Molek* (Sheffield, 1985); J. Day, *Molech: A God of Human Sacrifice in the Old Testament* (Cambridge, 1989).

57 Bivar suggests that a cult similar to those of the Semitic underworld deities Nergal and Moloch made headway in Iran during the era of Median supremacy prior to the rise of Cyrus the Great ('Religious Subjects on Achaemenid Seals', pp. 103ff.; 'Mithra and Mesopotamia' in Hinnells, *Mithraic Studies*, vol. 2, pp. 275–89). In 'Mithra and Mesopotamia' Bivar presents arguments for a blending of features of the cult of Nergal with pre-Zoroastrian Iranian religious traditions, such as Mithra-worship, in a syncretistic religion which in the early Achaemenid era was suppressed and forced westwards, eventually providing the basis of later Roman Mithraism (pp. 285–9). While much of Bivar's hypothesis remains conjectural, evidence exists of a local identification of Nergal and Mithra in Cilicia (Boyce, *A History of Zoroastrianism*, vol. 2, p. 273).

58 The theory that Zurvanism was a pre-Zoroastrian religion which evolved in western Iran was advanced by Benveniste in Chap. 4 of *The Persian Religion* and, similarly, Nyberg regarded Zurvan as an ancient western Iranian deity, indeed the god of the Median Magi (*Die Religionen des alten Iran*, pp. 105, 380ff.). According to Widengren, during the Parthian era (250 BC–AD 226) in Iran Zurvanism was independent of Zoroastrianism (*Les Religions de l'Iran*, pp. 244ff., 314ff.), but the weight of evidence indicates that Zurvanism did emerge as a religious trend in Zoroastrianism and was affected by Babylonian astronomical and astrological speculations (U. Bianchi, *Zaman i Ohrmazd: lo zoroastrismo nelle sue origini e nella sua essenza* (Turin, 1958), pp. 130–89; Boyce, *A History of Zoroastrianism*, vol. 2, pp. 232–43). Gnoli also argues that the dualist

formula of Ohrmazd versus Ahriman was itself a feature of the Zurvanite system (*Zoroaster's Time and Homeland*, p. 212). Boyce offers arguments that Zurvanism was promoted by Persian Magi in Babylon, who in the latter half of the fifth century combined new interpretations of the Gathic teaching of the twin Spirits with elements of Babylonian astronomical–astrological lore and the new movement gained the support of Darius II (*A History of Zoroastrianism*, vol. 2, pp. 240ff.). The influence of Zurvanism seems to have been particularly strong and lasting in western Iran and Asia Minor (F. Cumont, *Textes et monuments figurés relatifs aux mystères de Mithra* (Brussels, 1896–9), pp. 9–10).

59 The principal Zurvanite myth is preserved in non-Zoroastrian works like the work of the Armenian Christian apologist Eznik of Kolb, *Wieder die Sekten* [Against the Sects], tr. J. M. Schmidt (Vienna, 1900); and in *Zurvan* Zaehner reproduces the four parallel versions of the myth (pp. 419–29). The second part of Zaehner's book (pp. 257–453) reproduces fragments from the *Avesta*, from extra-Avestan Zoroastrian texts and from polemical (Christian, Manichaean and Islamic) works relevant to Zurvanism and Zurvanite myths.

60 This account of the alternative 'garments', 'implements' or 'weapons' of Ohrmazd and Ahriman follows Zaehner's reconstruction of the Zurvanite myth of their investiture, *Zurvan*, pp. 113–25, which is based on fragments from the *Greater Bundahishn*, *The Selections of Zadspram* and the *Denkart*. Zaehner's argument seems to demonstrate that the forms of Ohrmazd's creation from the substance of light, 'a form of fire – bright, white, round, and manifest afar', and the 'black and ashen' form of Ahriman's creation from the substance of darkness in the *Greater Bundahishn* (1:44–9) were seen in Zurvanism as 'gifts' of Zurvan to his two sons who invested them with their respective 'selfhood' or 'essence' (Zaehner, *Zurvan*, pp. 116ff., 124ff.). The Denkart fragment reproduced by Zaehner, *Zurvan*, pp. 374–8, elaborates the myth of the alternative weapons of Ohrmazd, the robe of priesthood, his brilliance and 'shining white garment' versus Ahriman's weapon, the robe of false priesthood, 'the ordering of evil in its pure estate', the ash-coloured garment associated with Saturn. The fragments from *The Selections of Zadspram* that allude to the 'implement' or 'form' delivered by Zurvan to Ahriman are reproduced in Zaehner, *Zurvan*, pp. 342ff. and 351, and while the first passage describes the implement as fashioned from the 'very substance of darkness mingled with the power of Zurvan', in the second fragment the form brought by Zurvan to Ahriman is 'the black and ashen garment', the implement 'like unto fire, blazing, harassing all creatures, that hath the very substance of Az (greed or lust)'.

The second fragment alludes also to the treaty by which Ahriman's creation is doomed to be devoured by Az if Ahriman fails to fulfil his threat to make all material creation to hate Ohrmazd and love him, which is seen as 'the belief in the one principle' that identifies the increaser and destroyer.

61 The myth of the creation of the luminaries through heavenly incest after Ahriman's instruction is preserved in Eznik's *Wieder die Sekten* and a translation of the relevant fragment may be found in Zaehner, *Zurvan*, pp. 438ff. Eliade suggests that the myth was introduced to justify the renowned incestuous practices of the Magi, see *A History of Religious Ideas*, vol. 2, p. 525.

62 Zaehner, *Zurvan*, p. 78. This Zurvanite system, in which the creation of fire and water precedes the creation of Ohrmazd and Ahriman, is preserved in the tract, *Ulema i Islam* (Zaehner, *Zurvan*, pp. 409–16). The fatalist and materialist Zurvanite circles are discussed in Zaehner, *The Dawn and Twilight*, pp. 197ff., 205ff.

63 M. Eliade, *The Two and the One* (London, 1965), p. 83. Zurvanism is defined as a 'major heresy' by Zaehner, *Zurvan*, p. 5, and as a 'deep and grievous heresy' by Boyce, *Zoroastrians*, p. 69, but according to Shaked, Zurvanism was not considered heretical but was a 'fairly inoffensive variant of the Zoroastrian myth of creation', seen by its opponents as 'mildly deviant', S. Shaked, 'The Myth of Zurvan: Cosmogony and Eschatology', in I. Gruenwald, S. Shaked, G. A. G. Stroumsa (eds.), *Messiah and Christos* (Tübingen, 1992), pp. 232–3.

64 The Bon triad, its Zurvanite colouring and the question of Iranian religious influences in Tibet are discussed, for example, in G. Tucci, *The Religions of Tibet*, tr. G. Samuel (London/Berkeley, 1980), pp. 214ff.; M. Eliade, *A History of Religious Ideas*, tr. A. Hiltelbeitel and D. Aspostolos-Cappadona (Chicago, 1985), vol. 3, pp. 267, 270.

65 Such presentation by the priesthood of the king as a heretic has been defined as 'a novelty in Mesopotamian religious politics', A. I. Oppenheim, 'The Babylonian evidence of Achaemenian rule in Babylonia', in I. Gershevitch (ed.), *Cambridge History of Iran* (Cambridge, 1985), vol. 2, p. 541. Apart from the *Cyrus Cylinder* (published by H. C. Rawlinson in *The Cuneiform Inscriptions of Western Asia*, 101.5, plate 35, tr. in J. B. Pritchard, *Ancient Near Eastern Texts Relating to the Old Testament*, 3rd edn with suppl. (Princeton, 1969), pp. 315–16) and the *Verse Account of Nabonidus* (published by S. Smith, *Babylonian Historical Texts Relating to the Capture and Downfall of Babylon* (London, 1924), pp. 27–97, tr. in Pritchard, *Ancient Near Eastern Texts*, pp. 312–15), another cuneiform document that recounts the story of Nabonidus' reign and Cyrus'

NOTES

conquest of Babylon in a less prejudiced manner is the *Nabonidus Chronicle* (published in Smith, *Babylonian Historical Texts*, pp. 110–18, tr. in Pritchard, *Ancient Near Eastern Texts*, pp. 305–7; A. K. Grayson, *Assyrian and Babylonian Chronicles* (Locust Valley, New York, 1975), pp. 104–111). Cyrus' assumption of Babylonian kingship in the context of Babylonian royal ideology and his ceremonial acts on assuming the duties of the Babylonian kings are discussed in A. Kuhrt, 'Usurpation, Conquest and Ceremonial: From Babylon to Persia', in D. Cannadine and S. Price (eds.), *Rituals of Royalty* (Cambridge, 1987), pp. 48–67.

66 The problem of Nabonidus' religious reforms has been examined in detail in P.-A. Beaulieu, *The Reign of Nabonidus, King of Babylon 556–539 BC* (New Haven and London, 1989), where the exaltation of Sin in Nabonidus' inscriptions is described on pp. 43–65 and the proclamation of Esagila and Ezida as temples of Sin on pp. 61ff. In the last years of his reign, 'Nabonidus was no longer hesitant to publicize his fanatical devotion to Sin and his intention to relegate Marduk to nearly total oblivion' (Beaulieu, *The Reign of Nabonidus*, p. 62). However, the promotion of serious religious reforms under Nabonidus and his conflict with the Babylonian priesthood have been questioned by A. Kuhrt, 'Nabonidus and the Babylonian Priesthood', in A. Beard and J. North (eds.), *Pagan Priests* (Ithaca, New York, 1990), pp. 117–55.

67 Although questioned by some scholars, the authenticity of Cyrus' edict has been well established in E. J. Bickerman, 'The Edict of Cyrus in Ezra' in *Studies in Jewish and Christian History* (3 vols., Leiden, 1976–86), vol. 1, pp. 72–108, where he demonstrates that Cyrus' proclamation was intended to legitimize his succession to the Davidic throne (pp. 94ff.). In 'The Biblical Portrayal of Achaemenid Rulers' (Kuhrt and Drijvers, *Achaemenid History*, vol. 5, pp. 1–17), Ackroyd recognizes in Ezra's narrative of Cyrus' actions both Persian and Jewish perspectives: from the first 'it can be seen to constitute a claim for Cyrus to be the legitimate successor to the Davidic line' and from the latter 'the claim that Cyrus is moved in this by the command of Yahweh, God of heaven' (p. 3). A. Netzer argues that Yahweh's recognition of Cyrus as 'his anointed' (Isaiah 45:1) gives Cyrus a 'true place in the line of David' and makes him a 'legitimate king of Israel', A. Netzer, 'Some Notes on the Characterization of Cyrus the Great in Jewish and Judeo-Persian Writings', *Commémoration Cyrus, Hommage Universel* 11 (Teheran/ Liège, 1974), p. 41. Later Jewish traditions concerning Cyrus and the Throne of Solomon are assembled in L. Ginzburg, *The Legends of the Jews*, vol. 6 (Philadelphia, 1946), pp. 433ff., 453ff.

68 The contrasting historical fortunes of the Jews under Babylonian and

Persian rule and the developments in exilic and post-exilic Judaism are charted in P. R. Ackroyd, *Israel under Babylon and Persia* (Oxford, 1970), while his *Exile and Restoration* (London, 1968) traces the principal themes in the prophecy of the exile and restoration. The phenomenon and the evolution of the prophetic tradition in Israel has been the subject of numerous studies. See, for example, J. Lindblom, *Prophecy in Ancient Israel* (Oxford, 1962), or the more recent R. Coggins, A. Phillips and M. Knibb (eds.), *Israel's Prophetic Tradition: Essays in Honour of Peter R. Ackroyd* (Cambridge, 1982). The figures and reforms of Nehemiah and Ezra have been examined, sometimes with different conclusions, in W. Rudolph, *Esra und Nehemiah* (Tübingen, 1949); Ackroyd, *Israel under Babylon and Persia*, pp. 173–96; M. Smith, 'Palestinian Judaism in the Persian Period' in Bengston, *The Greeks and the Persians*, pp. 386–401. Among the studies of Jewish messianism see, for example, S. Mowinckel, *He That Cometh* (Oxford, 1959), pp. 155–87, for the belief in the Davidic messiah. Various theories have been put forward to explain the sudden disappearance of the Davidic scion Zerubbabel from the biblical narrative: according to Smith, 'Palestinian Judaism', p. 391, the messianic claims of Zerubbabel led to his assassination in a conspiracy organized by other members of the House of David.

69 Boyce provides an interesting historical parallel between the situation of the Jews in the Achaemenid empire and the Parsis in British India which allowed their continuous exposure to and unconscious assimilation of Zoroastrian and Christian influences respectively, *A History of Zoroastrianism*, vol. 2, p. 195.

70 The continuous influence of Iranian law on Judaism in the Achaemenid era and later is discussed in R. N. Frye, 'Iran and Israel' in G. Wiessner (ed.), *Festschrift für Wilhelm Eilers* (Wiesbaden, 1967), pp. 74–85. The problem of Iranian religious influences on post-exilic Judaism has provoked much controversy and literature, most of which is referred to in D. Winston, 'The Iranian Component in the Bible, Apocrypha and Qumran: A Review of the Evidence', *History of Religions*, 5 (1966), pp. 183–216. A more recent treatment of Zoroastrian influences on Jewish eschatological, angelological, and demonological notions in Jewish writings, from the canonical Daniel to the Qumran scrolls, was undertaken by Boyce in *A History of Zoroastrianism*, vol. 3, pp. 389–436. The chronological problem affecting the studies of the religious contacts between Iran and Israel has been dealt with by S. Shaked in 'Qumran and Iran: further considerations', *Israel Oriental Studies*, 2 (1972), pp. 433–46.

71 J. B. Russell, *The Devil: Perceptions of Evil from Antiquity to Primitive Christianity* (New York, 1977), pp. 176ff. Russell does not exclude Iranian influence on the emergence of the concept of the Devil in Hebrew thought (p. 218) and defines finally the Hebrew theodicy as standing 'between the monism of the Hindus and the dualism of the Zoroastrians' (p. 220). The development of the concept of Satan in the Old Testament is the subject of R. S. Kluger's *Satan in the Old Testament*, tr. H. Nagel (Evanston, 1967), where the principal thesis is that the influence of Ahriman on the figure of Satan was exercised not on the Old Testament level but at the further, Judeo-Christian, stage of development (p. 157). Kluger also suggests that there might have been Persian influences in the later version of the Satan figure in Chronicles and that 'Ahriman in his polar opposition to Ahura Mazda may have been a prototype for the Old Testament Satan detaching himself from the personality of God' (p. 158). However, Persian influence on the figure of Satan is accepted as certain only after 'the detachment of Satan from God, who is then "cleansed" of his darkness' (p. 159), a differentiation process in which 'the decisive factor is the immanent development as a prerequisite for such influence' (p. 158). N. Forsyth, in his *The Old Enemy: Satan and the Combat Myth* (Princeton, 1987), advances the thesis that the newly independent figure of Satan in Chronicles, who 'substitutes for God as the *agent provocateur* in human affairs' (p. 121), came to be fused in Jewish apocalyptic literature with the figure of the adversary of the combat mythology of the ancient Near East (pp. 124ff.).

72 The Enochic apocalyptic cycle and its role in early Jewish apocalyptic thought has been widely debated and studied but many important problems concerning the origins of the Enochic traditions have not yet been resolved. Among the important works on Jewish Apocalyptic are: D. S. Russell, *The Method and Message of Jewish Apocalyptic* (Philadelphia, 1964); P. D. Hanson, *The Dawn of Apocalyptic* (Philadelphia, 1975); C. Rowland, *The Open Heaven* (New York, 1983). Some new studies of the Enochic traditions have reinforced the traditional theory about the Mesopotamian background of the figure of Enoch. See: J. C. Van der Kam, *Enoch and the Growth of an Apocalyptic Tradition* (Washington, 1984) and H. Kvanvig, *Roots of Apocalyptic* (Neukirchen-Vluyn, 1988). J. Charlesworth (ed.), *The Old Testament Pseudoepigrapha* (2 vols., New York and London, 1983–5), includes new translations of the oldest Enochic apocalyptic cycle of 1 (Ethiopic Apocalypse of) Enoch, 2 (Slavonic Apocalypse of) Enoch and 3 (Hebrew Apocalypse of) Enoch. 2 Enoch, a much debated and often enigmatic Enochic apocalypse, has

been preserved only in the Slavonic Orthodox world and influenced important Bogomil teachings. The books of Enoch and the development of Enochic traditions have been treated comprehensively, sometimes controversially, in J. T. Milik and M. Black, *The Books of Enoch* (Oxford, 1976). 1 Enoch and the Sibylline Oracles, The Martyrdom and Ascension of Isaiah and The Testaments of the Twelve Patriarchs are quoted from the translations in Charlesworth, *The Old Testament Pseudo-epigrapha*. The account of the teachings of the 'two ways' and Belial in the Testaments of the Twelve Patriarchs on pp. 45–6 is based on the Testament of Asher 1:3–5; Testament of Judah 20:1–2; 25:3; Testament of Dan 5:6–11; 6:2; Testament of Gad 4:7; 5:1; Testament of Benjamin 7:1–2.

73 The theme of Satan poisoning the tree is developed in the Life of Adam and Eve 19, while the tree was planted by Satan in 3 Baruch, or the Greek Apocalypse of Baruch, which dates from the early Christian era and has been preserved in Greek and Slavonic versions. The apocalyptic narrative of 3 Baruch, with its rich and complex imagery, came to influence some Bogomil beliefs in the Middle Ages.

74 The Martyrdom and Ascension of Isaiah is a composite work and its last section (Chaps. 6–11) was an independent apocalyptic text, which, known as The Vision of Isaiah and preserved in Latin and Slavonic translations, came to enjoy considerable popularity among the Bogomils and the Cathars.

75 A discussion on the background of the Persian Sibylline Oracles and the Zoroastrian influences in the Jewish–Christian Sibylline Oracles can be found in Boyce, *A History of Zoroastrianism*, vol. 3, pp. 371–87 and 389–401 respectively.

76 Apart from the continuing publication of the Dead Sea Scrolls, considerable literature exists on the Qumran sect, its teachings, its role in Second Temple Judaism and its relevance to the beginnings of Christianity. See: J. M. Allegro, *The Dead Sea Scrolls*, 2nd edn (Harmondsworth, 1975); F. M. Cross, *The Ancient Library of Qumran* (New York, 1961); H. Rinngren, *The Faith of Qumran* (Philadelphia, 1963); M. Black, *The Scrolls and Christian Origins* (London, 1961); G. R. Driver, *The Judaean Scrolls* (New York, 1965); D. Flusser, 'The Dead Sea Scrolls and the New Testament', Part 1 in *Judaism and the Origins of Christianity* (Jerusalem, 1987). For the quotations from the Community Rule (The Manual of Discipline) and the War Rule (The War of the Sons of Light and the Sons of Darkness) the translations of both Vermes and Gaster have been used, as follows: G. Vermes, *The Dead Sea Scrolls in English*, 3rd edn (Harmondsworth, 1987), pp. 65–6, 118–19; T. H. Gaster (tr.),

The Scriptures of the Dead Sea Sect (London, 1957), pp. 49–50, 53–6, 277, 282.

77 Shaked, 'Qumran and Iran', pp. 436–8; also the comments in R. N. Frye, 'Qumran and Iran: The State of Studies' in J. Neusner (ed.), *Judaism, Christianity and Other Graeco-Roman Cults: Studies Dedicated to Morton Smith* (Leiden, 1975), vol. 3, pp. 167–73 and particularly pp. 172–3. According to Zaehner in *The Dawn and Twilight*, p. 52, God's attitude to the spirits of truth and falsehood in the Community Rule offers 'an exact parallel' to Ahura Mazda's attitude to the Holy and Destructive Spirits.

78 Parallels between Zurvanite and Qumranite myths, including the focus on predestination, are discussed in Duchesne-Guillemin, *The Western Response to Zoroaster*, pp. 92–4. Arguments for Zurvanite influence on Qumran are presented in H. Michaud, 'Un mythe zervanite dans un des manuscrits de Qumran', *Vetus Testamentum*, 5 (1955), pp. 137–47.

2   Syncretism and Orthodoxy

1 J. M. Balcer, 'Alexander's Burning of Persepolis', *Iranica Antiqua*, 13 (1978), p. 133. According to Balcer, 'Fundamental to Alexander's sovereignty of Asia, the key regal centres of Memphis, Thebes and Babylon bound him within the agelong mythological ceremonies of ancient Near Eastern cosmic kingship, to rule as the Achaemenid "Great King, King of Kings, King of Many Countries"' but the 'Achaemenid resistance to Alexander's invasion and usurpation of the kingship of Asia denied this assumption to rule' (p. 126). In this line of argument the burning of Persepolis led not only to the 'conclusive disruption of the Achaemenid cycle of cosmic kingship' (p. 131) but also prevented Alexander from 'obtaining the sovereignty of Asia' and opened the millennium of Persian 'resistance to Hellenism and the West' (p. 133). Literature and views on the figure and the conquests of Alexander are abundant, from W. W. Tarn's *Alexander the Great* (2 vols., Cambridge, 1948), where Alexander is credited with the ideal of the 'union of mankind', to more recent works like R. Lane Fox, *Alexander the Great* (London, 1973) and A. B. Bosworth, *Conquest and Empire* (Cambridge, 1988).

2 The Persian tradition of Alexander and his association with Ahriman appears in later Pahlavi texts like *Arda Viraf Namak* 1:3–11 or the *Bahman Yasht* 2:19, and is discussed from a Parsi perspective by Dhalla, in *History of Zoroastrianism*, p. 293; there are further comments in S. K.

Eddy, *The King is Dead* (Lincoln, 1961), pp. 11–19; Boyce, *A History of Zoroastrianism*, vol. 3, pp. 384ff. Eddy's book reconstructs, sometimes controversially, the patterns of Near Eastern reaction to the penetration of Hellenism and touches upon the origins of the alternative Persian tradition, recorded in the *Shah Nameh* 18:3–4, which converts Alexander into a son of Darius III and a Macedonian princess (pp. 73ff.).

3 The Iranian apocalyptic tradition of Macedonian rule as the fourth and final age is discussed in Boyce, *A History of Zoroastrianism*, vol. 3, pp. 384–7; D. Flusser, 'The four empires in the Fourth Sibyl and in the Book of Daniel', *Israel Oriental Studies*, 11 (1972), pp. 148–75. Pahlavi fragments alluding to Alexander's burning of the Avesta are assembled in Bailey, *Zoroastrian Problems*, pp. 151–7, while the story of Alexander's visit and restoration of Cyrus' tomb is narrated in Arrian (6:28.4–8) and Strabo (730).

4 The Hellenistic age and civilization have been surveyed in works like W. W. Tarn, *Hellenistic Civilization*, 3rd edn (London, 1952); M. Hadas, *Hellenistic Culture: Fusion and Diffusion* (New York and London, 1959); C. Schneider, *Kulturgeschichte des Hellenismus* (2 vols., Munich, 1967–9); while F. E. Peters' *Harvest of Hellenism* (New York, 1967) charts the history of the Near East from the time of Alexander's conquests to the victory of Christianity over paganism in the fourth Christian century. The history of the Hellenistic kingdoms has received extensive treatment, including works on individual Hellenistic states, such as E. J. Bickerman, *Institutions des Seleucids* (Paris, 1938), but new studies continue to shed fresh light on various aspects of the Hellenistic civilization; see, for example, the contributions in A. Kuhrt and S. Sherwin-White (eds.), *Hellenism in the East* (Berkeley, 1987), on subjects like the Seleucid rule in Babylonia or the interaction of Greek and non-Greek elements in the art and architecture of the Hellenistic east. An overview of the approaches and stereotypes in the study of the Greek mysteries and the 'mystery religions' and the attempts at dating the latter can be found in W. Burkert, *Ancient Mystery Cults* (Harvard, 1987), pp. 1–4, which offers a 'comparative phenomenology' of the mysteries of Eleusis, Dionysus, Meter, Isis and Mithras. Burkert's book (pp. 2ff.) and the earlier, classical work of R. Reitzenstein, *Hellenistic Mystery-Religions*, tr. J. Steely (Pittsburgh, 1978), Chap. 2, 'Oriental and Hellenistic Cults', pp. 169–237, offer two different approaches to the Oriental influences in Hellenistic religions. Since the publication of F. Cumont's work, *The Oriental Religions in Roman Paganism* (Chicago and London, 1911), most of the cults have received extensive separate treatment in other works: see M. P. Nilsson, *The Dionysiac Mysteries of the Hellenistic and Roman Age* (Lund, 1957); M. J. Vermaseren,

Cybele and Attis: The Myth and the Cult, tr. A. M. H. Lemmers (London, 1977); R. Merkelbach, *Isisfeste in Griechisch-römischer Zeit* (Meisenheim-am-Glan, 1963). The spread of Oriental cults in the Thracian lands has also been thoroughly surveyed in the recent work of M. Tacheva-Hitova, *Oriental Cults in Moesia Inferior and Thracia* (Leiden, 1983).

5 These missions to the Hellenistic world were proclaimed in the Thirteenth Major Rock Edict of Ashoka; the five kings alluded to in the edict are identified as the Seleucid Antiochus II, Ptolemy II of Egypt, Antigonus Gonatas of Macedonia, Magas of Cyrene and Alexander of Epirus (G. P. Carratelli, *Gli editti di Aśoka* (Florence, 1960), pp. 40–42). The legends about Ashoka are discussed in E. J. Thomas, *The History of Buddhist Thought* (London, 1932), Chap. 3, and further in Chap. 12, with an assessment of Ashoka's Buddhism, pp. 153ff.

6 Early standard works on the Greeks, Scythians and the Sarmatians in the north Pontic area, such as E. H. Minns, *Scythians and Greeks* (Cambridge, 1913); M. I. Rostovtzeff, *Iranians and Greeks in South Russia* (Oxford, 1922), have been followed by numerous new publications, particularly in Russian, on the history of Graeco-Iranian co-existence and interchange in the area. The remarkable Scythian art is well represented in M. Artamonov, *The Treasures in the Scythian Tombs* (London, 1969), while many recent Russian works have illuminated further aspects of the history of the Scythians, Sarmatians and the Hellenistic Bosphorus kingdom. Much obscurity surrounds Sarmatian religious beliefs, which are discussed, with suggestions for Zoroastrian influences, in T. Sulimirski, *The Sarmatians* (London, 1970), pp. 34–8.

7 A fresh overview on Hellenism in the Seleucid kingdom is offered in Kuhrt and Sherwin-White, *Hellenism in the East*, while the conflict between the Jewish Hellenizers and the Hasidim and Antiochus IV's measures against Judaism have been treated extensively in works such as V. Tcherikover, *Hellenistic Civilization and the Jews* (Philadelphia, 1959), and E. J. Bickerman, *Der Gott der Makkabäer* (Berlin, 1937). The history of the Graeco-Bactrian kingdom is surveyed, sometimes with differing conclusions, in W. W. Tarn, *The Greeks in Bactria and India*, 2nd edn (Cambridge, 1951), and A. K. Narain, *The Indo-Greeks* (Oxford, 1957). Boyce's discussion of the religious aspects of the Graeco-Iranian encounter in Central Asia at the time of the Graeco-Bactrian kingdom (*A History of Zoroastrianism*, vol. 3, pp. 157–93) summarizes the evidence of the crucial recent archaeological discoveries in Bactria.

8 On the history of Parthia, the sixth 'Oriental Monarchy' in Rawlinson's *Seven Great Oriental Monarchies of the Ancient World*, N. C. Debevoise's *A Political History of Parthia* (Chicago, 1938) remains the standard work,

while more recent and updated surveys are offered in A. Bivar, 'The Political History of Iran under the Arsacids' in E. Yarshater (ed.), *The Cambridge History of Iran*, vol. 3 (1) (Cambridge, 1983), pp. 21–100 and R. N. Frye, *The History of Ancient Iran* (Munich, 1984), pp. 205–49. Many problems and controversies plague the study of the religious situation in the Parthian empire and the evolution of Zoroastrianism in the Arsacid era: compare Boyce, *Zoroastrians*, pp. 80–100 and J. Duchesne-Guillemin, *La Religion de l'Iran ancien* (Paris, 1962), pp. 224ff. Among the studies of Graeco-Iranian syncretism in Commagene a recapitulation can be found in J. Duchesne-Guillemin, 'Iran and Greece in Commagene' in *Études mithriaques* (Leiden, 1978), pp. 187–201.

9 The connection between the Yueh-Chih movement into Bactria and the Sarmatian migration to the Pontic area is made in J. Harmatta, *Studies in the History and Language of the Sarmatians* (Szeged, 1970), pp. 31–4, 40. There are many uncertainties about the identity and early history of the Yueh-Chih and opinion is still divided over whether they were originally of Indo-European extraction. A reconstruction of the nomadic influx and conquest in Bactria may be found in Tarn, *Greeks in Bactria*, pp. 270–311. The translation of the name Yueh-Chih as 'Lunar Race' is suggested by J. M. Rosenfield, *The Dynastic Art of the Kushans* (Berkeley, 1967), pp. 7–8, with arguments for its connection with the mythology and the lunar emblems in the costumes of the Yueh-Chih, whose pre-Bactrian history is reviewed briefly on pp. 9ff. The reconstruction of the early history of the Yueh-Chih in A. K. Narain, 'Indo-Europeans in Inner Asia', in D. Sinor (ed.), *The Cambridge History of Early Inner Asia* (Cambridge, 1990), pp. 151–77, associates the Yueh-Chih problem with that of the supposed Inner Asian homeland of the Indo-Europeans (pp. 152–4).

10 Frye, *History of Ancient Iran*, p. 257. With reference to the Kushan king Kanishka, see p. 58. On Kushan history an overview is provided in B. Staviskii, *La Bactriane sous les Kushans*, tr. P. Bernard, M. Burda, F. Grenet, P. Leriche (Paris, 1986), pp. 127–57.

11 An extensive survey of the complex Kushan pantheon, as recovered from Kushan coinage, can be found in Rosenfield, *The Dynastic Art of the Kushans*, pp. 60–104, which is a good guide to the uniquely syncretistic character of Kushan civilization, in both the fields of culture and religion. For a complex picture of the religious and cultic traditions in Kushan Bactria general orientation is provided in Staviskii, *La Bactriane sous les Kushans*, pp. 195–231.

12 There are various valuable surveys of Mahayana Buddhism, for example, E. Conze, *Buddhist Thought in India* (London, 1962), pp. 195–237; B. L.

Suzuki, *Mahayana Buddhism*, 4th edn (London, 1981). The teaching of the Bodhisattva has also received extensive treatment in works like H. Dayal, *The Bodhisattva Doctrine in Buddhist Sanskrit Literature* (London, 1932), with arguments for Zoroastrian influence on the Bodhisattva doctrine and the cult of sun-worship in India, p. 39. Iranian influence on the Bodhisattva teaching is also proposed, for example, in M. T. de Mallmann, *Introduction à l'étude d'Avalokiteçvara* (Paris, 1948). The influence of the Zoroastrian teaching of the Saoshyant on the emergence of the Maitreya belief in northern Buddhism is put forward, for example, in Boyce, *Zoroastrians*, p. 84; Gnoli, 'Saoshyant' in Eliade, *Encyclopedia of Religion*, vol. 13, p. 68; Mithraic influence on the figure of the Maitreya is proposed, for example, in A. M. Dani, 'Mithraism and Maitreya' in *Études mithriaques*, pp. 91–9; cf. Frye, *History of Ancient Iran*, p. 269. There is extensive literature on the syncretism of the Gandhara art school and differing conclusions as to the source of the western influences in Gandhara which are variously recognized as Roman or Graeco-Bactrian. An account of the evolution of the Gandhara school and its pioneering elaboration of the Buddha image is provided in J. Marshall, *The Buddhist Art of Gandhara* (Cambridge, 1960).

13 The offerings to Ahriman, as described by Plutarch, are seen by Boyce as a 'conscious inversion' of the 'sacred rituals of the *yasna*', *A History of Zoroastrianism*, vol. 3, p. 457. She also suggested that this 'dark rite' might have 'owed something to what appears to have been a recognized observance of the Old Iranian religion, namely the making of offerings to chthonic beings in shady places' (pp. 457–8). Plutarch's version has been read as an authentic form of Zurvanism by Benveniste, *The Persian Religion*, p. 113, where the position of Mithras as a mediator between the forces of good and evil is regarded as a Zurvanite idea (pp. 89ff.). Zaehner, however, recognized in Plutarch's description a 'half-way house' between catholic Zoroastrianism and Roman Mithraism, *The Dawn and Twilight*, pp. 123–5.

14 F. Cumont, *The Mysteries of Mithra*, tr. T. McCormack (New York, 1956), p. vi.

15 E. Renan, *Marc-Aurèle et la fin du monde antique* (Paris, 1923), p. 579. It is worth noting that Julian's adherence to Mithraism has been questioned recently by R. Turcan in his *Mithras Platonicus* (Leiden, 1975), but his objections have been met by P. Athanassiadi, 'A Contribution to Mithraic Theology: The Emperor Julian's *Hymn to King Helios*', *Journal of Theological Studies*, 28 (1977), pp. 360–71.

16 It would be impossible to refer here to all theories that try to trace the beginnings of the Mithraic mysteries. Yet mention should be made of

an interesting attempt to associate early Mithraism with the Bosphorus kingdom: see P. Beskow, 'The Routes of early Mithraism', *Études mithriaques*, pp. 7–19; and the arguments for a solar cult of Mithra in the Kushan empire and its potential affiliations with Roman Mithraism occur in D. W. MacDowall, 'Mithra's Planetary Setting in the Coinage of the Great Kushans', *Études mithriaques*, pp. 305–17; A. D. H. Bivar, 'Mithraic Images of Bactria: Are they related to Roman Mithraism?' in U. Bianchi (ed.), *Mysteria Mithrae* (Leiden/Rome, 1979), pp. 741–61. The traditional Anatolian theory is referred to below.

17 R. N. Frye, 'Mithra in Iranian history' in Hinnells, *Mithraic Studies*, vol. 1, p. 64. The claim for a 'proto-Mithraic cult' in the Persian army has been advanced on the basis of Aramaic inscriptions in Persepolis in R. A. Bowman, *Aramaic Ritual Texts from Persepolis* (Chicago, 1970). According to G. Widengren, 'The Mithraic Mysteries in the Greco-Roman world with special regard to their Iranian background', *La Persia e il mondo Greco-Romano* (Rome, 1966), pp. 433–6, Mithra was indeed the high god of the 'warrior societies' who had their 'military forms of initiation' and these were the source of the initiatory rites in the Mithraic Mysteries of the Roman age. The theses of Bowman and Widengren have met much resistance, but in regard to a cult of Mithra among the Persepolis soldiers Frye remarks that 'there is no reason why such a kind of special organization or cult should not exist within the Mazdayasnian religion at Persepolis' (p. 64).

18 Bivar, 'Religious subjects on Achaemenid seals'; 'Mithra and Mesopotamia'. Some of Bivar's arguments have been subjected to criticism by H. J. W. Drijvers, 'Mithra at Hatra' in *Études mithriaques*, pp. 151–87.

19 This reconstruction of the symbolism of the *tauroctonia* follows the interpretation of J. Hinnells, 'Reflections on the bull-slaying scene', in *Mithraic Studies*, vol. 2, pp. 290–313; 'The Iranian Background of Mithraic Iconography', *Commemoration Cyrus, Hommage Universel*, I (Teheran/Liège, 1974), pp. 242–50, which rejects Cumont's thesis of the *tauroctonia* as a reflection of the Iranian theological dualism of good and evil in a specific Mithraic version in which Mithra sacrifices the primeval bull to create the world but creation and life is attacked, as in the *Greater Bundahishn*, by Ahriman and his demons (Cumont, *The Mysteries of Mithra*, pp. 136ff.; M. J. Vermaseren, *Mithras the Secret God*, tr. T. and V. Megaw (London/Toronto, 1963), pp. 67–70). According to Boyce, in its pre-Zoroastrian form, the myth of the slaying of the bull might have been referring to a sacrifice, its death being considered 'a creative and useful act' which led to the generation of 'all other good creatures and plants' (*A History of Zoroastrianism*, vol. 1, p. 139).

20 M. P. Spiedel, *Mithras–Orion: Greek Hero and Roman Army God* (Leiden, 1980). Another recent work, by D. Ulancey, *The Origins of the Mithraic Mysteries* (Oxford, 1989), argues that in Mithraism, Mithras was associated with the constellation Perseus and was seen as a cosmocrator, responsible for the precession of the equinoxes, which was symbolized in Mithraic *tauroctonia*.

21 J. P. Arendzen, 'Mithraism' in *The Catholic Encyclopedia*, vol. 10 (New York, 1911), p. 403.

22 U. Bianchi, 'The religio-historical question of the mysteries of Mithra', in Bianchi, *Mysteria Mithrae*, p. 27, though he argues that the 'dynamic and heroic Mithra of the Roman mysteries is not without connexion with the Iranian Mithra' (p. 27). In *Mithras Platonicus*, Turcan argues that by the second century Greek philosophical circles were well acquainted with Mithraic teachings and began the process of accommodating Mithras into the Platonic system. The traditional theory that Mithraism was essentially a Roman version of Zoroastrianism can be found in Cumont, *The Mysteries of Mithra*.

23 J. F. Hansman, 'Some Possible Classical Connections in Mithraic Speculation', in Bianchi, *Mysteria Mithrae*, p. 610.

24 Bivar, 'Mithra and Mesopotamia', p. 280; U. Bianchi, 'Mithraism and Gnosticism' in Hinnells, *Mithraic Studies*, vol. 2, p. 458.

25 The identification of the lion–man with Aion–Zurvan is suggested, for example, in Cumont, *The Mysteries of Mithra*, pp. 107ff., where he is regarded as being 'at the pinnacle of the divine hierarchy and at the origin of things', and 'Lord and master of the four elements that compose the universe', who 'creates and destroys everything' (p. 109). His identification with Ahriman has been accepted by Zaehner, *The Dawn and Twilight*, p. 129; Duchesne-Guillemin, *Ormazd et Ahriman*, pp. 126ff. (where he is held to represent both Aion and Ahriman); Duchesne-Guillemin, *The Western Response to Zoroaster*, p. 95 (where the lion-headed figure, 'this cruel, ugly deity, clearly appears with his serpent, his signs of the Zodiac, his four wings, as the master of the world'). The association with the lion-headed portrayals of Nergal is in Bivar, 'Religious subjects on Achaemenid seals'; 'Mithra and Mesopotamia'; this Mesopotamian, 'Nergalian' background of the Mithraic lion-headed statues is supported by H. von Gall, 'The Lion-Headed and the Human-Headed God in the Mithraic Mysteries', *Études mithriaques*, p. 515.

26 J. Hansman, 'A Suggested Interpretation of the Mithraic Lion–Man Figure', *Études mithriaques*, pp. 215–27, 'Some Possible Classical Connections in Mithraic Speculations', pp. 608ff. Jaeger sees Plato's 'bad

world–soul that opposes the good one in the *Laws* as a 'tribute to Zoroaster' (*Aristotle*, p. 132).

27 Hansman, 'A Suggested Interpretation', p. 226.

28 The relevant fragments from the *Denkart*, 182.6ff.; 211.1; 355.6, after D. Madan (ed.), *Dinkard* (Bombay, 1911) and the *Greater Bundahishn* concerning the religion of the sorcerers and the rite of the 'mystery of the sorcerers' are translated and discussed in Zaehner, *Zurvan*, pp. 14ff. Duchesne-Guillemin supports the identification of the 'Ahrimanic' sorcerers with the 'Magians' described by Plutarch ('Notes on Zervanism in the light of Zaehner's *Zurvan*, with additional references', *Journal of Near Eastern Studies*, 15:2 (1956), p. 110).

29 Zaehner, *The Dawn and Twilight*, pp. 128ff.; *Zurvan*, pp. 19ff. Similarly, Duchesne-Guillemin (n. 25, above) sees 'the master of this world' in the lion-headed figure.

30 Bianchi, 'The religio-historical question of the mysteries of Mithra', pp. 24ff.; and 'Mithraism and Gnosticism'; R. L. Gordon, 'Franz Cumont and the doctrines of Mithraism' in Hinnells, *Mithraic Studies*, vol. 1, p. 222.

31 Bianchi, 'The religio-historical question of the mysteries of Mithra', p. 39.

32 H. M. Jackson, 'The Meaning and Function of the Leontocephaline in Roman Mithraism', *Numen*, 32 (1985), pp. 19, 33, with a detailed overview of the evidence and theories concerning the nature of the lion-headed god in the Mithraic Mysteries.

33 The notions of *yetser ha-tov* and *yetser ha-ra* are discussed in E. Urbach, *The Sages: Their Concepts and Beliefs* (Jerusalem, 1975), vol. 1, pp. 471–83. The 'heretical' tradition of the 'Two Heavenly Powers', as attested in the rabbinic records, has received extensive treatment in A. Segal, *Two Powers in Heaven* (Leiden, 1977), while according to I. P. Culianu, 'The Angels of the Nations and the Origins of Gnostic Dualism' in R. Van den Broek and M. J. Vermaseren (eds.), *Studies in Gnosticism and Hellenistic Religions* (Leiden, 1981), pp. 78–92, its transformations in the first century AD could have influenced Gnostic dualism. Later Jewish lore about Satan and the powers of evil is surveyed in J. Trachtenberg, *The Devil and the Jews* (New Haven, 1943); *Jewish Magic and Superstition* (New York, 1939); L. Jung, *Fallen Angels in Jewish, Christian and Mohammedan Literature* (Philadelphia, 1926).

34 In 3 Enoch Samael appeared as Prince of the Satans (14:2) and Prince of Rome (26:12), while in the quoted rabbinics, Samael was styled the 'great prince in heaven' in Pirke de-Rabbi Eliezer 13, 'Samael the Wicked' prince of the evil angels in Deuteronomy Rabbah 11, and was

portrayed as standing alongside Michael before the *Shekhinah* during the Jewish exodus in Exodus Rabbah 18:5. Samael's war against Michael, his defeat, fettering and surrender to Israel were recounted in Bereshit Rabbah, whereas he appeared as the angel of death, for example, in Abodah Zarah 20b, and in Jewish astrological literature was associated with Mars. Michael was given the title Prince of the World in Pirke de-Rabbi Eliezer 27 and his association with the 'foundation' of Rome is brought forward in Shir ha-Shirim Rabbah (1:6,4). A convergence between the figures of Satan, the 'Prince of the World' (as chief of the national angels) and Samael (as an angel of death and Rome) is posited in Culianu, 'The Angels', pp. 84ff., which might have changed the Prince of the World into Creator of the World and further an evil Creator of the World in a dualist system (Culianu, 'The Angels', p. 91).

35 Quoted after J. B. Russell, *The Prince of Darkness* (London, 1989), p. 70. In an earlier book, *The Devil*, Russell provided an instructive summary of the features of the Devil in the New Testament, while in *Satan: The Early Christian Tradition* (New York, 1981), he surveyed in detail the perception of the Devil and evil in early Christian thought. Among other studies of the role of the Devil and the powers of evil in the New Testament and the early Christian tradition are: T. Ling, *The Significance of Satan* (London, 1961); N. Forsyth, *The Old Enemy*, pp. 248–307; J. Hick, *Evil and the God of Love* (New York, 1966).

36 Russell, *The Devil*, p. 256.

37 It is impossible to survey here the development of the study of Gnostic origins, revolutionized with the discovery of the Nag Hammadi Library in 1945, and the existing theories about the phenomenon of Gnosticism. The contributions to the Messina Colloquium on the origins of Gnosticism – U. Bianchi (ed.), *Le origini dello Gnosticismo* (Leiden, 1967) – highlighted the multifarious approaches to the problem. While for the early Church the Gnostic sects largely represented forms of Christian heresy that had to be combated, in the various more recent attempts to explain the nature of Gnosticism it has been defined as a Hellenization of Christianity (Harnack), as a pre-Christian phenomenon rooted in Iranian mysticism and redemption myths (Bousset, Reitzenstein), an outcome of a crisis in Jewish apocalyptic thought following the catastrophy of AD 70 (Grant), and the presence of Jewish and Jewish–Christian apocalyptic traditions in Gnostic systems have been acknowledged in recent studies. At the same time, the view that Gnosticism represents essentially an inner Christian development or a Christian heresy remains influential and continues to provoke debate. Yet with the publication and the studies of the texts of the Nag Hammadi Library it is becoming

increasingly apparent that Gnosticism, in the words of J. Robinson, 'seems not to have been in its essence just an alternate form of Christianity' but 'a new syncretistic religion', 'drawing upon various religious heritages', *The Nag Hammadi Library* (Leiden, 1973), pp. 9–10. The Nag Hammadi texts referred to below are quoted from the translations in *The Nag Hammadi Library*.

38 An overview of the figure of Christ in Gnostic systems and Gnostic Christologies can be found in K. Rudolph, *Gnosis,* ed. and tr. R. McL. Wilson (Edinburgh, 1983), pp. 148–71; also in G. Filoramo, *A History of Gnosticism* tr. A. Alcock (Oxford, 1990), pp. 116–27; while Gnostic Docetism is discussed by U. Bianchi, 'Docetism: A Peculiar Theory about the Ambivalence of the Presence of the Divine' in his *Selected Essays on Gnosticism, Dualism and Mysteriosophy*, pp. 303–11.

39 The tradition of Eve's seduction by Samael, who comes to her, 'riding on the serpent', to beget Cain is recorded in Pirke de-Rabbi Eliezer 22. The tradition that Eve had conceived the angel from Samael and declared that with the birth of Cain she had acquired the angel of the Lord as a man occurs in Targum-Pseudo-Jonathan 5:1–3, where Cain is described 'as those on high, not like those below' (quoted after J. Bowker, *The Targums and Rabbinic Literature* (Cambridge, 1969), p. 132).

40 The duality between Cain, as father of the generations of the wicked, and Seth, as father of the generations of the just, is emphasized in Pirke de-Rabbi Eliezer 22, while the notion of the kingdom of the house of David as planted by Seth is discussed in G. A. G. Stroumsa, *Another Seed: Studies in Gnostic Mythology* (Leiden, 1984), p. 74.

41 The notion of the Gnostic spiritual race as the 'children' or 'seed' of Seth appeared in Nag Hammadi tracts like the Apocryphon of John, the Three Steles of Seth and the Gospel of the Egyptians. The nature of 'Sethian' Gnosticism has been explored in Stroumsa, *Another Seed* and in the contributions in B. Layton (ed.), *The Rediscovery of Gnosticism*, vol. 2, *Sethian Gnosticism* (Leiden, 1981). In Epiphanius' account of the Sethian Gnostic system Jesus Christ was identified with Seth, while the Nag Hammadi treatise Melchizedek implied that Melchizedek might have been regarded as Seth's incarnation. The equation between Seth and Zoroaster is discussed in W. Bousset, *Hauptprobleme der Gnosis* (Göttingen, 1907), pp. 379–82; also by B. A. Pearson, 'The Figure of Seth in Gnostic Literature' in Layton, *The Rediscovery of Gnosticism*, vol. 2, pp. 494, 498.

42 The main Christian sources for the Gnostic theology of Valentinus were the polemical writings of Irenaeus, Hippolytus and Epiphanius, Tertullian's *Against Valentinus* and others. Some of the Nag Hammadi texts like The Gospel of Philip betray Valentinian influences, while The

Gospel of Truth is sometimes attributed to Valentinus himself. Valentinian Gnosticism has received extensive treatment in A. Orbe, *Estudios valentinianos* (4 vols., Rome, 1955–61); more recently in B. Layton (ed.), *The Rediscovery of Gnosticism*, vol. 1, *The School of Valentinus* (Leiden, 1980). The teachings of the Alexandrian theologian Basilides are known from the differing versions of Irenaeus, Hippolytus and Clement of Alexandria. Marcion's writings have been lost but accounts of his teachings are presented in the works of anti-heretical polemicists like Irenaeus and Tertullian. Marcion's dualism is discussed in E. G. Blackmann, *Marcion and his Influence* (London, 1948), pp. 66ff; while Harnack's book, *Marcion: Das Evangelium vom fremden Gott*, 2nd edn (Leipzig, 1924), still remains the classic treatment of Marcion.

43 The association between the portrayal of the Demiurge as an arrogant archon and Isaiah's parable against the king of Babylon has been demonstrated in N. A. Dahl, 'The Arrogant Archon and the Lewd Sophia' in Layton, *The Rediscovery of Gnosticism*, vol. 1, pp. 689–713, with further arguments for Sophia herself being cast in the role of the 'virgin daughter of Babylon'.

44 Jackson, 'The Meaning and Function of the Leontocephaline in Roman Mithraism', p. 32. G. Quispel argues for the influence of the Orphic teriomorphic Demiurge Phanes, sometimes described as a roaring lion, on both the Mithraic lion–man and on Yaldabaoth, 'The Demiurge in the "Apocryphon of John"' in R. McL. Wilson (ed.), *Nag Hammadi and Gnosis* (Leiden, 1978), pp. 1–34. According to Jackson, however, it is impossible to establish any genealogy between the three figures, which are seen as the result of 'independent development of late Roman representatives of celestial eternity on solar and/or Saturnine exemplars' (p. 32).

45 A. J. Welburn, 'Reconstructing the Ophite Diagram', *Novum Testamentum* 23:3 (1981), p. 271.

46 Quoted from the *Denkart* fragment in Zaehner, *Dawn and Twilight*, p. 301. The link between Zoroastrianism and the Sassanid empire is discussed on pp. 284ff., while a survey of the religious situation in the Sassanid period in Iran is advanced in Zaehner, *Zurvan*, pp. 35–53; cf. Boyce's arguments that the Sassanid dynasty was of Zurvanite orientation, *Zoroastrians*, pp. 118ff. The concepts of royalty and religious policy in the Sassanid empire have been surveyed in G. Gnoli, 'Politica religiosa e concezione della regalità sotto i Sassanidi', in *La Persia nel Medioevo*, pp. 225–51.

47 J. R. Russell, *Zoroastrianism in Armenia* (Harvard Iranian Series v, Cambridge, Massachusetts, 1987), p. 126, with an account of the

Christian–Zoroastrian encounter in Armenia and a scrutiny of Zoroastrian traditions in Armenia and their survival, pp. 113–53. 'Iranian' Armenia has been the subject of two pioneering studies by N. G. Garsoïan, reprinted in her *Armenia between Byzantium and the Sasanians* (London, 1985): 'Prolegomena to a Study of the Iranian Elements in Arsacid Armenia' and 'The Locus of the Death of Kings: Iranian Armenia – the Inverted Image'.

48 Quoted after Shaked's translation, *The Wisdom of the Sasanian Sages* (*Denkard* VI), p. 79. The notion of threefold religious hierarchy in Sassanid Zoroastrianism is scrutinized by Shaked in his 'Esoteric Trends in Zoroastrianism' where he demonstrates its association with a 'hierarchy of religious truths' and the division between popular and higher Zoroastrianism, some aspects of the latter being considered restricted religious mysteries.

49 This threefold division is reported by Eznik of Kolb in his work *Against the Sects*, in Schmidt's translation, *Wieder die Sekten*, p. 87. The interpretation of the adherents of the three principles as Zurvanites follows Zaehner's reading of Eznik's report in *Zurvan*, pp. 28–9.

50 These two forms of Zoroastrianism are attested by later Islamic writers like al-Baghdadi and al-Shahrastani and their evidence is discussed in Zaehner, *Dawn and Twilight*, pp. 180–81.

51 Madan, *Dinkard*, p. 154, quoted after Zaehner's translation of the names of the sects in *Zurvan*, p. 13.

52 Quoted from the recent translation of Kartir's inscription by D. N. MacKenzie in *Iranische Denkmäler*, Reihe 2, *Lief* 13 (Berlin, 1989), p. 58.

53 al-Biruni, *Chronology of the Ancient Nations*, tr. E. Sachau (London, 1879), p. 190.

54 The Babylonian sectarians, joined by Mani's father, are called *Mughtasilah* by al-Nadim, in *The Fihristi of al-Nadim*, tr. B. Dodge (2 vols., New York, 1970), p. 774; and *katharioi* in the Manichaean work *Kephalaia*, ed. and tr. H. J. Polotsky and A. Böhlig (vol. 1, Stuttgart, 1940), 1.27, p. 44. They have been identified with the Elchasaites on the basis of the recently deciphered *Cologne Mani Codex* (see n. 56 below). Hippolytus' *Refutation of All Heresies* along with Epiphanius' *Panarion* are the principal sources for Elchasai and the Elchasaites. The relevant passages are quoted from the translations provided in A. F. Klijn and G. J. Reinink, *Patristic Evidence for Jewish-Christian Sects* (Leiden, 1973).

55 These Zurvanite–Elchasaite parallels are emphasized in W. Bousset, *Hauptprobleme der Gnosis* (Göttingen, 1907), pp. 153, 156; and critically discussed in Zaehner, *Zurvan*, pp. 72ff.

56 Mani's Elchasaite background and his conflict with the Elchasaites came

to light with the recent decipherment and publication by A. Henrichs and L. Koenen of the important Greek document, the *Cologne Mani Codex* (*CMC*), now available in L. Koenen and C. Römer (eds.), *Der Kölner Mani-Codex* (Opladen, 1988), which is used for the references below. The document relates the account of Mani's childhood, his revelations and the crystallization of his sense of mission, the customs and the purification rituals of the Elchasaites, Mani's collision with Elchasaite traditionalists and his breaking with the sect. His arguments against the Elchasaite ablutions and purifications are contained in *CMC* 80:18–83, 19, pp. 55–7. The account of Mani's conflict with the Elchasaites follows the evidence of the *CMC* 80:22ff.

57 *CMC* 18:8–19:18. On Mani's celestial Twin and revelations see A. Henrichs, 'Mani and the Babylonian Baptists: A Historical Confrontation', *Harvard Studies in Classical Philologies*, 77 (1973), pp. 33–5, which charts the characteristic ritualist customs of the Elchasaites and their conflict with Mani.

58 Quoted after *CMC* 26:7–15; 43:3–7 and *Kephalaia*, vol. 1, ed. and tr. H. J. Polotsky and A. Böhlig (Stuttgart, 1940), 15:3ff. The esotericism in Elchasaite and Manichaean thought has been well demonstrated by G. Stroumsa in his 'Esotericism in Mani's Thought and Background' in L. Cirillo and A. Roselli (eds.), *Codex Manichaicus Coloniensis* (Cosenza, 1986), pp. 153–69.

59 *CMC* 102:5ff.; 108:17ff. The diverse sources for Manichaean apocalypticism and its syncretic character are surveyed in depth by L. Koenen in his 'Manichaean Apocalypticism at the Crossroads of Iranian, Egyptian, Jewish and Christian Thought' in Cirillo and Roselli, *Codex Manichaicus Coloniensis*, pp. 285–333.

60 This apocalyptic scheme is recounted in the 'Great War Sermon' in H. J. Polotsky (ed.), *Manichäische Homilien* (Stuttgart, 1934), 7:8–42:7.

61 C. R. C. Alberry (ed.), *A Manichaean Psalm Book*, Part 2 (Stuttgart, 1938), p. 16.

62 al-Nadim, *Fihristi*, p. 802.

63 Bardaisan rejected and polemicized against Marcion's teaching of two gods. On the intriguing figure of Bardaisan, his system and teachings of fate and free will, see H. J. W. Drijvers, *Bardaisan of Edessa* (Assen, 1966).

64 Among the principal non-Manichaean sources for Manichaeism are: Alexander Lycopolitanus' opus against Manichaeism; the *Acta Archelai*; Augustine's works such as *Contra Faustum PL*, vol. 42, cols. 207–518; Theodore bar Konai's *Liber Scholiorum*; al-Nadim's account of Manichaeism in his *Fihristi*. The Turfan fragments were written in various

languages (Middle Persian, Sogdian, Parthian, Uighur, Bactrian), while the Coptic finds included the Manichaean *Psalm Book*, *Homilies* and *Kephalaia* (Discourses) – the sayings of Mani collected after his death. Along with the decipherment of the *Cologne Mani Codex*, the discovery and publication of these Manichaean documents were of crucial importance for testing the validity of the non-Manichaean accounts of the Manichaean system and for providing new insights into the teachings and history of the Manichaean church and its founder, Mani.

65 al-Nadim, *Fihristi*, p. 778.

66 al-Nadim, *Fihristi*, pp. 783–6.

67 al-Nadim, *Fihristi*, p. 798. Manichaean Christology is surveyed in E. Rose, *Die Manichäische Christologie* (Wiesbaden, 1979).

68 T. Olsson, 'The Manichaean Background of Eschatology in the Koran' in P. Bryder (ed.), *Manichaean Studies: Proceedings of the First International Conference on Manichaeism* (Lund, 1988), pp. 273–82.

69 N.-A. Pedersen, 'Early Manichaean Christology' in Bryder, *Manichaean Studies*, p. 169, with an examination of the Jesus figures in Manichaeism and their parallels in Gnosticism, Marcionism, et cetera.

70 *Kephalaia* 154, tr. I. Stevenson, *A New Eusebius* (London, 1968), p. 282.

71 B. A. Pearson, 'The Figure of Seth in Manichaean Literature' in Bryder, *Manichaean Studies*, pp. 153–5. Sethel (i.e. Seth) was praised as an 'Apostle of Electship' in *A Manichaean Psalm Book*, p. 144.

72 al-Nadim, *Fihristi*, p. 796.

73 This eschatological chronology is developed in the 'Great War Sermon' in the *Manichäische Homilien*, pp. 12–41.11.

74 S. N. C. Lieu, *Manichaeism in the Later Roman Empire and Medieval China*, 2nd rev. edn (Tübingen, 1992), p. 218. Lieu's book presents a detailed and updated survey of the history of Manichaeism in the Roman empire, the subject also of an earlier general work, E. de Stoop, *Essai sur la diffusion du manichéisme dans l'empire romain* (Ghent, 1909).

75 On Mani as the Maitreya and the Buddha of Light and on Mani's assimilation to Lao-Tzu see Lieu, *Manichaeism*, pp. 255–61. Lieu's work offers a penetrating survey of the spread and decline of Manichaeism in medieval China and its eastern transformations, which are also the subject of P. Bryder, *The Chinese Transformations of Manichaeism: A Study of Chinese Manichaean Terminology* (Lund, 1985).

76 On the circumstances of the inclusion of the work in the canon see Lieu, *Manichaeism*, pp. 268–70.

77 On Marco Polo's encounter with Manichaeans in Fukien see L. Olschski, 'Manichaeism, Buddhism and Christianity in Marco Polo's China', *Zeitschrift der schweizerischen Gesellschaft für Asienkunde*, 5 (1951), pp. 1–21.

The suppression of Manichaeism under Chu Yüan-Chang and its later recoverable traces in China are surveyed in Lieu, *Manichaeism*, pp. 298–304.

78 The evidence for the late survival of Zoroastrian traditions in Armenia is examined in Russell, *Zoroastrianism in Armenia*, pp. 514–39.

79 The Arewordik are discussed in Russell, *Zoroastrianism in Armenia*, with allusions to the allegations of Paulician association with the 'Sons of the Sun'. According to N. G. Garsoïan, *The Paulician Heresy* (The Hague and Paris, 1967), p. 95, n. 46, although the Arewordik remained distinct from the Paulicians, the two sects may have been in 'close relation with each other, since the Paulicians were favoured by the Persian authorities', while it is possible that some Paulician groups adopted Persian practices.

80 Garsoïan, *The Paulician Heresy*, with a critical reconstruction of Paulician history, pp. 112–51, and original Paulician doctrine, pp. 151ff.

81 Garsoïan, *The Paulician Heresy*, pp. 183–5.

82 Petrus Siculus, *Historia Manichaeorum*, *PG*, vol. 104, col. 1252.

83 The views on the Massalians, treated in I. Hausherr, *Études de spiritualité orientale* (Rome, 1969), pp. 64–96 and R. Staats, *Gregor von Nysa und die Messalianer* (Berlin, 1968), appear somewhat divergent. According to S. Runciman, *The Medieval Manichee: A Study of the Christian Dualist Heresy* (Cambridge, 1946), p. 24, the Massalians were 'the agents that were to keep alive the rich Gnostic tradition in Byzantium' and had 'preserved for the heretics of the future a vast bulk of Gnostic literature', but this is difficult to ascertain. The Massalians are also discussed in D. Obolensky, *The Bogomils: A Study in Balkan Neo-Manichaeism* (Cambridge, 1948), pp. 48–51, part of Chap. 2 'Neo-Manichaeism in the Near East', which scans the complicated picture of sectarian and heretical trends in the Near East and Byzantium.

84 The background to the Serbs and the Croats coming to the Balkans, their Iranian origins and Slavicization, can be found in J. V. A. Fine, *The Early Medieval Balkans: A Critical Survey from the Sixth to the Late Twelfth Century* (Ann Arbor, Michigan, 1983), pp. 49–59. On the Sarmatian origins of the Serbs and Croats see also R. Browning, *Byzantium and Bulgaria* (London, 1975), p. 44; Sulimirski, *The Sarmatians*, pp. 188–94; F. Dvornik, *The Slavs: Their Early History and Civilization* (Boston, 1956), pp. 26–7. The extensive Iranian influences on the Slavs and Slavonic religion are treated more generally in Dvornik, *The Slavs*, pp. 47ff.; M. Gimbutas, *The Slavs* (London, 1971), pp. 151–70; I. Dujčev, 'Il mondo slavo e la Persia nell'alto medioevo' in *Medioevo bizantino-slavo* (3 vols., Rome, 1965–71), vol. 2, pp. 321–424; R. Jacobson, 'Slavic

Mythology', in the *Standard Dictionary of Folklore, Mythology and Legend* (New York, 1950), vol. 2, pp. 1025–8, with arguments that the 'Slavs participated in the Iranian evolution into a clear-cut dualism' (p. 1025).

85 Bianchi, 'Dualistic Aspects of Thracian Religion', p. 231.

86 Bianchi, 'Dualism' in M. Eliade (ed.), *Encyclopedia of Religion* (New York, 1987), vol. 4, p. 511.

3   The Rise of the Great Heresy

1 Frye, *The Heritage of Persia*, p. 159, with a discussion of the Iranian presence and cultural influence in the steppes prior to the advent of the Huns.

2 The Bulgars were placed between Iran and Turkestan in a seventh-century Armenian geographical tradition. There is also evidence of an early Bulgar presence in Armenia and in the northern Caucasus, where they were reported to have founded their own cities in Zacharias Rhetor's *Ecclesiastical History* (mid sixth century): Zacharias Rhetor, *Die Sogenannte Kirchengeschichte des Zacharias Rhetor*, XII, 7, p. 253. The academic search for the origins of the Bulgars still continues, although at one stage a consensus for a Turkic descent seemed to be nearly reached despite suggestions that the Bulgars were originally of Iranian extraction and that their assimilation of Turkic elements was a later process: V. F. Genning and A. H. Halikov, *Rannie bolgari na Volge* [The Early Bulgars on the Volga] (Moscow, 1964), pp. 184, 190–91. A number of inconsistencies in the Turkic theory have been recently exposed in P. Dobrev, *Prabălgarite* [The Proto-Bulgars] (Sofia, 1991), which draws attention to a body of material on the association of the Bulgars with Bactria and Sogdiana. The strong links between the Bulgars and the Alans in the northern Pontic steppes remain undisputed.

3 O. Pritsak, *The Origin of Rus*: vol. 1, *Old Scandinavian Sources other than the Sagas* (Cambridge, Massachusetts, 1981), p. 61, with extensive discussion of the cultural and religious situation in the Eurasian steppes in the period (pp. 56–73). According to Pritsak, in the Eurasian steppes and particularly in the Bosphorus area, Hellenism, understood as a 'marriage of cultures', survived the decline of classical Mediterranean Hellenism after 31 BC and 'continued to flourish until the tenth and eleventh centuries' (*The Origin of Rus*, p. 72).

4 B. B. Piotrovskii (ed.), *Istoriya narodov severnogo Kavkaza s drevneishikh*

vremen do kontsa XVIIIv [History of the peoples in the North Caucasus from ancient times until the end of the 18th century] (Moscow, 1988), pp. 112–14, 136–7.

5 Besides some novel studies of Khazar Judaism, following the publication of D. M. Dunlop, *The History of the Jewish Khazars* (Princeton, 1954), new works, based primarily on archaeological evidence, have indicated the role of the Bulgars and the Alans in maintaining and developing Sarmato-Alan cultural traditions in the areas under Khazar supremacy: M. Artamonov, *Istoriya Khazar* [History of the Khazars] (Leningrad, 1962), pp. 308–16; S. A. Pletneva, *Ot Kochevi k gorodam* [From Nomadism to City] (Moscow, 1967). S. A. Pletneva, *Khazari* [The Khazars] (Moscow, 1976), pp. 56–8, presents arguments that the Bulgaro-Alan nobility might well have exploited the dual kingship system of the khaganate by establishing a permanent hold on the seat of the khagan's secular co-ruler (bek or khagan-bek) and surrounding the khagan himself with a system of taboos.

6 S. Runciman, *A History of the First Bulgarian Empire* (London, 1930), p. 21. Runciman's book still remains the standard full-length treatment of the First Bulgarian Empire in English. More recent surveys can be found in D. M. Lang, *The Bulgarians* (London, 1976), Chap. 3, 'From Khanate to Imperium'; R. Browning, *Byzantium and Bulgaria* (London, 1975), a comparative study of Bulgaria and Byzantium in the 9th–10th centuries; Fine, *The Early Medieval Balkans*, Chaps. 3–6.

7 al-Nadim, *Fihristi*, pp. 36–7. In a recent work, I. Zimonyi, *The Origins of the Volga Bulgars* (Szeged, 1990), examining the evidence about the Volga Bulgars in Islamic sources, the author suggests that al-Nadim had confused the Bulgars with the Manichaean Uighurs.

8 The art of Volga Bulgaria and its indebtedness to Sarmato-Alan culture has been examined in considerable detail in F. H. Valeev, *Drevnee i srednevekovoe iskusstvo srednego povolzhia* [Ancient and Medieval Art in the Middle Volga Region] (Joshkar Ola, 1975), with references to some Zoroastrian themes in Volga Bulgar art, seen as indications of the Sarmato-Alan influence, pp. 76, 97–9.

9 Lang, *The Bulgarians*, p. 121. The imperial structure of the Bulgar state is surveyed in detail in V. Beshevliev, *Părvobulgarite* [The Proto-Bulgars] (Sofia, 1981), pp. 39–66, with a discussion of the possible dual-kingship type of Bulgar monarchy (pp. 45–50) and some parallels between the Sassanid and Bulgar classes of nobility (p. 41).

10 Lang, *The Bulgarians*, p. 121. The strong Sassanid influence on Bulgarian art and architecture has also been recognized and discussed by, among others, D. Talbot Rice, 'Persia and Byzantium', in A. J. Arberry (ed.),

The Legacy of Persia (Oxford, 1953), p. 49; B. Fiov, *Geschichte der altbulgarischen Kunst bis zur Eroberung des bulgarischen Reiches durch die Türken* (Berlin and Leipzig, 1932), pp. 5–35; S. Vaklinov, *Formirane na staro-bulgarskata kultura 6–9 vek* [The Formation of the Old Bulgarian Culture in the Sixth to Ninth Centuries] (Sofia, 1977), pp. 92–3, 148–9. The thesis that Sassanid elements of design might have reached Byzantium through the Bulgarian medium has been advanced by Talbot Rice, 'Persia and Byzantium', p. 49.

11 These parallels have been well demonstrated by B. Brentjes, 'On the Prototype of the Proto-Bulgarian Temples at Pliska, Preslav and Madara', *East and West* (Rome), New series, vol. 21, pp. 213–16. Arab evidence defining the Bulgars as Magians can be found in J. Marquart, *Osteuropäische und ostasiatische Streifzüge* (Leipzig, 1903), pp. 204–5.

12 Brentjes, 'On the Prototype of the Proto-Bulgarian Temples', p. 215.

13 M. Kiel, *Art and Society of Bulgaria in the Turkish Period* (Assen, 1985), p. 1, with a brief survey of the history of medieval Bulgaria until the Ottoman conquest in the late fourteenth century.

14 *Scriptor incertus*, in Leo Grammaticus, *Chronographia*, ed. I. Bekker (Bonn, 1842), p. 348. R. Browning, *Byzantium and Bulgaria*, p. 50, argues that Krum did not intend to take Constantinople but was waiting instead for a *coup d'état* in the besieged city.

15 In the Salic law, compiled during the reign of the first Christian Merovingian king, Clovis I (481–511), the Franks were extolled as an 'illustrious tribe', 'of immaculate purity', established by God the Creator, converted to Catholicism and 'free of heresy'. See H. Fichtenau, *The Carolingian Empire* (Oxford, 1963), pp. 1–3.

16 The numerous monumental inscriptions in Greek, left by the Bulgar Kans, traditionally praised their deeds and theocratic rule. Concerning the Kans' collisions with Byzantium, Bulgar royal propaganda used formulas such as 'May God grant the divine ruler that he tramples underfoot the emperor . . .', while an inscription of Kan Persian (836–52) states: 'The Bulgars rendered many favours to the Christians [i.e. the Byzantines] and the Christians forgot but God sees all', V. Beshevliev, *Purvobulgarskite nadpisi* [The Proto-Bulgar Inscriptions] (Sofia, 1979), pp. 132–9, 200–209.

17 Folkloric relics of the Thracian worship of Dionysus in modern Thrace are examined in K. Kakouri, *Dionysiaka: Aspects of the Popular Thracian Religion of To-day* (Athens, 1965); vestiges of Thracian Orphism in south-eastern Thrace are treated in A. Fol, *Trakiiskiyat Orfizăm* [Thracian Orphism] (Sofia, 1986); M. Wenzel, 'The Dioscuri in the Balkans', *Slavic Review*, 26 (1967), pp. 363–81, argues that a complex of rituals preserved

in the western Balkans includes surviving relics from the mysteries of Samothrace.

18 The evidence of the sect of the Athingani is discussed in J. Starr, 'An Eastern Christian Sect: the Athinganoi', *Harvard Theological Review*, 2 (1936), pp. 93–106.

19 N. Garsoïan, *The Paulician Heresy*, pp. 183–5.

20 Petrus Siculus, *Historia Manichaeorum qui et Paulicani dicuntur*, *PG*, vol. 104, col. 1241.

21 The 'Paulician' legend and its relation to the Paulician influx in Bulgaria are discussed in I. Ivanov, *Bogomilski knigi i legendi* [Bogomil Books and Legends] (Sofia, 1925), pp. 10–12.

22 al-Nadim, *Fihristi*, pp. 802–803, acknowledged the rapid decline of Manichaeism after al-Muqtadir's caliphate: in the mid tenth century he knew 300 Manichaeans in Baghdad, but around twenty-five years later there were not even five Manichaeans left, while the *archegos* himself 'sought out any place where he could be safe'.

23 R. Browning, *The Byzantine Empire* (London, 1980), p. 82; cf. the position of A. Toynbee, *Constantine Porphyrogenitus and His World* (London, 1973), p. 367, with the conclusion that if Symeon's imperial designs had succeeded, his reign might 'have seen the beginnings of a fusion between the East Roman empire and Bulgaria with a minimum of resistance and bloodshed'. In 913, with his troops at the gates of Constantinople, Symeon was indeed crowned a *Basileus* by Patriarch Nicholas I Mysticus (although it remains unclear whether he was crowned *Basileus* of the Bulgars or co-emperor with the young Constantine VII) but the validity of his coronation was rejected after the ensuing Constantinople coup. Inevitably, Symeon's coronation in Constantinople and his bid for the imperial throne have attracted much comment and differing conclusions: see, for example, Fine, *The Early Medieval Balkans*, pp. 148ff.; D. Obolensky, *The Byzantine Commonwealth: Eastern Europe 500–1453* (London, 1971), pp. 108–15.

24 The circumstances of the adoption of the Slavonic liturgy in Bulgaria following the collapse of the mission of the Apostles of the Slavs in Moravia are expounded in F. Dvornik, *Les Slaves, Byzance et Rome au IXe siècle* (Paris, 1926), pp. 312–13; D. Obolensky, 'Sts. Cyril and Methodius, Apostles of the Slavs', *St Vladimir's Seminary Quarterly*, 7 (1963), pp. 6–7, with a discussion of the role of the literary movement under Symeon for the transmission of the Slavo-Byzantine culture to the Russians and the Serbs and making 'Byzantine sacred and secular literature accessible to all Slavs'.

25 Ivanov, *Bogomilski knigi i legendi*, p. 20.

26 Obolensky, *The Bogomils*, p. 95.

27 According to Theophanes Continuatus, *Chronographia*, ed. I. Bekker, *CSHB*, 1838, pp. 411–12, Romanus Lecapenus was persuaded by a certain astrologer that one of the statues in the Constantinople quarter of Xerolophus was in reality Symeon's double and ordered its decapitation, which caused the immediate death of Symeon.

28 Arguments for Manichaean influences among the Pechenegs can be found in V. G. Vasilevskii, 'Vizantiya i Pechenegi 1048–1094' [Byzantium and the Pechenegs 1048–1094], *Trudi* (St Petersburg, (1) 1908), pp. 38–57. Cf. O. Pritsak, *The Pečenegs: A Case of Social and Economic Transformation* (Lisse, 1976), p. 24, and Ivanov, *Bogomilski knigi i legendi*, pp. 19–20, with suggestions for Zoroastrian influences on the Pechenegs.

29 In *Antapodosis* (3:29), Liudprand of Cremona, Otto the Great's ambassador to Constantinople, portrayed Benjamin (Boyan) as an adept of magic, who could transform himself into a wolf or any other shape: see *Die Werke Liudprands von Cremona*, ed. J. Becker (Hanover and Leipzig, 1915), p. 88. The figure of the 'princely magus by blood' has been discussed in V. Flint, *The Rise of Magic in Early Medieval Europe* (Princeton, 1991), pp. 350–55. I. Dujčev, 'Boyan Magesnik' [Boyan the Magician], in *Prouchvaniya vårhu bålgarskoto srednovekovie* [Studies on Medieval Bulgaria] (Sofia, 1945), pp. 9–51, associated the pursuits of the Prince with the Byzantine secret arts, while V. Pundev, *Boyan Magiosnik* [Boyan the Magician] (Sofia, 1925), p. 18, attempted to link the Prince with the Bogomil heresy.

30 Theophylact's letter to Tsar Peter, the earliest certain evidence of the rise of Bogomilism, has been recently edited and discussed in I. Dujcev, *Medioevo bizantino-slavo* (Rome, 1965), vol. 1, pp. 283–315.

31 Translation into French and comments in H.-C. Puech and A. Vaillant, *Le Traité contre les Bogomiles de Cosmas le prêtre* (Paris, 1945); partially translated into English in E. Peters (ed.), *Heresy and Authority in Medieval Europe* (London, 1980), pp. 108–17.

32 The statement that Bogomil preachers taught their followers to defy the Tsar and nobility has been voluminously developed and over-elaborated in Marxist historiography, which largely treats the Bogomil sect as a broad social movement against 'feudal oppression', while notions of the Bogomils as vehicles of social protest occur in some general works on Bulgarian or Balkan history. The lack of evidence for such theses and for the speculation that the Bogomils might have been a strong social or peasant movement have been well demonstrated in J. Fine, 'The Bulgarian Bogomil Movement', *East European Quarterly*, 11:4 (1977), pp. 385–412.

33 Puech and Valliant, *Le Traité contre les Bogomiles*, pp. 190–92.

34 E. Esin, 'The Conjectural Links of Bogomilism with Central Asian Manichaeism', in *Bogomilstvoto na balkanot vo svetlinata na najnovite istraju-vanja* [Bogomilism in the Balkans in the Light of the Latest Research] (Skopje, 1982), p. 108. In A. Sharenkoff, *A Study of Manichaeism in Bulgaria with Special Reference to the Bogomils* (New York, 1927), Bogomilism is treated as a direct continuation of old Manichaeism in the medieval Balkans.

35 See, for example, I. Dujčev, 'I Bogomili nei paesi slavi e la loro storia', in *L'Oriente Cristiano nella storia della civiltà* (Rome, 1963), p. 628.

36 Zaehner, *Zurvan*, pp. 70, 450, where the related doctrine of the three principles of the Thracian 'Euchites' is defined as dependent on Zurvanism; Eliade, *The Two and the One*, pp. 83–4; the parallels between Zurvanism and Bogomilism are also noted by Toynbee, *Constantine Porphyrogenitus*, p. 657, where the mythologies of the two religious systems are defined as 'identical in essence', although affiliation between them is being rejected.

37 I. Dujčev, 'Aux origines des courants dualistes à Byzance et chez les Slaves méridionaux', *Revue des Études Sud-est Européennes*, 1 (1969), pp. 57ff.

38 T. Sulimirski, 'Sarmatians in the Polish Past', *The Polish Review*, 9:1 (1964), pp. 7–8.

39 S. Runciman, *The Medieval Manichee* (Cambridge, 1946), p. 91, considers Jeremiah a 'co-founder of the Bogomils' along with Bogomil, while D. Mandić, *Bogomilska crkva bosanskih krstjana* [The Bogomil Church of the Bosnian 'Krstjani'] (Chicago, 1962), p. 127, argues that Jeremiah was the first leader of the heretical church in Bosnia under the name of Eremis. Jeremiah is more commonly seen, however, as an author and compiler of apocryphal legends; cf. Obolensky, *The Bogomils*, pp. 271–4.

40 The evidence of the activities of the two 'Franks' appears in an index of forbidden books and is reprinted and discussed in Ivanov, *Bogomilski knigi i legendi*, pp. 50–51.

41 D. Angelov, 'Rationalistic Ideas of a Medieval Heresy' in *Bulgaria's Share in Human Culture* (Sofia, 1968), p. 69.

42 *The Bulgarian Apocryphal Chronicle* 13, published and discussed in Ivanov, *Bogomilski knigi i legendi*, pp. 273–87, with comments on the Bogomil elements in the work (pp. 275–6).

43 Although the early Aaronids were often implicated in mutinies and plots, the lineage intermarried with the prominent Byzantine houses of the Ducas and Comneni and by the end of the twelfth century had already given two imperial wives to Comnenian emperors, Catherine

and Irene Ducaina. Two of Irene's female scions soon entered the new royal house of Jerusalem by marrying the Angevin kings of Jerusalem, Baldwin III (1143–62) and Amalric I (1162–74).

44 Cf. Eliade, *A History of Religious Ideas*, vol. 3, p. 182, with arguments that following the influx of Bulgarian nobles in Constantinople Bogomilism penetrated Byzantine aristocratic and monastic circles and shaped its theology. Basil's design for defeating Bulgaro-Byzantine hostility through intermarriage is reported in Yachya of Antioch, *Historiae*, quoted after the translation in V. P. Rozen, *Imperator Vasili Bolgaroboïtsa* [Emperor Basil the Bulgar-Slayer] (St Petersburg, 1883), p. 59.

45 These controversial accusations are advanced in a Greek version of the *Life of St Vladimir*, which abounds in errors, and are usually regarded as unreliable. The evidence of the religious situation under Samuel allows various interpretations and some scholars continue to consider Samuel a Bogomil supporter. Obolensky, *The Bogomils*, p. 151, suggests that in the course of his wars with Byzantium Samuel tolerated the Bogomils for political reasons and this toleration gave rise to popular legends, associating him with Bogomilism; cf. also Fine, *The Early Medieval Balkans*, pp. 196–7.

46 A. Toynbee, *A Study of History* (London, 1939), vol. 4, p. 72.

47 The letter is contained in *PG*, vol. 131, cols. 47–58, but is erroneously attributed to a later theologian, Euthymius Zigabenus. Another edition is to be found in G. Ficker, *Die Phundagiagiten: Ein Betrag zur Ketzergeschichte des byzantinischen Mittelalters* (Leipzig, 1908), pp. 3–86.

48 An English translation of both versions of the Cathar ritual can be found in Wakefield and Evans, *Heresies in the High Middle Ages*, pp. 468–94.

49 Michael Psellus, *Dialogus de daemonum operatione*, *PG*, vol. 122, cols. 819–76.

50 Zaehner, *Zurvan*, p. 450, with a reproduction of the relevant fragment.

51 Obolensky, *The Bogomils*, p. 186, with an analysis of the teachings that could be considered Bogomil and those which seem to have been imposed by Psellus on the Euchites. The demonology in Psellus' tract, including the third trend, is more commonly attributed to his knowledge of Chaldean systems through Neoplatonic authors like Porphyry and Proclus but some scholars accept the existence of a third 'satanic' trend among the Thracian sectarians. See, for example, M. Wellnhofer, 'Die Thrakischen Euchiten und ihr Satanskult im Dialoge des Psellos', *Byzantinische Zeitschrift*, 30 (1929–30), pp. 477–84, with Near Eastern parallels.

52 J. Gouillard, 'Une source grecque du Sinodik de Boril, la lettre inédit du Patriarche Cosmas', *Travaux et mémoires*, 4 (1970), pp. 361–74.

NOTES

53 In 1463 a copy of the *Corpus Hermeticum* was brought to the founder of
the Platonic Academy in Florence, Cosimo de' Medici, where it was
translated by the Platonist Marsilio Ficino. A survey of the recoverable
history of the manuscript of the *Corpus Hermeticum* and the role of
Psellus can be found in W. Scott, *Hermetica* (Oxford, 1924), vol. 1, pp.
25ff.

54 Gouillard, 'Le Synodicon de l'orthodoxie', *Travaux et Mémoires,* 2 (1967),
pp. 59–61. According to Obolensky, *The Bogomils*, p. 202, there seems to
have been contact between Italus' disciples and Bogomilism and through
similar encounters with philosophical ideas in Byzantium during the
eleventh and twelfth centuries Bogomilism 'assumed the character of a
philosophical sect'.

55 Anna Comnena, *The Alexiad*, tr. E. Dawes (London, 1928), p. 236.

56 Comnena, *The Alexiad*, p. 385.

57 Comnena, *The Alexiad*, p. 386.

58 Comnena, *The Alexiad*, p. 412 (the following quotes are from Dawes's
translation, pp. 412–15).

59 Comnena, *The Alexiad*, p. 418.

60 Comnena, *The Alexiad*, p. 415.

61 Zigabenus Euthymius *Panoplia Dogmatica* (*PG*, vol. 130). The Bogomil
section is edited by Ficker in *Die Phundagiagiten*, pp. 89–111.

62 Runciman, *The Medieval Manichee*, pp. 72–3. It is worth noting that the
association between Niphon and Patriarch Atticus is presented as a
much closer relationship in Joannes Cinnamus, *Historiae*, ed. A. Meineke,
CSHB, Book 2, 1836, pp. 63–6, than in Nicetas Choniates, *De Manuele
Comneno*, in *Historia*, ed. I. Bekker, *CSHB*, Book 2, 1835, p. 107, where
it was used by Atticus' adversaries in their intrigues against the patriarch.
English translations of both accounts can be found in C. M. Brand (tr.),
Deeds of John and Manuel Comnenus (New York, 1976), pp. 56–8, and H.
J. Magoulias, *O City of Byzantium: Annals of Niketas Choniates* (Detroit,
1984), pp. 4–7.

63 An important source for the encounters between Orthodoxy and heretical movements in Macedonia, *The Life of St Hilarion*, was edited by E.
Kalužniacki in *Werke des Patriarchen von Bulgarien Euthymius* (Vienna,
1901), pp. 27–58.

64 Theodore Balsamon, *Photii Patriarchae Constantinopolitani Nomocanon*, *PG*,
vol. 104, col. 1148.

65 Hugo Etherianus and his work against the heretics in Byzantium has
been surveyed by A. Dondaine in 'Hugues Ethérien et Léon Toscan',
Archives d'histoire doctrinale et littéraire du moyen âge, 27 (1952), pp. 67–
113, with fragments of the text itself.

4   The Dualist Communion

1 J. Havet (ed.), *Les Lettres de Gerbert* (Paris, 1889), No. 180, pp. 161–2. Among the historians suspecting heretical inclinations in Gerbert are Runciman, *The Medieval Manichee*, p. 117; I. da Milano, 'Le eresie popolari', in *Studi Gregoriani*, 2, pp. 44–6.

2 The incidents with Leutard and Vilgard are reported in Ralph Glaber (the Bald), *Historiarum libri quinque* 2:11–12, in *Raoul Glaber: Les cinq livres de ses histoires [900–1044]*, ed. M. Prou (Paris, 1886), pp. 49–50.

3 The Aquitanian 'Manichaeans' are reported in Adémar of Chabannes, *Chronique* 3:49, ed. J. Chavanon (Paris, 1897), p. 173.

4 Among the accounts of the Orléans heretics a short version is provided in Adémar of Chabannes, *Chronique* 3:59, pp. 184–5; while a longer account appears in Paul of Saint Père de Chartres, *Gesta synodi Aureliansis*, in M. Bouquet (ed.), *Recueil des historiens des Gaules et de la France*, vol. 10, pp. 536–9.

5 The Montforte episode is recorded in Ralph Glaber, *Historiarum* 4:2, in Prou, *Raoul Glaber*, pp. 94–6 and Landulf the Elder, *Historia Mediolanensis*, 2:27, *MGH SS*, vol. 8, pp. 65–6, quoted after the translation in Wakefield and Evans, *Heresies of the High Middle Ages*, pp. 86–9.

6 M. Lambert, *Medieval Heresy* (London, 1977), p. 33, where the western 'proto-dualism' is defined as a 'half-way house between Western dissidence and Eastern Dualism'. A. Dondaine, 'L'Origine de l'hérésie médiévale: A propos d'un livre récent', *Rivista di storia della Chiesa in Italia*, 6, (1952) pp. 47–78, discerns a decisive Bogomil influence on the earliest appearances of heresy in medieval western Christendom. Conversely J. B. Russell, *Dissent and Reform in the Early Middle Ages* (Berkeley, 1965), p. 215, argues that prior to the mid twelfth century there are no obvious traits of eastern dualism in the teachings of the western heretics, although they were 'tending in the direction of dualism', which made them receptive to the influence of eastern dualist missionaries after 1140. In between these positions there exist a number of intermediary opinions concerning the measure of Bogomil impact on early western heresy.

7 An account of the beliefs and practices of the Cologne heretics is given in the letter of Eberwin of Steinfeld to St Bernard of Clairvaux, *PL*, vol. 182, cols. 676–80.

8 Bernard's letter to Alphonse Jordan is reproduced in *PL*, vol. 182, cols. 434–6; the quotations are from the translation provided in Wakefield and Evans, *Heresies of the High Middle Ages*, pp. 122–4.

9 The letter is reproduced in *PL*, vol. 179, cols. 937–8; the quotations are from the translation in Wakefield and Evans, *Heresies of the High Middle Ages*, pp. 140–41.

10 Lambert, *Medieval Heresy*, p. 43.

11 Anselm of Alessandria, *Tractatus de hereticis*, ed. A. Dondaine, 'L'Hiérarchie cathare en Italie', Part 2: 'Le "Tractatus de hereticis" d'Anselme d'Alexandrie', *Archivum Fratrum Praedicatorum*, 20 (1950), pp. 308–24. The quotations are from the translation in Wakefield and Evans, *Heresies of the High Middle Ages*, pp. 168–70.

12 *De heresi catharorum in Lombardia*, ed. A. Dondaine, 'L'Hiérarchie cathare en Italie', Part 1, *Archivum Fratrum Praedicatorum*, 19 (1949), pp. 305–312.

13 C. Thouzellier, 'Hérésie et croisade au xiie siècle', *Revue d'histoire ecclésiastique*, 49 (1954), pp. 855–72.

14 Eckbert of Schönau, *Sermones tredicim contra Catharos*, *PL*, vol. 195, cols. 11–102.

15 William of Newburgh, *Historia rerum anglicarum* 1:13, ed. R. Howlett, *Chronicles of the Reigns of Stephen, Henry II and Richard I* (London, 1884), vol. 1, pp. 131–4.

16 G. Scholem, *The Origins of the Kabbalah*, tr. A. Arkush (Princeton, 1987), draws attention to some interesting parallels between Cathar and early Kabbalistic themes, but studies and debates on this matter continue without any clear conclusions as yet. See, for example, S. Shahar, 'Écrits cathares et commentaire d'Abraham Abulafia sur "Le Livre de la Création", Images et Idées Communes', in *Juifs et Judaïsme de Languedoc* (Toulouse, 1977), pp. 345–63; and the criticism of Shahar's views in M. Idel, *Studies in Ecstatic Kabbalah* (New York, 1988), pp. 33–45.

17 Bernard Gui, *Manuel de l'inquisiteur*, ed. G. Mollat (2 vols., Paris, 1926–7), vol. 1, p. 20.

18 The *Acts* were published by G. Besse in *Histoire des ducs, marquis et comtes de Narbonne* (Paris, 1660), pp. 483–6. Their authenticity has been conclusively established by A. Dondaine in 'Les Actes du concile albigeois de Saint-Félix-de-Caraman', *Miscellanea Giovanni Mercati*, vol. 5, *Studi e Testi*, Vatican City, 125 (1946). The text of the *Acts* has recently been reproduced by B. Hamilton in 'The Cathar Council of Saint-Félix Reconsidered', *Archivum Fratrum Praedicatorum*, Rome, 48 (1978), pp. 51–3.

19 Rainerius' tract has been printed in Dondaine, *Un traité néo-manichéen*, pp. 64–78.

20 Dondaine, 'Les Actes', p. 345.

21 Hamilton, 'The Cathar Council', p. 39.

22 Joachim of Fiore, *Expositio in Apocalypsum* (Venice, 1527), f. 134r–v.

23 *De heresi catharorum in Lombardia*, p. 306.

24 Runciman, *The Medieval Manichee*, p. 73.

25 *De heresi catharorum in Lombardia*, p. 306.

26 Mark's doubts, journey, imprisonment and death are recounted in Anselm's *Tractatus de hereticis*, pp. 309–10.

27 The split of Italian Catharism into separate churches and their missions to the Balkan mother-churches is recorded in *De heresi catharorum in Lombardia*, pp. 306–8.

28 Recently edited with an extensive commentary by E. Bozoky, *Le Livre secret des cathares* (Paris, 1980). An English translation appears in Wakefield and Evans, *Heresies of the High Middle Ages*, pp. 458–65. On Nazarius and the tract in Catharism, see Bozoky, *Le Livre secret*, pp. 26ff.

29 The letter exists in two versions, reproduced in J. D. Mansi, *Sacrorum conciliorum nova et amplissima collectio* (54 vols., reprint of 1901–27 edn, Graz, 1960–61), vol. 22, cols. 1201–2, 1203–6.

30 Hamilton, 'The Cathar Council', pp. 46ff.

31 Borst, *Die Katharer*, pp. 98, 108, 142. According to Obolensky, *The Bogomils*, pp. 157–62, the Drugunthian church was actually the Paulician Balkan church, with its traditional absolute dualist orientation. A recent synthesis of the evidence in B. Hamilton, 'The Origins of the Dualist Church of Drugunthia', *Eastern Churches Review*, 6 (1974), pp. 115–24, has demonstrated that the Bogomil character of the Drugunthian church and indicated that the schism in Balkan dualism followed cultural lines: 'the Byzantine areas of Drugunthia in Thrace and Constantinople accepted absolute dualism, while Slavonic areas in Bulgaria and Bosnia remained faithful to the traditional moderate dualist teaching of Pop Bogomil' (p. 121).

32 Cf. Hamilton, 'The Origins of the Dualist Church of Drugunthia', p. 119.

5   The Crusade Against Dualism

1 A. Theiner, *Vetera monumenta Slavorum Meridionalium historiam illustrantia* (Rome, 1863), vol. 1, p. 41. The religious and messianic overtones of the Assenid rebellion and restoration of the Bulgarian monarchy are discussed in I. Dujčev, *Prouchvania*, pp. 46ff. Alternatively, Nicetas Choniates, *Historia*, p. 485, stated that the rebels were incited by 'demoniacs' and 'soothsayers' who prophesied that God had assented to their freedom.

2 Theiner, *Vetera monumenta*, vol. 1, p. 6.

3 Theiner, *Vetera monumenta*, p. 20.

4 Alberic of Trois-Fontaines, *Chronica*, p. 886.

5 The *Synodicon of Tsar Boril* has been edited by M. G. Popruzhenko in *Bălgarski Starini* [Bulgarian Antiquities], vol. 8, Sofia, 1928.

6 Arnold Aimery, *PL*, vol. 216, col. 139.

7 E. Martin-Chabot (ed. and tr.), *La Chanson de la Croisade Albigeoise* (3 vols., Paris, 1931–61) vol. 3, pp. 208–9. Among the accounts of the Albigensian Crusade see J. R. Strayer, *The Albigensian Crusade* (New York, 1971). There exists a considerable literature on the Crusade in French: a recent exhaustive treatment of the theme is M. Roquebert, *L'Epopée cathare* (3 vols., Toulouse, 1970–86).

8 Matthew of Paris, *Historia Anglorum*, ed. F. Madden (3 vols., London, 1868–91), vol. 3, p. 278. Cf. vol. 2, pp. 338, 415. The mass burning at Mont-Aime is recorded in Alberic of Trois-Fontaines, *Chronica*, pp. 944–5.

9 The events in Catalonia are reconstructed by V. Subirats, 'Le catharisme en Catalogne', *Cahiers d'études cathares*, 14 (1963), 2e serie No. 19, pp. 3–25; cf. M. Loos, *Dualist Heresy in the Middle Ages* (Prague, 1974), p. 204. Apart from the standard treatment of the Inquisition by H. C. Lea, *A History of the Inquisition in the Middle Ages* (3 vols., New York and London, 1888), recent works include B. Hamilton, *The Medieval Inquisition* (London, 1981), W. Wakefield, *Heresy, Crusade and Inquisition in Southern France* (London, 1974).

10 Germanus' encyclical is published in Ficker, *Die Phundagiagiten*, pp. 115–26.

11 Gregory's letter to Bela is reproduced in A. Theiner, *Vetera monumenta historica Hungariam sacram illustrantia*, vol. 1 (2 vols., Rome, 1859–60), pp. 159–160.

12 Theiner, *Vetera monumenta historica*, vol. 1, pp. 166–7.

13 F. Rački, '*Bogomili i Patareni*', *Rad jugoslovenske akademije znanosti i umjetnosti*, Zagreb, 7 (1869), p. 144.

14 Theiner, *Vetera monumenta historica*, pp. 55, 72.

15 An overview of the evidence and reconstruction of the course of the Crusade is provided in J. V. A. Fine, *The Bosnian Church: A New Interpretation* (New York and London, 1975), pp. 137–48. The failure of the Crusade is apparent in Innocent's statement in 1247 that the Bosnian Church had relapsed 'totally into heresy' (Theiner, *Vetera monumenta historica*, pp. 204–5).

16 Suibert's commentary is quoted after Mandić, *Bogomilska crkva*, pp. 439–40.

17 The evidence of Luciferian sects and 'heretic witches' is given in J. B. Russell, *Witchcraft in the Middle Ages* (Ithaca, New York and London, 1972), pp. 159–63, 177–81, where they are defined as professing 'a curious perversion of Catharism', 'a heresy of a heresy', p. 178. Cf. the position of N. Cohn, *Europe's Inner Demons* (London, 1975), pp. 56–9, who rejects the existence of such a Luciferian doctrine developed out of medieval dualism. On the impact of medieval dualism on the concept of witchcraft, see also J. B. Russell, *A History of Witchcraft* (London, 1980), pp. 58–63; J. C. Baroja, *The World of Witches*, tr. O. N. V. Glendinning (Chicago, 1961), pp. 77–8.

18 Cf. Barber, *The Trial of the Templars*, pp. 181, 186–8.

19 F. Legge, 'Western Manichaeism and the Turfan Discoveries', *Journal of the Royal Asiatic Society* (1913), p. 73.

20 Quoted after the translation provided in Wakefield and Evans, *Heresies of the High Middle Ages*, p. 88.

21 Bech's statement may be found in I. von Döllinger, *Beträge zur Sektengeschichte des Mittelalters*, vol. 2 (2 vols., Munich, 1890, repr. 1968), p. 206.

22 The Patarene articles are refuted in Juan Torquemada, *Symbolum pro informatione manichaeorum*, ed. N. L. Martines and V. Proano (Burgos, 1958). A translation of the articles can be found in Fine, *The Bosnian Church*, pp. 355–7, with a commentary that questions their relevance for the Bosnian church.

23 Theiner, *Vetera monumenta historica*, vol. 2, p. 91.

24 B. Hamilton, *Religion in the Medieval West* (London and New York, 1986), p. 177.

25 Fine, *The Bosnian Church*, particularly pp. 148ff.

26 S. Ćircović, 'Die Bosnische Kirche', *L'Oriente cristiano nella storia della civiltà* (Rome, 1964), pp. 552–5; *Istorija srednjovekovne bosanske drzave* (Belgrade, 1964), pp. 58–69. Another view of the Bosnian church as influenced by the mysticism and structure of eastern monasticism is in D. Dragojlovic, *Kristjani i jereticka crkva bosanska* [The Kristjani and the heretical church of Bosnia] (Belgrade, 1987).

27 Pius II, *Europa Opera quae extant omina*, ed. M. Hopperus (Basel, 1551), p. 407.

28 The so-called Radosav ritual. Cf. Fine, *The Bosnian Church*, p. 83; F. Sanjek, *Les Chrétiens bosniaques et le mouvement cathare* (Paris, 1976), pp. 185ff.

29 Loos, *Dualist Heresy*, p. 298. On the letter of John XXII, see n. 31 below.

30 Fine, *The Bosnian Church*, pp. 151, 295–6.

31 T. Smičiklas, *Codex Diplomaticus regni Croatiae. Dalamatiae et Slavoniae*, 9, 1911, p. 234.

32 Quoted after the documents published in M. Esposito, 'Un Auto-da-fé à Chieri en 1412', *Revue d'histoire ecclésiastique*, 42 (1947), pp. 422–32.

33 The events surrounding the accusations against Niphon Scorpio and Callistus' defence were told by Nicephorus Gregoras, *Historia Byzantinae*, vol. 3, pp. 260–61, 532–46; whereas the penetration of heresy into Mount Athos is discussed in vol. 2, pp. 714, 718–20.

34 The account of Theodosius' struggles against heresy follows the version of these events in the *Life of St Theodosius*, ed. V. Zlatarski (Sofia, 1904).

35 Obolensky, *The Bogomils*, p. 264.

36 *Zakonik Stefana Dushana, cara Srpskog*, ed. S. Novakovic (Belgrade, 1898).

37 The episode of Euthymius' struggle with the two heretical sorcerers is examined in D. Angelov, *Bogomilstvoto v Bulgaria* (Sofia, 1980), with observations on the growing popularity of magic and demonology in this period.

38 Symeon of Thessalonica, *Dialogus contra haereses*, *PG*, vol. 155, cols. 33–176.

39 *Oeuvres complètes de Gennade Scholarios*, ed. L. Petit, X. Sideridès, M. Jugie (Paris, 1935), vol. 4, p. 200.

40 W. Miller, *The Balkans* (New York and London, 1896), p. 287.

41 Fine suggests that the term 'pagan' could have been 'a pejorative term for members of the Bosnian Church' (*The Bosnian Church*, p. 235). An overview of Hrvoje's career is provided in *The Bosnian Church*, pp. 232–7.

42 Fine, *The Bosnian Church*, p. 295, with further suggestions that the religious situation might have been misunderstood in Rome or was a 'deliberate frame-up' of the Bosnian church, pp. 297–9.

43 W. Miller, *Essays on the Latin Orient* (Cambridge, 1921).

44 A critical overview of the evidence alleging Patarene co-operation with the Ottomans can be found in Fine, *The Bosnian Church*, pp. 338–41, along with a brief survey of Bosnian religious history after the Turkish conquest, pp. 375–87, and criticism of the theory of Patarene mass conversion to Islam, p. 385. Cf. S. Džaja, *Die 'Bosnische Kirche' und das Islamisierungsproblem Bosniens und der Herzegowina in den Forschungen nach dem Zweiten Weltkrieg* (Munich, 1978). Still other interpretations and conclusions are presented in M. Hadžijahić, *Porijeklo bosanskih Muslimana* (Sarajevo, 1990) and S. Balič, *Das unbekannte Bosnien* (Cologne, 1992), pp. 90–127.

45 The Bosnian gravestones were associated with Bogomilism by A. J. Evans, *Through Bosnia and Herzegovina on Foot during the Insurrection* (London, 1876), pp. 174–7, and the theory was developed further by A.

Solovjev in 'Le symbolisme des monuments funéraires bogomiles', *Cahier d'Études Cathares*, 18 (1954), pp. 92–114; 'Les Bogomiles vénéraient-ils la Croix?', *Bulletin de l'Académie royale de Belgique, Classe des lettres*, 35 (1949), pp. 47–62; O. Bihalji-Merin and A. Benac, *Steine der Bogomilen* (Vienna and Munich, 1964), pp. viiiff., and others. Among the opponents of the Bogomil thesis is M. Wenzel who has published and catalogued the motifs on the *stecci*, with maps showing the distribution of each motif, in *Ukrasni motivi na steccima* [Ornamental Motifs on the *Stećci*] (Sarajevo, 1965). Along with other scholars, M. Wenzel links some of the *stećci* with the horse-breeding Vlach clans, who were numerous and influential in medieval Bosnia and Herzegovina.

46 On the theory of Manichaean influences in the *stecci* carvings, see Solovjev, 'Le symbolisme des monuments funéraires bogomiles', p. 100; a discussion of the themes of *stecci* symbolism in the light of Uighur Manichaean iconography can be found in Esin, 'The conjectural links of Bogomilism with Central Asian Manichaeism', pp. 109–14.

47 The survival of classical cultic symbolism in some figurative and ornamental *stećci* carvings has been demonstrated in a series of publications of M. Wenzel, 'O nekim simbolima na dalmatinskim steccima' [Some Symbols on the *Stećci* in Dalmatia], *Prilozi povijesti umjetnosti u Dalmaciji*, (Split) 14 (1962), pp. 79–94; 'The Dioscuri in the Balkans'.

48 Fine, *The Bosnian Church*, p. 10, with a discussion of the strong pagan survival in Bosnia, and a suggestion for the late survival of a classical mystery cult, p. 18. The evidence for a medieval mystery cult in Bosnia is presented in M. Wenzel, 'A Medieval Mystery Cult in Bosnia and Herzegovina', *Journal of the Warburg and Courtauld Institute*, 24 (1961), pp. 89–107, with suggestions of links between the cult and the underground chambers in the castle of the Patarene duke, Hrvoje Vukcic, pp. 103–5.

49 Cf., for example, Kakouri, *Dionysiaka*, with a discussion of the association between heresy and the survival of Dionysian worship in Thrace; pp. 61ff.; R. Vulcanescu, *Mitologie Romana* (Bucharest, 1985), pp. 233–4.

50 Wenzel, 'Medieval Mystery Cult'; 'The Dioscuri in the Balkans'.

51 The eighteenth-century evidence of the Patarenes and 'Manichaeans' in Bosnia is discussed in Fine, *The Bosnian Church*, pp. 376–7.

52 Nineteenth-century references to alleged current Bogomil remains in Bosnia were discussed in J. Asboth, *An Official Tour through Bosnia and Herzegovina* (London, 1890), pp. 98–100.

53 Obolensky, *The Bogomils*, p. 267.

6 The Dualist Legends

1 D. Obolensky, *The Byzantine Commonwealth: Eastern Europe 500–1453* (London, 1971), p. 123, with the observation that the Bogomil leaders were 'mostly drawn from the lapsed clergy and monks'. Obolensky also discusses the 'occultism' of the Bogomils, in which the 'doctrines of the sect had an outward and inward esoteric aspect' and the 'latter was communicated only to a relatively small group of initiates' (p. 123). Similarly, according to Loos, *Dualist Heresy*, p. 89, the account by Euthymius Zigabenus of the Bogomil doctrines revealed 'some of the hidden depths – the things which the sect kept carefully hidden from the uninitiated'.

2 The 'Manichaean' treatise was copied into the *Liber contra Manichaeos* of the anti-Cathar polemicist Durand de Huesca for the purpose of refutation.

3 The Cathar teaching of the angel, sent by God and imprisoned in a prison–body, was recorded by Moneta of Cremona, *Adversus Catharos et Valdenses libri quinque* ed. T. Richini (Rome, 1743), Book 2, Chap. 1, p. 110.

4 This doctrine is recorded in the *De heresi catharorum* and was held by two groups of Italian Cathars, whose bishops, Caloiannes and Garattus, drew their consecration from Sclavonia and Bulgaria respectively.

5 Moneta, *Adversus Catharos*, Book 2, Chap. 1.2, p. 112, referred to a Cathar belief that when Satan proceeded to destroy the human race, God saved Noah his wife, sons, et cetera.

6 This system of Cathar absolute dualism is recorded in Moneta, *Adversus Catharos,* Book 1, Preface, pp. 2–4.

7 Rainerius Sacchoni, *Summa*, p. 71.

8 The beliefs of the Desenzano Cathars were recorded in *De Heresi catharorum*, pp. 308–10.

9 The heresy of the Albanenses is recorded in the treatise *Brevis summula contra herrores notatos hereticorum*, ed. C. Douais, *La Somme des authorités à l'usage des prédicateurs méridionaux au XIIIe siècle* (Paris, 1896), pp. 114–43. The quotations are from the translation provided in Wakefield and Evans, *Heresies of the High Middle Ages*, pp. 353–61.

10 The exposé is printed in Dondaine, 'Durand de Huesca et la polémique anti-cathare', *Archivum Fratrum Praedicatorum*, 29 (1959), pp. 268–71.

11 Peter of Vaux-de-Cernaym, *Historia albigensis*, Part 1, 2, ed. P. Guébin and E. Lyon, *Petri Vallium Sarnii monachi Historia albigensis* (3 vols., Paris, 1926–39) vol. 1, pp. 11–12.

12 J. N. Garvin and J. A. Corbett, eds., *The Summa contra haereticos Ascribed to Praepositinus* (Notre Dame, 1958), Appendix B, p. 292.

13 The Dualist system of John de Lugio is recorded in Rainerius Sacchoni, *Summa*, pp. 72–6.

14 Moneta, *Adversus Catharos*, Book 2, Chap. 1:1, p. 110.

Index

PENGUIN
ARKANA

NEW AGE BOOKS FOR MIND, BODY & SPIRIT

With over 200 titles currently in print, Arkana is the leading name in quality books for mind, body and spirit. Arkana encompasses the spirituality of both East and West, ancient and new. A vast range of interests is covered, including Psychology and Transformation, Health, Science and Mysticism, Women's Spirituality, Zen, Western Traditions and Astrology.

If you would like a catalogue of Arkana books, please write to:

Sales Department – Arkana
Penguin Books USA Inc.
375 Hudson Street
New York, NY 10014

Arkana Marketing Department
Penguin Books Ltd
27 Wrights Lane
London W8 5TZ

PENGUIN

ARKANA

NEW AGE BOOKS FOR MIND, BODY & SPIRIT

A SELECTION OF TITLES

Neal's Yard Natural Remedies
Susan Curtis, Romy Fraser and Irene Kohler

Natural remedies for common ailments from the pioneering Neal's Yard Apothecary Shop. An invaluable resource for everyone wishing to take responsibility for their own health, enabling you to make your own choice from homeopathy, aromatherapy and herbalism.

Zen in the Art of Archery   Eugen Herrigel

Few in the West have strived as hard as Eugen Herrigel to learn Zen from a Master. His classic text gives an unsparing account of his initiation into the 'Great Doctrine' of archery. Baffled by its teachings – that art must become artless, that the archer must aim at himself – he gradually began to glimpse the depth of wisdom behind the paradoxes. While many Western writers on Zen serve up second-hand slogans, Herrigel's hard-won insights are his own discoveries.

The Absent Father: Crisis and Creativity   Alix Pirani

Freud used Oedipus to explain human nature; but Alix Pirani believes that the myth of Danae and Perseus has most to teach an age that offers 'new responsibilities for women and challenging questions for men'. It is a myth that can help us face the darker side of our personalities and break the patterns inherited from our parents.

Power of the Witch   Laurie Cabot

In fascinating detail, Laurie Cabot describes the techniques and rituals involved in charging tools, brewing magical potions and casting vigorous, tantalizing spells. Intriguing and accessible, this taboo-shattering guide will educate and enlighten even the most sceptical reader in the ways of an ancient faith that has much to offer today's world.

Water and Sexuality   Michel Odent

Taking as his starting point his world-famous work on underwater childbirth at Pithiviers, Michel Odent considers the meaning and importance of water as a symbol.

PENGUIN
ARKANA

NEW AGE BOOKS FOR MIND, BODY & SPIRIT

A SELECTION OF TITLES

The Revised Waite's Compendium of Natal Astrology
Alan Candlish

This completely revised edition retains the basic structure of Waite's classic work while making major improvements to accuracy and readability. With a new computer-generated Ephemeris, complete for the years 1900 to 2010, and a Table of Houses that now allows astrologers to choose between seven house systems, it provides all the information on houses, signs and planets the astrologer needs to draw up and interpret a full natal chart.

Aromatherapy for Everyone   Robert Tisserand

The therapeutic value of essential oils was recognized as far back as Ancient Egyptian times. Today there is an upsurge in the use of these fragrant and medicinal oils to soothe and heal both mind and body. Here is a comprehensive guide to every aspect of aromatherapy by the man whose name is synonymous with its practice and teaching.

Tao Te Ching   The Richard Wilhelm Edition

Encompassing philosophical speculation and mystical reflection, the *Tao Te Ching* has been translated more often than any other book except the Bible, and more analysed than any other Chinese classic. Richard Wilhelm's acclaimed 1910 translation is here made available in English.

The Book of the Dead   E. A. Wallis Budge

Intended to give the deceased immortality, the Ancient Egyptian *Book of the Dead* was a vital piece of 'luggage' on the soul's journey to the other world, providing for every need: victory over enemies, the procurement of friendship and – ultimately – entry into the kingdom of Osiris.

Astrology: A Key to Personality   Jeff Mayo

Astrology: A Key to Personality is designed to help you find out who you *really* are. A book for beginners wanting simple instructions on how to interpret a chart, as well as for old hands seeking fresh perspectives, it offers a unique system of self-discovery.

PENGUIN

ARKANA

NEW AGE BOOKS FOR MIND, BODY & SPIRIT

A SELECTION OF TITLES

Weavers of Wisdom: Women Mystics of the Twentieth Century
Anne Bancroft

Throughout history women have sought answers to eternal questions about existence and beyond – yet most gurus, philosophers and religious leaders have been men. Through exploring the teachings of fifteen women mystics – each with her own approach to what she calls 'the truth that goes beyond the ordinary' – Anne Bancroft gives a rare, cohesive and fascinating insight into the diversity of female approaches to mysticism.

Dynamics of the Unconscious: Seminars in Psychological Astrology II
Liz Greene and Howard Sasportas

The authors of *The Development of the Personality* team up again to show how the dynamics of depth psychology interact with your birth chart. They shed new light on the psychology and astrology of aggression and depression – the darker elements of the adult personality that we must confront if we are to grow to find the wisdom within.

The Myth of the Eternal Return: Cosmos and History   Mircea Eliade

'A luminous, profound, and extremely stimulating work ... Eliade's thesis is that ancient man envisaged events not as constituting a linear, progressive history, but simply as so many creative repetitions of primordial archetypes ... This is an essay which everyone interested in the history of religion and in the mentality of ancient man will have to read. It is difficult to speak too highly of it' – Theodore H. Gaster in *Review of Religion*

The Hidden Tradition in Europe   Yuri Stoyanov

Christianity has always defined itself through fierce opposition to powerful 'heresies'; yet it is only recently that we have begun to retrieve these remarkable, underground traditions, buried beneath the contempt of the Church. In this superb piece of scholarly detective work Yuri Stoyanov illuminates unsuspected religious and political undercurrents lying beneath the surface of official history.

PENGUIN

ARKANA

NEW AGE BOOKS FOR MIND, BODY & SPIRIT

A SELECTION OF TITLES

Working on Yourself Alone: Inner Dreambody Work
Arnold Mindell

Western psychotherapy and Eastern meditation are two contrasting ways of learning more about one's self. The first depends heavily on the powers of the therapist. *Process-oriented* meditation, however, can be used by the individual as a means of resolving conflicts and increasing awareness from within. Using meditation, dream work and yoga, this remarkable book offers techniques that you can develop on your own, allowing the growth of an individual method.

The Moment of Astrology   Geoffrey Cornelius

'This is an extraordinary book ... I believe that within the astrological tradition it is the most important since the great flowering of European astrology more than three hundred years ago ... Quietly but deeply subversive, this is a book for lovers of wisdom' – from the Foreword by Patrick Curry

Homage to the Sun: The Wisdom of the Magus of Strovolos
Kyriacos C. Markides

Homage to the Sun continues the adventure into the mysterious and extraordinary world of the spiritual teacher and healer Daskalos, the 'Magus of Strovolos'. The logical foundations of Daskalos's world of other dimensions are revealed to us – invisible masters, past-life memories and guardian angels, all explained by the Magus with great lucidity and scientific precision.

The Eagle's Gift   Carlos Castaneda

In the sixth book in his astounding journey into sorcery, Castaneda returns to Mexico. Entering once more a world of unknown terrors, hallucinatory visions and dazzling insights, he discovers that he is to replace the Yaqui Indian don Juan as leader of the apprentice sorcerers – and learns of the significance of the Eagle.

PENGUIN

ARKANA

NEW AGE BOOKS FOR MIND, BODY & SPIRIT

A SELECTION OF TITLES

The Ghost in the Machine   Arthur Koestler

Koestler's classic work – which can be read alone or as the conclusion of his trilogy on the human mind – is concerned not with human creativity but with human pathology. 'He has seldom been as impressive, as scientifically far-ranging, as lively-minded or as alarming as on the present occasion' – John Raymond in the *Financial Times*

T'ai Chi Ch'uan and Meditation   Da Liu

Today T'ai Chi Ch'uan is known primarily as a martial art – but it was originally developed as a complement to meditation. Both disciplines involve alignment of the self with the Tao, the ultimate reality of the universe. Da Liu shows how to combine T'ai Chi Ch'uan and meditation, balancing the physical and spiritual aspects to attain good health and harmony with the universe.

Return of the Goddess   Edward C. Whitmont

Amid social upheaval and the questioning of traditional gender roles, a new myth is arising: the myth of the ancient Goddess who once ruled earth and heaven before the advent of patriarchy and patriarchal religion. Here one of the world's leading Jungian analysts argues that our society, long dominated by male concepts of power and aggression, is today experiencing a resurgence of the feminine.

Shiatzu   Yukiko Irwin with James Wagen Voord

Employing thumbs, fingers and palms to apply pressure to various parts of the body, Shiatzu gives relief to a wide variety of ailments, although its main purpose is to maintain good health and vitality. In this clear and easy-to-follow book Yukiko Irwin gives step-by-step instructions and explains the various techniques of Shiatzu for you to use alone or with a partner.